The Science of Intimate Relationships

The Science of Intimate Relationships

Garth Fletcher, Jeffry A. Simpson,
Lorne Campbell, and Nickola C. Overall

A John Wiley & Sons, Ltd., Publication

This edition first published 2013
© 2013 Garth Fletcher, Jeffry A. Simpson, Lorne Campbell, and Nickola C. Overall

Blackwell Publishing was acquired by John Wiley & Sons in February 2007. Blackwell's publishing program has been merged with Wiley's global Scientific, Technical, and Medical business to form Wiley-Blackwell.

Registered Office
John Wiley & Sons Ltd, The Atrium, Southern Gate, Chichester, West Sussex, PO19 8SQ, UK

Editorial Offices
350 Main Street, Malden, MA 02148-5020, USA
9600 Garsington Road, Oxford, OX4 2DQ, UK
The Atrium, Southern Gate, Chichester, West Sussex, PO19 8SQ, UK

For details of our global editorial offices, for customer services, and for information about how to apply for permission to reuse the copyright material in this book please see our website at www.wiley.com/wiley-blackwell.

The right of Garth Fletcher, Jeffry A. Simpson, Lorne Campbell, and Nickola C. Overall to be identified as the authors of this work has been asserted in accordance with the UK Copyright, Designs and Patents Act 1988.

Library of Congress Cataloging-in-Publication Data
Fletcher, Garth J. O.
  The science of intimate relationships / Garth Fletcher, Jeffry A. Simpson, Lorne Campbell, and Nickola C. Overall
      pages cm
    Includes bibliographical references and index.
    ISBN 978-1-4051-7919-5 (pbk.) – ISBN 978-1-118-35516-9 (epub) – ISBN 978-1-118-37870-0   1. Intimacy (Psychology)   2. Sex (Psychology)   3. Interpersonal relations.   I. Title.
    BF575.I5F543 2013
    158.2–dc23
                          2012042775

A catalogue record for this book is available from the British Library.

Cover image: Cupid and Psyche, 1986. © Calum Colvin.
Cover design by Simon Levy Associates

Set in 10.5/13 pt Minion by Toppan Best-set Premedia Limited

1   2013

Contents

Contents

Part Four: Maintaining Relationships: the Psychology of Intimacy   155

About the Authors

Garth Fletcher is professor of psychology at Victoria University Wellington. He is a fellow of five societies including the Royal Society of New Zealand, the Association for Psychological Science, and the Society for Personality and Social Psychology, and has been associate editor of both *Personal Relationships* and the *Journal of Personality and Social Psychology*. Fletcher has published over 100 articles and book chapters, and has authored and edited six books.

Jeffry A. Simpson is professor of psychology and director of the doctoral minor in interpersonal relationships (IREL) at the University of Minnesota. He has been the editor of the journal *Personal Relationships* and is currently the editor of the *Journal of Personality and Social Psychology: Interpersonal Relations and Group Processes* (JPSP-IRGP). Simpson is the incoming president of the International Association for Relationship Research, and has published nearly 200 articles and chapters along with several edited books.

Lorne Campbell is associate professor of psychology at the University of Western Ontario. He has published over 40 articles and book chapters, serves on the editorial board of the *Journal of Personality and Social Psychology* and *Personality and Social Psychology Bulletin*, and has been the editor of the journal *Personal Relationships*.

Nickola C. Overall is senior lecturer of psychology at the University of Auckland, New Zealand. She has published over 40 articles and book chapters, serves on the editorial board of the *Journal of Personality and Social Psychology*, and is currently associate editor for *Personal Relationships*.

Preface: The Science of Intimate Relationships

The front cover of this textbook is by the noted artist Calum Colvin, who is professor of fine art photography at the University of Dundee in Scotland, UK. The picture is a contemporary reading of a classic statue from the eighteenth century depicting Cupid and Psyche by Canova (currently in the Musée du Louvre). The Greek legend of Cupid and Psyche can be traced to the second century AD. It starts with Cupid being sent by Venus (Cupid's mother) to pierce Psyche with his arrow so she would fall in love with a vile creature (placed there by Venus) when she awoke. Venus was jealous of Psyche because of her renowned beauty. The plan goes awry when Cupid accidentally pricks himself with his own arrow and falls head over heels in love with Psyche. The legend, as legends do, goes through many twists and turns before they finally get together and live happily ever after (literally, as Psyche was rendered immortal like Cupid).

If you look closely at the picture on the cover, you can see that it is not quite what it seems at first glance. It was created in a rather complicated fashion by arranging a collage of material from an ordinary lounge (a radio, a couch, a light bulb, a book, and so forth), then partly painting and photographing the arrangement from a certain angle. The image is finally printed as a large-scale photograph. This picture illustrates a major theme in this textbook; namely, that love, passion, and intimacy are powerful forces that can seem exotic, yet at the same time are woven through the fabric of ordinary life, forming part, as they do, of the bedrock in human nature.

When teaching courses on intimate relationships, we (the authors) sometimes ask our students to what extent personal experiences in relationships might help or hinder the scientific study of relationships. We typically find that students are divided in their views. Some point out that personal experiences of love, jealousy, intimacy, interpersonal conflict, sex, and so forth, all too readily blind the perceiver to the variability across individuals in how such phenomena are experienced, and such experiences are not especially informative about the causes for such phenomena. Others argue, again quite reasonably, that personal experiences can lead to insights and should not be thought of as existing outside the science of intimate relationships. Most agree that experiencing emotions like love, jealousy, and grief (illustrated in the legend of Cupid and Psyche) are, if nothing else, convincing demonstrations of their power.

We suspect that many scientists who study intimate relationships are initially motivated one way or another by their own personal experiences, but scientists also understand the severe limitations of relying on such personal experiences to build a scientific understanding of intimate relationships. The problem is that personal experiences typically come seamlessly packaged with implicit beliefs, causal attributions, scripts, and predictions. As we emphasize throughout the book, taking a scientific approach requires the suspension, or at least a critical examination, of such personal views and beliefs (difficult though that may be).

This book is aimed at university courses on relationships taught at an upper-level undergraduate or postgraduate level. We had several goals in mind when writing the book. We wanted to write a rigorous book that was true to the science, but was also intriguing and at times provocative. Thus, we attempt to strike a lively and enthusiastic tone that accurately represents the excitement in the field. We also wanted to write a genuinely interdisciplinary but accessible book – challenging aims indeed! We leave it to you, the reader, to decide how successful we have been.

Science can be a harsh environment because of the often forceful public criticism and scrutiny of ideas and research. However, a spirit of generosity and collegial support also prevails. We thank our colleagues who reviewed and read chapters, including Gina Grimshaw and Alan Dixson. We also thank Chelsea Rose, Janet Craig, Kim Nathan, and five anonymous reviewers who read the whole book, providing thoughtful and constructive suggestions and criticisms.

We thank the team at Wiley-Blackwell for their support, patience, and enthusiasm for the project, especially Julia Kirk, Karen Shield, and Matt Bennett. We also owe a great debt of gratitude to the untiring and expert help of Chelsea Rose in creating the PowerPoint slides for the book, sorting out the flood of copyright issues involved, and preparing and coordinating the ancillary materials. We could not have written the book without her considerable help.

Finally we give grateful thanks to our respective partners and families for their understanding and support, especially when working on the book during countless evenings and weekends.

Part One

Introduction

The Science of Intimate Relationships 1

Focus of the book – domains of scientific study – interdisciplinary links – relationship mind and body – common sense and pop psychology – research methods – book overview – summary and conclusions

> The emergence of a science of relationships represents a frontier – perhaps the last major frontier – in the study of humankind.
>
> Berscheid and Peplau, 1983

The first known academic treatise on intimate relationships was *Plato's Symposium*, written approximately 2300 years ago. In this historic document, Aristophanes tells a tale of a curious mythical being that is spherical in form with two complete sets of arms, legs, and genitalia. Because of the strength and speed of these creatures (they cartwheeled around on four arms and four legs), they posed a threat to the gods. Accordingly, Zeus split them in half and rearranged their genitals so that they were forced to embrace each other front on to have sexual relations. Some of the original beings had two sets of male genitalia, some had two sets of female genitalia, and some had one set of female and one set of male genitalia. Thus, procreation of the species was possible only by members of the original male–female creatures getting together. Possibly in deference to the sexual orientation of some of his audience (or to the tenor of that time), Aristophanes was quick to add that males who sought union with other males were "bold and manly," whereas individuals who originated from the hermaphrodite creatures were adulterers or promiscuous women (Sayre, 1995, p. 106). Regardless of sexual orientation, the need for love is thus born of the longing to reunite with one's long-lost other half and to achieve an ancient unity destroyed by the gods.

As this allegory suggests, individuals are alone and incomplete – an isolation that can be banished, or at least ameliorated, when humans pair off and experience the

The Science of Intimate Relationships, First Edition. Garth Fletcher, Jeffry A. Simpson, Lorne Campbell, and Nickola C. Overall.
© 2013 Garth Fletcher, Jeffry A. Simpson, Lorne Campbell, and Nickola C. Overall.
Published 2013 by Blackwell Publishing Ltd.

intimacy that can only be gained in a close, emotionally connected relationship. Such intimacy, the experience of reuniting with one's long-lost other half, reaches its peak in parent–infant bonding and in the intimate high of romantic sexual relationships. But such intimacy is also experienced quite powerfully and deeply in platonic relationships, familial relationships, and in the long sunset of sexual relationships that have lost their passionate urgency and settled into a deep form of close companionship.

Just like Plato's mythical beings, then, humans have a basic need to be accepted, appreciated, and cared for, and to reciprocate such attitudes and behaviors – in short, to love and to be loved (Baumeister and Leary, 1995). This is especially true for finding a sexual or romantic partner, a quest that can range from a one-night stand to seeking out a mate for life. Indeed, for most people the goal of forming a permanent, sexual liaison with another person is a pivotal goal in life in which a massive outlay of energy is invested.

In this textbook, we confine our attention largely to intimate relationships that are sexual or romantic rather than other types of relationships, such as parent–child relationships, platonic friendships, casual friendships, or co-worker relationships. Obviously, intimate relationships can be, and often are, influenced by these other types of relationships. When these connections are important or salient, we will address them. Moreover, we discuss certain categories of non-sexual relationships that are centrally related to adult intimate relationships, the most important being parent–child relationships. And we discuss both heterosexual and same-sex relationships, including their similarities and differences. Nevertheless, our attention is focused on heterosexual relationships, simply because most scientific research has investigated heterosexual relationships.

This introductory chapter sets the scene for the book by tracing the history of scientific work on relationships, dissecting what is true (and false) about common-sense and pop psychology, briefly discussing basic research methods in the field, and finally presenting a brief overview of the book's contents. We have boldfaced all technical terms the first time they appear in each chapter of the book, and provide brief definitions of each term in the glossary at the end of the book.

The Science of Intimate Relationships: a Brief History and Analysis

As Plato's symposium attests, humans have been theorizing about relationships for eons. This is not surprising, given the proclivity of humans to develop causal models and explanations, many of which are based on culturally shared understandings. Indeed, this is one hallmark of our species. Consistently, many of the topics covered in this book have been discussed in literature and plays hundreds of years before any rigorous scientific investigation of relationships appeared (think Homer, Shakespeare, and Jane Austen).

The first scientific forays into intimate relationships did not take place until the twentieth century. To give you some idea of the way in which scientific work has taken

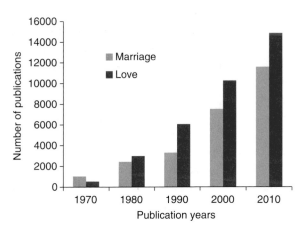

Figure 1.1   Publications from 1970 to 2010 – love and marriage

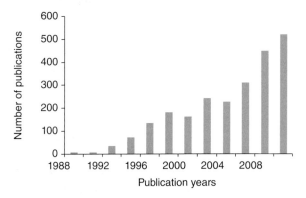

Figure 1.2   Publications from 1988 to 2010 – sexual or romantic relationships

on tsunami proportions in relatively recent years, we used a popular academic data base – the Web of Science – to assess the number of publications in scientific journals devoted to the topic of relationships during the past 40 years (from 1970 to 2010). We first used the key words *love* and *marriage*. As shown in Figure 1.1, the number of publications has rapidly increased over the last 40 years. We then used the key words *sexual* or *romantic relationships* and looked at the number of publications in two-year periods from 1987 to 2010. The results, shown in Figure 1.2, also reveal a dramatic rise in publications, in this case from 12 in 1987/1988 to 520 in 2009/2010! These results show that nearly 70% of all the publications in scientific journals in these domains have appeared during the past 20 years, with about 40% of the articles published within the last decade.

Domains of study

Publications relevant to romantic relationships have appeared across a diverse set of disciplines, including cross-cultural and anthropological studies, neuroscience, clinical

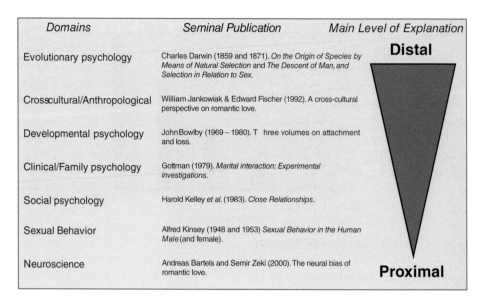

Domains	Seminal Publication	Main Level of Explanation
		Distal
Evolutionary psychology	Charles Darwin (1859 and 1871). *On the Origin of Species by Means of Natural Selection* and *The Descent of Man, and Selection in Relation to Sex.*	
Crosscultural/Anthropological	William Jankowiak & Edward Fischer (1992). A cross-cultural perspective on romantic love.	
Developmental psychology	John Bowlby (1969 – 1980). Three volumes on attachment and loss.	
Clinical/Family psychology	Gottman (1979). *Marital interaction: Experimental investigations.*	
Social psychology	Harold Kelley *et al.* (1983). *Close Relationships.*	
Sexual Behavior	Alfred Kinsey (1948 and 1953) *Sexual Behavior in the Human Male* (and female).	
Neuroscience	Andreas Bartels and Semir Zeki (2000). The neural bias of romantic love.	**Proximal**

Figure 1.3 Major scientific domains studying sexual relationships from distal to proximal levels, along with seminal publications

and family psychology, developmental psychology, the science of sexual behavior, evolutionary psychology, and social and personality psychology. Figure 1.3 gives our take on the pioneering contributions in each field. Notably, all of the pioneering contributions were published in the second half of the twentiethcentury, with two stunning exceptions – two publications in the second half of the nineteenth century by Charles Darwin (more on Darwin later).

Scientific approaches to the study of intimate relationships differ according to their goals and level of focus (see Figure 1.3). At the most general level, all human sciences have the same core aims – the explanation, prediction, and control of human behavior – although certain aims are sometimes emphasized depending on the particular approach. For example, clinical psychology emphasizes the prediction and control of relationship phenomena (especially relationship functioning, success, and stability), whereas social psychology and evolutionary psychology focus more on explanation.

Different approaches to the study of human relationships concentrate on different goals or questions, and, thus differ in their specific domain(s) of investigation. The study of social development, for example, is interested in understanding the development of bonding and attachment in childhood and how it relates to the development of intimate relationships across the life span (termed an **ontogenetic** approach). Evolutionary psychology is primarily concerned with understanding the evolutionary origins of human courting, sexual behavior, mate selection, parenting, and so forth. Thus, evolutionary psychology is primarily concerned with **distal** causes stemming from our remote evolutionary past in order to clarify current human behavioral, cognitive and emotional tendencies. Social psychology, in contrast, takes human dispositions (behavioral, cognitive, and emotional) as givens, and seeks to model the way in which our dispositions combine with external contingencies in our local environment to produce important behavior, social judgments, and emotions. Thus, social psychology offers much more fine-grained predictions and explanations of particular behaviors and cognitions that occur in specific situations (a **proximal** level) than does evolutionary psychology. Anthropological and cross-cultural approaches, on the other hand, focus on the way in which broad cultural and institutional contexts frame and guide the behavior of individuals and couples. Whereas social psychology tends to focus on the links between the individual and the dyadic relationship (e.g. how one person's traits influence his or her partner and relationship outcomes), anthropological approaches tend to focus on connections between the couple (e.g. the rules and norms in relationship) and the wider culture in which the relationship is embedded.

An example A social psychological approach to understanding how people select mates might be to postulate a psychological model examining the importance that each partner places on particular characteristics (which will vary across individuals) are treated as cognitively stored standards, such as the perceived importance of finding an attractive and healthy mate. Individuals may then use these ideal standards to make choices between different potential mates or to evaluate how satisfied they are with their current mate. Resultant levels of satisfaction and relationship commitment, in turn, might then affect their own behavior, which might influence their partner's behavior, resulting in the couple deciding to live together or break off the relationship. Thus, a social psychological model describes *how* cognitions, emotions, and behaviors interact (combine) within each person, and also how individuals in relationships communicate and influence each other (see Chapter 3). These models can be quite detailed, describing, as they do, a complex reality. Nevertheless, they deal only with a certain slice of what influences individuals and relationships at a given point in time, much of which operates at the proximal level (see above) rather than at the distal level emanating either from the remote evolutionary past or wider cultural forces.

Evolutionary psychology, on the other hand, asks important questions that social psychologists usually do not ask, such as why do people want mates who are attractive and healthy in the first place, or what are the origins of certain gender differences? (To avoid confusion, throughout the book we will use "gender" to refer to males versus females, and "sex" to refer to sexual intercourse or related behaviors and attitudes.) Answers for evolutionary psychologists often lie in the evolutionary history of humans, particularly in the adaptive advantages that should have accrued to our ancestors in ancestral environments if they were attracted to and chose certain kinds of mates, such as those who were relatively attractive and healthy.

Interdisciplinary links

Scientists are increasingly working in an interdisciplinary fashion across all the domains shown in Figure 1.3. For example, social psychologists now are beginning to team up with evolutionary psychologists, developmental psychologists, and neuroscientists.

Indeed, the whole field is becoming inter-disciplinary. Covering all these aspects in a single book is a tall order, and this cannot be accomplished in just one theory. Nevertheless, we attempt to address this broad and diverse body of work in this book (which makes this textbook unique among relationship texts). Our ecumenical strategy is based on our conviction that the most appropriate way to deal with the wide range of scientific approaches to relationships is in terms of a theory-knitting approach that focuses on different levels of explanation, ranging from proximal to distal causes. Different theories focus on different claims and deal with different parts of the very complex causal nexus that drives human behavior, including how people think, feel, and act in their intimate relationships. Accordingly, such theories are not necessarily in conflict; rather, they are often complementary, providing different ways to view and understand how different parts of the proverbial elephant can be combined (see the final chapter).

The relation between mind and body

In this book, we constantly move between biological and psychological processes. In Chapter 3, we cover the relationship mind. In Chapter 4, we discuss the relationship body and brain – which raises a longstanding debate in philosophy and science about the connection between minds and brains. The standard scientific stance, to which we adhere, is termed a **materialist** perspective. According to this view, the human mind and brain are one and the same, but they describe what is happening at different explanatory levels. A computer analogy clarifies this esoteric-sounding claim. The same computer software or program can be used to access and manipulate the stored information in the memory of two computers that differ in their internal hardware. A precise description of the two computers in terms of their electrical currents, stored electrical potentials, and hardware can also be provided. These latter descriptions, however, fail to give an adequate description and explanation of what the two computers actually do, which may be identical according to a higher-order description of how the information is processed in each computer (as specified by the programming software).

This computer analogy of the human brain and mind is irresistible – the mind is akin to a higher-order description of the brain's hardware that details how information is stored, accessed, organized, and the specific functions it is used for. Both cognitive and social psychology operate at the software level. A neurological description of the brain, on the other hand, describes the hardware.

Interestingly, the common-sense psychology of human behavior is typically pitched at the software level of the brain. When we say that Mary believes that George is unhappy and buys him a gift to cheer him up, we are explaining Mary's behavior in terms of information that is stored and acted upon in the same way that we explain how other intelligent systems work (such as non-human animals and computers). If anyone believes that human behavior can be described and interpreted without the spectacles of common-sense psychological theory, try to imagine someone baking a cake without perceiving their actions as intentional, or developing a good explanation for why George drove his car to Mary's place without mentioning any of his goals, beliefs, wishes, wants, personality traits, abilities, attitudes, intentions, or motives. Although both cognitive and social psychology approaches extend far beyond common-sense psychology, these former domains operate at the same explanatory level as common-sense theories of mind and behavior.

Common sense and pop psychology

Let's address two other claims that are often associated with the scientific study of intimate relationships. These two propositions are typically expressed as follows: (i) studying relationships and love scientifically will destroy the magic of it all; and (ii) studying intimate relationships scientifically only tell us what we already know based on common sense – like "good communication produces successful relationships" or "arguing and getting angry are bad for relationships" or "men are more aggressive in relationships than women."

Loud boos to both claims! There is no evidence that studying any phenomenon makes it less puzzling or enthralling. Indeed, the very opposite is true, especially in psychology, where what appear to be mundane and everyday behaviors (such as speaking or explaining someone else's behavior) become mysterious – even magisterial – feats when investigated more closely. Whether studying relationships tells us only what we already know, the proof of the pudding is in the eating – once you have read this book, you will be able to make a much more informed judgment of this claim. However, we have already laid a trap by citing three commonly accepted notions that extensive research suggests are either questionable or flat-out wrong. It turns out that the relation between communication and relationship satisfaction is not straightforward (Chapter 9), that arguing and getting angry are not necessarily bad for relationships (Chapter 9), and that men are not more frequently physically aggressive than women in relationships (Chapter 11). It does not pay to be overly confident about maxims learned at one's caregiver's knee, or gleaned from the latest column one has read about relationships in a magazine. Some popular stereotypes about relationships are true, others are false, and many are half-truths, as we will see.

On the other hand, we do not claim that all lay beliefs or theories (whether shared, common-sensical, and/or idiosyncratic) should be automatically dispensed with as unscientific rubbish. After all, laypeople have the same set of aims as do scientists – to explain, predict, and control their own lives and relationships. Common-sense theories and aphorisms regarding love and relationships have developed over eons of time. Given that we (humans) are still here and prospering, it is unlikely that all lay theories are utterly false, and therefore useless as tools for people to predict, explain, and control their own personal lives and relationships. However, this does not mean that lay wisdom is necessarily correct, or that it provides an adequate scientific theory. To adopt a scientific approach entails subjecting a theory or body of knowledge to the same critical methodological scrutiny, regardless of whether it comes from the Bible, from common sense, or from renowned authorities. Common-sense theories are a valuable resource that scientists can use to generate ideas, but common sense offers a partial, limited, and sometimes false account of relationship phenomena (Fletcher, 1995).

However, even if common-sense theories or maxims are totally false, this does not mean that they are not worthy of scientific study. People's beliefs and theories influence their behavior, regardless of whether or not their mental states are true or false. For example, a man may believe (quite irrationally) that his wife is being unfaithful and, accordingly, he has an extramarital affair of his own in retaliation. The man's belief, although false, partly explains his behavior. Thus, if we wish to explain a person's behavior, thoughts, or feelings, we must take his or her common-sense beliefs and theories into account.

We also reject the claims that scientists should not investigate or report findings that might maintain or justify behavior judged as bad or inappropriate. Such claims are a dagger aimed at the heart of science, which is not in the business of suppressing truth or conforming to current commonplace views. Science investigates phenomena and strives to attain the truth. Arguments that evolutionary theories, for example, are wrong or detrimental to certain people because they justify differences between men and women and legitimate discrimination or prejudice confuse the "is vs. ought" distinction. To be sure, scientific theories and findings can be used for invidious purposes by unscrupulous or prejudiced individuals. But the real problem lies in how such theories are applied. For example, if men and women are different in certain ways as a matter of empirical fact, and there exists a desire to prevent discrimination and encourage equality, then we need to understand the causes of such differences – otherwise misdirected and expensive societal efforts are likely to fail and better ones not developed.

In sum, this is not a pop psychology book about relationships. It is not intended to save people's relationships or render instant nirvana. Indeed, one goal of this book is to counteract the avalanche of pop psychology information (and sometimes misinformation) dealing with intimate relationships. We do not believe that all pop psychology books are rubbish, or that self-help books may not be useful for some people. Our rule is *caveat emptor* – let the buyer beware – because, frankly, there is a considerable amount of relationship "snake-oil" promoted on talk shows, books, TV programs, the internet, and so forth. Much pop psychology, with its sloganeering and quick-fix solutions, is false or misleading. Intimate relationships are fascinating and complex – too complex to be captured in terms of achieving relationship utopia in five easy steps. Over the many years we have spent studying relationships scientifically, we have developed a great deal of respect for the many ways in which couples heroically struggle, often against long odds, to predict, control, and understand their own intimate relationships and lives. All too often, pop psychology fails to connect to the real psychological world of most intimate relationships, and sells people well short.

Research methods

It is difficult to interpret and understand the results of scientific research without having some basic understanding of the research methods and statistics employed. For this reason, we will briefly describe the scientific methods and data analytic approaches used in different studies when we describe and discuss them in each chapter. However, to give a heads up, all of the studies that we will discuss either observe something or manipulate something involving relationships. In social psychology, the former are termed **correlational** studies, and the latter are **experimental** designs. The advantage of experimental studies (in combination with random assignment of participants to experimental conditions) is that they can isolate and offer compelling evidence for whether an experimentally manipulated variable actually causes changes in an outcome (dependent) variable. In contrast, correlational studies leave causal claims more difficult to pin down. For example, relationship satisfaction is typically positively correlated with good communication (both of which can be measured with self-report scales). However, this result is consistent with relationship satisfaction causing good communication, good communication causing relationship satisfaction, or some **third variable** (say depression) causing communication and satisfaction to move up and down together, giving the illusion that the two are causally linked.

However, things are not quite this simple. First, even though experimental studies can provide evidence for causality, the conclusions reached depend on how well the experiments are done and how valid and effective the experimental manipulations are. Some experiments, even published ones, may not faithfully represent what happens in the real world of relationships. Second, it is often impossible ethically to do certain types of experiments. For example, relationship satisfaction or communication cannot ethically be manipulated in ongoing relationships. Third, correlational designs (using a statistical technique such as **multiple regression**) can identify which variable might be causing which by tracking both variables over time and calculating the paths that go from relationship satisfaction at Time 1 to changes of good communication at Time 2, and from good communication at Time 1 to changes in relationship satisfaction at Time 2. The problem of third variables sometimes can also be overcome, to some extent, by calculating the path between good communication and relationship satisfaction, while statistically controlling for the effects of, say, depression. If the paths remain statistically significant, depression is not likely to be a third variable.

Incidentally, we will often report correlations in this book, so a quick primer is in order. Correlations between two variables can range from −1.0 to 1.0, where the midpoint (zero) is equivalent to no relationship at all. If the correlation is negative, then this means that one variable goes up while the other goes down. For example, studies typically report that depression is negatively correlated with relationship satisfaction, which means that more depressed people have lower relationship satisfaction. The size of the correlation also counts. As a rule of thumb, a correlation of .10 is usually considered low, .30 is a medium correlation, and .50 a large correlation. For a familiar example, the correlation between height and weight is large at about .70.

The range of methods used in the studies reported in this book are extensive and often clever. Relationship scientists have invented intriguing ways of measuring and manipulating variables in the laboratory, such as using computers to measure reaction times (indicating the cognitive accessibility of specific thoughts) and to assess unconscious mental processes. They also gather different kinds of self-reports via the internet, from dating agencies, and across different cultures, on emotions, expectations, memories, preferences, attitudes, evaluative standards, and mind-readings of partner's thoughts and feelings. They sometimes ask questions of partners' friends or family members, and occasionally eavesdrop on people's everyday experiences via the use of hand-held computers or cell phones. And they observe and video-record relationship interactions in both the laboratory and in couples' homes (sometimes surreptitiously), use **brain imaging** techniques, gather genetic evidence, analyze **natural experiments** in which certain groups have set up local subcultures (e.g. religious cults, Israeli kibbutz), compare humans with other species, and conduct computer simulations.

Along with an array of new methods, the last two decades have also witnessed rapid growth in the development of new statistical tools for modeling the psychological processes between partners and across time, and measuring changes in variables as relationships develop. We won't go into detail on such methods (you may be pleased to know!), but will give enough information as we proceed to give you an intuitive grasp of how such methods work.

Contents of the book

In the second chapter of this introductory section of the book, we outline some key theories in the interdisciplinary science of intimate relationships, and discuss the multiple threads that tie intimate relationships and human nature together. In Part Two of the book, we discuss the nature of the human relationship animal in two chapters that focus on the relationship mind and the relationship body. In Part Three, we address the initial development of intimate relationships, with chapters discussing **attachment theory** and mate selection. Part Four delves into major relationship topics that deal with the maintenance phases of intimate relationships – love, mind-reading, communication, sex, and violence. In Part Five, we summarize the causes and consequences of relationship dissolution. Finally, in the concluding chapter, we attempt to join all the dots and provide an integrated summary of the science of intimate relationships.

Because this book deals with the scientific study of relationships, we offer few unadorned or iron-clad conclusions. Relationship science is a hotbed of argument and disagreement about issues, big and small. Many intriguing questions and current controversies will be raised, a few of which remain unanswered or unresolved. Science is like that. Whenever possible, we attempt to present integrated accounts of what is currently known about each area of investigation based on the best available scientific evidence. In many ways, science operates like a courtroom, with the jury being the wider scientific community, the judge being the editors and board members of scientific journals (who set the rules about admissible evidence), and the lawyers being the warring factions presenting their own versions of the truth. When students get into the controversies and arguments in the scientific literature, they are sometimes tempted to throw up their hands in despair, thinking "You can prove anything!" We hope to show that such an attitude is unnecessary and wrong, that a balanced analysis of scientific findings often lays the facts bare, and that an intelligent evaluation of the available theories that account for the facts usually reveals the best scientific paths to pursue.

Summary and Conclusions

In this opening chapter, we postulated what you may reasonably think is a no-brainer – that intimate relationships are important, very important, to most people. Thus, the way they work (or sometimes don't work!) have been central themes in classic litera-ture, plays, and the media for as long as writing has existed. Moreover, lay theories and beliefs about intimate relationships almost certainly predate the invention of writing by millennia. In contrast, scientific investigations of relationship phenomena have been a recent arrival. With the exception of Darwin's magisterial works on evolution (pub-lished in the latter half of the 1800s), all the seminal contributions to relationship science across different domains were published between 1948 and 2000 (see Figure 1.3), with about 70% of all scientific publications appearing within the past 20 years (see Figure 1.1).

We pointed out that different disciplines approach intimate relationships with dif-ferent goals and often examine them at different levels of analysis. For example, evo-lutionary psychology is interested in the distal origins of love, sex, and mate selection, whereas social psychology focuses more on the proximal forces in the immediate environment that influence how we think, feel, and behave in relationships. We also suggested that integrating the best parts of these two approaches of scientific investiga-tion can yield novel insights and a deeper, more nuanced understanding of intimate relationships. To put it bluntly, this book is an evidence-based argument for the value of adopting an interdisciplinary approach to understanding intimate relationships.

Finally, we made a plea for "parking" what you know, or think you know, about relationships at the front door before you enter this academic house. This is not because we think that all common-sense beliefs are false or wrong. On the contrary, many common-sense and culturally based beliefs have more than a grain of truth, as we shall see. Rather, a scientifically based approach to the topics covered in this book demands a willingness to face new and perhaps challenging ideas about intimate relationships.

To conclude, this book illustrates how scientific work on relationships has a double-barreled role. It increases our understanding of intimate relationships, while simulta-neously informing our understanding of the basic building blocks of psychology: cognition, affect, and behavior. This is primarily because so much of human cognition, emotion, and behavior is deeply interpersonal in nature. At the beginning of this chapter, we cited a famous quote from two pioneers of the field, advanced 28 years ago, that the emergence of a science of relationships may represent the last major frontier in the study of humankind. This textbook illustrates the many ways in which this final frontier has more or less been breached.

2 Intimate Relationships in Context
Key Theories, Concepts, and Human Nature

Social psychology – evolutionary psychology – genes – life history theory – human development – culture – summary and conclusions

There's nowt so queer as folk.

Everyday expression from Yorkshire, UK

The nature of human nature has generated passionate arguments and disagreements across the decades. One of the principal controversies is the extent to which humans are born as **blank slates** (to be written on by cultures and experiences) versus a set of genetically determined dispositions and specialized instincts (Pinker, 2002). Humans are, of course, the products of evolution, just like all other species. But, the oddness of the human species creates special problems (and tensions) when trying to create a sound, scientific account of our origins and unique nature. Indeed, one theme uniting even the most bitter of opponents concerning human nature is acceptance of the proposition that humans are a weird and a wonderful species (summed up in the piece of folk wisdom quoted above.

In this chapter, we discuss the way in which humans rear children (often in the context of pair bonding and broader family networks) was probably a major factor in the evolution of the special qualities of *Homo sapiens*. This section develops a theme previously canvassed; namely, that intimate relationships can really be understood only within the context of human nature itself. However, this is a two-way street. Because intimate relationships provide the backdrop to the twin fulcrums of human evolution – sexual reproduction and child-rearing – understanding how and why intimate relationships function is an essential requirement for understanding human nature.

The Science of Intimate Relationships, First Edition. Garth Fletcher, Jeffry A. Simpson, Lorne Campbell, and Nickola C. Overall.
© 2013 Garth Fletcher, Jeffry A. Simpson, Lorne Campbell, and Nickola C. Overall.
Published 2013 by Blackwell Publishing Ltd.

Of the fields noted in Chapter 1 (see Figure 1.3), we devote most attention in this book to social psychology and evolutionary psychology, given the central roles they have played in the development of the science of intimate relationships. Thus, we initially provide brief descriptions of each field to provide a firm foundation for what will be covered in the remaining chapters. Next, we discuss genes, the evolution of development and human nature, and how these aspects tie into intimate relationships. We cover a lot of material in this chapter, but stick with it – the key theories and concepts that we introduce are central to the science of intimate relationships, and we will use them repeatedly throughout the book.

Social Psychology

A brief history

When Ellen Berscheid and Elaine Hatfield got a small grant from the National Science Foundation (NSF) in 1975 to study romance and love, nothing prepared them for what followed (Hatfield, 2006). They received the first Golden Fleece Award in 1975 from US Senator William Proxmire, which he gave for many years to recipients of research grants from government agencies for projects that he judged to be particularly foolish. The senator's complaints were replete with some basic misconceptions this book tackles head on (from Harris, 1978):

> I object to this not only because no one – not even the National Science Foundation – can argue that falling in love is a science; not only because I'm sure that even if they spend $84 million or $84 billion they wouldn't get an answer that anyone would believe. I'm also against it because I don't want the answer. I believe that 200 million other Americans want to leave some things in life a mystery, and right at the top of things we don't want to know is why a man falls in love with a woman and vice versa. . . So National Science Foundation – get out of the love racket. Leave that to Elizabeth Barrett Browning and Irving Berlin.

The media firestorm and political pressure that accompanied this pronouncement had unfortunate consequences. Ellen Berscheid almost lost her faculty position at the University of Minnesota and Elaine Hatfield was informally advised by NSF not to bother applying for any more research grants. Fortunately, they both survived and went on to become two of the most influential social psychologists and relationship scholars in the field.

A social psychological approach to intimate relationships focuses on the interaction between two individuals, paying close attention to both behavior and what goes on in people's minds (emotions and cognitions). Up to the late 1970s, most social psychological research on relationships concentrated on interpersonal attraction; namely, identifying the factors that lead people to be attracted to one another during the initial stages of relationship development. This research was largely atheoretical, and the findings read like a laundry list of variables that influence attraction, including the importance of similarity, proximity, physical attractiveness, and so forth (for a nice overview of this research, see Finkel and Baumeister, 2010).

By the 1980s, the psychological zeitgeist had shifted toward the much greater complexity inherent in the development, maintenance, and dissolution of dyadic romantic relationships. This shift was prompted by several key developments. First, John Gottman and other clinical psychologists began research that, for the first time, observed and carefully measured the dyadic interchanges of married couples in an attempt to predict divorce (Gottman, 1979) (see Chapter 12). Second, Zick Rubin (1973) and others became interested in love, and devised reliable self-report scales that measured love well (see Chapter 7). Third, Harold Kelley and his colleagues produced a seminal book published in 1983 titled *Close Relationships*, which presented the first comprehensive treatment of intimate relationships from an interactional, social psychological perspective.

The explosion of research on intimate relationships that occurred over the next two decades was marked by six major developments. First, there was a continuing stream of research inspired by the early work of Kelley and others on the nature and process of interdependence – the behavioral, emotional, and cognitive ties that bind partners together in romantic relationships (see Chapters 3 and 9). Second, considerable attention was paid to understanding the inner workings of the intimate relationship mind by studying the role that social cognitions and emotions play in intimate relationships (see Chapter 3). Third, the topic of love attracted considerable scientific attention (see Chapter 7). Fourth, prompted in part by the development of new statistical and methodological tools, the study of communication enabled an increasingly illuminating analysis of interaction in intimate relationships (see Chapter 9). Fifth, there was burgeoning interest in how attachment and bonding processes, forged in childhood, contribute to adult romantic relationships (reflecting the interface between developmental psychology and social psychology; see Chapter 5). Sixth, scientists increasingly examined the links between evolutionary psychology and social psychology (a theme witnessed in virtually every chapter of this book).

Interdependence theory

The backbone of a social psychological approach to intimate relationships is provided by **interdependence theory**, which can be traced to two books produced by Kelley and Thibaut that were published in 1959 and 1978 (Kelley & Thibaut, 1978; Thibaut & Kelley, 1959). This theoretical approach has several interlocking components. In general, the theory is framed in terms of the rewards that partners can provide each other in different types of situations. However, the relationship evaluations and decisions that are made in specific situations (e.g. "Should I go or should I stay?") are not based on the objective nature of rewards, but rather on the consistency between perceptions of rewards in relation to two kinds of standards – expectations about what benefits are deserved (**comparison level** or CL), and the perceived quality of available alternative partners or relationships (**comparison level alternatives** or CLalt). If the perceived rewards in the current relationship are higher than both CL and Clalt, people

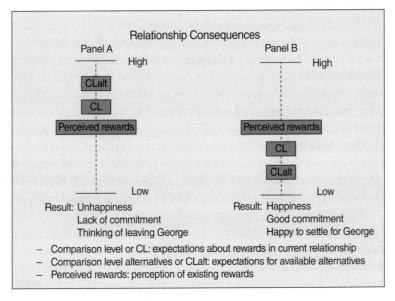

Figure 2.1   Interdependence theory: perceived costs, rewards, and standards
Source: Adapted from Kelley and Thibaut, 1978, and Thibaut and Kelley, 1959

should be relatively satisfied and committed. Keeping rewards constant, but moving CL or CLalt higher than perceived rewards should lower a person's relationship satisfaction and commitment in the current relationship (see Chapter 12).

Consider the example shown in Figure 2.1. In both cases, Mary has the same perceived rewards in her relationship with George. In Panel A, however, Mary's perceived rewards are lower than she thinks she deserves (given what she brings to the relationship), and she also believes that other romantic partners might be able to offer her more and better rewards than can George. As a result, Mary is dissatisfied and is thinking of leaving George. In contrast, in Panel B, although the perceived rewards are at the same level, Mary is happy to stay in her relationship with George, given that her CL and Clalt are at lower levels.

This component of the theory may not seem earth shattering today. However, one needs to remember that **behaviorism** (the dominant theoretical approach in psychology during the 1950s and 1960s) posited that the main causes of behavior resided in the environment rather than in the mind. During the heyday of behaviorism, attributing the causes of behavior to internal states, such as attitudes or beliefs, was regarded as quaint, unscientific nonsense (Fletcher, 1984). By locating rewards and costs primarily in the perceiver's mind, interdependence theory helped usher in the cognitive revolution, which had effectively supplanted radical behaviorism by the late 1970s. Interdependence theory also anticipated the development of social cognitive theories and approaches in social psychology by more than a decade.

A second key feature of interdependence theory is the manner in which two partners in a relationship coordinate their daily interactions to sustain cooperation and concern for each other, rather than selfishly pursuing their own personal goals and benefits. Using concepts drawn from **game theory**, this aspect of the theory focuses on the power and influence partners have over one another, and how they respond to one another when their interests either conflict or overlap. The two most important forms of control are **fate control** and **behavior control**. Fate control occurs when an individual decides to do something that affects his or her partner and the partner has little if any say in what happens. An example is arranging a surprise party for one's partner – the partner does not have any control over either whether this event happens or what it entails. Relationships in which fate control is pervasive are problematic because one partner is consistently deprived of control and often becomes unhappy as a result. An example of mutual behavior control is negotiating who will do what in organizing a party. In this situation, both partners are involved and they have more or less equal power and control over the final outcome – organizing a successful party – which is equally desirable for both partners.

Of course, many situations in real life are blends of the two processes (Kelley, 1979). For example, Kelley and one of his colleagues asked 100 heterosexual couples to answer hypothetical questions about how satisfied they would be if either one of them or both of them cleaned their apartment (Kelley, 1979). The mean satisfaction ratings on the 21-point scales couples used are shown in Figure 2.2. These numbers show the amount of satisfaction gained by men and women, depending on how their cleaning behavior is coordinated. Men are happier than women if no-one does any cleaning or if only one person does the cleaning. On the other hand, women are happier than men if they share the cleaning burden (which is mutual behavior control). These gender differences reflect traditional sex role stereotypes, which still exist today (women may be both happy and shocked if their male partners decide to clean the toilet!).

The third feature of interdependence theory is the central role of **interpersonal attributions**, such as trust, commitment, and attitudes toward one's partner. Greater trust, commitment, and more positive partner attitudes facilitate the often automatic shift that partners make from a selfish frame of mind to a relationship or partner-

Figure 2.2   Example of mutual influence in who cleans the house
Source: Adapted from Kelley, 1979

centered orientation (Rusbult and Van Lange, 2003). As we will see in later chapters (e.g. Chapters 3 and 9), research has documented the pivotal status of these relationship-level attributions in making relationships happier and more stable across time (Rusbult and Van Lange, 2003).

It is hard to exaggerate the importance of interdependence theory in the study of intimate relationships. This is not because the specific details of the theory have all been accepted, as originally formulated, but rather because the three main components of the approach – internal standards, mutual influence, and interpersonal attributions – have continued to guide some of the most important questions, theories, and research conducted on intimate relationships. We return to these concepts many times throughout this book.

Evolutionary Psychology

Darwin

Coincidentally, a draft of this chapter was being written on the 150th anniversary of the day that the most important and influential theory in the history of science was published: the theory of evolution by natural selection. The publication was Charles Darwin's book *On the Origin of Species by Means of Natural Selection*, which

Figure 2.3 Charles Darwin (1809–1882) in his 20s
Source: Image in public domain, see http://commons.wikimedia.org/wiki/File:Charles_Darwin
_by_G._Richmond.jpg

was published on November 24, 1859. The basic ideas in *The Origin of Species* (as we shall refer to it) had been developed by Darwin nearly 20 years prior to its publication, based on the extensive observations that he made as a young man on *The Beagle*, the ship on which he circumnavigated the world on a five-year journey. Darwin delayed publication of his groundbreaking ideas because he was acutely aware of the truly revolutionary nature of his theory and the firestorm of criticism it would provoke, challenging as it did the religious and scientific conventional wisdom of the day.

Darwin was especially sensitive about the risks to his reputation for several reasons, including his reclusive personality, his painful sensitivity to criticism from his friends and peers, and his lifelong, undiagnosed affliction, which produced a range of stress-related symptoms, including flatulence, rashes, trembling, crying bouts, exhaustion, and vomiting (Desmond and Moore, 1991). Darwin was an agnostic, whereas his wife (Emma) held strong, traditional Christian beliefs. However, they more or less resolved this difference of opinion, and ultimately had a long and happy marriage. This enduring problem in their relationship is illustrated by a letter from Emma to Charles during the first year of their marriage, where she shares her deep fears about the intellectual path he is taking, combined with expressions of love and support. At the bottom of the letter is a touching scribbled note by Charles, which reads: "When I am dead, know that many times have I kissed and cried over this." This difference in viewpoints only heightened his fears about the effects on his family from making his heretical ideas public.

Darwin initially developed his ideas in private and only shared them slowly over time with a few carefully chosen individuals. He was finally provoked into publication after receiving a short paper outlining essentially the same basic theory from the naturalist William Wallace in 1858. Wallace had independently arrived at the same set of ideas and conclusions, but without the body of evidence and arguments that Darwin had obsessively compiled over many years. After feverishly working night and day on his book, Darwin sent it off to the publisher with great trepidation, and his debilitating illnesses in full swing (Desmond and Moore, 1991).

We introduce evolutionary theory (and its recent off-shoot, **life history theory**) in detail here for three reasons. First, concepts and ideas from this approach constitute a cornerstone for much of the material covered later in the book. Second, evolutionary ideas and concepts can be difficult to intuitively appreciate or understand, partly because of the vast sweeps of time involved in how different species evolved. Third, rightly or wrongly, evolutionary ideas often run up against erroneous beliefs or misunderstandings.

Darwinian evolutionary theory

Selection for survival A confusion sometimes made in criticisms of **Darwinian evolutionary theory** is between the fact of evolution and the theory of evolution, the latter of which explains the underlying mechanisms of evolutionary processes. The enduring persuasiveness of Darwin's original evolutionary treatise is tied to both factors. Darwin was not the first person to suggest that life on earth had evolved. However, in the *Origin*

Figure 2.4 One of the many caricatures of Charles Darwin published in response to his theory of evolution
Source: From the *Hornet*, 1871. Image in public domain, see http://commons.wikimedia.org/wiki/File:Editorial_cartoon_depicting_Charles_Darwin_as_an_ape_(1871).jpg

of Species, he presented a meticulously detailed and very well organized array of evidence that rendered the fact that evolution had occurred inescapable. Darwin's masterstroke was to also hypothesize mechanisms that explained how evolution occurred. The evidence since 1859 has now accumulated to the point that the theory of evolution has essentially become a scientific fact, tied to the rest of science by countless threads (see Coyne, 2009; Dawkins, 2009).

The Darwinian engine of evolution involves three core elements: **variation, inheritance,** and **selection.** To begin with, there must be variation in the characteristics of the organisms within a given species. Second, some of these variations must be inherited genetically, that is, reliably passed on to offspring. The third element – selection – specifies that environmental elements (such as competing animals, access to food, access to mates, weather conditions, diseases, etc.) influence the extent to which particular individuals survive and reproduce successfully.

Those individuals who are less well adapted tend to either not survive or not reproduce as successfully, so their genes (and associated traits or features) are not passed on to future generations. As a result, natural selection determines which genetic variations survive, thus regulating changes in a species over eons of time. Together, these three elements provide a powerful mechanism that explains why most organisms in nearly all species are well adapted to the environments in which they live, and why as many as 99% of all the species that have ever lived are now extinct (Dennet, 1995)! However, Darwin's theory does more than explain how different species develop and adaptations evolve; it also explains how complex physical features like the eye, or complex behaviors like birds building intricate nests or spiders spinning massive webs, could slowly evolve over millennia under the sway of selection forces.

Sexual selection Darwin actually proposed two distinct ways in which selection could function. The first dealt with factors that increased the chances of survival, such as success at obtaining food and defending against predators. According to this part of his theory, any variation that improved the chances of survival (and ultimately repro-duction) is likely to be selected for. The second evolutionary account – termed **sexual selection** – was outlined by Darwin in his second major book in 1871, titled *The Descent of Man, and Selection in Relation to Sex*. This second part of his theory of evolution explains why male and female animals are so often different in appearance and behavior (sometimes to the point where they were mistakenly believed to be dif-ferent species).

According to Darwin, sexual selection is generated by mate choice – typically with females choosing males as mates in most (but not all) species (Trivers, 1972). In the vast majority of mammals, males compete vigorously with one another to increase their chances of being chosen as a mate by the females. This has resulted in the devel-opment of male weapons (such as antlers in deer) and large differences in physical size and power between males and females (such as in gorillas). The difference in size or appearance between the sexes is referred to as **sexual dimorphism**. Humans, for example, are moderately sexually dimorphic compared to other mammals. In addition, the male features that most females favor in mates typically evolve into increasingly exaggerated forms (and sometimes relatively rapidly), whether it be the redness of the band around a male woodpecker's leg or the flashy tail of a male peacock.

Why do females concentrate on certain features or traits of males when choosing mates? Many species of female birds, for example, are drawn to the bright colors of portions of their mate's anatomy, while others are attracted to the size and magnifi-cence of their mate's tails. Yet, being brightly colored or dragging round an enormous tail seems likely to increase the chances of being attacked or killed by predators, decreasing the chances of survival and reproductive success. Indeed, because of this puzzle, Darwin admitted to "feeling sick" at the sight of a peacock feather (Coyne, 2009).

Darwin's explanation for the odd mating predilections of different species was that it came down to taste or fashion in both humans and peahens. Evolutionary biologists, however, did not give up on the notion that mating taste or fashion might be governed by Darwinian adaptational logic. One recent theory exploits the idea that big tails, large antlers, bright colors, and the like tend to **handicap** males who have these ornate fea-tures (see Figure 2.5). Males who can afford to maintain these exaggerated, costly

Figure 2.5 Sexual selection and the handicap principle
Source: Image ©Jennifer Johnson, BlueCherry Graphics/Shutterstock.com

impediments honestly signal to females that they are healthy specimens from good genetic stock. Support for this theory has mounted. For example, male peacocks that have more elaborate tails produce both more offspring and healthier offspring than do their tail-challenged male competitors (Petrie, 1994; Petrie and Halliday, 1994).

Darwin's (1871) ideas about sexual selection were not taken as seriously as the mighty theory of natural selection in relation to survival (Cronin, 1991). This may have been attributable to the fact that most male biologists at the time paled at the thought that females in most species – by exercising choice in mate selection – controlled the evolutionary direction of males and their species. However, research and theoretical developments on sexual selection theory have burgeoned during the last few decades, with some profound implications for the study of human mating relationships (Miller, 1998, 2000).

Parental investment theory To take a key example, Robert Trivers (1972) developed a revolutionary theory based on sexual selection theory: **parental investment theory**. Trivers argued that the sex investing the most time, energy, and resources into producing and raising its offspring (usually the female in virtually all mammals) should have evolved to be more discriminating when choosing mates. In contrast, the sex that commits less time, energy, and resources to offspring should evolve to be less choosy, and should also compete more strenuously with members of the same sex to mate with the more discriminating sex. In other words, Trivers explained what Darwin had assiduously documented, but could not fully explain – why in many species males court and females choose.

Parental investment theory has been a major success story in predicting and helping explain gender differences in mate selection across a variety of species. For example, in those rare species in which the males invest more in offspring than females do, the anticipated reversal of the classic sex differences is found (Eens and Pinxten, 2000). In seahorses, for example, the males incubate the eggs (given to them by their female mate) in a pouch before the males eventually "give birth." In some species of pipefish, females produce more eggs than any one male can brood (care for). This motivates female pipefish to compete for males that might brood their eggs. Female pipefish are less choosy than male pipefish, and they are predictably physically larger and more brightly colored than males. In the much studied and spectacularly unusual case of the spotted sandpiper, females lay up to five clutches in succession with different males, after which the males do all the rearing of offspring, but only with one clutch. This means that there are usually many more available female birds than male birds. Sure enough, contrary to the standard pattern, female sandpipers are larger than male sandpipers, and they are also more aggressive because they must compete vigorously for access to males and defend the multiple nests of their male partners.

For humans, where both females and males typically commit considerable time, energy, and resources into rearing offspring, both sexes should be discriminating when choosing mates. However, women tend to invest somewhat more time and energy into having and raising children than do men; consequently, men should (and do) a little more of the courting, and women should be (and are) a little more choosy. We revisit this issue in subsequent chapters.

Key features of evolutionary psychology

Toward the end of his final chapter in the *Origin of Species*, Darwin speculated that, in the distant future, the study of psychology "will be based on a new foundation." With this mantra in mind, modern-day evolutionary psychology seeks to understand the nature and origins of the cognitive and emotional mechanisms that define the human mind and guide social behavior. Disagreements among proponents of this broad approach are a dime a dozen. Nevertheless, there is reasonable agreement on three basic principles, which were originally introduced by Leda Cosmides and John Tooby in the late 1980s and early 1990s (for a good primer by Cosmides and Tooby see Tooby and Cosmides, 1997).

First, evolutionary psychology attempts to explain and understand how human cognition and emotions evolved. Human behavior is not ignored, and behavioral repertoires certainly have evolved, but the human mind (which directs behavior) is the critical evolved organ rather than a collage of specific instincts or behavioral patterns. One often hears objections to evolutionary psychology, such as "If the evolutionary goal is to reproduce, how come men are not queuing up to place their sperm in sperm banks, and why are so many women using birth control?" The answer is that evolution has not instilled a general behavioral strategy – I must produce offspring – into the brains of humans, or any other animal for that matter. Rather, a suite of emotional and cognitive proclivities has evolved that are associated with patterns of sexual behavior, mate selection, and attraction to the opposite sex that would have enhanced reproductive success under the conditions that existed in our ancestral environments (which obviously did not contain sperm banks or contraception). To understand human behavior, we must look to the normal emotions, thoughts, and goals that humans possess, because they contain the imprint of our evolutionary past, or so it is argued.

Second, the notion that humans evolved as general learning machines is not viewed as plausible from an evolutionary perspective. Human ancestors faced a host of different, specific problems in their ancestral environments, not one general problem. Accordingly, our minds should consist of specific sets of learning abilities, desires, and proclivities that evolved to solve the specific problems faced in our ancestral environments, including detecting cheating, gathering food, mating, raising children, maintaining territory, cooperating with allies, and so forth. The human mind is similar to a cognitive Swiss army knife rather than a general problem solver, so it is argued. This is termed the **modularity** assumption.

Third, an evolutionary approach is historical. It attempts to identify the selection forces that made specific mental modules functional within environments that existed tens of thousands of years ago. What being functional means is not that what was selected for felt good, led people to lead happy lives, or even increased longevity. Functionality refers to whether reproductive success was enhanced. For example, being hyper-competitive with others may not make a person feel happy, but if such behavior produced greater reproductive success across hundreds of generations, it would have been selected for in our species. On the flip side, if a common human behavior is functional in modern environments (i.e. currently leads to greater reproductive success), this does not mean it was necessarily functional during our ancestral past.

Indeed, certain characteristic behaviors of modern-day humans appear almost designed to hinder reproductive success (e.g. violence within families), but may have been functional in ancestral environments. We describe many examples of such pernicious human traits in romantic relationships in due course, including male violence toward female partners and sexual jealousy.

The next sections develop a theme already summarized; namely, that intimate relationships can be understood only within the context of human nature, and vice versa. In the remainder of this chapter, we lay the groundwork, which we will elaborate on in the other chapters of the book. We start with genes, then discuss the evolution of human development, and finally move into culture.

Human Nature and Genes

Based on Mendel's theory of genetic inheritance – and the discovery of the molecular structure of the blueprint of life (**DNA**) in 1953 – modern theories of genetics are remarkably consistent with the basic principles of Darwinian evolution (Carroll, 2006) (for a great primer on genes, see http://www.dnaftb.org/). Indeed, the discovery that DNA is the basis of reproduction for all life on earth (from microbes to humans) provides stunning support for Darwinian evolutionary theory.

DNA molecules can be gigantic, containing billions of atoms. If the DNA in a single human cell were rolled out into a straight line, it would be about 7 feet (2.13 m) long, yet it is crammed into the miniscule nuclei in most of the millions of cells in the human body. When DNA was initially discovered, it was thought that genes would simply map onto separate hunks of each molecule in a straightforward fashion. However, research has revealed a far messier reality, with less than 5% of the DNA in humans being transcribed and used to generate proteins. What is the other 95% doing there? One idea is that some of the remaining DNA is "junk," perhaps representing the genetic fossils of evolutionary history. Yet some of this apparent junk controls important genetic tasks that regulate when and how DNA is expressed (i.e. generates proteins). These **regulatory genes** promote or inhibit the production of protein by the DNA genes, allowing the development of the organism over its life span to be attuned to the environment and giving it flexibility to respond depending on new or changing information from the environment. Genes, therefore, do not function in a one-time fashion as a general road-map at the beginning of life; they are constantly directing our emotions, cognitions, and behavior throughout our lives.

At the beginning of the twenty-first century, the fossil evidence, the development of more accurate dating methods based on radioactive decay, and evidence from studies of genetic variation in human populations around the globe have produced three firm conclusions about the evolutionary origins of our species (*Homo sapiens*). First, humans originally evolved in Africa. Second, we are a young species, evolving into our current biological state around 150 000 to 200 000 years ago. Third, roughly 70 000 years ago, we migrated from Africa to every region of the earth (apart from the poles and a few small Pacific islands), with this migration being completed at least 1000 years ago (Stringer and McKie, 1996). This is the most remarkable and rapid dispersion of a large animal species that has ever happened on earth.

The story, however, has become more complicated, thanks to Svante Pääbo and his colleagues, who recently discovered that DNA from fossilized Neanderthal bones indicates that Europeans shared between 1% to 4% more DNA mutations with Neanderthals than with modern-day Africans (Green *et al.*, 2010). Their interpretation is that interbreeding between modern (out of Africa) humans and Neanderthals occurred about 50 000 years ago in the Middle East, before their ancestors eventually migrated farther to the east and to the west (toward Europe). Two or three percent might not seem much, but it is close to the genetic inheritance that you received from your great, great, great grandfather! Upon hearing about this stunning finding, the first author of this book walked around his house repeatedly singing "I'm an ape-man" (a famous line from a song recorded by the Kinks in 1970) until his wife politely asked him to desist! Comical anecdotes aside, the general account that humans evolved from Africa in fairly recent times remains accurate.

Some of the most far-reaching findings concern the degree of genetic similarity both within and between different species. Genetic variability can be used like a genetic clock because DNA across individuals becomes more dissimilar over time (because of mutations) at a rate that can be calculated (Carroll, 2006). This evidence needs to be treated cautiously because the precision of such estimates is poor; for example, estimates of the genetic divergence between humans and chimpanzees range from 4 to 11 million years ago (Hawks, 2010). However, all of the current evidence converges in suggesting that *Homo sapiens* and the other **great apes** (i.e. gorillas and orangutans) are closely related. The closest relative to *Homo sapiens* is the chimpanzee, with whom humans share between 94% and 99% of their genes.

This last figure of gene overlap may be misleading, given other recent evidence that the differences between chimps and humans in regulatory genes (see above) are much more marked than within the genes themselves (Nowick *et al.*, 2009). Moreover, humans and chimps share only about 70% of their genes on the **Y chromosome** (Hughes *et al.*, 2010). The Y chromosome is inherited only by males (not females). This 70% figure may seem unsurprising until one appreciates the incredible extent to which genes are conserved over vast stretches of time across species. For example, humans share about 50% of their genes with fruit flies, carrots, and bananas. Even microbes share 100–200 genes with humans, which implies that some genes are virtually immortal, having been around for about 3 billion years (Carroll, 2006). Thus, the evidence suggests that the selection pressures producing the very different mating patterns seen in humans and chimpanzees were quite powerful. (Chimpanzees live in free-flowing social groups, with females and males regularly having sex with one another in a relatively promiscuous fashion; humans typically do not.)

What is Human Nature?

The ancestral evolutionary environments, within which hominids evolved during the past 2 million years or longer, were in Africa. This period of time, known as the **Pleistocene**, was replete with numerous changes in habitat and relatively rapid climate changes. In these early environments, *Homo sapiens*, and our immediate ancestors, lived in relatively small family-based groups of **hunter-gatherers** of up to 150 people. Settled agrarian cultures, which included the development of cities and modern forms of culture, did not appear until after the last ice age about 11 000 years ago. Thus, over 95% of the last 2 million years of human evolution occurred with *Homo* species living as semi-nomadic hunter-gatherers. For this reason, anthropologists and evolutionary psychologists use modern hunter-gatherer societies, such as the **!Kung San** (Bushmen) of the Kalahari Desert in Africa or the **Ache** of Paraguay, to gain at least some idea of what life was probably like in ancestral environments.

There is, however, one indisputable fact about human nature and the workings of the intimate relationship mind: evolutionary and cultural forces produced the human animal that exists today. Moreover, the degree of similarity between other species and modern humans correlates with how recently humans shared the same ancestors. Genetically speaking, our closest relatives are the other great apes. Sure enough, compared to other animal species, humans are most similar in appearance and behavior to the other apes, especially chimpanzees. Yet humans are also remarkably unique animals, distinguished from other species by a suite of characteristics that, if present at all elsewhere in the animal kingdom, exist only in embryonic and much less extreme forms. These include:

- an exceptionally large brain given our size, with a massively developed **cerebral** and **prefrontal cortex**;
- a fully developed capacity for language;
- a complex **folk psychology**, with associated theories of how the mind as well as other people function, based on cognitive representational attributions such as beliefs, desires, and so on;

- an extraordinary facility and motivation to imitate others' behavior, and associated high levels of social intelligence;
- upright walking along with considerable dexterity and hand–eye coordination, which allow remarkable accuracy in throwing objects (such as spears) over long distances;
- the ability and motivation to practice and master complex cognitive and behavioral activities of all kinds, regardless of their novelty or apparent utility (e.g. chess, music, stamp collecting, playing air guitar);
- sophisticated cultural knowledge and beliefs, which are passed on to each generation both informally and formally;
- the ability and motivation to generate complex causal models of the world;
- the ability to make mental plans that extend far into the future in a deliberate fashion, and to coordinate plans with others;
- the ability and motivation to invent sophisticated tools, including weapons, literature, computers, and all the other paraphernalia of modern technology;
- a remarkable motivation and ability to cooperate and coordinate plans and activities in social groups.

This is not a complete list, and it excludes traits and skills associated with art, humor, religion, politics, and music, which are also characteristic of the human species. But it will do for the moment. We will argue that intimate relationships have played a central role in the evolution of our unique species. To do so, we now shift attention to an off-shoot of evolutionary psychology that integrates knowledge and findings across the life sciences – life history theory.

Life History Theory

Goals of life history theory

Life history theory is based on the profound observation that it is not only the biological and behavioral makeup of individual organisms that evolve, but also their developmental patterns from birth to death. The theory was originally developed to explain how and why different species (e.g. rabbits versus elephants), as well as different individuals within a species, invest time, energy, and resources in particular traits, behaviors, and life tasks rather than others. With respect to humans, for instance, life history theory explains how and why humans differ in the way they develop compared to other species. It also explains how and why different individuals within the human species are directed down different types of developmental pathways.

Life history mysteries and the critical role of tradeoffs

The cornerstone construct in life history theory is the notion of tradeoffs and how organisms make them across the life course. For example, should individual animals pour energy and time into growing big and strong and delay reproduction, or grow rapidly and reproduce early? Alternately, should organisms pour energy into caring for a few progeny (concentrating on the quality of each offspring), or invest in the overall quantity of offspring and forgo extensive parental effort? It turns out that many of the behavioral strategies and tactics adopted by different organisms evolved in bundles; adopting one type of strategy (e.g. a reproduce fast strategy) tends to force changes in other, correlated dimensions (e.g. sexually maturing at an earlier age). We focus on life history theory in this chapter to explain how and why humans differ from other species. We delay until Chapter 5 to show how this theoretical approach helps explains individual differences in social development across the life span leading to different **mating strategies** and romantic attachments.

The life history of each species differs as a function of the tradeoffs made over evolutionary history. An important cluster of characteristics revolve around a dimension that runs from "be small, live fast, and die young" to "be large, grow slow, and live long" (Konner, 2010). A good exemplar of the "be small, live fast, die young" strategy in mammals is the mouse. The female house mouse is able to breed when 6 weeks old, can have five to ten litters each year with six to eight young in each litter, and lives for about a year in the wild. Not surprisingly, such rapid reproduction can lead to massive population explosions and crashes over very short periods of time. At the other end of the mammalian scale is the elephant, which can breed at 13 years of age, has one calf at a time, and lives for about 60 years (see Figure 2.6).

Although a good start, this kind of analysis reveals many puzzling inconsistencies across mammalian species. For example, there is a mouse-sized bat that lives much longer than a house mouse (about 20 years versus one year) and reproduces much more slowly and invests much more in each offspring than a house mouse. The

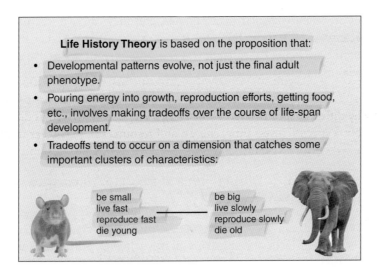

Life History Theory is based on the proposition that:

- Developmental patterns evolve, not just the final adult phenotype.
- Pouring energy into growth, reproduction efforts, getting food, etc., involves making tradeoffs over the course of life-span development.
- Tradeoffs tend to occur on a dimension that catches some important clusters of characteristics:

be small
live fast
reproduce fast
die young

be big
live slowly
reproduce slowly
die old

Figure 2.6 Basic life history dimension
Source: Images (left) ©Pakhnyushcha/Shutterstock.com; (right) ©Talvi/Shutterstock.com

South American crab-eating fox (which – you may have guessed – eats crabs) is considerably more populous and successful reproductively than its land-locked fox counterpart. These differences are a function of both the biological features of each species and lifestyle options. Small bats can fly and have superb echo-location to track down prey at night. But they also often live in caves, which provide good protection from predators. Crab-eating foxes have access to a regular supply of a high-protein diet – crabs – unlike their land-locked cousins, who have a much less nutritious diet (Konner, 2010).

Having the ability to avoid predation and protect offspring enables species to exploit and develop a "be large, grow slow, live long" strategy without necessarily being enormous. Mouse-sized cave-dwelling bats are a good example. On the other hand, large size can really help. Elephants, for example, are so large that they are virtually immune to predation (except, unfortunately, from humans). Female elephants also adopt another strategy, which turns out to be an important component in the story of human evolution; namely, they live in tight family groups made up of mothers, daughters, sisters, and aunts, and the members of this group provide invaluable assistance in helping to rear and protect each calf (Moss, 2000).

The Strange Nature of Human Development

Humans are developmental oddities in the primate world. Compared to all other primates (controlling for body size), humans have lengthier childhoods and live much longer lives than other primate species, with women often living for 20 or 30 years after the ability to reproduce has ceased (**menopause**). These differences are not subtle – they represent a stretching of human development by about 50% compared to the other great apes (Konner, 2010). Consider our nearest genetic relative, the chimpanzee. Chimpanzees are slightly smaller than humans, and they can live well past 45 years. However, because of high mortality rates (three to seven times higher than humans depending on the age being considered; Hill *et al.*, 2001), only about 3% of chimpanzees in the wild make it past 45; they also reach sexual maturity at roughly nine years of age, and they die soon after menopause (Thompson *et al.*, 2007).

The unique nature of human development in the primate world is linked to one basic feature – the nature and size of the human brain. The human brain is large. Very large! It is about three times bigger than the brain of a chimpanzee or a gorilla. A large brain, of course, means a large head, which leads to the well-known problems with human birth (not shared by other primates). It also means that humans are obliged to be born early in developmental terms (the nine-month period of human gestation is similar to that of chimpanzees and other apes). Consequently, human babies are relatively helpless and non-social during the first three months of life. The growth of the human brain after birth also outstrips all other higher primates (Konner, 2010). Chimpanzees reach 50% of their adult brain size at birth, whereas human brains reach the 50% mark at 36 weeks after birth. Large brains are also expensive to maintain and run. Very expensive! Although constituting only 2.3% of body weight in humans, they require about 20% of the energy extracted from eating food for adults when resting, compared to 13% for chimpanzees, and only 8.5% for the mouse (Isler and van Schaik, 2009).

Offloading the heavy lifting: the role of alloparents

How do humans manage the evolutionary trick of living a long time while having relatively few progeny that stubbornly stay young and need protection for a long time? Traditional models of life history have difficulty with such cases because they assume that the only energy available is that acquired by each individual's own efforts (Sear and Gibson, 2009). This is where intimate relationships move to center stage. Researchers have recently begun to appreciate that females in social groups (not just humans) can offload some of the heavy lifting involved in child care to other individuals, including their older offspring and kin. These helpers of child-rearing are known as **alloparents,** and the process is often termed **cooperative breeding**. It turns out the elephant is not alone (Hrdy, 2009).

Analyses of hunter-gatherer cultures show that although mothers remain the primary source of protection and caregiving to their infants, alloparents provide considerable additional help in gathering resources and directly caring for offspring. One excellent example is the !Kung San hunter-gatherers. Konner (2010) found that, during the first three months of a child's life, 20% to 25% of physical contact with the baby is with individuals other than the birth-mother, and this figure increases to 50% from three months well into the second year of life. Thus, analyses of both hunter-gatherer groups and non-nomadic traditional cultures confirm the adage that "it takes a village to raise a child" (Hrdy, 2009; Konner, 2010).

There is nothing terribly unusual across species in the use of alloparents to help raise offspring. As we have noted, the elephant does it, and about 9% of bird species do it (Cockburn, 2006). Such a strategy is also not uncommon in primates that live in family groups. However, humans add a few special twists to the general game plan, all of which rely on the development of powerful attachment bonds. As mentioned above, one unique feature of human development is that women live for many years after menopause. Evolutionary theories have no problem with the standard non-human pattern in which adults die shortly after they stop reproducing. Remember that the sole driving force of evolution at the end of the day is reproductive success, so why bother investing energy and effort in staying alive if reproduction is impossible. What, then, explains this curious human pattern?

One hypothesis is that this is a uniquely human evolutionary adaptation. Grandmothers typically form very strong attachments with their grandchildren, often make substantial contributions to childcare, and do a lot of foraging for food in hunter-gatherer cultures. Grandmothers in modern settings do not forage for food (although they may shop for food), but they often help their offspring and their grandchildren with childcare, housework, financial resources, and cooking. This is not only a plus for their children and grandchildren, it is also good for the grandmothers because it increases the likelihood that their own genes are sent into the future. Grandmothers share 25% of their genes with their grandchildren and 50% of their genes with their own children. Thus, genetically speaking, helping two grandchildren reach maturity is equivalent to helping one son or one daughter reach maturity.

Indeed, having grandmothers around enhances the survival rates of most children, sometimes dramatically (Hrdy, 2009; Sear and Mace, 2008). In one study, the presence of grandmothers reduced their grandchildren's mortality by 50% in the Mandinka horticulturalists of Gambia in West Africa (Sear et al., 2000). Moreover, studies of modern industrial states show that greater involvement of grandparents and kin in terms of providing material and emotional support to their own offspring (when they are parents) predicts higher quality parenting and more secure attachments between mothers and their children (Konner, 2010).

Inclusive fitness

This **grandmother hypothesis** represents an application of an influential evolutionary theory known as **inclusive fitness**. It was developed by William Hamilton in 1964 to explain why infertile worker bees and ants spend their entire lives helping their nests to survive and unceasingly assisting some of their siblings to survive and reproduce. The evolution of infertile insects initially posed a potentially fatal problem for evolutionary theory, one that Darwin himself wrestled with for many years, because it seemed to rule out reproductive fitness as the driving force behind evolution for these species. Inclusive fitness theory solved Darwin's dilemma long after he died. Infertile worker bees and ants cannot send their own genes directly into the future, but by sacrificing their own lives for the good of the hive or nest, they can send the genes they share with their siblings (50% between full siblings) into the next generation.

Of human bondage

Humans are a pair bonding species. The presence of fathers to help raise children, provide protection, and provide food for the family was almost certainly a major factor in extending the human life span, building large brains, and reducing mortality. Pair bonding is also common in other species. About 81% of birds, for example, form pair bonds to help raise their chicks (Cockburn, 2006), although pair bonding is relatively uncommon in mammals (only about 3% of mammals pair bond). None of the **great apes** pair bond monogamously with one glaring exception – us. Moreover, human males are unique among **primates** and all the apes in the extent to which they provide food and resources for their infants. When chimpanzees, gorillas, and orangutans are weaned from their mothers, they are more or less on their own in the constant quest for food. When humans are weaned, they remain utterly dependent for many years for their food supplies on their family members, their fathers, and members of their wider social group.

The combination of alloparents and the extensive parental care that pair bonding allows, has permitted one more feature to emerge in human females that is also unique among the apes – the ability to wean infants relatively early and thereby reduce time periods between pregnancies. In nomadic hunter-gatherer cultures, for example, the average time between pregnancies is three to four years, whereas it is between six to eight years for chimpanzees, gorillas, and orangutans (Hrdy, 2009). This unique feature also gave our species a distinct reproductive edge over our close ape relatives, allowing for relatively rapid growth of the population when environments were stable and resources plentiful.

What evolutionary factors produced such big brains and high levels of social intelligence in humans? Recent research suggests that mating patterns and offspring rearing arrangements may have played important roles. Shultz and Dunbar (2010) compared brain size (controlling for body weight) with mating patterns in 135 bird species. The crucial factor was that stronger pair bonding was associated with long periods of time caring for immature offspring. For example, the rook (like other corvids) is one of the brightest birds in the animal kingdom, rivaling the social intelligence of primates and dolphins (Emery *et al.*, 2007). It develops strong and life-long monogamous partnerships with a single mate, and exhibits a great deal of cooperative behavior in building nests, sharing food, provisioning for young, and defending local territories. What goes for pair bonding also goes for cooperative breeding in that it is associated with the evolution of larger brains and greater social intelligence in birds (Emery *et al.*, 2007), in mammals such as foxes and wolves, and in **new world monkeys** like marmosets and tamarinds (Burkart and van Schaik, 2010) (see Figure 2.7).

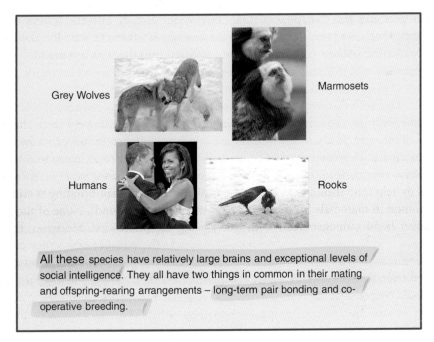

All these species have relatively large brains and exceptional levels of social intelligence. They all have two things in common in their mating and offspring-rearing arrangements – long-term pair bonding and co-operative breeding.

Figure 2.7   Examples of species with comparatively large brains and high social intelligence
Source: Images from left to right: © Judy Zechariah; Spencer Wright; Comparative Cognition Lab., University of Cambridge; dbking

A few technical terms about different mating arrangements need to be clarified at this juncture. The two most common mating arrangements in human cultures are **monogamy** (sustained romantic involvement with one partner) and **polygyny** (when one man is romantically involved with more than one woman at a time). The term monogamous is also (confusingly) used to refer to couples or individuals who are sexually faithful and do not indulge in extramarital sexual relations, but we reserve the term "monogamous" to refer to a one man/one women relationship to avoid ambiguity. The term for one woman being romantically involved with more than one man is **polyandry**, which is very rare in human cultures. The same terms are used to refer to mating arrangements in non-human species with the additional category of **multi-male/multi-female** mating arrangements, which involve relatively promiscuous mating for both males and females (as, for example, in chimpanzee troops).

Darwin was the first to observe that competition between males, as well as the need to guard female mates, could explain sexual dimorphism; indeed, he was correct (Dixson, 2009). In polygynous species such as the gorilla, in which competition between males is intense, males are much bigger than females, by a factor of 2.4. In contrast, human males are 10 to 20% or 1.1 to 1.2 times bigger than females (Dixson, 2009), which is closer to the standard monogamous mating pattern. Thus, sexual dimorphism in hominid fossils can be treated as a rough indicator of past mating arrangements in a species. The fossil evidence is fragmentary and estimates vary, but it suggests that the degree of sexual dimorphism in modern humans (about 1.2) is similar to *Homo erectus* (that lived one to two million years ago). However, sexual dimorphism is more substantial in earlier hominids, reaching 1.5 in **Australopithecus afarensis**, which lived three to four million years ago in Africa. This evidence suggests that the mating systems of *Homo sapiens* witnessed today (which are predominantly monogamous with a dose of polygyny – see Chapter 7) are not recent innovations, but were set in place long ago in our ancestors.

Consistent with this conclusion, Carles Lalueza-Fox and his colleagues (2010) analyzed the DNA of 12 Neanderthal specimens and found startling evidence that this group of 12 died at about the same time (perhaps butchered and eaten by other Neanderthals). They were part of an extended family group that consisted of three men, three women, three teenage boys, and three infants. The men were closely related (possibly brothers or uncles), but the three women came from different lineages, which suggests they left their own family groups to live with these three men. This marital arrangement (termed **patrilocal**) is typical in contemporary hunter-gatherer cultures.

To summarize, although the evidence is fragmentary, the extended family units seen today in *Homo sapiens* were almost certainly well established half a million years ago (Eastwick, 2009).

Humans are cultural animals

The development of language and culture, which allow information to be shared and communicated across individuals and down generations, has played a crucial role in generating some of the unique attributes and skills that humans now have. The development of hunting technology (e.g. spears, hatchets), the evolution of the ability to hunt effectively in cooperative male bands for meat (a highly nutritious food source), and the invention of cooking (which allowed for easier digestion and the extraction of more calories) were probably major forces that allowed the final stages of human evolution to unfold in the late Pleistocene. However, these quintessential human skills and attributes could only have evolved alongside (or in combination with) the life history of *Homo sapiens*, with intimate relationships and mating arrangements playing a pivotal role.

The power of human culture poses problems for an exclusively evolutionary account of human behavior. Humans are unique in possessing sophisticated cultural knowledge and beliefs, which are passed on from generation to generation through formal and informal channels. This form of transmission is non-Darwinian because it involves the transmission of acquired knowledge, beliefs, or skills to the next generation that is not accomplished via genetic inheritance. This **transmitted culture** can be accepted, altered, or rejected by individuals. Thus, the shared beliefs and knowledge of any given culture are capable of much more rapid transmission and change than is true of biological evolution. Moreover, cultures are stuffed full of rules, norms, beliefs, guidelines, rituals, and sanctions, linked to love, sex, child-rearing, and marriage. Thus, a lot of transmitted culture directly concerns intimate relationships.

How can scientists (or anyone) tell when human behavior is a product of social learning shaped by a specific culture or is the product of our genes as an evolved, evolutionary adaptation? At first blush, one might think that such a question is easily answered by examining behavior across cultures. That is, if the behavior is different across cultures, it is probably an outcome of culture, and if it is universal it should be genetically determined. However, matters are not this simple.

Consider, as an example, the arrowleaf plant, which develops leaves that look like arrowheads when it grows on land, like lily pads when it grows in shallow water, and like seaweed ribbons when submerged in deeper water (Wilson, 1998). The arrowleaf plant has genetic flexibility built into its **genome**, allowing it to alter its growth according to changes in the environment. The same kind of process can be found in many plants and animals including humans. Thus, variable behavior across cultures could be a function of evolutionary adaptations that are directing behaviors as a function of individuals interacting with different social or physical environments. The behaviors may be linked to cultural norms, but they are essentially produced via the evolutionary adaptation. This process is termed **evoked culture** by Tooby and Cosmides (1992) (see Eastwick, in press, for a good discussion of the differences between transmitted and evoked culture).

Likewise, a universal pattern of behavior does not necessarily mean that the behavior is a product of evoked culture. A particular form of behavior may be universal because it has been culturally learned and applied in similar ways across thousands of years and is transmitted socially. For example, the practice of wearing clothes of some kind is universal, but clothes-wearing genes are unlikely to exist determining what kind of clothes each culture develops. Similarly, everyone in Japan can use chopsticks, but this is not because Japanese people possess chopstick genes, and there are almost certainly no utensil genes that switch humans onto using chopsticks, knives and forks, or whatever, depending on the environment.

In spite of these difficulties, it is possible sometimes to determine which behaviors constitute a product of evoked versus transmitted culture. However, an awful lot of human behavior is likely not to be purely a product of either evoked culture or transmitted culture but a combination of the two forces acting interactively. Humans are cultural animals shaped by evolutionary processes to live, learn, and develop within intensely social groups. Human mind-reading, language, cooperation, and attachment instincts form a unique suite of abilities that equip us to live successfully within a cultural environment that teaches us the skills, attitudes, and beliefs needed to survive and reproduce.

Cultural transmission has also almost certainly influenced biological evolution in humans. Consider *Homo heidelbergensis*, a species often regarded as the immediate ancestor of *Homo sapiens* that lived half a million years ago in Africa, Europe, and Asia. Their brains were similar in size to modern *Homo sapiens*, and some amazing archaeological finds suggest that by 350000 to 400000 years ago, they built huts, controlled fire for cooking, and constructed beautifully designed 2-m long wooden spears for hunting (Tattersall & Schwartz, 2009). Such cultural inventions, which probably date back much farther in time, must have played a powerful role in Homo evolution.

Figure 2.8 A reconstruction of *Homo heidelbergensis*, our probable ancestor
Source: Image © Jose Luis Martinez Alvarez

A more recent example of the effects of cultural transmission on genes (and also illustrating that evolution did not stop when *Homo sapiens* migrated out of Africa some 70 000 years ago) is the widespread variability among humans in the tendency to produce the **enzyme lactase** in adulthood. This enzyme is needed to digest sugars (lactose) in unprocessed milk. Everyone has a gene that produces this enzyme, but in many people, as with most mammals, this gene switches off after infancy. This is understandable: why bother to produce an enzyme to digest milk after an age when milk is no longer consumed? Some people, however, have inherited a mutated control gene that fails to switch off the lactase gene in childhood. This genetic variability is related to how one's ancestors lived during the past few thousand years.

Individuals who descended from cultures with a long history of herding cows or goats, and consumed dairy products, tend to be lactose tolerant as adults. Thus, they can digest milk products. The opposite is true of individuals from cultures that did not herd animals or consume milk products. Thus, in Africa, 90 to 100% of Tutsi populations (who are milk-dependent pastoralists) are lactose tolerant throughout their entire lives, whereas none of the hunter-gatherer !Kung are lactose tolerant as adults. About 70% of western people have acquired the mutation, which allows them to drink milk as adults (Ridley, 1999). If you have trouble digesting milk products, your distant ancestors probably did not herd cows and goats.

Arguments about the causal effects of culture and genes on behavior do not, and should not, reduce to claims that human nature is completely a product of one or the other. Indeed, most evolutionary models factor in the power and influence of human cultural practices. However, they emphasize that many cultural practices, the human mind, and much of human behavior are products of longstanding evolutionary selection pressures. According to this view, humans are not blank slates at birth upon which the environment and culture simply write. Rather, the way in which genes are expressed tends to be flexible and operates in terms of the interaction between the organism and the cultural and physical environment. This, in turn, implies that we should focus on how individual humans develop in their environments across time.

Summary and Conclusions

In this chapter, we have introduced several key concepts and theories to which we will return many times throughout the book. We first described a foundational theoretical approach from social psychology – interdependence theory – that focuses on the immediate, proximal-level forces in intimate relationships. This theory posits that three major proximal-level variables influence relationships: expectations and standards, mutual influence between partners, and interpersonal attributions.

We next outlined the core features of Darwin's theory of evolution by natural selection, on which modern evolutionary psychology is based. The driving forces of evolution boil down to three factors: genetic variation in a population, inheritance, and selection forces. So much evidence has piled up supporting this theory that Darwinian evolutionary theory is now considered a scientific fact explaining the evolution of all species (including *Homo sapiens*). Darwin's theory of sexual selection, in particular, has special relevance to intimate relationships in humans. We will refer to it often as we proceed, along with parental investment theory, which was derived from Darwin's theory in 1972 by Robert Trivers.

Evolutionary psychology has three fundamental principles. First, it is a cognitive approach that seeks to understand how the human mind evolved to deal with the myriad threats, challenges, and opportunities of ancestral environments. Second, it assumes that the human mind is modular, having evolved to handle many different specific problems in our ancestral past. Third, it is historical, meaning that adaptations forged in our evolutionary past may or may not be adaptive in our modern environments.

A brief sortie into the nature and function of genes revealed that humans are an exceptionally young species (less than 200 000 years old). Although humans are very similar to the great apes in many ways (especially chimpanzees), they are also spectacularly unique. We then argued that understanding the unusual way in which humans have evolved may explain some of the mysteries, such as our massive brains and our prodigious skills and abilities. More specifically, we suggested that the way intimate relationships work in humans may well have played a central role in the evolution of our human oddities.

To summarize our argument, none of the other great apes (gorillas, chimpanzees, and orangutans) monogamously pair bond or make extensive use of alloparents, whereas humans have both kinds of intensive social and material support when raising their children. This combination most likely helped to vault the high levels of intelligence and social skills in our ape-like ancestors to new and unprecedented levels. First, it allowed humans to stretch out their developmental life histories well past the normal reproductive years. Second, it produced strong selection pressures for empathy, social monitoring, mind-reading, social intelligence, and the ability and motivation for the type of sophisticated cooperation that is a hallmark of our species. All of these factors helped to promote the existence and power of human cultures, which we believe turned humans into cultural animals. For humans, to a much greater extent than any other animal, cultures and evolutionary adaptations interact to produce the variability in behavior we see both across and within cultures.

Having set the scene and introduced the key theories and concepts in Chapters 1 and 2, we will now dive into two broad areas of research investigating intimate relationships in the next two chapters: the relationship mind, and the relationship brain and body.

Part Two

The Relationship Animal

The Intimate Relationship Mind **3**

Structure and functions of relationship cognition – relationship goals – general versus specific lay relationship theories – functions of lay relationship theories – controlled versus automatic processing – self regulation – emotions – origins of the intimate relationship mind – summary and conclusions

> There is nothing so practical as a good theory.
>
> Lewin, 1951

Consider the following question. How do you know whether you are in a good relationship or a bad one? If you are anything like the students in the classes we teach your response may be "I just know," or maybe "Good relationships feel good." The second answer is close to the mark, even if it seems tautological. If you want a quick and effective evaluation of your relationship, you are likely to consult your feelings – do I love my partner?, how committed am I to my relationship?, do I feel satisfied with my relationship?, how do I feel about my partner? For scientists (or even lay people), however, such an answer is superficial, and invites a second step – what lies behind and causes these judgments?

One major goal of the science of intimate relationships is to answer this last question posed, and explain how and why people make evaluations of the state of their relationships. However, the sweep of related research and theory is broad, dealing with every imaginable kind of relationship judgment and decision, from those that occur at the very genesis of the relationship ("he looks interesting"), to the kind that occur at its end ("This relationship will never work!"), to the myriad of less momentous judgments that accompany every relationship, every day.

The Science of Intimate Relationships, First Edition. Garth Fletcher, Jeffry A. Simpson, Lorne Campbell, and Nickola C. Overall.
© 2013 Garth Fletcher, Jeffry A. Simpson, Lorne Campbell, and Nickola C. Overall.
Published 2013 by Blackwell Publishing Ltd.

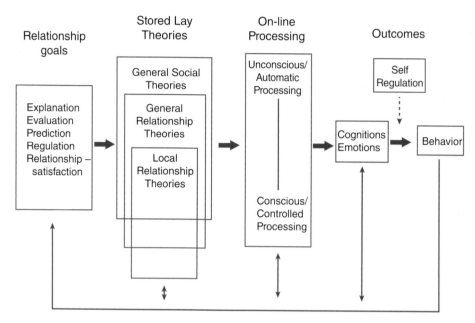

Figure 3.1 The intimate relationship mind

In this chapter we will explore the nature of the intimate relationship mind, the origins and causes of relationship cognition, and the role of emotions and feelings. We show that the human (intimate) relationship mind is a remarkable instrument, honed by evolution and culture to meet pre-ordained goals.

The model of the intimate relationship mind presented contains our own spin on work in the field, but is more or less consistent with extant research and theorizing. It is both general and complex, but we will anchor it to specific examples to render it digestible. Relationships are composed of two people but to simplify matters we will deal initially with just one individual in the dyad and his or her relationship mind. We start with a diagram showing the elements and associated causal links (see Figure 3.1).

Here is an example to give a feel for the way the model shown in Figure 3.1 works before exploring it in detail:

Mary's partner gives her a gift of flowers, which leads her to feel happy (Emotions Outcome). She had begun to think her husband was taking her for granted (Local Relationship Theory), something that she had avoided talking about (Self-Regulation). She recalls with pleasure (Emotional Outcome), the way her husband (George) used to flood her with gifts and romantic notes when they first got together (Conscious, Controlled Processing) and thinks what a loving person he usually is (Cognition Outcome). Mary decides to make his favorite meal (Behavioral Outcome).

Mary's general belief that close relationships need a lot of work to stay successful (general relationship theory), and her positive evaluation of her relationship (local relationship theory), are strengthened (feedback arrow from Outcomes). Finally, some of the goals shown in the model are heavily involved, including Explanation, Evaluation, Regulation, and Relationship Satisfaction.

We will work through the central elements from left to right in the model, starting with the relationship goals. A cautionary note – although the model is shown going from left to right, and split into different elements, in reality these processes will often occur simultaneously in the mind or work from right to left (as both the above example and the diagram illustrate).

Relationship Goals

We previously sketched out some reasons why intimate relationships are important to the wider scientific enterprise. However, relationships are not just important to scientists, but are pivotal concerns for almost everyone. If an alien anthropologist dropped on earth, listened to pop music for a day or two, and browsed through a random assortment of self-help books, movies, and novels, it would quickly come to the conclusion that humans are obsessed with love, sex, and intimate relationships. Indeed, research has confirmed that finding a mate and forming a warm, intimate relationship (to love and be loved) are recognized by most people as key goals in their lives (see Reis and Downey, 1999).

Other kinds of life goals, that at first glance seem not to be about intimate relationships, are also linked to this search for a satisfying sexual relationship including the drive for status, attractiveness, fitness and good health. The reason is that these qualities are highly valued in mates in sexual relationships. And, of course, raising children and enjoying family life are also often (but not always) linked to the goal of finding and retaining a mate.

The five general goals listed in Figure 3.1 (explanation, evaluation, prediction, regulation, and relationship satisfaction) kick powerfully into action from the moment a potential partner is met, and they remain potent throughout the course of the relationship (see Chapter 9):

George meets Mary at a party – what sort of a person is she? Does she come close to my ideal? Will she agree to come out on a date? Am I happy? Is Mary happy? How can I persuade Mary to have sex with me? Will the relationship go on to bigger and better things, or crash like my last one? How will Mary get on with my parents? Why doesn't my mother get on with Mary? Should we live together? How can I convince Mary to marry me? Why was she upset at our wedding? Why wouldn't she lend me her car when I asked her? What present should I get her for her birthday? Will I get jealous when I meet her ex-boyfriend? Why does she want to talk about the relationship all the time? Why is Mary depressed? How can I get her to pay more attention to me? How can I add spice to our sex life? Will she find out about my affair at the office? Why are we having so many problems? How do I persuade Mary to visit a marriage counselor? Why did our relationship break up? How can I meet a new partner?

These questions represent a tiny percentage of the countless number of problems, questions, and associated goals that arise in the course of a relationship, ranging from the mundane (how will Mary react when George tells her he will be late?) to the momentous (should they get married? have a baby? get divorced?). However, they illustrate the degree to which the five general goals are intertwined. For example, explanations for relationship behavior are tied into attempts to both control and predict the course of that behavior. Take the question asked above that posed a question about prediction – "How will Mary react when George tells her he will be home late for dinner?" The answer will depend on his understanding of Mary, which in turn will influence how he might frame his message to avoid any negative ramifications. If he believes Mary is thin-skinned, and that the relationship is shaky, then he might bend over backwards to apologize and bring flowers home. On the other hand, if George thinks Mary is imperturbable and that the relationship is rock solid, he might adopt a more matter-of-fact approach and not bother to express the message diplomatically.

Although these goals are intertwined in lay psychology, they may nevertheless function autonomously depending on the circumstances. For example, people are often intrinsically interested in how other relationships work, even when the outcomes of such relationships cannot be controlled, and the relationships have no direct impact on their lives. Examples include fictional relationships in books and films and television, and the (often prurient) interest people have in the lives and loves of celebrities or other famous people.

Many questions remain about these goals in intimate relationships. For example, how do people try and achieve them, and why and how do they differ across cultures and across individuals within cultures? We will answer these, and many other questions, in due course. But, first, we need to examine the contents and processes of the intimate relationship mind.

Lay Relationship Theories

The relationship mind is split into two basic components, which are intertwined: stored relationship theories or dispositions and on-line thinking. This division is standard fare in traditional cognitive models, although the two components are often termed long-term memory versus short-term or working memory. The notion that humans store every single event and behavior experienced as memory traces in long-term memory has long since been discarded as wildly implausible. Instead, according to stock cognitive theory, humans encode, organize, store, and recall events and behaviors in terms of stored knowledge structures, in which the details are often lost or blurred. Of course, a small amount of information can be retained in working memory, but this memory store is severely limited both in terms of the amount of information it can retain (typically considered as close to seven items) and in the length of time it remains available.

As can be seen from Figure 3.1, the relationship memory store consists of three overlapping knowledge structures. We will discuss each one in turn, and outline how the overlapping components are crucial to understanding how thinking works in intimate relationships. The term "relationship theories" denotes a general class of mental constructs that are relatively stable over time. These include things like memories, attitudes, beliefs, motives (and goals) that have indirect causal links to behavior.

General social theories

People have a variety of rules, beliefs, expectations, and so forth that apply generally to interpersonal relations (from strangers to lovers). These include a general folk theory (often termed **theory of mind**) that specifies when and how to attribute beliefs, attitudes, intentions, and personality traits. Hence, as can be seen in Figure 3.1, they apply to intimate and non-intimate relationships alike.

A case study: attribution theory We give an example using a much-researched theory in social psychology, known as **attribution theory**, that deals with the way in which people explain (attribute causes) to their own and other people's behavior. Imagine explaining, for example, why your partner forgot your birthday. It could be that he (or she) was under stress at work, or that he is generally forgetful, or that his level of commitment is waning, or that he is paying you back for forgetting his birthday, and the list could go on almost unendingly.

Even a minimal level of anecdotal observation suggests that people try to understand and explain each other's behavior a lot, especially in relationship contexts. This impression is backed up by research. First, people talk a lot about relationships. When Dunbar and Duncan (1997) surreptitiously listened to conversations in cafeterias, bars, and trains in England they found that talk about personal relationships typically featured strongly in the conversations (up to 50% of the conversation time across three different samples). These results are shown in Figure 3.2. This level of interest is not confined to western countries. Ethnographies of traditional cultures, including hunter-gatherer cultures, also often note that sex and adult sexual relationships are favorite topics of conversation (Haviland, 1977; Shostak, 1981). Second, people often produce causal attributions spontaneously when they are asked to describe their relationships (Fletcher *et al.*, 1987) and in the way they think about relationships and relationship events (Fletcher *et al.*, 1990; Holtzworth-Munroe and Jacobson, 1985).

However, a central difficulty in developing a scientific theory about the underlying cognitive processes involved is that laypeople use a vast array of causes and reasons to explain behavior. The way that attribution theorists have dealt with this problem is to hypothesize that it is not the content of the cause that matters so much, as where the putative causes are located along a handful of dimensions including stability, specificity, and locus of attribution.

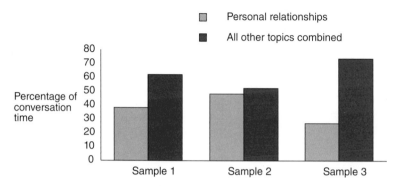

Figure 3.2 Talking about relationships in casual conversations
Source: Adapted from Dunbar and Duncan, 1997

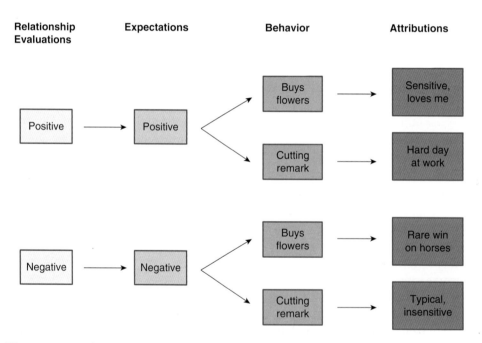

Figure 3.3 Attributions in intimate relationships

To understand how such a model works in a close relationship consider the following example shown in Figure 3.3. Mary is unhappy with her marriage and is distrustful of her husband, George. George comes home and surprises her with a gift of flowers. Mary explains his action with the attribution "George has had a rare gambling win." Thus, Mary writes George's positive behavior off using attributions that are unstable, specific, and external to George. The unstable nature of the cause means that the positive behavior will not continue, the specificity of the cause means that it will not lend a positive hue to George's personality or behavior, and the external nature of the cause means that George is not really responsible for the behavior of bringing home the flowers.

Contrast this response with the likely scenario if George were to come home and make a cutting remark, in response to a polite query about his day. In this case, Mary makes an attribution to George's insensitivity. Now the implications are reversed. The stable nature of the cause means that the negative behavior is likely to continue, the generality of the cause means that it will leak through to negatively color the rest of George's personality or behavior, and the internal nature of the cause means that George is responsible for his insensitive behavior. This entire set of attributions, for both positive and negative behaviors, is bad for the relationship.

Now, instead, imagine that Mary is in a state of marital bliss. George comes home with the surprise gift of flowers. Mary explains this behavior in a relationship-positive fashion according to his sensitivity (a stable, general, and internal cause). Conversely, a cutting remark by George will be written off with an unstable, specific, and external attribution (had a hard day at work). This set of attributions is good for the relationship.

A considerable body of research in western cultures has supported this attribution model in close relationships (for reviews, see Fincham, 2001; Fletcher and Fincham, 1991). This research has used a range of methods and has examined relationships both cross-sectionally and longitudinally using correlational designs. Strong connections have been found between the nature of the attributions and the level of relationship satisfaction. In particular, large amounts of blame attributed to the partner for relationship problems, or for negative features of the relationship, are especially corrosive in close relationships (see Chapters 9 and 12).

Of course, as we noted in Chapter 1, these methods suffer from the dreaded third variable problem. That is, more negative attributions might be correlated with lower relationship satisfaction, but this does not necessarily mean either variable is doing any direct causal work. A third variable like depression might cause attributions to become more negative and also cause relationship satisfaction to plummet, producing the correlation. However, if this was the case, then the link between attributions and relationship satisfaction would disappear when a variable like depression was statistically controlled for. And, research in this area has shown the correlational link between relationship satisfaction and attributions is robust, and is not influenced much when a range of third variables have been statistically controlled (see Fincham, 2001; Fletcher and Fincham, 1991).

One important feature of this attribution model is that attributions function to maintain existing levels of relationship satisfaction, regardless of the behavior of the partner. George is essentially powerless in terms of shifting his wife's evaluation of the relationship or himself. Regardless of whether he buys his wife flowers or barks at her, Mary will maintain her existing impression of George and her attitude toward the relationship. This feature is linked to a central tenet of attribution theory first enunciated by Fritz Heider (1958); namely, people have a basic need to sift out and maintain judgments of the dispositional and stable properties of the world, including the social world. Causal attributions are powerful means by which the relative permanence of any pre-existent belief, attitude, or social knowledge structure can be maintained, including relationship and partner theories. Potent levels of love and positive personality impressions are money in the cognitive bank that allow people to ride out bursts of bad behavior. On the other hand, the way in which relationship cognition works also explains why it is difficult for relationships that have gone sour to be turned around (but see Chapter 12).

Such a cognitive strategy cannot hold out forever against behavior, otherwise relationships and relationship judgments would never change – which they obviously do. However, we are claiming here that lay theories and beliefs are resistant to change, not incapable of change. Ordinary people, just like scientists, are conservative. They do not jettison their relationship theories according to every behavioral nuance and day-to-day experience. To do so would be to live in a nightmarish social world, in which levels of love and commitment, and related mental models of relationships and partners (not to mention ourselves) would inexplicably zoom around.

Self-esteem Self-esteem is an example of a general disposition that influences the intimate relationship mind. Self-esteem can be thought of as an attitude toward the self, and is exquisitely sensitive to how other people view and react to the self. In an influential theory, Mark Leary and colleagues (Leary *et al.*, 1995; Leary, 2001) posited that self-esteem is essentially like a fuel gauge (or sociometer) that monitors the extent to which the individual is well regarded by others. Evidence has steadily accumulated supporting this theory in intimate relationship contexts. For example, self-esteem is positively correlated with self-perceived mate value, such as attractiveness (Anthony *et al.*, 2007), and with a secure orientation to relationships characterized by openness and trust (Bylsma *et al.*, 1997).

Sandra Murray and her colleagues have shown that lower self-esteem is associated with underplaying the amounts of love and satisfaction actually reported by the partner (Murray *et al.*, 2000). Diary studies by Murray and others also document the subtle and dynamic nature of these processes over short periods of time (typically 3 weeks) in romantic relationships (Murray *et al.*, 2000; Murray *et al.*, 2003a; Murray *et al.*, 2003b, 2006). These studies suggest that when the partner is perceived as being insensitive or transgressing in some way, low self-esteem, or the possession of negative beliefs about how the partner views them, motivates withdrawal from the relationship, the production of uncharitable attributions, and a slide in relationship satisfaction.

General relationship theories

This category includes concepts (and related emotions) such as love, beliefs, expectations, and ideal standards that concern hypothetical relationships or beliefs about relationships in general (see Figure 3.1). This category is distinct from the first category (general social theories) in two ways. First, it is more content-loaded. Second, it is specifically concerned with intimate relationships. Of course, a certain amount of idiosyncrasy exists with such beliefs. However, there is substantial evidence that people's general relationship theories are similar in some basic ways, both across cultures and within western cultures. Research within western cultures, for example, shows that both men and women share similar concepts and understandings concerning the meaning of love and commitment (Fehr, 1999; see Chapter 7), what emotions mean in relationship settings (Fitness, 1996), what a good relationship looks like (Hassebrauck, 1997), and what criteria are used in searching for a mate (Fletcher *et al.*, 1999; see Chapter 7).

A critical feature of this category of lay theories is that they exist as mental constructs that individuals bring with them into specific relationships. Consider the following vignette and note the multitude of ways in which items from George's general theory overlap with the information generated from a specific relationship.

George first met Mary at a party. She was poised and confident, which reminded him of his previous girlfriend. Almost unconsciously, he felt the old vague feelings of inadequacy surface. However, these feelings subsided when he got to talk to her over the carrot sticks and humus, and he discovered they both liked "Mad Men" (his old girlfriend hated "Mad Men"). Mary laughed at a joke he made, her eyes seemed warm, and she had a quizzical look that intrigued him. She wasn't exactly good-looking, but George had never really gone after a conventionally pretty woman. He did not fit the tall, dark, and handsome stereotype, and beautiful women intimidated him. At one point in the conversation, Mary touched his arm, and he felt her breast press briefly against him. He casually slid his hand into his pocket to hide his sexual arousal. Could she be interested in him? He wanted to put his arm around her, but held back. "If women think you are after only one thing, that can put them off," George thought. The discussion became more personal, they asked about each other's jobs, what they wanted out of life, and their hobbies. George thought they were quite similar in many ways, and he warmed to her – she seemed interesting and intelligent. Mary's girlfriend (who he vaguely knew) came over and talked about leaving. George glanced at her hand – no wedding ring. Maybe this was the one? He took the plunge: "Does anyone feel like going for a coffee?" Mary smiles: "Why not – this party's dying."

George's evaluations, his emotions, his decisions, and his behavior only make sense when we understand that they have been generated as a function of what George's relationship mind brings to the interaction. Relationship scientists have extensively studied virtually every aspect illustrated in the above story including the role that previous relationship experiences have, the characteristics people look for in a mate, the role of similarity in mate selection, how self-perceptions influence mate selection, the role of physical attractiveness, the causes of interpersonal attraction, the longitudinal development of relationships, the predictors of relationship satisfaction or longevity, sex and passion, and gender differences. This book duly covers all this work, and more.

A major thesis of this chapter is that focusing on the overlap between general lay theories and local lay relationship theories is a powerful lever in explaining how the intimate relationship mind works. That is, people routinely compare their partner and their relationships with what they expect to have, or what they desire to have, or what they think they can get elsewhere (see Chapter 2).

Local relationship theories

Local relationship theories concern theories that people build up about specific people and specific relationships. What do lay local theories of intimate relationships look like? I will take as an example, the following representative short account from a participant in one of our studies, who was asked to briefly describe her current relationship (she had been dating her partner for three months):

> I first met my partner at a party. We hit it off immediately – he is attractive and outgoing and also seemed to lead an interesting life. We have since developed a rather warm and sweet relationship. He is sensitive and kind, although we have both had our problems with past relationships, and he seems a bit insecure. We do a lot of things together, and we talk about our hopes and dreams. The one problem we do have is getting our schedules together – he likes to spend a lot of time with his friends, which I think is fine (I don't want to have a relationship with someone who is super-dependent on me). But, I think we need some time on our own. I am not sure where the relationship is going, and I am happy keeping it fairly light at the moment, which seems to suit us both.

This written account represents a truncated version of this person's mental model (sex, for example, is not mentioned at all, which is typical of such brief accounts). Moreover, there are substantial differences in the sophistication and complexity of such accounts. If we had asked a person who was married to talk about his or her relationship (and if they did so frankly and freely) the resultant transcription would be likely to run into pages (if not a book for some of our friends). Nevertheless, this short description exemplifies some key points about the nature of local relationship accounts that researchers repeatedly find. First, the account has a story form, with the individual starting from the time they had met. Second, both the partner and the relationship are described in dispositional or trait terms that are quite abstract (sensitive, kind, warm) – there is little in the way of specific episodes or activities mentioned. Third, there is a tendency to link the items mentioned in terms of causal connections (e.g. he is kind but insecure – perhaps because of past relationship experiences).

From the time that a prospective partner is met, people begin to build a mental model of the partner and the relationship (self vis-à-vis the other). This model will become more complex and integrated over time, with causal connections of various kinds drawn between the elements. Many kinds of judgments will be involved, including personality judgments of the other, relationship-level judgments, and interactions between the relationship and outside situations and other relationships. Within the context of the local relationship model, people will also develop sometimes elaborate explanations of specific problems or issues that concern them (one can see an embryonic version of this in the above short account).

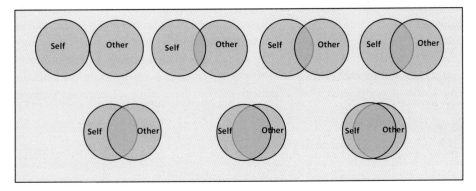

Figure 3.4   The inclusion of the other in the self scale
Source: From Aron *et al.*, 1992; © 1992 American Psychological Association, Inc.

Self theories As local relationship theories develop, they steadily become entwined with self theories. Art and Elaine Aron have documented this point in an extensive program of research, showing how perceptions of the self and the partner influence one another over time. As part of this research, they have developed a simple scale, shown in Figure 3.4. This one-item scale is reliable and seems to work as well as more complex and lengthy scales in measuring perceived closeness. Their research suggests that as couples become more intimate, they build and cognitively access a relationship theory, which represents the overlap between the self and the partner (Aron *et al.*, 2001).

In one study, Aron *et al.* (1991) found that married participants took shorter times to make decisions about whether traits applied to the self when these traits were true for both spouses and when the couples were closer (as measured by the scale shown in Figure 3.4). They interpret these results as showing that when a trait (e.g. extroversion) is perceived as applying equally to both spouses, then this renders the relevant self-judgment more accessible and automatic. In contrast, when couples are close, the centrality and power of the local relationship model makes it more confusing (and therefore increases the response latencies) when the individual, for example, believes he is an extrovert and his partner is an introvert.

Anecdotal observations of couples who have been married for 40 years or more being interviewed illustrate how far such a process can go. Some of these couples will answer questions for one another and routinely complete each other's sentences. They seem close to comprising a single unit, both cognitively and behaviorally.

Relationship evaluations At the center of lay local relationship theories exists a set of relationship evaluative judgments that are continuously updated on the basis of relevant information. The most studied evaluative categories include overall satisfaction, passion, commitment, trust, closeness or intimacy, and love. Social psychologists and social scientists have carried out a massive amount of research on such constructs. The number of self-report scales designed to measure relationship quality judgments runs into the hundreds. Just one of the most popular scales developed in 1976 by Spanier (the **Dyadic Adjustment Scale**) had been cited 2970 times in research articles (just before sending the completed manuscript to the publishers in 2012). As will be seen throughout this book, there is overwhelming evidence that these kinds of judgments play a critical role in generating relationship behavior, cognition, and emotion.

A perennial debate in the scientific literature concerns the following issue. Do people simply perceive and judge their relationship along a simple positive–negative dimension, which then drives every evaluatively loaded judgment? Or do people distinguish between, and cognitively store, separate judgments about relationship domains such as satisfaction, passion, commitment, trust, closeness or intimacy, and love? The former assumption has guided the development of several scales designed to assess overall levels of perceived relationship quality, and is reflected in John Gottman's (1990) claim that "in fact, if one selects a sample with sufficient range in marital happiness, it is difficult to measure anything other than marital satisfaction that involves the couple's perception of their relationship" (p. 78). Supporters of this thesis can point to the fact that self-report measures of constructs like relationship satisfaction, commitment, trust, and so forth are normally very highly correlated (typically around .70). Such data suggest that people evaluate their relationship in a holistic fashion: "If my relationship is great, then everything about it is great;" "If my relationship is horrible then everything about it is horrible."

However, there is good reason to believe that people develop evaluative judgments of their relationships that differ across domains to some extent. First, it is easy to envision plausible examples that support such a thesis: "George loves his wife and is highly committed to his relationship, but is vaguely dissatisfied because he does not entirely trust her," or "Mary trusts her husband completely, and feels very close to him, but she is disillusioned about the waning of the fires of passion." Second, various studies have shown that self-report measures of commitment predict relationship breakup, over and above reports of relationship satisfaction (Bui *et al.*, 1996; Rusbult and Martz, 1995). Third, using a fancy data-analytic technique known as **confirmatory factor analysis**, research has supported a model in which individuals do keep their evaluations reasonably consistent across such domains, but which also allows systematic variability of the sort outlined previously (Fletcher *et al.*, 2000a).

As romantic relationships develop, intimacy and closeness are also on the move. Harry Reis and colleagues (Reis and Patrick, 1997; Reis and Shaver, 1988), taking a leaf out of interdependence theory as described in Chapter 2, argue that a key element in developing intimacy is the way in which the partner responds; specifically, to what extent does the partner communicate that he or she understands, validates, and cares for the other. The associated kinds of attributions (what you think your partner thinks and feels about you), sometimes termed **reflected appraisals**, are crucial in intimate relationships (as will be documented in later chapters). We noted previously that research has showed that the most corrosive class of attributions for relationship prob-

"My ex had a problem with me always asking him if he had a problem with me. Would you have a problem with me always asking you if you had a problem with me?"

Figure 3.5
Source: © 2009 Liza Donnelly and Michael Maslin

lems is partner blame. The reason for this is may be because such attributions undercut perceptions that your partner understands, validates, and cares for you.

To understand further how these three levels of relationship cognitive modules are psychologically linked (general social theories, general relationship theories, and local relationship theories) we turn to the functions of these lay theories.

The Functions of Lay Relationship Theories: Back to the Goals

What are lay relationship theories for? The standard (social) psychological explanation is in terms of their goals or functions. Perhaps the most central route by which people explain, predict, and control their relationships is via the development and use of key relationship quality judgments. If you are satisfied with your relationship and trust your partner implicitly, for example, this will allow you to make rapid predictions about the likelihood of the relationship lasting in the medium term, and also to give an immediate (albeit superficial) explanation for, say, why you communicate so smoothly.

Recall that we began this chapter by asking the question "How do you know when you are in good or a bad relationship?" We are finally in a position to advance an answer. People do so by comparing what they perceive they have in the relationship with pre-existing expectations, ideal standards, and beliefs concerning what constitutes a good relationship or partner. In short, individuals integrate and compare components of their local relationship theories with their general relationship theories (as depicted in Figure 3.1).

A plenitude of evidence for this general proposition will be offered throughout the book. However, we present one illustrative example here. If George enters a relationship with the belief and expectation that plenty of passion and hot sex are indispensable elements (generally speaking) in producing a successful long-term relationship, then his satisfaction with the relationship will be pinned to his perceptions of how the sex and passion is going. In contrast, if Mary enters a relationship with the belief that passion and sex are not really important elements in long-term relationships, then her general levels of satisfaction with the relationship will not be influenced much by perceptions of her sex life. If George and Mary get together, then they may strike problems.

Fletcher and Kininmonth (1992) found evidence for exactly this scenario. For individuals who strongly believed that sex and passion were important in intimate relationships, their overall levels of relationship satisfaction were quite strongly connected to how passionate the relationship was ($r = .75$). In contrast, for individuals who did not believe that sex and passion mattered so much, their relationship satisfaction was less strongly related to the amount of passion and sex in the relationship ($r = .46$). The same pattern of findings was obtained for other beliefs such as the importance of intimacy and the role of favorable external factors.

As noted previously, one of the main goals in life is to have a satisfying sexual relationship. However, even a cursory analysis of this goal reveals its complexity. First, such goals vary from a one-night stand to a life-long commitment (see Chapter 7). Second, as relationships change over time so do the nature of the goals (George might simply be after a good time initially, but this goal will change after his love and commitment for Mary deepens over time). Third, the way in which people achieve satisfying intimate relationships varies as a function of how they cope with a conundrum posed by developing a close sexual relationship; namely, the potential of relationships to provide succor and support versus pain and misery. Intimate relationships, to put it bluntly, pose an approach-avoidance problem (see Gable and Impett, 2012).

This conundrum has been recognized repeatedly in social psychological approaches to intimate relationships. It can be found, for example, as a central component in **attachment theory** (see Chapter 5), and the **risk regulation model** (see Chapter 9). We will discuss these theories and associated research in due course. However, we simply note here that they share a common proposition that individuals vary in the way they set their relationship goals along a dimension that ranges from the confident desire to promote intimacy, closeness, and commitment versus the defensive need to protect the self and thus to restrict intimacy and dependence to manageable levels.

On-line Cognitive Processing: Unconscious and Automatic versus Conscious and Controlled

When do people think about their intimate relationships? If our general model is correct, then online cognitive processing should not normally occur without also, willy-nilly, calling up various stored dispositional constructs that are relevant to the relationship, and these may include aspects from all three knowledge categories (general social theories, general relationship theories, and local relationship theories). Relationship cognition can be elicited by almost anything. Simply sitting on the couch together watching TV (without any interaction) may evoke some relationship cognition or affect. However, watching a play, reading a book, or merely noticing a stranger who resembles one's partner may elicit some thought or feeling concerning one's partner. Feeling angry with one's boss, or admiring the handsomeness of a stranger, might also serve to remind one of an existing local relationship. Reflecting this point, Fitness and Fletcher (1993) reported that 40% of their sample recalled strong feelings of love while they were daydreaming or simply thinking about their partner in his or her absence.

However relationship cognition is evoked, an important distinction (or dimension) is between unconscious/automatic processing and conscious/controlled processing, as shown in Figure 3.6. The existence of two basic forms of cognition has been widely postulated in cognitive psychology and cognitive science. The unconscious/automatic processing end of things is typically seen not only as unconscious and automatic, but also as relatively fast and effortless, not readily verbalizable, and as relatively undemanding of cognitive capacity. The conscious/controlled end of the dimension can be described in exactly opposite terms; that is, conscious, controlled, relatively slow, more readily verbalized, and quite demanding of cognitive capacity. In cognitive processing terms, many automatic/unconscious processes can occur simultaneously (or in parallel), whereas conscious/controlled processing tends to occur most efficiently one process at a time (or serially).

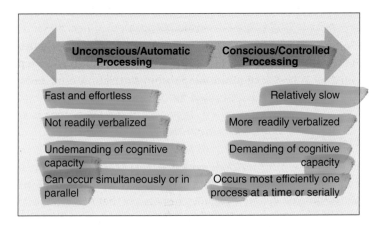

Figure 3.6 A basic dimension in cognitive processing

This kind of distinction is typically presented in terms of a dimension, rather than a hard and fast set of categories. The reason is to capture the point that many cognitive processes represent mixtures of the two processes, and also that cognitive processes that may start out with people sweating blood at the conscious/controlled end of the spectrum end up as automated and automatic (e.g. piano-playing, driving a car, learning how to please one's partner).

Consider a standard conversation in an intimate dyad, which only seems ordinary because adults have mastered the complex psychological processes involved. Each person in the dyad needs to encode and interpret the barrage of verbal and nonverbal information emanating from his or her partner, while simultaneously controlling the expression of his or her own verbal and nonverbal behavior (including facial expressions, eye contact, gestures, and body position), and blending a suite of cognitive, affective, perceptual, and behavioral processes into a performance that is smoothly coordinated in an interactive dance with the other. At the same time, each person will be making rapid judgments, guided and influenced by a set of stored relationship theories, and according to higher-order goals of the kind already described, which will vary from the mundane (e.g. "I want my partner to take the rubbish out") to the pivotal (e.g. "I am trying to avoid my partner becoming suspicious about the affair I am keeping secret"). The only way such regular interactions can be effectively accomplished is if a huge amount of cognitive and perceptual processing is routinely carried out automatically, unconsciously, and simultaneously.

When do people think consciously about relationships?

The amount and extent of conscious and in-depth analysis of a given relationship will vary tremendously depending on the stage of the relationship, individual personality differences, and the local environment. In a relationship that has reached a stable plateau, and has a long history, complex interactional episodes will become over-learned and stereotypical in nature, with very little conscious attention or thought required. Research has clearly shown that even in the most stable and well-regulated relationship, two kinds of events will snap people back into consciously regulated analysis: negative events and unexpected events (see Weiner, 1985; Fletcher and Thomas, 1996). If your partner forgets your birthday or unexpectedly buys you a present out of the blue, then you will ask why. However, your answer will be guided and conditioned by your background relationship theories in a largely unconscious fashion, in ways we have already discussed.

Evidence for this distinction

There is a massive amount of research evidence that generally supports the existence of the unconscious/automatic versus conscious/controlled processing dimension, from cognitive and social psychology (Wegner and Bargh, 1998). Automatic processing comes in various forms. In one variety, outside events may be perceived and processed, but in an automatic and unconscious fashion. This kind of automatic processing

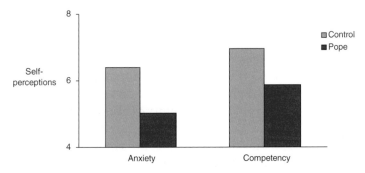

Figure 3.7 Subliminal perceptions can influence perceptions
Source: Adapted from Baldwin *et al.*, 1990

implies that people can process (at some level) what their partner is saying, even when the TV is on, the baby is crying, and they are reading the newspaper. An experimental demonstration of this kind of unconscious and automatic processing was provided by Mark Baldwin and others (Baldwin *et al.*, 1990) in a piece of research intriguingly titled "Priming relationship schemas: My advisor and the Pope are watching me from the back of my mind." Graduate students who were exposed to a briefly presented scowling picture of their departmental chair (outside of self-reported awareness) lowered subsequent ratings of some of their own research ideas, compared to a control group. In a replication of the effect, Roman Catholic women who had just read a sexually permissive passage, and were subliminally exposed to a picture of Pope John Paul II with a disapproving expression on his face, reported higher levels of anxiety and negative self-perceptions, than did control participants who were not shown the subliminal slide (see Figure 3.7). In both cases, participants reported being unaware of perceiving the stimulus figure.

Role of stored relationship theories

However, even when paying complete attention to one's partner, thinking will still be automatically and unconsciously influenced by stored knowledge structures. Thus, general relationship theories or knowledge structures (e.g. expectations, ideals, and beliefs) are silently and constantly at work, subtly influencing online judgments of local relationships and partners. For example, Fletcher *et al.* (1994) used a memory-loading technique in which participants made yes/no judgments as to whether specific words (e.g. passionate) were true of their own relationships, while at the same time they had to memorize a string of digits. These authors reported that the addition of this memory task slowed down such judgments for those individuals who had weak (general) beliefs about the role of passion (or intimacy) in intimate relationships. In contrast, adding this memory task did not slow down those who had strong beliefs in the importance of passion or intimacy. Moreover, when the same participants rated whether items, which are largely irrelevant to relationship success, applied to their relationships then memory loading slowed down for everybody. These results suggest that strong relationship beliefs are more readily accessible and thus allow people to make related judgments unconsciously, fast, and automatically.

A lot of other research makes the same point. Murray and Holmes (2009) review research showing that people automatically respond to the goal of enhancing intimacy. For example, subliminal priming of the name of an accepting other increases the willingness to disclose (Gillath *et al.*, 2006) and forgive transgressions (Karremans and Aarts, 2007). Exposing people to stress also seems to automatically trigger the goal of seeking support from a current romantic partner (Mikulincer *et al.*, 2000).

Other research suggests that those in committed relationships will automatically avoid paying attention to other attractive mates. Jon Maner and colleagues (Maner *et al.*, 2009) first **primed** participants who were either single or in committed relationships with a mating goal by unscrambling words that included words like "erotic". A control group was also included that did not have mating relationships primed. Then, participants completed a task (supposedly measuring cognitive ability) in which they had to pull their attention away from attractive faces on a computer screen to another part of the screen, and say whether a circle or a square appeared. The results, shown in Figure 3.8, suggest that when people are reminded they are in committed relationships, this automatically cuts off the mate search mechanism thus protecting commitment and satisfaction with the current relationship (also see Plant *et al.*, 2010).

Self-regulation

If everyone openly expressed every passing cognition and emotion honestly, many relationships would implode – consider such revelations as "I wish your penis were bigger," "I always liked your sister more than you," "I stole some money from you years

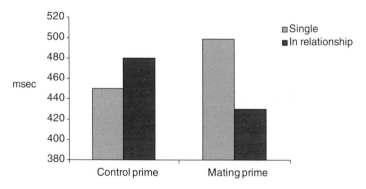

Figure 3.8   Time in milliseconds to switch attention from attractive faces
Source: From Maner *et al.*, 2009; © 2008 Elsevier

ago," "I have always hated the shape of your nose," or even "Actually, you do look fat in those trousers." Fortunately, as shown in our model (Figure 3.1), the expression of thoughts and feelings are routinely controlled and censored in relationships.

This censoring process is revealed in many ways. For example, studies investigating the private thoughts and feelings that partners report while having discussions about relationship problems (see Chapter 8 for more detail) reveal that the behavior exhibited during these problem-solving discussions is relatively sunny and positive compared to the underlying reported cognitions and emotions, which present a bleaker picture (Fletcher and Fitness, 1990; Fletcher and Thomas, 2000). The same research shows that the two spheres (thoughts/emotions and behavior) are correlated, but that the negativity of the thoughts and feelings are typically softened and packaged for public consumption, or leak through in subtle ways in nonverbal behavior (see Fletcher et al., 1999).

Moreover, people tell lies quite a lot in relationships. A study by Bella DePaulo and Debbie Kashy (1998) asked people to keep a diary of the lies they told to others over one week. In that period those in non-marital romantic relationships told an average of close to one lie in every three interactions, whereas for married individuals this rate dropped to just under one lie for every 10 interactions. Many of these lies were white lies designed to protect the feelings of the other person (e.g. "you look great in those trousers"), but a good many were also classified as protecting the self in some way ("I said I did not know why the computer crashed because I did not want to admit I might have caused the problem").

A recent review of self-regulation in relationships by Luchies et al. (2011) shows that those who are more skilled and practiced at regulating themselves tend to have better romantic relationships and handle relationship stressors in a more constructive fashion. Moreover, there is evidence that relationships are higher in quality and have higher longevity if both partners are superior in the self-regulation stakes (Vohs et al., 2011).

We will have a lot more to say about self-regulation in relationships in other chapters, but we summarize this section by simply making the point that thoughts or emotions in relationship contexts can be hidden or expressed in behavior (in either a muffled or full-blown fashion). Accordingly, relationship behavior can be an uncertain guide to what is happening in the mind of the other.

Interlude and a Caveat

So, let's summarize where we have got to thus far. We have laid out a model in which relationship thinking occurs as a function of goals, stored lay relationship theories, and on-line processing. These factors are inextricably intertwined in relationship contexts and drive cognition, affect, and behavior. Because the goals of finding a mate and building intimate relationships are basic to human nature, humans spend a good deal of time thinking about relationships and building theories about them. Most people don't consciously analyze their own relationships every minute of every day. Yet, as the research convincingly shows, relationship theories continue to unconsciously guide relationship thoughts and behavior even when the individual is not explicitly paying attention to their partner or the relationship.

The critical reader at this point may think our treatment sounds rather too cerebral for comfort. Certainly, individuals develop relationship theories that they use to reach goals. However, surely (it could be argued) a key feature of intimate relationships is that they are shot through with powerful emotions including love, anger, jealousy, and even hatred. Moreover, relationship cognitions are typically not dispassionate intellectual judgments, but are "hot" cognitions, suffused with positive or negative feelings.

We plead guilty. Our cognitive treatment requires buttressing regarding the role of emotions. Indeed, intimate interpersonal relationships constitute the crucible within which emotions are expressed, learnt, and used both in infancy and throughout life. Consider basic emotions like anger, love, hate, jealousy, guilt, and shame. These are largely social or interpersonal emotions, and are almost certainly experienced and expressed most frequently within the contexts of intimate relationships. As will be seen, however, understanding how emotions function within intimate relationships by no means implies that we can disregard the role of cognition.

Emotions in Relationships

Functions of emotions

The functions of emotions in relationships are no different from their role generally (Fitness et al., 2003). First, emotions (such as fear, anger, or love) both attract attention and provide the motivation to attain a goal. Second, they provide information that helps people decide how to attain their goals. Thus, in relationship settings there is evidence that feelings of love are associated with the desire to be physically close to the partner, and to express such urges. Anger is associated with urges to confront the partner and seek redress, whereas hate is marked by the urge to avoid or escape from the partner (Fitness and Fletcher, 1993).

However, negative emotions present a problem, given that their automatic full-blooded expression is likely to accelerate the demise of many relationships. Thus, individuals actively control and manage the expression of emotions like jealousy or anger (Fletcher et al., 1999), as we have previously argued. Indeed, the expression of emotions serves a range of communication goals that are important in intimate relationships. Drawing on Darwin's (1872) pioneering account, Clark and her colleagues have argued, for example, that the expression of emotions, such as anxiety and sadness, signal the need for comfort and support whereas anger sets the scene for the partner to seek forgiveness (Clark et al., 2001; Clark et al., 1996).

Moreover, Clark and her colleagues have argued that, whereas in exchange (e.g. workplace) relationships, people may feel uncomfortable or even manipulated by the other's expression of negative emotions (see Clark and Taraban, 1991), individuals in intimate relationships expect and welcome their partners' expressions of emotions because they feel responsible for meeting their partners' needs. Similarly, in intimate relationships, people expect that their partners will be responsive to their own needs, and may feel betrayed when such responsiveness is not forthcoming (e.g. Fitness, 2001). Consistent with this functional argument, research shows that individuals in close relationships generally regard emotional expressiveness as positive and desirable. For example, Huston and Houts (1998) found that emotionally expressive spouses tend to have happier partners. Similarly, more secure attachment styles in intimate relationships are associated with freer expressions of anxiety and sadness (Feeney, 1995, 1999).

Lay emotion theories and scripts

Fitness *et al.* (2003) have argued that emotion lay theories can be categorized according to the same tri-partite division that we previously laid out for cognitive lay theories. At the most general level, people hold theories about the nature of "emotional" versus "non-emotional" stimuli and about the features (e.g. causes, physiological symptoms, urges, and outcomes) of specific emotions like anger and happiness. Such lay emotion theories are often referred to as **emotion scripts,** in recognition that emotion episodes often involve more than one person, and, like dramatic productions, unfold predictably over time (Fitness, 1996).

At the next level of specificity, people hold theories about the causes and features of emotions in relational contexts. Think back to the last time that you felt angry with your partner in an intimate relationship. What caused you to feel this way? What physiological experiences did you have? What urges did you have? What behavior did you actually perform? What did you feel like afterwards? To the extent that you expressed the emotion what did your partner say or do? To what extent did you blame your partner? How much control did you have over the emotion? How predictable was the emotion?

Researchers, like Julie Fitness (Fitness, 1996) and Beverley Fehr (Fehr and Baldwin, 1996) have asked exactly these kinds of questions (and many more) about emotions that people experience in intimate relationships. The results have shown that different emotions are distinguished by a set of characteristics that cohere into core themes or scripts. For example, if you responded according to the prototypical script for anger revealed in participants' reports, you would have said that your partner triggered the emotion by treating you unfairly, that you felt a good deal of muscle tension and felt a strong urge to express yourself (which you probably did), that your partner responded in kind (angrily), that despite the short-lived nature of the anger you felt tense or depressed afterwards, that you perceived that you had reasonable control over yourself and the situation, and finally that it was mainly your partner's fault. Your partner, in turn, should respond by asking for forgiveness. For a stripped-down version of this sort of script see Figure 3.9.

Similar thumbnail sketches of emotions like jealousy, hatred, love, and guilt are provided by the same research. Each emotional prototype has the same general script-like form that unfolds in a particular way, with the raw feeling being enveloped in a set of perceived causes and effects, and with appropriate accompanying states and behaviors. In short, the self-perception and expression of emotions involves a lot of

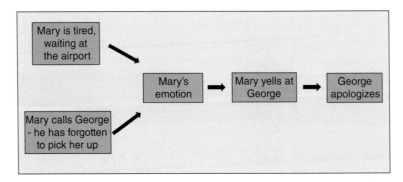

Figure 3.9   Emotion Script: What do you think the emotion is?

cognition, and, in intimate relationship settings inevitably drags in both general and local relationship theories of the sort previously described. If Mary's husband buys her a bunch of roses she may experience love toward him, or anger if she knows, that he knows, she hates roses.

This kind of analysis answers a thorny question in psychology; namely, without access to the emotional experiences themselves, how do you accurately attribute emotions to other people. The answer suggested is that you come well equipped for such tasks with the possession of mini-theories that locate emotions within a network of causes and consequences. Moreover, such theories are also pressed into service when making self-attributions of emotions. They often do so in an automatic fashion creating the illusion that we are directly observing them in our minds. Of course, emotions are a function of internally experienced feelings, brain states, and processes (more of this in Chapter 4), but such raw experiences are nevertheless interpreted and labeled in the light of the rich store of information and theories in the layperson's mind.

Basic emotions

Another way in which emotions are accurately attributed to others is via their facial expressions. Darwin initially proposed (with some evidential support) that the principal emotions were expressed in the same way across different aboriginal populations in his book, *The Expression of the Emotions in Man and Animals*, published in 1872. However, it took another 90 years before Paul Ekman provided telling evidence for Darwin's thesis in his investigations with pre-literate tribes in New Guinea (the South Fore) that had little prior contact with Europeans or western culture. We say "compelling" because prior research with western or literate cultures was subject to the objection that participants may have learnt western emotional displays from watching movies and reading magazines (see Russell, 1994). Ekman reported that members of the South Fore culture were quite accurate in identifying posed pictures of individuals displaying the **basic emotions** of anger, fear, disgust, surprise, happiness, and sadness

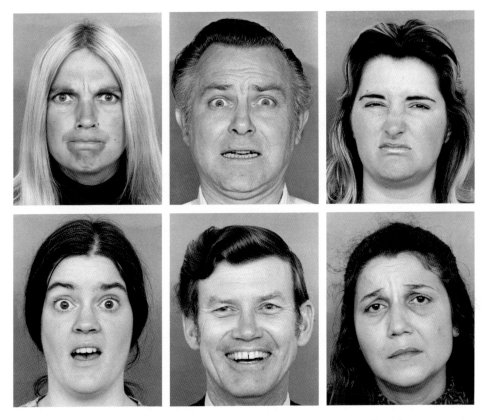

Figure 3.10 Basic emotion running counter clockwise from left: anger, fear, disgust, surprise, happiness and sadness
Source: Image © Paul Ekman, PhD/Paul Ekman Group, LLC

(the same emotions as shown in Figure 3.10 which we hope you all recognized) (see Ekman, 1994).

In 1994, James Russell published a wide-ranging critique of the general cross-cultural work in this area (which by this time included 31 literate cultures and five pre-literate cultures), which was followed by a vigorous debate among Russell (1995), Ekman (1994), and Carroll Izard (1994). The debate and re-analyses of prior data revealed that the levels of accuracy were very high with western literate cultures, went down a notch with non-western literate cultures, and were the lowest for the isolated non-literate cultures of New Guinea. However, even in the New Guinea cultures respondents typically chose the right label (from a list of three emotions) over 80% of the time (Ekman, 1994, table 4). Interestingly, however, Ekman (1994) reports that simply presenting a picture with an emotional display without any context produced various difficulties. For example, because the participants could not read they had to recall the list of emotions words, which they found difficult. Thus, the researchers

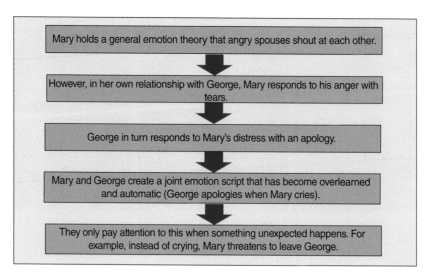

Figure 3.11   Mary, George, and emotion scripts

altered the procedure by telling a short story to accompany the visual image. In short, the emotion label was now being chosen with the help of an emotion script along with the facial expression. This is still good evidence for the universality of such basic emotions, but with a cognitive twist added.

At the third level of specificity, partners develop local, idiosyncratic theories about how emotions work within their own relationships. Such local lay theories may conflict with general higher-order emotion theories. For example, Mary may hold a general emotion theory that angry spouses are likely to shout at one another, but within her own relationship, she may typically respond to George's anger with tears. He, in turn, may reliably respond to her distress with an apology. In this way, relationship partners can create joint emotion scripts that can become over-learned and "run off" automatically, with each partner only really paying attention when something unexpected happens (e.g. George continues to shout at Mary, despite her distress, or instead of crying Mary threatens to leave the relationship). This scenario is shown in Figure 3.11.

Do emotions get in the way of rational thought?

Antonio Damasio (1994) has argued persuasively that emotions are indispensable for motivating people to make good decisions and to behave rationally. Damasio bases this argument partly on case studies of individuals who had suffered localized forms of brain damage (to regions of the **prefrontal cortex**) that specifically incapacitated their ability to experience emotions, but left other abilities and functions intact. For example, Elliot, one of Damasio's favorite cases, was incapable of making even the most basic decisions, such as what clothes to wear, and his intimate relationships became dysfunctional. Yet, he scored normally on personality and intelligence tests, and could reason perfectly well. Damasio's explanation for the crippling effects of such deficits is that the absence of emotion removes an essential element (with a long evolutionary history) that people routinely use to make choices among different actions or activities.

Damasio's (1994) theory has the ring of truth when applied to relationship settings. Imagine making decisions and judgments in relationship contexts while experiencing no emotions or feelings. If you were to meet a few people at a party, who do you phone up for a date? If you go on a date with someone, how do you decide whether to go out on another date? How do you respond when your partner tells you he or she loves you, or that he or she wants to go to bed with you? If you do decide that your partner can be trusted or not trusted, is warm or cold, is patient or bad-tempered, how do you act on those judgments? Without any emotions or affective tone to go on, we suspect individuals would become like rudderless ships – indeed, just like those described by Damasio who suffered from specific damage to regions of the brain centrally involved in emotions and affect.

The point here is that cognition and emotion are thoroughly intertwined. Mary decides to date George because she likes him and is attracted to him – the automatic and conscious processing that underlies such a judgment may be complex, but it is likely to be the resultant hedonic feel to her interaction with George she uses as the final output in making some sort of decision. It is the lack of introspective access to the complex cognitive and neuropsychological machinery at work, which informs and produces emotions like "love," that is (we suspect) one reason why people often pronounce love as a mysterious and inexplicable.

Again, we will have a lot more to say about the role of emotions in intimate relationships in later chapters. However, there are two general take-home messages to this section. First, emotions and cognitions are thoroughly intertwined, and work together in normal social cognition. Second, emotions are indispensable rather than inimical to good decision-making in relationship settings.

The Distal Origins of the Intimate Relationship Mind: Evolution and Culture

In the introduction we mentioned three critical domains that explain the origin and nature of any psychological phenomenon: ultimate causation in terms of evolutionary and cultural processes; ontogeny, which deals with developmental processes; and proximate causation, which deals with on-going, situationally specific processes. However, these sources do not exert their influence in terms of main effects but rather in interactions with one another. This is a crucial point that will be exemplified again and again in the coming chapters, but we will set the scene here with a brief overview, mentioning chapters in passing that deal with the same questions.

In the model we proposed (Figure 3.1) the intimate relationship mind is split into three kinds of overlapping stored theories: general social theories, general relationship theories, and local relationship theories. Although there is some domain specificity

involved, we argued that lines of influence are likely to operate among all three categories, which will tend to keep them roughly in synchronization. For example, explaining
why Mary left George will influence George's general theories about intimate relationships, reading an article about intimate relationships (scholarly or pop) can influence
George's local relationship theory about his relationship with Mary (perhaps he was
not assertive enough about his own needs and wishes), and George can use his understanding of a restaurant script to impress his new partner on a first date.

Such stored knowledge structures are constantly available, being pressed into action
and conditioning our cognitions, emotions, and behaviors often unconsciously and
automatically. This notion nicely squares with both evolutionary and cultural origin
accounts. For example, in evolutionary approaches nascent rules and tendencies
encoded genetically need to operate in exactly this kind of omnipresent background
way, ready to exert their influence when the developmental or environmental context
call them into action.

As noted previously, the standard model of evolutionary psychology developed
principally by John Tooby and Lida Cosmides (1992) assumes that human cognition
and emotion is modular. That is, humans evolved to develop hundreds if not thousands of cognitive and emotional rules or strategies specifically designed to solve the
problems faced in the ancestral environment, including the myriad problems faced in
the intimate relationship domain.

This is probably the most controversial component of this approach, even among
evolutionary psychologists. The concept of modularity was pioneered by Jerry Fodor
(1983) who used it to refer to cognitive or perceptual capacities that are hard-wired
and automatic, such as visual or auditory perception. In an oft-cited example, he
pointed out that a visual illusion still remains potent, even when observers know that
what they are looking at is wrong. The visual system is, thus, insulated against the
influence of other cognitive systems, such as higher-order knowledge or beliefs, and
proceeds in an automatic and encapsulated fashion. On the face of it, the idea that
conscious and controlled cognition is controlled by thousands of if–then programs
that operate in an insulated and automatic fashion (like the visual system) adds up to
a rather stupid organism, rather than a flexible and intelligent organism.

Indeed, Fodor (1983) believed that higher-order human cognition is not fundamentally modular. Conscious, controlled cognition appears to be highly permeable, open
to suggestion and influence from all quarters, and actively non-modular in its operation. The development of scientific theories, for example, almost always involves the
deliberate and imaginative comparison between two or more domains, as does the
everyday use of metaphors and similes. The ability to generate highly abstract and
hypothetical knowledge structures (e.g. logic and mathematics) that are context-free,
and can be applied across domains, also seems inherently non-modular.

The non-modularity of the intimate relationship mind is represented in the following aphorism that one sees occasionally emblazoned on T-shirts – "A woman needs a
man like a fish needs a bicycle." Understanding what this means, and why it is funny,
relies on the human ability to compare and understand relations among disparate
domains (fishes, modes of transport, and sexual relationships). A highly modular mind

would be dumbfounded at such an expression. Indeed, language itself is a device that appears wonderfully adapted to non-modular, cross-domain cognition.

One useful way of approaching this issue is to concede that the human mind possesses both modular and non-modular features (Hirschfeld and Gelman, 1994). We will compile evidence throughout this book that the intimate relationship mind is shaped and composed of a range of distinct phenomena that have specific biological features, developmental trajectories, and causal etiologies, which often operate in modular ways (automatically, and relatively independently of other traits and processes) – these include attachment processes (Chapter 5), romantic love (Chapter 7), sexual jealousy (Chapter 10), sexual passion and behavior (Chapter 10), mate selection processes (Chapter 6), and physical attraction (Chapters 6 and 10).

However, the intimate relationship mind is a product of interactions between culture and our evolutionary heritage. We stressed previously our view that humans are cultural animals, and gave some examples of how biological evolution and culture almost certainly influenced each other over many thousands of years in human history. However, they continue to interact at the proximal level, shaping the intimate relationship mind.

Let's give an example. As we show in later chapters, there is good evidence that physical attractiveness has universal appeal in prospective mates, that men give it more weight than women, and that the features that go toward making some people more attractive than others are also universal. We will in due course also describe why this is the case in terms of evolutionary arguments and evidence. However, culture also has a role to play.

Take Ken and Barbie. Barbie dolls have been around since 1959, and have become the most popular doll in the world, with 99% of 3–10-year-olds owning one in the USA (Rogers, 1999). Barbie's dimensions are odd, but her face is classically pretty. Setting her height as 1.75 meters (5 ft 9 inches), her approximate measurements if she was scaled up to life size would be chest 88 cm (35 inches), waist 55 cm (21 inches), and hips 76 cm (30 inches). Barbie is often derided as having abnormally large breasts, to the point that she would fall over if she was a real person, but this is an illusion created by her tiny waist. Ken is more life-like, with a body that is closer to a stereotypical chiseled, well-muscled male frame. This did not stop him from being dumped by Barbie, however, on Valentine's Day in 2004, after dating him for more than 40 years, although they were reunited on Valentine's Day 2011, after an extensive digital campaign by Mattel (check out what Ken had to do to get Barbie back on YouTube).

When Cindy Jackson looked at the Barbie doll, when she was six, she said in a TV interview in 2004 that she thought "This is what I want to look like." Indeed, 31 operations later at the age of 48, she became a living Barbie doll (although her body, it has to be said, is considerably more buxom than Barbie's slim figure). This is clearly not a typical response. However, when Helga Dittmar and other researchers exposed girls aged from five to eight years of age to images of Barbie dolls, their desire to be thin increased and their body self-image suffered a hit (probably temporarily) (Dittmar *et al.*, 2006). More generally, the surge of eating disorders, such as bulimia and anorexia that has afflicted western and industrialized cultures, has often been thought to be linked to the incessant bombardment of sexy (and thin) images of women in various ways, including music videos and the media.

Indeed, there is some evidence for such a link. In one study, Anne Becker and colleagues (Becker *et al.*, 2002) surveyed samples of high school students living in the Nagroda province of Fiji at two time points – one month after the wide-spread introduction of TV in 1998, and two years later, by which time most homes had TV sets. The results revealed a startling increase in just two years in terms of body dissatisfaction and behaviors like induced vomiting to control weight.

This example is just one of many, which show how mate selection goals and self-perceptions of mate value (which have a long evolutionary history) are profoundly influenced by information from the culture. They also illustrate the point that our evolutionary heritage was developed over many thousands of years during which we were *not* bombarded daily with attractive images of other people and web-based dating a mouse-click away. No wonder the responses to such features of contemporary culture can all too often be dysfunctional or even life-threatening.

Summary and Conclusions

The intimate relationship mind can be usefully split into different components: goals, stored lay theories, on-line processing, and self-regulation. In this chapter, we discussed the links among these categories, and how they drive emotions, thoughts, and behaviors in relationships. A few take-home messages stand out. First, the goals are critical motivating factors. Second, the overlap between general and local relationship theories enables people to evaluate their partners and relationships. Third, a lot of relationship thinking is unconscious and automatic – conscious thoughts represent the tip of the iceberg. Fourth, self-regulation is ubiquitous in relationships. Fifth, emotions and cognitions are inextricably intertwined in intimate relationships. Finally, the only way of understanding the ultimate origins of the intimate relationship mind is to untangle the dual roles played by evolution and culture.

The relationship mind, as we have seen, is both busy and complex. In this chapter we have given our take on how the relationship mind works, how and why people evaluate their intimate relationships, and how partner and relationship judgments are produced. The way the relationship mind works, of course, shares many features with the way it works more generally. However, it also has some special characteristics, about which we have a lot more to say in future chapters.

The Intimate Relationship Body 4

sexual reproduction – human genitalia – orgasms, nipples, adaptations, and by-products – the human body and behavior are windows into our mating past – hormones, sex and relationships – the relationship brain – health and intimate relationships – summary and conclusions

The brain is wider than the sky.

Emily Dickinson, 1924

René Descartes (1596–1650), who coined the famous phrase "I think therefore I am," argued for a version of **mind–body dualism** – the view that the mind and the body are entirely different entities. Descartes likened the material body to a machine that performed its functions according to the laws of nature. In contrast, the mind (made up of thinking, conscious experience, moral judgments, and the like) was not governed by the laws of nature.

Descartes' ideas on mind–body dualism have been extraordinarily influential in science and philosophy. Nevertheless, mind–body dualism has been steadily losing steam over the last few decades as different streams of scientific work have coalesced into supporting a materialist approach to the human mind; namely, although cognitive and biological approaches may operate at different explanatory levels, the mind and the relationship brain are really one thing, not two things (see Chapter 1).

One stream of research, supporting a materialist approach, is concerned with what is termed **embodied cognition**. The central axiom of this research domain posits that bodily and perceptual processes and cognition work to influence one another within an integrated biological system. It is replete with cute experimental examples, such

The Science of Intimate Relationships, First Edition. Garth Fletcher, Jeffry A. Simpson, Lorne Campbell, and Nickola C. Overall.
Published 2013 by Blackwell Publishing Ltd.

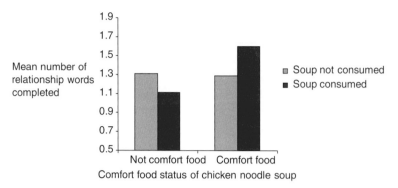

Figure 4.1   Priming food can influence relationship cognition
Source: From © Troisi & Gabriel, 2011

as the finding that warming one's hands with a hot cup of coffee heightens perceptions of interpersonal warmth when meeting a stranger (Williams and Bargh, 2008), or eating comfort food like chicken soup automatically brings relationship words to mind (Troisi and Gabriel, 2011), as can be seen in Figure 4.1. A second scientific stream concerns the progress toward understanding how human minds have evolved (in conformity with the laws of nature), some of which we have already discussed. Yet a third example of such work is the burgeoning of research on the human brain and body, especially in relation to social judgments, relationships, and illness. This chapter focuses on this third category of scientific work, specifically, of course, in terms of sexual relationships.

If a materialist approach is worth its salt, then scientific work on the relationship mind and body should be consistent and fit together in an informative fashion. In this chapter we will test this assertion by outlining what scientists currently know about the biology of the relationship brain and body (specifically as they are linked to sexual relationships), and broadly comparing this to the major propositions emanating from the scientific study of the relationship mind (and behavior) as outlined in the previous two chapters.

We begin by addressing two basic questions that are often taken for granted; namely, why there are two sexes (male and female) in almost all species, including humans, and what explains the structure of human genitalia. These questions reside at the extreme distal end of the continuum we described in Chapter 1 (see Figure 1.3), requiring answers from deep evolutionary time. The remaining topics deal mainly with the proximal end of the same dimension. Specifically, they concern the role of hormones in relationships, and how the different areas of the brain affect the initiation, functioning, and maintenance of intimate relationships. We conclude the chapter by reviewing how and why intimate relationships influence health outcomes.

Why Sexual Reproduction?

Given the commonplace status of the basic facts of **sexual reproduction** today, you may find it surprising that they were more or less a mystery until the seventeenth century, when three medical students from Holland worked out that the union of female eggs and male sperm is required to produce human offspring (Cobb, 2006). Sexual reproduction (requiring genetic contributions from both males and females) has been around for an astonishingly long time (about 1 billion years), and most species reproduce this way. But, there are considerable costs attached to such a reproductive system. It is cumbersome, and the process of sexual selection obliges males and females in many species to devote enormous efforts to attracting and mating with suitable mates. It is also often a risky business for (usually) males who, in advertising their mating credentials, may also advertise their location to predators (the peacock being an example), or face injury or even death in competing for access to females.

Asexual reproduction, which simply clones the organism to (usually) produce identical offspring, on the face of it, seems a simpler, safer, and more efficient system. This form of reproduction is the primary form of reproduction for single-cell organisms, such as microbes. But several animals also have the ability to switch to asexual reproduction when male genes are in short supply including jellyfish, aphids, and even some species of sharks. These points raise two questions. Why do species that can switch to asexual reproduction bother with sexual reproduction at all, and why did such a cumbersome, inefficient arrangement (sexual reproduction) become so popular in the first place?

The most common answer given to these thorny questions is that sexual reproduction randomly shuffles genes from the male and female to produce offspring. This process reliably produces myriad individual differences across offspring from the same parents, which is grist for the Darwinian evolutionary mill. Recall that an essential component of Darwinian evolutionary theory is the existence of variability across individuals in the same species, thus providing natural selection something to work on. In essence, this explanation suggests that sexual reproduction caught on long ago because it allowed evolutionary processes to produce adaptations more effectively – that is, the process of evolution itself has evolved.

A powerful application of this general argument concerns how organisms deal with the ever-present threat of parasites. All living things rely, in part, on mutations to produce variability in genetic make-up, and bacteria also have the ability to exchange genes in cell-to-cell contact. However, parasites can reproduce at a fantastically fast pace compared to humans. Some bacteria, for example, can asexually reproduce once every 20 minutes. Starting with one bacterium, and assuming unlimited food and no deaths, this is fast enough to cover the entire earth 8 feet deep (2.44 meters) in bacteria after only 39 hours! This gives bacteria a massive advantage in the evolutionary arms race between parasites and humans. However, shuffling the genetic deck to create novel genetic combinations, via sexual reproduction, is a powerful engine for creating variability across individuals in their constitutions and immune systems, boosting the chances that even when devastating plagues strike human populations, some or even many individuals will be able to survive the disease and eventually reproduce, thus passing on their resistance (see Ridley, 1999). Indeed, this is what generally happens.

Human Genitalia and their Origins

Figures 4.2 and 4.3 may prove useful in following this necessarily ultra-brief account of a complicated process. Human sexual organs are both external and internal. A huge number of sperm (from 200 to 500 million) are ejaculated into the **vagina** courtesy of an erect male penis and a male orgasm, but by the time they swim up the **fallopian tube** (about 10 cm or 6 inches in length) only about 200 are left (Dixson, 2012). Over a period of some hours these sperm are exposed to a range of chemicals that will increase their motility and ability to penetrate the egg. If the few sperm left are lucky, they may meet an **ovum** passing along one of the Fallopian tubes from the **ovary** where

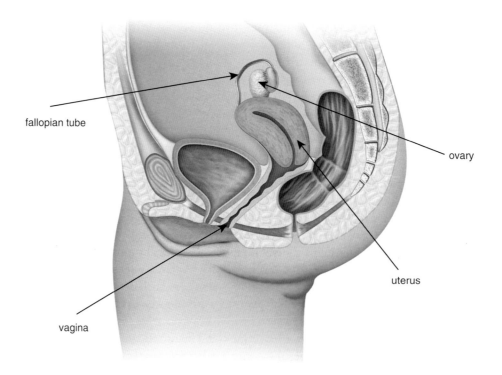

Figure 4.2   Human female reproductive organs
Source: Image © Andrea Danti/Shutterstock.com

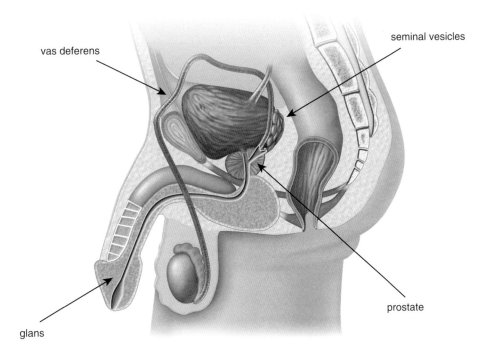

Figure 4.3 Human male reproductive organs
Image © Andrea Danti/Shutterstock.com

ova are stored and released about once a month. If fertilization is successful, the egg
is attached to the **uterus** and a human fetus starts its uncertain journey. We say uncertain because the chances of a spontaneous miscarriage are high at the early stages of
implantation, up to 50%, although the chances of success substantially improve over
the first 12 weeks and beyond.

The external parts of the male reproductive system involve the penis (including the
glans and the foreskin covering the glans), and the testicles (which produce and create
the sperm). Located internally, the **seminal vesicles** and the **prostate** produce the
seminal fluid (making up to 95% of semen), which contains a diverse array of chemicals to help sperm on their way and to counteract the slightly acidic environment of
the vagina. Sperm, by the way, can stay in the vagina perhaps as long as four to five
days and still produce fertilization.

In many fish and denizens of the ocean, fertilization of female eggs occurs outside
the bodies of both male and female organisms. However, once the evolution of animals
on land got cracking (about 350 million years ago), sexual reproduction via internal
fertilization became the norm, presumably because external fertilization is no longer
a viable strategy. And, internal fertilization in females can only evolve in tandem with
a male device able to deliver sperm internally into the female. Not all male animals

have a penis to accomplish this task (most male birds get by without one), but many do, including all the mammals. Moreover, variability in the form and shape of the penis, and associated behavior of males and females, across the animal kingdom is staggering (Birkhead, 2000).

Over the last four decades, scientists have picked up the key elements of Darwin's ideas in sexual selection theory (see Chapter 2) to help explain the variability in genitalia and reproductive behavior across species (see Birkhead, 2002; Eberhard, 1985). This work has demonstrated that the evolutionary history of sexual reproduction is a battleground, in which both sexes attempt to exert control over the reproductive process, the result often being an uneasy compromise. More specifically, competition between males, along with female mate choices, not only operate prior to copulation (as Darwin proposed) but also often after copulation (so-called **sperm competition**). Moreover, different mating systems adopted by particular species are evolutionarily intertwined with the nature of their reproductive organs and their mating behavior. We illustrate and apply these points to human reproduction and genitalia.

The human body and behavior are windows into our mating past

In species in which multiple matings take place between females and males, dozens of adaptations have been documented in the battle to control fertilization, and the evolution of the penis itself was often influenced by sperm competition. For example, the penis of some species of male dragonflies contains barbs and spikes for the purpose of removing the sperm of rival males (Waage, 1979). And, in one species of squirrel, the penis is shaped like a knife, enabling it to cut through the dried and hardened sperm of other males that block the vaginal opening (Birkhead, 2000). A standard behavioral strategy (seen for example in the chimpanzee) is to have sex as frequently as possible with a range of eligible males and females. Indeed, the reproductive systems of male chimpanzees are purpose-built to provide the staying power needed, with huge testes and fast-swimming, high quality sperm (Dixson, 2009).

But is there evidence for sperm competition in humans? This is an important question because the answer throws light on the recent evolutionary history of human mating systems. Sperm competition in humans requires the co-existence of sperm capable of fertilization from at least two men in a woman's vagina, thus requiring that a woman mates with two men in the space of up to five days (Goetz et al., 2007). Certainly this is possible, and the existence of sperm competition in humans is argued for by some evolutionary psychologists (see, for example, Baker and Bellis, 1995; Goetz et al., 2007). In many species, including monogamous ones, males and females stray sexually from their primary mates. Humans are no exception. For example, about 14% of women under 30 in liberal western countries like France and the US report that they had sexual intercourse with a man when involved in an existing sexual relationship (Simmons et al., 2004).

However, the effects of sperm competition in evolutionary terms are dependent on the frequency with which these extra-pair dalliances occur within the presumptive five-day fertile period, as it is only then that conception can take place. Baker and Bellis's (1995) British nationwide survey reported that between 6 and 9% of women had sex with an interloper within five days of having sex with their main partner. Now the chances of conception of any given act of sexual intercourse are 3%. Thus, the overall chances of conception occurring in these circumstances turn out to be fairly remote (0.23%). This figure is consistent with an estimate by James (1993) that 1 in 400 (0.25%) of non-identical twins have been fathered by different men. More generally, the rates of extra-pair paternity from DNA fingerprinting in the general population, according to a review of published data by Simmons *et al.* (2004), are quite low at 1.82%, although they are considerably higher for certain traditional cultures (at about 10%). The lower rate of extra-pair paternity in modern cultures could be partly a function of the availability of contraception.

On the other hand, some fascinating genetic analysis by Bryan Sykes and Catherine Irven (2000) of the male (Y) chromosome of people sharing the surname of Sykes, which goes back 700 years in England, revealed that about 50% of the respondents had exactly the same Y chromosome. The other 50% might be a function of people simply assuming the name, or through adoption, or by illegitimacy. It can be worked out using these data that the average rate of infidelity was lower than 2% every generation, otherwise less common matching of the Y chromosome would have been found in those who happen to share the surname of Sykes. Further work along the same lines by Mark Jobling and his colleagues (2011), analyzing many different surnames in England, have found similar results. Thus, it appears that married women living in the United Kingdom over the last 700 years or so, mostly without access to modern contraception, were generally sexually faithful to their partners.

Although variability across individuals and cultural settings certainly does not rule out sperm competition being a factor in human reproduction, these data suggest that sperm competition in humans living today is not exactly a thriving enterprise. However, the most compelling evidence against the sperm competition thesis has been documented by Alan Dixson (2009). In a rigorous and systematic analysis, he showed that virtually all the features of human sexual organs and reproduction fall into a pattern characteristic of primates and other mammals that are monogamous or polygynous, not multi-male/multi-female. Sperm competition is characteristic of the latter mating system for obvious reasons. If the depositing of sperm by a male is likely to be displaced by a rival male, then the competing males will evolve biological features designed to win the competition to fertilize the female.

Dixson (2009) has shown that when comparing human males to apes and other primates that have multi-male/multi-female species, human males (relatively speaking) have (i) smaller testes that contain lower volumes of sperm; (ii) slower replacement of sperm; (iii) less vigorous sperm; (iv) lower sperm quality; (v) a longer and less muscular vas deferens (connecting the testes to the seminal vesicles); and (vi) smaller prostate glands and seminal vesicles (which provide the seminal fluids) (see Figure 4.3).

In yet another take on the sperm competition thesis, Gordon Gallup repeats an often claimed "fact" that in comparison to other species the human penis is unusually long, based on some influential data by Short (1984), and that it has an unusually well-developed glans (see Figure 4.3) – a good design, so it is argued, for engaging in sperm competition. To demonstrate the plausibility of this thesis, Gallup *et al.* (2003) used artificial genitals and simulated semen to show that the human penis can displace rival semen in the reproductive tract of women with relatively deep penetration. Consistently, Goetz *at al.* (2005) found that men in more committed relationships with more attractive women reported thrusting deeper, using more thrusts, and having sex of longer duration. They suggested that because physically attractive women are likely to draw the attention of other men, these sexual behaviors may represent an unconscious attempt to displace rival semen.

One difficulty with Gallup's claims is that using updated information on penis length in non-human species, Dixson (2009) showed that the pervasive claims in the literature about the unusual length of the human penis are wrong. The human penis is not in fact unusually long compared to many other species (such as the chimpanzee), although it does appear to be thicker than other species. Again, the glans is relatively bulbous, but not unusual compared to other species (see Dixson). It is plausible that the length and thickness of the human penis has evolved over the last million years or so simply to match the evolution of the increasing width and length of the female vagina, which in turn was driven by the need to accommodate giving birth to the increasing size of the human head.

Finally, the human penis is smooth in contrast to those of many other animals, such as the chimpanzee, which is studded with small hard spines. The presence of penile spines is strongly linked to the presence of multi-partner mating systems (like the chimpanzee) in which sperm competition is alive and well (see Dixson, 2009). Thus, penile spines could be adaptations designed to remove sperm from recent copulations with male competitors, although the evidence for primates is limited concerning this function (Dixson, 2012). Intriguingly, a recent study has succeeded in pinpointing the regulatory gene switch in the chimpanzee (our closest relative) that is responsible for their penis spines and shown it is missing in humans (McLean *et al.*, 2011).

On balance, we think the evidence weighs against sperm competition playing a large role in recent hominid evolution. In the previous chapter, we noted that evidence concerning sexual dimorphism of humans and hominids as far back as *Homo erectus* (living one to two million years ago) suggests – consistent with the evidence compiled here – that the current mating systems of humans have been in place for at least two million years. However, as we also previously noted, polygyny is a commonplace mating arrangement across cultures. Thus, some have argued that the current flexible system of human mating, ranging from polygyny to monogamy (but either way involving powerful bonding between partners) has evolved from a gorilla-like form of polygyny, which may have been practiced by *Australopithecus afarensis* (living three to four million years ago in Africa) (see, for example, Geary *et al.*, 2011).

To end this section with a few caveats, our conclusions do *not* imply that either men or women are perfectly sexually faithful, or always mate for life, or that they don't adjust their mating strategies to suit different circumstances, or that there are not important gender differences in mating strategies, as we shall see in further chapters.

Orgasms, Nipples, Adaptations, and By-products

Let's turn to gender differences in orgasms. Relative to men, women can experience multiple orgasms within very short time periods (sometimes even only a few minutes), but they are also more likely to rarely or never experience orgasms during sex. A well-conducted 1994 sex survey by Michael and colleagues (1994), which sampled a representative cross-section of US adults, found that 29% of married women and 30% of single women reported that they always had orgasms during sexual intercourse, whereas 6% of married women and 14% of single women reported that they rarely or never had orgasms. Men reported very different figures. Seventy-five percent of men said they always had orgasms during sexual intercourse, whereas only 2% claimed they never had them. Women are also more likely to seek professional help for and suffer from low sexual desire than men (Baumeister *et al.*, 2001). And, surveys of heterosexual couples have revealed that low sexual desire or low interest in sex is much more common in women than men (Frank *et al.*, 1978).

One possible reason for women's greater variability in having orgasms during sex could be the location of their **clitoris**, which lies several centimeters away from the penis during sexual intercourse. Another major gender difference is that men usually must achieve orgasms in order to inseminate women and, therefore, reproduce. Women, of course, can reproduce without experiencing orgasms, although orgasms may at times help them become pregnant (Baker and Bellis, 1995), as we discuss further below. These differences have led some theorists, most notably Steven Gould (1992) and Donald Symons (1979), to suggest that the clitoris is not an evolved adaptation; rather, it is just a **biological homologue** – a byproduct of the human penis that serves no special functions.

If this idea strikes you as ridiculous, consider nipples in humans. Nipples serve important biological functions in women because they play an essential role in delivering milk to infants. Nipples, however, have no obvious function for men. So why do men have nipples? The answer has to do with evolutionary constraints on the design of the human body. From a biological standpoint, the human fetus within the womb is unisex – it is sex-undifferentiated – until the sixth week of physical development. At six weeks, if a fetus is a male (if it has an X and a Y pair of chromosomes), a potent form of **testosterone** is produced that leads the fetus to develop as a male. If the fetus is a chromosomal female (if it has a pair of X chromosomes), there is no surge of testosterone, and the fetus develops into a female. Both sexes, therefore, start life with the same body plan and the same basic parts. In other words, all of the organs specific to one gender are also present in the other gender in the womb, at least in rudimentary form. Male and female genitalia also develop from the same genital ridge in the developing fetus, with a clitoris eventually developing in females and a penis in males. Male nipples are thus biological byproducts for men, being functionally designed for women who use them to nurse young.

The explanation that female orgasms are similar to male nipples, however, is less clear-cut for three reasons. First, in primates closely related to humans, such as chimpanzees, females often seem to have orgasms during sexual intercourse (Slob and van der Werff Ten Bosch, 1991). Second, the clitoris has approximately 8000 nerve fibers, twice as many as in the glans of the penis. Third, the human clitoris is connected to a series of important physiological changes during sexual activity, including an infusion of blood into the vagina, **vulva**, and uterus, the release of lubricating fluids into the vagina to facilitate sexual intercourse, and the production of specific hormones that coordinate sexual responses. The human clitoris, therefore, shows evidence of complex adaptive design as indicated by these well-orchestrated biological systems that stimulate the desire for sexual intercourse when sexual arousal reaches its peak.

Whether or not orgasms serve an evolutionary function in women remains hotly debated. Robin Baker and Mark Bellis (1995) have proposed that women's orgasms might increase the chances of fertilization. The evidence for this hypothesis is sparse, but the biological mechanism they suggest seems plausible. When a woman has an orgasm, her **cervix** pulses rhythmically and dips into the pool of semen left by her mate, drawing the semen closer to the cervix and toward her egg. However, there is little direct evidence for the links between orgasm and fertility, and Levin (2012) argues that if female orgasm increases the flow of sperm via the cervix (as Baker and Bellis propose), it would be likely to cause problems rather than help conception take place.

A more plausible possibility may be that female orgasms in species such as the chimpanzee initially evolved to heighten sexual enjoyment and facilitate the motivation for frequent sexual intercourse, then was picked up in humans to become part of the female romantic bonding process. Sexual satisfaction is certainly positively linked to love and relationship satisfaction (see Chapter 10) and, as we describe later, female orgasms trigger a surge of cuddle hormones that enhance bonding.

Hormones, Sex, and Relationships

We start with a few facts and definitions to help navigate this section. **Hormones** are substances that regulate or control other cells or organs, continually being released into the bloodstream, and picked up by receptors all over the body. Their effects are often relatively slow and often long-lasting. **Neurotransmitters** are released in the brain into the **synapses** (the gaps between **neurons**), and produce fast responses linked to activity in specific brain regions. Some substances (like **oxytocin** or **epinephrine**) can be either hormones or neurotransmitters, but because of the **blood–brain barrier** they exert their effects differently either in the brain or the body, depending on where they are released. We will deal in this section with some of the important hormones released in the body by different glands, and how they are controlled, and reserve our coverage of neurotransmitters for the next section on the relationship brain.

The **half-lives** of hormones in the blood vary tremendously (from seconds to hours), and their effects can be rapid (e.g. speeding up the heart) or super slow (e.g. body growth). They are multi-purpose tools, regulating the growth and development of the body, motivating behavior, and often being released in response to events that happen in the environment. Hormones are created and released from many parts of the brain

Major Endoocrine Glands

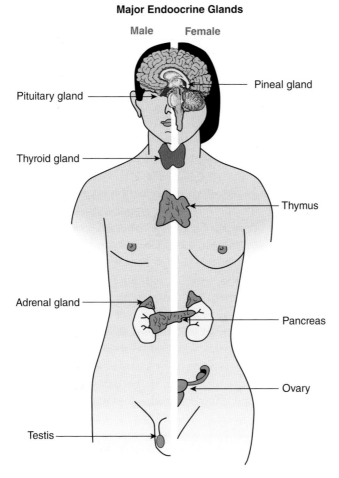

Figure 4.4   Major endocrine glands
Source: Image © US Federal Government

including the **endocrine glands** (**pituitary** and **pineal**) and glands in the body (**thymus, thyroid, pancreas, adrenal glands, testes,** and **ovaries**) (see Figure 4.4).

There are lots of hormones (for example, there are about 100 neurotransmitters) and scientists are still on the road to understanding what they all do. We focus our treatment on those that play pivotal roles in human mating and relationships in terms of three main categories: the **sex hormones,** the **cuddle hormones,** and the **fight or flight hormones.** As we shall see, hormones play a critical role in orchestrating the human body and brain in the furtherance of goals linked to sex and relationships. Moreover, reflecting human evolutionary history, the hormones we discuss (or similar variants) have been around for hundreds of millions of years playing a role in sexual reproduction and mating. The same or very similar hormones, for example, are found in fish, mammals, and birds playing roles linked to sexual reproduction and mating (see Insel, 2010). Evolution truly plays by the maxim "if it ain't broke don't fix it."

Sex hormones

Testosterone plays a dominant role in adult sexual activity (Dabbs & Dabbs, 2000; Regan, 1999). It is often thought of as a male hormone, but this is not entirely true, as we shall see. Overall testosterone levels differ from person to person, but the level also varies within each person depending on several factors, such as the time of the day, the degree of sexual arousal, and the amount of competition. Men, on average, produce about 5 milligrams of testosterone each day, 10 times more than women. Only about 2% of the testosterone that is produced each day has effects on the metabolism, but this invisibly small amount exerts powerful effects on human behavior and biology, especially in men.

For both women and men, testosterone production is controlled by the **hypothalamus** in the brain, but is made and secreted by glands in the body. The hypothalamus, located at the base of the brain (see Figure 4.4), operates like a thermostat, constantly monitoring the level of testosterone in the blood and increasing production by sending signals to the pituitary gland, which is located beneath the hypothalamus, and is connected to the brain by the pituitary stalk. The pituitary gland, in turn, produces hormones that signal the testes (in men) and the ovaries (in women) to produce hormones such as testosterone.

Testosterone is clearly linked to sexual arousal in men (for a review see Bancroft, 2005). For men who have problems with testosterone production from their testes, administration of testosterone restores their normal sexual functioning (including increasing the frequency of masturbation). If the testosterone is withdrawn, sexual functioning goes downhill, and if it is restored it goes back to its original levels (com-

Figure 4.5   *Source:* © 2009 Liza Donnelly and Michael Maslin

pared to participants given placebos). The same results were obtained in one study in which normal male samples had their levels of testosterone production first suppressed (for 6 weeks) then restored via the administration of a different hormone (Bagatell, *et al.*, 1994).

Testosterone plays an important role in long-term sexual relationships. Gray and his colleagues (2002, 2004; Gray and Campbell, 2009), for example, have shown that single men in North America have higher testosterone levels than (i) married men, (ii) married men who have fathered children, and (iii) non-married fathers. Recent longitudinal research following single men over time showed that men experience steep declines in testosterone levels soon after they enter a long-term relationship and become fathers, particularly when they spend more time with their children (Gettler *et al.*, 2011). These results are consistent with the notion that men in long-term relationships reduce their mating effort (i.e. they no longer compete for mates), and their testosterone levels therefore drop.

However, there is also evidence that differing stable levels of testosterone reflect different mating orientations; namely, men with higher testosterone adopt more short-term mating strategies rather than long-term strategies (see Chapters 5 and 6). In line with this hypothesis, van Anders and Watson (2006) found that single men with lower testosterone levels were more likely to enter relationships than men with higher levels. It is not surprising, therefore, that single men have higher testosterone than men who are in relationships – these men are less likely to enter relationships in the first place! In addition, men with higher testosterone are about 43% more likely to divorce than men with lower levels (Booth and Dabbs, 1993), and men who remain married over time have 9% lower testosterone compared to men who get divorced or remained single over a similar length of time (Mazur and Michalek, 1998). When men with higher testosterone do enter relationships, in other words, they are more likely to break up than men with lower testosterone levels.

The hormones that govern sexual behavior in women are more complicated than for men. To begin with, the production of two hormones – **estrogen** and testosterone – systematically vary a lot over time because of the nature of women's menstrual cycles (see Chapter 6). The production of testosterone peaks in the menstrual cycle for women just before ovulation on about the 14th day of the cycle. Correspondingly, there is evidence that sexual desires and the initiation of sexual activity also peak at about the same time (Bancroft, 2005). The effects of administering testosterone (via patches or injections) on sexual desires and activity have also been extensively studied in women who either report low sexual desire, or have problems or surgery impacting on their normal hormonal secretions. There is evidence from this research that testosterone withdrawal or replacement can influence female sexuality, but, in contrast to men, the results are inconsistent, and there are stronger individual differences among women than among men (Bancroft, 2005).

Estrogen is not thought to directly influence sexual drive in women (see Dixson, 2012). One primary sexual function of estrogen seems to be the regulation of lubrication and elasticity in the vagina during sexual intercourse. Estrogen also plays a critical role in the development of secondary sexual characteristics in women (e.g. breast

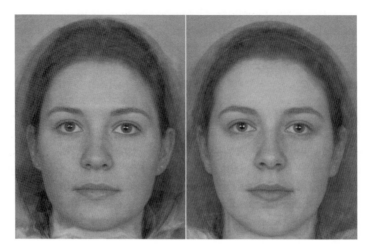

Figure 4.6   Composite faces of the (left) 10 women with highest and (right) 10 with lowest levels of urinary estrogen
Source: From Law Smith *et al.*, 2006; © 2005 The Royal Society

development, feminine facial appearance). Moreover, estrogen inhibits fat from accumulating in the abdominal region and stimulates fat accumulation in the buttocks and thighs, resulting in the classic hour-glass shape of women's bodies.

Indeed, women with higher estrogen levels have a curvier appearance (i.e. low waist-to-hip ratios, or waists that are approximately 70% the size of their hips) and larger breasts than women with lower estrogen levels, resulting in a more feminine-looking body shape (Jasieńska *et al.*, 2004). Women with high estrogen levels also have more feminine facial features (e.g. large, round eyes, small jaws and chins, smaller noses). The pictures shown in Figure 4.6 are composite pictures based on 10 women with the lowest estrogen levels and 10 women with the highest estrogen levels, taken from research by Law-Smith *et al.* (2006).

Interestingly, women with higher estrogen also report a stronger desire to have more children (between three and four children) than women with lower estrogen levels (between one and two children; Law Smith *et al.*, 2012). In this particular study, women with higher maternal tendencies (and also higher estrogen levels) were also rated as more feminine-looking by independent observers. Higher estrogen levels are also associated with greater desire for, and comfort with, intimate relationships (Edelstein, Stanton, Henderson, & Sanders, 2010) (also see Chapter 7).

To summarize, the research on the role of hormones in sexual activity, desires, and physical appearance reveals a simpler and less nuanced picture for men than for women. For men, testosterone is the key hormone producing both a masculine physique and on-going levels of sexual desire and activity. For women, estrogen is a key hormone linked to fertility and desirability as a mate, whereas the production of testosterone seems to be linked to ongoing sexual desire activity but in a weaker and more inconsistent fashion than for men. This pattern of gender differences is consistent with our prior discussion of strong gender differences in the reliability of orgasms, and with our later discussion of mate selection (Chapter 6), and sex and passion (Chapter 10). In the meantime a few cautionary notes are in order.

First, there is good evidence that once normal levels of circulating testosterone are attained, there is not a lot to be gained by increasing levels still further by the use of testosterone patches or the like (Bancroft, 2005). Second, it is tempting to think that human behavior is completely at the mercy of hormones and what goes in the brain. Not so. For example, testosterone not only pushes sexual desires and behavior around, but also gets pushed around by sexual desires and behavior. There is evidence, for example, that thinking sexy thoughts or viewing erotica increases testosterone levels in both men and women (Goldey & van Anders, 2011).

Cuddle hormones

Oxytocin and **vasopressin** are closely related hormones linked to important aspects of reproduction and mating. Oxytocin (and vasopressin) are secreted from many parts of the brain and spinal cord, and also by the pituitary gland at the base of the brain (see Figure 4.4). Oxytocin is released in relatively large quantities in women during and immediately after labor, and during breast-feeding, producing a sense of well-being and enhancing feelings of closeness and warmth with the infant (i.e. bonding) (Nelson and Panksepp, 1998; Neumann, 2008).

Oxytocin levels in the bloodstream, and oxytocin receptors in the brain, are turned on by the presence of estrogen (Sanchez et al., 2009). In contrast, both vasopressin levels and the expression of vasopressin receptors are turned on by the presence of testosterone (Sanchez et al., 2009). Consistent with these findings, as we shall see, oxytocin is the prime cuddle hormone for women, whereas vasopressin seems to do the trick for men. However, research on the roles of these hormones in blood plasma (not acting as neurotransmitters in the brain) in intimate relationships has produced a somewhat confusing pattern of results.

One body of research appears to confirm their role as cuddle hormones. For example, oxytocin in women and vasopressin in males are released into the bloodstream during sexual activity (Carmichael et al., 1987; Murphy et al., 1987), and oxytocin levels in women are higher following orgasm (Blaicher et al., 1999). Oxytocin levels are also higher in women when they recall positive experiences involving their romantic partners, particularly for women who report being in love with their partners (Gonzaga et al., 2006). Grewen et al. (2005) found that oxytocin levels of both partners of 38 couples who had supportive relationships were consistently higher than non-supportive relationships when couples spent time talking with each other, watching a movie clip from a romantic movie, and then hugging for 20 seconds (also see Gouin et al., 2010).

However, (this is the confusing part) well-replicated findings also show that higher levels of oxytocin in women (and vasopressin in men) are associated with more distress in relationships (Taylor et al., 2010), and lower levels of forgiveness and more anxiety about hurtful behaviors by romantic partners (Tabak et al., 2011). Various explanations have been offered for these apparently inconsistent findings, not helped by the fact that the functions of these hormones in the body are anything but clear cut. One suggestion is that levels of these hormones might reflect individual differences in sensitivity to external events impinging on the relationship (good or bad) (see Tabak *et al.*, 2011). We return later to the roles these hormones play in the brain as neurotransmitters.

Fight or flight hormones

When stressful events are encountered, they usually trigger a **fight or flight** response, which produces changes in the **cardiovascular system** (increased heart rate and blood pressure), and the **endocrine system** (the release of hormones such as epinephrine and **cortisol**), which makes more glucose available. Glucose has the side effect of suppressing the immune system. These responses operate in unison to prepare the body to deal with the stressor, such as an approaching bear on a lonely wilderness trail, or an approaching partner suggesting the need for a serious talk about the future of your relationship. Stressors can also be psychological, as when simply imagining what it would feel like meeting a bear on a lonely trail or having a serious talk about the future of your relationship. Note the stressful event does not have to be negative – it could be exciting and enjoyable. The same systems are involved in either case.

When faced with a stressful event, the brain and the body work in concert using what is termed the **hypothalamic–pituitary–adrenal (HPA) axis** to generate and regulate these hormones. Cortisol is similar to epinephrine, but has much longer-term effects. For this reason, it is a principal marker of long-term stress in intimate relationships. High and sustained levels of cortisol can ultimately result in poor long-term health outcomes. Falling in love also releases cortisol into the body (Marazziti and Canale, 2004; Loving *et al.*, 2009), probably due to uncertainties about the future of the relationship (stress), the excitement generated, and the powerful desire to be together (passion).

One function of the hypothalamus is to regulate social soothing in response to threatening events (Carter, 2003; Coan *et al.*, 2006). When people feel threatened and someone comforts them, which is a core attachment process, activation of the HPA axis is reduced and distress lessens. Although the exact role of the hypothalamus in this process is still not entirely clear, it appears to coordinate the activity of these different systems (Coan, 2008).

The Relationship Brain

The profusion of technical terms and the unremitting pace of research in this area, makes this a difficult area to get your head around (to make a bad pun). A few tips to help neophytes. There are some cool web sites with 3D images of the brain that are worth a look. Certain common terms refer to spatial location in the brain (**dorsal** refers to the top part of the brain, **ventral** the bottom part, **anterior** is the front, and **posterior** is the back). Also keep in mind that the brain is split into two **hemispheres**, so that many structures come in twos (one in each hemisphere) – looking to the front, the right hemisphere of your own brain is on your right, and your left hemisphere is on your left. Thus, when research publications describe activation taking place in specific brain sections they tag them accordingly. For example, **bilateral activation** in the **amygdala** means that both almond-shaped organs are involved, whereas if only one is especially busy, then it is described as either the left or right amygdala. One final note of clarification – it is common practice in the neuroscience area to use abbreviations in capital letters to refer to areas of the brain. To avoid a blizzard of acronyms producing mental fog, but also help the assiduous student in reading articles in this area, we will routinely use both the full-blown terms and the acronyms here and throughout the book.

The human brain is a remarkable organ. Each adult brain has about 100 billion **neurons**, and each neuron has on average about 7000 potential connections (termed **synapses**) to other neurons, yielding from 100 to 500 trillion connections in adult brains. As we noted in Chapter 2, during the first two to three years of life, the human brain grows at a massive pace. Over the last three decades of neuroscience research it has become apparent that the brain is much more like a muscle than was previously thought. Thus, hundreds of hours playing music, juggling, learning the maps and roads in large cities (as do professional taxi drivers), or learning new languages, beefs up the grey matter in the parts of the brain most closely linked to these activities (see Woollett and Maguire, 2011).

Reflecting the central role that relationships occupy in human nature, a new field termed **social neuroscience** has emerged over the last two decades, investigating the neurological structures and processes undergirding all the phenomena explored in the last chapter, including social cognition, social memory, social emotions, and yes, even passionate love. Advances in this area have been rapid, thanks in part to the invention of non-invasive brain imaging techniques like **functional magnetic resonance imaging** (**fMRI**), which measures activity in different parts of the brain by assessing changes in blood flow. When specific parts of the brain work hard, they call up increased flows of blood (containing additional oxygen and glucose), peaking about 4 to 6 seconds after the neuronal event. The powerful magnetic field generated by the brain imaging machine is able to pick this up because oxygen-rich blood is more affected by magnetic fields than oxygen-thin blood. A more recent innovation, using a similar approach, is **diffusion tensor imaging** (**DTI**), which tracks and records the rate at which fluids (mainly water) in the connecting fibers (white matter) diffuse into the surrounding tissue. Because fluids diffuse more rapidly along the fibers than at right angles to the fiber, DTI allows the tracking and depiction of the interconnecting fibers that facilitate communication among the regions of the brain. Indeed, a good part of the brain is taken up with axons bundled together to form such interconnecting fibers.

One of the take-home messages of the flood of research using brain imaging is that specific parts of the brain seldom work alone; rather different neural systems are typically involved in any given task. This is consistent with the importance of neurotransmitters, given their central role in controlling communication among different parts of the brain. As noted in the introductory chapter, in this book we adhere to what is termed the materialist perspective. Thus, the scientific work on the relationship mind and body should be consistent and fit together in an informative fashion. Here, we will organize the material to test this proposition, examining some of the major themes we described in the prior chapter on the relationship mind. First, we take a look at social cognition in the brain, paying attention to goals and attribution processes. Second, we examine the link between emotions and cognitions, and how emotions are regulated. Third, we analyze the extent to which brain processes are consistent with the importance assigned by social cognition (and social psychology) to the distinction between controlled and automatic processing. Finally, getting a jump on the intensive examination of love in Chapter 7, we examine the brain's motivational and emotional systems designed to apply specifically to bonding and love in intimate relationships.

Social cognition and the brain

The Prefrontal Cortex (PFC) Comparisons between human brains and other ape brains suggest that the rapid increase in the brain size of humans across evolution was dominated by the development of the prefrontal neocortex. Consistently, this area of the brain is associated with some of the capacities that are unique to humans including language and reasoning ability. It is also the seat of humans' extraordinary social intelligence, including mind-reading, introspection, the capacity to make complex causal attributions, and the ability to process complex social information often rapidly and automatically (see Forbes and Grafman, 2010).

Mapping and working out the different regions of the **prefrontal cortex (PFC)** is a work in progress, but scientists have identified about half a dozen neural regions that have different functions (see Figure 4.7). For example, the **ventromedial prefrontal**

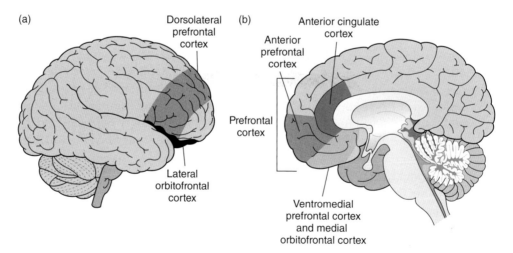

Figure 4.7   Major regions of the prefrontal cortex
Source: Images (left) © takito/Shutterstock.com (right) © Alena Hovorkova/Shutterstock.com

cortex (**VMPFC**) seems to play a particularly important role in perspective-taking, making attributions to the self or others, and regulating anxiety. The **dorsolateral prefrontal cortex (DLPFC)**, in contrast, seems to be mainly involved in controlling and directing behavior (see Forbes and Grafman, 2010). The **orbital frontal cortex (OFC)**, which is just above and behind your eyes, seems to be involved in regulating and planning behavior specifically linked to rewards and punishments. However, these neural areas typically work together in networks, and there is an extensive network of connecting fibers among the different regions of the prefrontal cortex (see Figure 4.7).

Emotions and cognitions work together Using brain imaging techniques, specifically fMRI and DTI, it has become apparent that regions in the prefrontal cortex (PFC) are heavily connected to the more evolutionarily ancient parts of the brain dealing principally with memory (the **hippocampus**) and the primary emotions such as happiness and fear (the amygdala) (Salzman and Fusi, 2010). Moreover, these influences seem to go both ways, suggesting that emotional states drive cognition and vice versa. Some regions like the **cingulate cortex (CC)**, which resembles a collar formed round the **corpus collosum** (a fibrous bundle connecting the left and right hemispheres) serve multiple functions linked to both cognitions and emotions, and are involved specifically in the regulation of emotions (see Figure 4.8).

In the previous chapter, we argued on the basis of the general psychological literature that emotions and cognitions are intertwined. The picture of the human brain based on neuroscience research reveals precisely the same theme, with a rich network of fibers

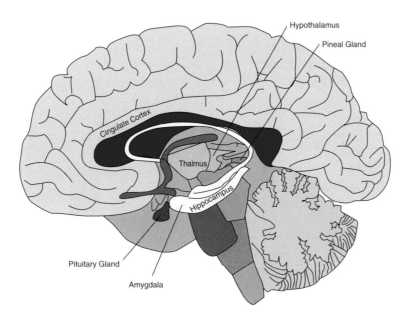

Figure 4.8   Major regions of the midbrain
Source: Image © Anita Potter/Shutterstock.com

between areas concerned with emotion regulation, such as the orbital cortex (OC), and other areas in the prefrontal cortex and the midbrain (see Figure 4.8). Indeed, a good part of the brain is taken up with axons bundled together to form such interconnecting fibers. If they could be stretched out into one continuous strand, they would be about 150000 km (90000 miles) long.

Research exploring how the brain reacts to threatening events provides a good example of how the neural circuits associated with cognition and emotion operate together when people are upset. In a landmark study by James Coan and colleagues (Coan *et al.*, 2006), 16 happily married women were given electric shocks while their brains were scanned in an fMRI experiment. Each woman was randomly assigned to one of three experimental conditions. In one condition, no one held the woman's hand while she was being shocked. In the other two conditions, women held the hand of either their husband or the male experimenter. Physical contact (hand holding), especially by the husband, led to the electric shocks being perceived as less painful. These results are shown in Figure 4.9. It also led to reduced neural activity in response to the threat in emotion-related action and body arousal circuits in the brain, such as the **ventral anterior cingulate cortex (vACC)**. In addition, the hypothalamus, which as we noted previously regulates the release of the stress hormone cortisol in the body, was more active for women who were less happily married.

A follow-up study by Eisenberger *et al.* (2011), which asked participants to look at both pictures of their partner and control images (strangers or objects) while receiving painful heat applied to their arm, replicated these findings. Moreover, consistent with other research, it also showed that our old friend the ventromedial prefrontal cortex (VMPC) (implicated in social cognitive processing and regulating anxiety) was especially active when viewing the comforting visages of their partners.

Controlled versus automatic processing In the previous chapter on the relationship mind, we proposed that the only way of understanding how people carry out the complex business of building relationship theories, conducting daily relationship

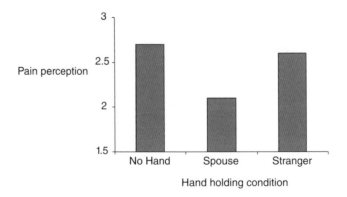

Figure 4.9   The power of hand holding
Source: From Coan *et al.*, 2006; © 2006 Association for Psychological Science

interactions, and making partner and relationship judgments is that a good deal of information processing is carried out in an automatic fashion – fast and unconsciously. However, controlled conscious processing is also often called for, which is relatively slow, conscious, and capable of being verbalized. And, many activities (simply talking with your partner about your respective days, or planning a birthday outing) involve both ends of the processing spectrum (controlled versus automatic) at the same time.

Social neuroscientists have used the same dimension (or similar ones such as explicit versus implicit processing) in studying the brain. In a recent review Chad Forbes and Jordan Grafman (2010) argue that, although both kinds of processing often take place at the same time for given neural regions, certain regions of the brain are dominant at either end of the dimension. Specifically, the areas we have already mentioned in the prefrontal cortex (PFC) are more often involved in conscious planning, monitoring, and the execution of actions. In contrast, the evolutionarily more ancient parts of the brain concerned with memory and emotions (such as the amygdala and the hippocampus) are more often the seat of unconscious processing.

Bonding and love

The cuddle hormones as neurotransmitters We noted previously the roles played by oxytocin and vasopressin, released in lactation and reproduction, and pointed out the somewhat inconsistent pattern of findings concerning the role these substances play as hormones released in the body. However, it is the roles of oxytocin, and its close relative vasopressin, as neurotransmitters (released in the brain) that have stolen the headlines over the last two decades. This is largely thanks to pioneering research on two species of voles (a small hamster-sized rodent) that live in the grasslands of North America – the montane vole and the prairie vole (Insel, 2010). These two species of voles are visually indistinguishable and virtually identical genetically (with 99% genetic overlap), but they vary in one crucial way. Prairie voles are monogamous, whereas montane voles are promiscuous, often living in solitary burrows. After a hectic 24 hours of copulation, prairie voles bond strongly for life, and the male voles subsequently help to care for the offspring and drive off competition from other males. Their montane cousins, in contrast, fail to bond and the males don't hang around, preferring to spend their time finding other female voles to mate with.

A remarkable program of research carried out by Thomas Insel and others has shown that oxytocin and vasopressin play a key role in producing these differences in mating behavior across the two species. Both species have plenty of these substances in the brain. However, prairie voles have a rich set of receptors in various specific parts of the brain that are simply missing in the brains of the montane voles (vasopressin receptors in the case of the males and oxytocin in the case of the female) (see Insel, 2010). By injecting oxytocin (or vasopressin in the case of the males) directly into the brains of the prairie voles the researchers were able to induce partner bonding. They also showed that when a substance was injected that blocked the action of this neurotransmitter in prairie voles, bonding but not sexual activity was inhibited. Moreover, injecting either oxytocin or vasopressin into the brains of the promiscuous montane voles had no effect on their bonding behavior because they lack the receptor sites to metabolize the hormones. Compelling data indeed!

Researchers currently cannot (as yet) directly measure the amounts of oxytocin or vasopressin in the brain, and they cannot (ethically) inject these substances directly into human brains (as they do with voles). Moreover, it is no good injecting these substances into the bloodstream – they have a short half-life, being digested and rendered inactive by the liver in short order, and thus not making it to the brain. However, a headline-grabbing study in 2005, by Kosfeld *et al.*, found that three or four puffs of oxytocin using a nasal spray not only makes it to the brain through the nasal membrane, but encourages individuals to trust their partners more and hand over more cash in investment games. Using the same kind of procedure, a robust, double-blind study carried out by Ditzen and colleagues (2009) found that, in comparison to a placebo group, couples exposed to oxytocin via nasal sprays exhibited more positive communication in conflict discussions as coded by observers. Moreover, the oxytocin group had lower cortisol levels in their saliva after the discussions, indicating they were less stressed by the experience. These findings are shown in Figure 4.10.

The bonding roles of oxytocin and vasopressin in humans are also consistent with research using brain imaging techniques. The pioneering research using fMRI to investigate romantic love in the human brain was published in 2000 by Andreas Bartels and Semir Zeki. Seventeen participants in heterosexual relationships were selected who professed to be truly, madly, and deeply in love. Their tasks were simply to look at pictures of their loved ones, along with those of friends of the same sex, while lying down in the fMRI machine. The brain activation patterns were then analyzed after subtracting the effects of the friends from the partners. Several studies have since used the same kind of methodology to explore the neural correlates of romantic love (Acevedo *et al.*, 2011; Bartels and Zeki, 2004; Xu *et al.*, 2011). The results show that regions rich in oxytocin and vasopressin receptors in the midbrain regions are exactly the same brain regions that are active when watching pictures of partners, particularly the **ventral tegmental area (VTA)** (see Figure 4.7). Reflecting a theme already emphasized, this area has rich connections with other areas of the brain including those in the prefrontal cortex (PFC) (see Figure 4.7).

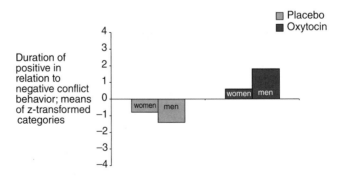

Figure 4.10 Effects of nasal spraying oxytocin on positivity of conflict discussions
Source: From Ditzen *et al.*, 2009; © 2009 Society of Biological Psychiatry

An important caveat to these fMRI findings is that the results reveal the differences between passionate sexual relationships and friendships. Thus, although increased brain activity does not show up in areas of the prefrontal cortex (PFC) in response to pictures of sexual partners, this does not mean that cognition is not important in romantic love (an implausible notion); rather it implies that the prefrontal cortex (PFC) may be equally busy when bringing either close friends or romantic partners to mind.

The dopamine system We have just one more important neurotransmitter to introduce. As it turns out the same midbrain areas (especially the ventral tegmental area or VTA) that are fired up when passionate love is experienced are also the seats of the **dopamine system**, which is associated with rewards and motivation. Dopamine is predominantly produced in the ventral tegmental area (VTA), and it produces goal-directed behavior in all mammals when it is released in the brain (Depue and Collins, 1999). Indeed, the dopamine system is so powerful that rats will forgo sex, food, and even water – sometimes to the point of death (Bozarth and Wise, 1996) – if they can increase dopamine activity in their brains by pressing levers that stimulate its production. The dopamine system, in other words, is an engine of goal-directed behavior, including those involved with the most rewarding features of sexual relationships (and, as it happens, addiction to drugs like heroin). Almost no work to date has been done specifically on the role of dopamine in human intimate relationships, but it seems likely that the dopamine system plays a role in romantic love.

Summary

Let's summarize this section by reframing a description of an initial meeting between George and Mary at a party that we presented in the previous chapter on the relationship mind. In this description (see p. 49), George was attracted to Mary's charm and looks. Mary seemed interested and George became sexually aroused when she brushed against him. He guessed she was single and took the plunge to ask her out. Let's recast our prior description in terms of the underlying neurological and bodily processes.

Meeting Mary immediately set George's neural networks humming. Information circulating between the memory and affective regions (including the amygdala and the hippocampus) and the prefrontal regions (including the ventromedial prefrontal cortex (VMPFC) called up long-term memories of his prior relationships and mating preferences. This produced positive judgments of Mary, and strenuous attempts to read her mind (especially what she was thinking about him). Working together, these brain networks, along with perceptions of Mary's behavior, sent signals to the hypothalamus, which, in turn, sent signals to the pituitary gland, which in turn produced hormones that instructed the testes to produce testosterone, which produced an increase in George's heart rate and sexual arousal, finally producing an erection. This brought the prefrontal cortex (PFC) into the action, especially the dorsolateral prefrontal cortex (DPC), leading George to inconspicuously attempt to hide his arousal. In addition, some dopamine and vasopressin were produced, which produced rewards and feelings of warmth in the medial brain structures, especially the ventral segmental area (VTA). Feedback to the prefrontal cortex (PFC) prompted George to take the plunge and ask Mary out for a coffee.

Mate selection and perhaps bonding have taken their first halting steps.

Health and Intimate Relationships

In 1897, Emile Durkheim first noticed a link between death (mortality) and social factors. He observed that people who had the fewest or weakest social ties to their families and communities were more likely to commit suicide. He coined the term **anomie** – a feeling of psychological detachment from others – and proposed that this sad, almost tortured psychological state tends to lead to suicide.

Research on the links between illness and intimate relationships have vindicated and expanded upon Durkheim's acute observations. Divorced adults, for example, are more likely to experience suicide, suffer from various physical and mental ailments, alcoholism, and even auto accidents compared to married couples who stay together (Bloom *et al.*, 1978). Data from the Charleston Heart Study, which followed 1300 people between 1960 and 2000, showed that people who were separated or divorced at the start of the study were more likely to die earlier in life, even after controlling for their initial health status and several other demographic variables (Sbarra and Nietert, 2009). Moreover, those who separated or divorced for longer periods of time were more likely to die, with heart problems probably being the primary cause of these early deaths (Stroebe and Stroebe, 1987). Indeed, the link between social isolation and heart disease was as strong as, or stronger than, other established risk factors for heart disease, such as smoking, lack of exercise, or poor diet (Atkins *et al.*, 1991).

These studies have motivated a surge of research into the factors behind social isolation and intimate relationships that either protect people against health problems or render them more susceptible to health problems. This research has focused on the roles of social support and stress, and exemplifies the point already made that what goes on in the brain and the body is intertwined with psychological processes.

Intimate relationships, social support, stress, and health

Social support can affect health outcomes in two basic ways (Cohen and Wills, 1985). First, receiving support directly from others can enhance wellbeing. For example, people who receive more support may be encouraged to take better care of themselves, eat better, exercise regularly, and keep off extra weight. Second, greater social support may protect wellbeing when stress rears its head. We focus our discussion on this latter form of stress buffering.

When people encounter a stressful event, they usually have a fight or flight response, which we discussed previously. To recap, this response triggers changes in the cardiovascular system (increased heart rate and blood pressure), and the endocrine system (the release of hormones such as epinephrine, and cortisol). According to standard models of stress, individual differences (e.g. personality, knowledge, experience, and skills), and how the individual interprets the stressor (e.g. as a threat, as a challenge, or as innocuous), together determine the coping response. For example, if you cognitively appraise an event (stressor) as non-threatening, you should not develop a full-fledged fight or flight physiological reaction.

Chronic stressors, which exist over long periods of time, can exact a toll on our health because they keep cortisol production high, which damages cells in our bodies (Miller and Chen, 2007). Chronic stressors also produce a lot of strain (termed **allostatic load**) on our bodies due to repeated changes in physiological responses and heightened activation of these systems as they continually respond to demands over long time periods. High allostatic load is indicated by sharp changes in blood pressure (from normal or baseline levels), higher cholesterol levels, and higher cortisol levels (Ryff *et al.*, 2001). People with higher allostatic load usually have weaker immune systems (Herbert and Cohen, 1993), more heart disease and memory loss, and are at greater risk for early death (Seeman, 2001).

How about stress that originates from our close partners or relationships? Interestingly, the first studies linking relationships and stress examined rats and monkeys. Rats exposed to stressors in the lab display less fear when they are with other rats than when alone (Latane and Glass, 1968). Young monkeys separated from their mothers at 6 months and then housed with other monkeys show better immune functioning than those housed alone (Coe and Lubach, 2001), although separation impairs the immune functioning of all separated monkeys. These and other findings suggest that maintaining attachment bonds with mothers early in life facilitates immune functioning, and that early relationship disruptions render organisms – including humans – vulnerable to life-long health problems. These findings are consistent with recent longitudinal health evidence in humans (Miller *et al.*, 2011).

Social support also reduces stress in humans, both during social interactions (Gerin *et al.*, 1992) and in chronically stressful environments (Seeman, 1996). For example, people who have persistent conflicts with family or friends are more likely to contract colds (Cohen *et al.*, 1998). People who both had more negative relationships with their parents when they were young, and have more negative interactions with their current romantic partners, have high allostatic loads because they must continually deal with these difficult social interactions (Ryff *et al.*, 2001). These findings, however, are stronger for men than women, indicating that men may be more susceptible to the health-damaging effects of negative social interactions. Indeed, a lot of research shows that social support tends to have greater health benefits for men than women (Stroebe and Stroebe, 1987).

Relationships with family members are especially important sources of support (and sometimes harm) for immune system functioning (Uchino *et al.*, 1996). And, findings consistently show that mortality and illness rates are lower for married than non-married people (Rendall *et al.*, 2011). However, this link is stronger for husbands than wives. For example, in the USA, an unmarried man's odds of dying at age 25 in the next year are 2.4 times higher than the odds for a married man, whereas unmarried women at age 25 are 1.72 times more likely to die in the next year than married women (Rendall *et al.*, 2011). No need to unduly panic if you are 25 and single – the overall chances of dying at age 35 in the next year is about one chance in a thousand in Western countries. Still, the protective effects of marriage are real and maintained through to old age.

Of course, it is quite possible that people who enter into marriage are already healthier or have healthier life styles than those who remain single, which would explain the results. However, when variables such as socio-economic status are statistically controlled for, the protective effects of marriage and the gender differences remain, although being reduced in size (Rendall *et al.*, 2011). The gender disparity may be because female partners (more than male partners) often take care of men and encourage them to engage in health-promoting behaviors, such as eating better, trying to lose weight, and going to the doctor for annual checkups.

These findings extend to physical and mental health outcomes, especially for happily married people. People in unhappy marriages are 2.5 times more likely to suffer from a major depression than happily married people (Weissman, 1987), and depression can lower immune system functioning (Herbert and Cohen, 1993). In a famous longitudinal study of Iowa farm families, unhappily married spouses were significantly more likely to become ill over time than happily married spouses were, controlling for levels of work stress, education, income, and other variables (Wickrama *et al.*, 1997). Although this evidence is correlational, other data by Conger and his colleagues (1999) suggests that low marital quality causes health problems, rather than the reverse.

Some of the most intriguing and influential experimental work on relationships and health has been carried out by Janice Kiecolt-Glaser and her collaborators. Kiecolt-Glaser *et al.* (1994) had healthy married couples enter the hospital for an overnight stay. Each couple discussed a major relationship conflict for 30 minutes while blood samples were drawn from their arms before, during, and after the conflict discussion. The amount of negative and particularly hostile behaviors displayed during the discussion seemed to suppress immune systems, especially for wives. However, the level of positive behaviors was not related to immune functioning or other health markers in either husbands or wives. This is one situation in which relationship health effects appear to be more deleterious for women than men. Many women feel greater responsibility for managing their relationships, and they often want more changes in their relationships than their male partners (see Chapter 9). Consequently, discussing a major relationship conflict in which they are more likely to want change, while still managing the relationship, may represent a more challenging stressor for women than men.

Similar effects are found in spouses providing long-term care to their chronically ill partners. Kiecolt-Glaser and colleagues (1994) studied changes in depression and immune functioning in people who were providing long-term care for their spouses, all of whom were suffering from **Alzheimer's disease**. Compared to a matched control group, caregivers experienced declines in immune system functioning and increases in depression across the 13 months of the study.

Finally, when one partner dies this takes a toll on health. Indeed, the death of a partner/spouse is perhaps the single greatest stressor that most people ever encounter (Holmes and Rahe, 1967). Durkheim (1897) was the first person to document an increase in suicide rates in widowed people only one week after the death of their spouse. His numbers were stunning: widowed men were 66 times more likely to commit suicide during this time period than married men, and widowed women were nine times more likely to kill themselves than married women (these figures are on low base rates of suicide, so they are not as disastrous as they sound). Contemporary research into suicide in western countries has shown that Durkheim's analyses still generally hold true. Men are more likely to commit suicide than women, and the dissolution of a sexual relationship remains an important risk factor.

Cardiovascular problems, such as sudden heart attacks, are responsible for most of the excessive deaths of very recently widowed people (Stroebe and Stroebe, 1987). Bereaved individuals also suffer from more debilitating health problems for the remainder of their lives. For example, they are significantly more likely to become depressed – especially widowed men – which compromises their immune functioning (Weisse, 1992) and results in greater susceptibility to a variety of other diseases.

Summary and Conclusions

One striking lesson from the comparative and evolutionary literature is the stunning extent to which human sexuality (from genitalia to hormones to brain structures) has an ancient evolutionary history, reflected in the similarity of hormonal and brain systems and basic reproductive processes between humans and other species. Once evolutionary processes stumbled across the trick of sexual reproduction (about one billion years ago) it caught on, most likely because of the boost given to pathogen resistance via gene shuffling. And, the hormones that evolved to regulate sexual reproduction are startlingly similar across many species. A snail version of oxytocin, for example, controls ejaculation in males and egg-laying in females, and the ancestral line leading to snails and humans diverged about 600 million years ago! (Donaldson and Young, 2008).

The comparative study of sexuality across apes and primates species also shows how similar humans are to our ape and mammalian cousins. Such comparative studies also allow strong conclusions to be drawn about the recent evolutionary past of humans; namely, over the last million years or so, our ancestors have evolved pair bonded mating systems. In particular, there is little evidence that sperm competition, combined with promiscuous sexual pairings like the chimpanzee, played a strong or recent role in the evolution of human genitalia or sexuality.

The evidence from the study of hormones, neurotransmitters, and the relationship brain, is also broadly consistent with the work covered in the prior chapter on the intimate relationship mind. First, in the relationship brain (as in the mind) goals are critical motivating factors. Second, a lot of relationship information processing occurs in regions of the brain that specialize in unconscious, automatic processing. Third, in relationship contexts, regions of the brain involved in self-regulation and emotion are especially active. Fourth, regions of the brain involved in emotions, cognitions, and self-regulation are heavily interconnected by neuronal fibers. Fifth, certain biological systems in the brain and body involving the reward centers (the dopamine system) and the bonding system (involving the cuddle hormones) are purpose-built to satisfy functions and goals that are specific to sexual intimate relationships.

This chapter does not mark the end of material concerning the brain and body. We will describe research on the brain and biological processes quite often in later chapters, and will comment further on the close links between illness, health, and intimate relationships in subsequent chapters. In this chapter, we have covered a complex and technical area in a brief fashion. However, we have revealed an impressive amount of convergence between the biological material covered here and the material in the previous two chapters dealing with the evolution of the human relationship body and brain (at the distal level) and the nature and functions of the relationship mind (at the proximal level).

Part Three

Beginning Relationships:
Attachment and Mate Selection

Born to Bond
From Infancy to Adulthood **5**

Claire's life – historical roots of attachment – normative features of attachment – individual differences in attachment – attachment in adolescence and adulthood – normative and individual difference attachment processes – life history models – controversies – summary and conclusions

> A child forsaken, waking suddenly,
> Whose gaze afeard on all things round doth rove,
> And seeth only that it cannot see
> The meeting eyes of love.
>
> George Eliot

"Claire," not her real name, has been a participant in a longitudinal study since the day she was born. At birth, her mother had dropped out of high school and was not living with Claire's biological father. During the first year and a half of her life, Claire's mother and father were unemployed, they had a turbulent "on-again/off-again" relationship, they struggled with money problems, and they moved several times before Claire was one year old. Although Claire's mother said she was delighted with Claire and being a new parent, Claire was classified as being insecurely attached to her mother at age one. When Claire was afraid, for example, her mother could not comfort her, no matter what her mother did.

Between ages two and five, Claire experienced a great deal of life stress. Her mother unexpectedly got pregnant again, and her father then suddenly died in a freak accident. At age three, when Claire and her mother were observed doing challenging tasks

The Science of Intimate Relationships, First Edition. Garth Fletcher, Jeffry A. Simpson, Lorne Campbell, and Nickola C. Overall.
© 2013 Garth Fletcher, Jeffry A. Simpson, Lorne Campbell, and Nickola C. Overall.
Published 2013 by Blackwell Publishing Ltd.

together, Claire's mother was rated as being unsupportive. Claire was described by observers as being withdrawn, immature, and hostile compared to her same-age peers. At preschool, Claire's teachers reported that she worried about a lot of things, was fearful and cautious, and was quick to fly off the handle. During elementary school, Claire's life improved, but unpredictable and stressful events continued to occur. One of her relatives was charged with a serious crime and her mother had a string of different live-in boyfriends. Fortunately, things were better at school. Claire was bright, her grades gradually improved during elementary school, and she started to develop new friendships.

Upon entering adolescence, Claire began engaging in high-risk behaviors. She started to use and abuse alcohol and drugs, and she reported having several sexual partners by the time she was 16. By age 19, Claire became pregnant, living with her mother, with no job and no steady boyfriend. At age 23, she claimed that her life revolved around her son, who she described as perfect. However, when Claire was observed doing the same challenging tasks with her son that she had done with her own mother 20 years earlier, she was rated as being relatively unsupportive, just like her mother. Today, Claire still lives with her mother, is unemployed, has difficulty maintaining romantic relationships, and worries that about her ability as a parent.

How can Claire's difficult and complex life be understood? How did her early life experiences lead her to become the person she is as an adult? Is Claire locked into her specific attachment pattern/style for life? Over the last 40 years, psychologists have learned a great deal about how the way in which basic attachment needs are met influence social development. Indeed, some of the most important theories in psychology speak to these important and intriguing issues.

We begin this chapter by introducing **attachment theory**, which is an evolutionary theory of human social behavior "from the cradle to the grave" (Bowlby, 1979, p. 129). We first discuss how and why attachment theory originated and some of its basic principles. We then review the universal features of the theory (those that apply to virtually all people) followed by when, how, and why certain people diverge from normal patterns of attachment (individual differences in attachment styles). We conclude the chapter by showing how attachment theory fits within another major evolutionary theory – **life history theory** – which helps us to understand how and why the early social experiences of Claire channeled her development to adulthood along particular paths.

Attachment Theory

Brief historical overview

The origins of attachment theory read like a movie plot. At the start of the Second World War, John Bowlby, a young and energetic psychiatrist who had just learned Freud's "talking cure" (now known as **psychoanalysis**), started treating juvenile thieves and delinquents in the East End of London. Armed with these new and presumably

Figure 5.1 John Bowlby (1907–1990) developed his grand theory of social and personality development across the life span, known as attachment theory, in three volumes (from 1969 to 1980)
Source: © Sir Richard Bowlby

powerful Freudian techniques, Bowlby was confident that he could cure most of the 13–17-year-old adolescents he had been assigned to treat. He was wrong; he failed miserably. Almost none of his clients improved, despite his best efforts. Bowlby went back to the drawing board. Instead of asking his young clients to talk about their dreams and fantasies and their sexual and aggressive urges, he asked them to talk about their lives, starting very early in life. He found a common theme running through their lives. Most of them had been separated from their mothers for a prolonged period of time early in life (Bowlby, 1944). This struck Bowlby as the smoking gun that could perhaps explain the truancy, crime, and emotional problems that plagued his adolescent clients.

Bowlby began reading the scientific literature voraciously in areas that were the forerunners of ethology, evolutionary biology, developmental psychology, cognitive science, and computer science. He was trying to figure out whether early maternal separation is associated with later social problems in species other than humans, and why it is so harmful to young organisms. He consulted with scientists such as Harry Harlow (1959), who was in the process of discovering that monkeys reared in total isolation from birth nevertheless possessed a powerful, innate need for physical contact that was as strong as thirst or hunger. Young rhesus monkeys in Harlow's famous experiments clung to wire mesh (fake) mothers covered in soft cloth nearly all of the time, even though the source of food (a bottle of milk) was implanted in a nearby wire mesh mother not covered in soft cloth. These findings do not seem surprising today, but they struck the field like a thunderbolt when they were first reported.

Harlow's now classic experiments suggested to Bowlby that all primates, including humans, have an innate **attachment system** that was shaped by evolution to keep vulnerable infants in close physical proximity to their stronger and wiser caregivers, particularly during infancy and young childhood.

With this knowledge in hand, Bowlby sketched a grand theory of social and personality development across the lifespan, now known as attachment theory, which he published in three seminal books from 1969 to 1980 (Bowlby, 1969, 1973, 1980). His theory was based on an astute observation. In all human cultures, and in all primate species, young, vulnerable infants show a specific **sequence of attachment reactions** when they are separated from their caregivers. Immediately following separation, nearly all infants protest loudly, often crying, screaming, or throwing temper tantrums as they frantically search for their missing caregivers. Bowlby believed that intense **protest** at the first sign of caregiver absence is a good initial strategy to promote infant survival, particularly for species born in a developmentally immature and dependent state, which is especially true of humans (see Chapter 2). Intense protests usually draw the attention of caregivers to their young children, who during evolutionary history would have been exceptionally vulnerable to injury or predation if left alone for very long.

But what if loud and persistent protests fail to bring caregivers back? If this occurs, infants enter a second stage, known as **despair**, in which they stop moving around, become quiet, and sometimes become despondent. Bowlby reasoned that becoming depressed is a good back-up strategy to promote infant survival. Excessive movement could result in accidents or injuries and, when combined with loud protests, it could attract dangerous predators. Thus, if protests fail to bring back an absent caregiver, the next best survival strategy should be to avoid doing things that increase the risk of predation.

After a long period of despair, which could last weeks, months, or even longer, Bowlby believed that young children who had not been reunited with their caregivers enter a third stage – **detachment**. During this final phase, infants resume normal activity without their caregivers, gradually learning to function in an independent and self-reliant fashion. Bowlby (1982) hypothesized that detachment paves the way for emotional bonds to develop with new caregivers. Detachment, in other words, allows infants to cast off old ties and begin forming new ones with caregivers who are available and may be able and willing to provide the time, attention, and resources necessary for their survival.

In sum, Bowlby believed that the cognitive, emotional, and behavioral reactions that characterize each of these stages reflect the operation of an innate attachment system that all primates are born with. The attachment system has evolved, and remains a central part of our human nature, because it provided a solution to one of the biggest challenges that our ancestors faced – how to survive the dangerous years of early childhood. Informed by Darwin (1859), Bowlby believed that the attachment system was genetically wired into all mammals via natural selection.

Attachment theory applies to everybody throughout life from birth to death. The theory has two main components: (i) **a normative component**, which explains typical features of attachment that apply to everyone, such as how and why attachment bonds form and remain fairly stable over time; and (ii) an **individual-difference component**, which explains how and why people who have different attachment styles think, feel, and behave in different social situations. We now discuss both of these components, beginning with the basic normative features of attachment.

Normative features of attachment

Human infants are born with large heads, courtesy of our large brains. This feature requires that humans are born in an underdeveloped physical state, compared to most other primates, to make it through the birth canal (see Chapter 2). Nevertheless, from the moment of birth, human infants enter the world ready, willing, and able to bond with their caregivers (Simpson and Belsky, 2008). Young children form strong emotional bonds quickly with their caregivers, even when they are neglectful or abusive (Moriceau and Sullivan, 2005). This bonding typically occurs when the brain is experiencing rapid neural development over the first two to three years of life, producing hundreds of millions of new connections (see Chapter 4). Following this explosive growth, synaptic connections are later pruned if they are not used early in life. This process allows environmental experiences to shape the development of each person's brain, allowing the individual to respond adaptively to the environment into which s/he has been born.

There are three normative developmental factors, all of which are critical to understanding how and why people form emotional bonds with others: (i) the way in which infants' reactions and behaviors are synchronized with their caretakers from the time the baby is born; (ii) young children's tendency to remain in close physical contact with and proximity to their caregivers, especially when they are upset or afraid; and (iii) the way in which attachment behaviors emerge and develop in a series of stages.

Mother–infant synchrony It takes two to tango. Mothers must synchronize their own behavior with their newborns' behavior to forge the strong infant–caregiver bonds that are needed for their infants to survive. Immediately after birth, mothers experience a rush of hormones that make them feel euphoric and receptive to emotional bonding, even though they are exhausted and in pain from just having given birth (Eibl-Eibesfeldt, 1989). Without being told what to do, mothers in all cultures hold and interact with their infants about 30 centimeters (1 foot) away from their own faces, which is the optimal distance for infants to clearly see their mothers' faces (Eibl-Eibesfeldt, 1989). Mothers also work hard to establish direct eye contact with their infants (Klaus and Kennell, 1976). And, when their infants reciprocate eye contact, mothers become livelier, speak with greater voice inflections (changing the pitch of their voice), and approach their infants more closely (Grossmann, 1978, cited in Eibl-Eibesfeldt, 1989). Mothers also enjoy establishing eye contact with their young infants, and they work hard to generate smiles, which they interpret as signs of genuine affection directed specifically toward them (Eibl-Eibesfeldt, 1989).

When interacting with their infants, mothers also exaggerate their facial expressions, change their expressions more slowly than normal, and maintain eye contact with their newborns for longer than normal periods of time (Eibl-Eibesfeldt, 1989). All of these actions are ideally suited to the infant's developing visual system. When talking to their infants, mothers deliberately slow down their speech, accentuate certain syllables, and talk one octave higher than normal speech (Anderson and Jaffe, 1972; Grieser and Kuhl, 1988). You probably have heard this sort of speech – "Does liddle bubby want to go beddy-bye? You are so, so cute, yes you are!" People also slip into this pattern of speech when talking to their pets or to their adult lovers, both of whom can also serve as attachment figures. This pattern of **baby talk** is preferred by young infants (Fernald, 1985), and is well suited to the developing hearing capacities of young infants.

These coordinated interactive behaviors between mothers (or other caretakers) and their young infants almost certainly evolved together, and maintain or increase the reproductive fitness of both mothers and their children. In other words, these complex and synchronized behaviors evolved because they increased the chances of both mothers and their infants passing their genes onto future generations.

Keeping close Both infants and parents like to stay close to one another (Bowlby, 1980). Young children establish or maintain proximity to their caregivers using three kinds of strategies (Belsky and Cassidy, 1994). By smiling broadly and squealing with joy across the room, infants draw caregivers toward them. Doing the opposite, and crying or screaming, also grabs the attention of the caregiver and typically leads to attempts to comfort the child and diagnose the problem. And, of course, the child may simply move toward the caregiver. All three of these broad classes of behaviors serve to keep infants in close physical proximity to their caregivers, thereby increasing the child's chances of survival. Because dying before sexual maturity is one of the main threats to successful reproduction, such processes almost certainly shaped the attachment system in humans, helping to establish the deep and profoundly social nature of our species.

Four phases of development Attachment behaviors develop across four phases in humans (Bowlby, 1969). In the first phase (between birth and two to three months), infants do not show strong preferences for being with any single caregiver or attachment figure. During the second phase (from two to three months to approximately seven months), most infants become more selective. For example, they begin to distinguish their daily caregivers and family members from strangers, they start to prefer certain people over others, and they begin to direct some of their attachment behaviors toward their mother, father, or other caregivers with whom they have begun to bond.

During phase 3 (from seven months to about three years), children start taking a more active role in seeking out their caregivers, especially when they are upset, and in initiating social contact with new people such as playmates. During this phase, children also start to develop what Bowlby termed **internal working models**, which are beliefs, expectancies, and attitudes about relationships based on earlier experiences with attachment figures. Working models exist both for the self (answering the question, "Am I worthy of love and attention?") and for significant others (answering the question, "Are my attachment figures going to be there for me when I really need them?") (Bowlby, 1973). Working models are a special category of general lay relationship theories, as we discussed in Chapter 2. They play a crucial role in adulthood, which will become clear later in this chapter.

During phase 3, the primary functions of attachment also emerge in the child's behavior. These functions are: (i) **proximity maintenance** (staying near to, and resisting separations from, the attachment figure); (ii) **safe haven** (turning to the attachment figure for comfort and support when distressed); and (iii) **secure base** (using the attachment figure as a foundation from which to engage in non-attachment behaviors, such as exploration and play). If children experience prolonged separations from their attachment figures in phase 3, they enter the three stages of response to separation discussed earlier (protest, despair, and detachment) unless their attachment figures return.

Phase 4, which starts at about age 3, marks the start of developing partnerships with attachment figures that are more flexible and strategic. Given their rapidly expanding language skills and their growing ability to infer the feelings, goals, and intentions of other people, children begin to see the world not only from their own viewpoint, but also from the standpoint of their attachment figures. They start to create more elaborate theories of how others view them and the world, and they gradually incorporate the plans, goals, and desires of their interaction partners – first their mothers and fathers, and then others – into their own decision-making. This, in turn, facilitates the negotiation of joint plans and activities with other people (see Chapter 2).

As children move through the toddler years and into middle childhood, the desire for physical proximity is slowly replaced by the desire to maintain psychological proximity, which is known as **felt security** (Sroufe and Waters, 1977a). Early in adolescence, observable signs of attachment bonds with parents begin to wane (Hinde, 1976). Nearly all adolescents remain attached to their parents, but the primary functions of attachment – proximity maintenance, safe haven, and secure base – are gradually transferred to peers and eventually to romantic partners as adolescents move into adulthood (Furman and Simon, 1999; Hazan and Shaver, 1994).

Each of these normative capabilities and tendencies has almost certainly been shaped by natural selection (Bowlby, 1969). During evolutionary history, reproductive fitness in both infants and their parents would have been enhanced by infants who: (i) initially forged stronger emotional bonds with their caregivers; (ii) maintained closer physical contact with their parents; and (iii) successfully moved through each attachment stage and transferred attachment functions from parents or caregivers to close friends and/or adult romantic partners. Because adults have more advanced cognitive, emotional, and behavioral skills and capabilities than children (e.g. the ability to self-soothe when upset, to think about attachment figures when regulating emotions), the attachment behaviors of adults are less visible than those of children. Nevertheless, the same basic normative processes are thought to operate in both children and adults (Bowlby, 1969; Mikulincer and Shaver, 2007).

Individual differences in attachment

Although infants are biologically prepared to form attachment bonds with their caregivers from the moment they are born, the specific type of bond they form depends on how they are raised and cared for (Ainsworth, 1979; Bowlby, 1969). Infants, of course, do not have the cognitive ability to judge the quality or safety of their environments. They cannot discern until they are much older, for example, whether or not their environment is plentiful, friendly, and rich in resources or threatening, harsh, and impoverished. However, infants and young children can gauge whether or not their caregivers are sensitive, responsive, and attentive to their needs. This kind of information incidentally provides information about the nature and quality of current, and perhaps even future, social and physical environments that they are likely to encounter during their lives (Belsky et al., 1991).

Consider an example. If caregivers in a hunter-gatherer culture living 70 000 years ago in Africa could devote the time, effort, and energy needed to be sensitive, responsive, and attentive parents, the social and physical environment is more likely to have been relatively safe and contain enough resources to live reasonably well. However, if caregivers were insensitive, non-responsive, and devoted little time and attention to their children, the environment was probably more dangerous (maybe there was serious conflict with other groups) or fewer resources were available (maybe food was scarce). Thus, as will become clear later, the quality of caregiving that children receive depends in part on local environmental conditions, which in turn affects how individuals view mating and parenting when they become adults (Ellis et al., 2009).

The first test that measured individual differences in attachment patterns in young children was developed by Mary Ainsworth. It is called the **strange situation.** In this hour-long lab test, 12- to 18-month-old children are exposed to two "danger cues" that were present in our evolutionary past: being left alone and being left with a strange person. When examining how young, frightened children reunite with their mothers after the mothers return from a short absence (leaving the lab room for one to two minutes at a time), Ainsworth and colleagues (1978) identified three primary attachment patterns in young children: **secure, anxious,** and **avoidant.**

When their mothers return to the lab room, securely attached children tend to directly approach their mothers, climb up on their lap, calm down fairly quickly, and then resume other activities (such as exploration and play in the lab room). Thus, securely attached children use their mothers as a safe haven and a secure base in order to control and reduce negative emotions when they are upset. Avoidantly attached children behave quite differently. They typically ignore and fail to approach their mothers when they return to the room, and act as if they really don't care if she is present or not, and they do not appear to be upset (even though there is evidence they are; Sroufe and Waters, 1977b). Avoidant children control and reduce their negative feelings in an independent and self-reliant way by not turning to their mothers for comfort and support. In contrast, anxiously attached children often behave in a distressed fashion when their mothers return to the room and make conflicted attempts to glean comfort and support from her. For example, they mix clinginess (grabbing on to their mother's clothes) with outbursts of anger (hitting her or pushing her away while still clinging tightly).

All three types of children are attached to their mothers – they simply display their attachment needs differently. Indeed, each pattern can be construed as an adaptive behavioral strategy that seems quite rational and sensible (Belsky, 1997; Main, 1981). Mothers of securely attached children tend to be more aware of and responsive to the needs of their children (Ainsworth *et al.*, 1978; de Wolff and van Ijzendoorn, 1997). For example, they are more attuned to signs that their infants are upset (Del Carmen *et al.*, 1993), they provide moderate and appropriate levels of stimulation (Belsky *et al.*, 1984), they engage in more synchronous interactions with their infants and children (Isabella and Belsky, 1990), and they behave in a warmer, more involved, and more appropriately responsive manner (Braungart-Rieker *et al.*, 2001). As a result, securely attached children are assured about the availability and responsiveness of their caregivers. This allows them to concentrate on other life tasks, such as playing, exploring the environment, and learning new skills. This partly explains why secure children are generally better adjusted, both emotionally and socially, in early and middle childhood (Sroufe *et al.*, 2005).

Anxiously attached children have a very different set of experiences. For the most part, they have caregivers who behave inconsistently toward them (Ainsworth *et al.*, 1978), often because of deficient parenting skills. Mothers of anxiously attached children, for example, respond erratically to their infants' needs and behavioral signs of distress, sometimes because they are under-involved or don't know how to be a good parent (Belsky *et al.*, 1984; Isabella *et al.*, 1989; Lewis and Feiring, 1989). Among children who have been maltreated, anxiously attached children are more likely to have been victims of parental neglect than physical abuse (Youngblade and Belsky, 1989). Thus, the demanding demeanor of anxious children may be designed to obtain, retain, or increase attention and care from unskilled or under-involved parents (Cassidy and Berlin, 1994; Main and Solomon, 1986).

In sum, the pattern of behaviors characteristic of anxious children – hypervigilance, persistent demands for attention, incessant worrying about being left or abandoned (Cassidy and Berlin, 1994) – may have evolved to counteract poor caregiving provided by young, naïve, over-burdened, or under-involved parents. For such children, this behavioral strategy would have increased proximity to their caregivers, solicited better care, and hence improved the child's chances of survival.

Avoidantly attached children have to deal with yet a different set of negative life experiences. Their caregivers tend to be cold, rejecting, and uncomfortable with their role as a parent (Ainsworth *et al.*, 1978). Mothers of avoidant children are less responsive to their infants' distress, they over-stimulate their children when interacting with them (e.g. playing in an overly animated or rough manner; Scholmerich *et al.*, 1995; Vondra *et al.*, 1995), and they dislike close body contact (Ainsworth *et al.*, 1978). Among maltreated children, avoidantly attached children are more likely to have been victims of physical or emotional abuse from their parents rather than of passive neglect (Youngblade and Belsky, 1989).

Avoidance may also serve several different purposes. Bowlby (1980), for example, believed that avoidance helps children to ignore or disregard events that might otherwise activate (turn on) their attachment systems. Without these defenses, avoidant children may recognize the true inaccessibility and rejecting demeanor of their caregivers, which could be incapacitating. Main (1981), on the other hand, claims that the independent, self-reliant behavior of avoidant children allows them to maintain reasonably close proximity to unhappy or overwhelmed caregivers without driving them away. Avoidance, in other words, could have evolved to overcome deficient caregiving by distressed, hostile, unhappy, or unmotivated parents. This behavioral strategy may have increased the survival of children who might have been abandoned if they had placed too many demands on their parents.

Attachment in Adolescence and Adulthood

In 1987, Cindy Hazan and Phil Shaver published the first study that applied what was known about attachment between parents and children to adult romantic partners. This was the "big bang" of adult attachment work, triggering a surge of research and theorizing on adult attachment that shows no signs of abating. Hazan and Shaver created a short self-report measure of adult attachment styles (see Figure 5.2) by first identifying the thoughts, feelings, and behaviors that Ainsworth *et al.* (1978) claimed were most characteristic of secure, anxious, and avoidant children.

They then asked a large sample of adults to indicate which paragraph – secure, avoidant, or anxious – best described their romantic relationships, while being allowed to choose only one attachment style. The results were striking. Secure adults reported being similar to secure children in terms of how they typically thought, felt, and acted in their romantic relationships. Furthermore, avoidant adults were quite similar to

> Hazan and Shaver (1987) asked their adult participants which paragraph best described their feelings (in romantic relationships):
>
> **Secure**: I find it relatively easy to get close to others and am comfortable depending on them and having them depend on me. I don't often worry about being abandoned or about someone getting too close to me.
> **Avoidant**: I am somewhat uncomfortable being close to others; I find it difficult to trust them completely, difficult to allow myself to depend on them. I am nervous when anyone gets too close, and often, love partners want me to be more intimate than I feel comfortable being.
> **Anxious**: I find that others are reluctant to get as close as I would like. I often worry that my partner doesn't really love me or won't want to stay with me. I want to merge completely with another person, and this desire sometimes scares people away.

Figure 5.2   Paragraphs used to assess the three main attachment styles in Hazan and Shaver's (1987) pioneering study
Source: © 1987 American Psychological Association, Inc.

avoidant children, and anxious adults were similar to anxious children. Even the percentages of adults who claimed they were secure (56%), avoidant (25%), or anxious (19%) more or less paralleled the percentages of children that Ainsworth and her colleagues had classified using the same three categories in the "strange situation."

One of the first questions that researchers posed in the early 1990s, following this groundbreaking research, was the extent to which people neatly fitted into one of the three specific attachment categories (Collins and Read, 1990; Feeney and Noller, 1990; Simpson, 1990). To answer this question, the individual sentences contained in the Hazan and Shaver paragraphs were converted to scale items and adults were asked to indicate how well each item described them personally. This method allows people to rate the different attachment styles independently instead of forcing them to choose only one style. For example, it would be possible to rate yourself as highly anxious and secure, or as avoidant and secure, or any combination you can think of.

What do people actually do? The results are the same across many studies. People see themselves as located independently somewhere on two different continuously distributed dimensions: (i) the degree of avoidance; and (ii) the degree of anxiety (see Figure 5.3). This two-dimensional model of adult attachment has become the standard in the adult attachment literature (Brennan *et al.*, 1998; Simpson *et al.*, 1996).

Adults who score high on avoidance tend to be uncomfortable with emotional closeness, they do not want to become interdependent with their romantic partners, they prefer being independent and self-reliant, and they use strategies to suppress their negative emotions when they are upset. Adults who score high on anxiety obsessively desire more closeness and greater felt security with their romantic partners, but they also worry that their partners do not truly love them and might leave them; thus, they use extreme strategies to control and reduce their negative emotions. Secure people (who score low in both anxiety and avoidance) trust their partners and want greater intimacy, are confident that their partners will be available and responsive if and when

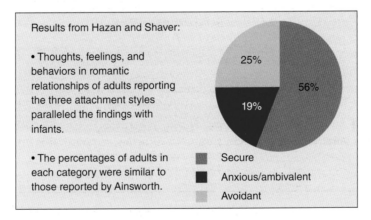

Figure 5.3   Percentages endorsing each attachment category
Source: From Hazan and Shaver, 1987

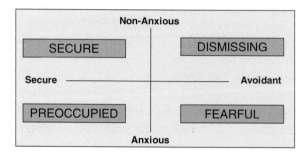

Figure 5.4 Factor analysis of independent attachment rating scales for adults in romantic relationships reveals two dimensions defining four categories
Source: From Fletcher, 2002; © 2002 Blackwell Publishers Inc.

needed, enjoy emotional closeness and mutual dependence, and use more adaptive strategies that are focused on solving problems to regulate their negative emotions (Mikulincer and Shaver, 2003).

When the two attachment dimensions are combined (see Figure 5.4), they form four attachment categories that can be thought of as defining four hypothetical individuals: **secure** (low anxiety/low avoidance), **preoccupied** (high anxiety/low avoidance), **dismissive** (low anxiety/high avoidance), and **fearful** (high anxiety/high avoidance) (Bartholomew and Horowitz, 1991). Importantly, however, most people do not fit neatly into any single category or type. Many people, for instance, are both moderately avoidant and moderately anxious. In what follows, we will often refer to secure, avoidant, or anxious people. These terms, however, refer to people who define the end-points of the two attachment dimensions.

How do adult attachment styles affect how people think, feel and behave in relationships? As shown in Figure 5.5, Mikulincer and Shaver (2003) have developed a process model that indicates: (i) what kinds of threatening situations should activate (turn on) and terminate (turn off) the attachment system; and (ii) how secure, avoidant, and anxious individuals react when threats arise. When potential threats are perceived, the positive working models of securely attached people allow them to remain confident that their attachment figures (e.g. romantic partners) will be attentive, responsive, and available to meet their needs, helping them control and reduce their negative feelings. These beliefs, in turn, increase their sense of felt security, which turns off the attachment system and allows secure people to use constructive, problem-focused coping strategies. A great deal of research, summarized below, supports this process model (Mikulincer and Shaver, 2007).

The pathways are different for the two kinds of insecurely attached people. When anxiously attached people perceive possible threats, they are uncertain that their attachment figures (partners) will be sufficiently attentive, available, and responsive to their needs. These worries keep their distress levels high and their attachment systems turned on, leading them to use emotion-focused coping strategies in which they

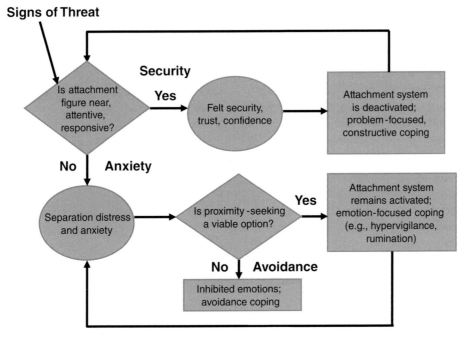

Figure 5.5   Attachment process model
Source: Adapted from Mikulincer & Shaver, 2003; reprinted from *Advances in Experimental Social Psychology*, © 2003, with permission from Elsevier

remain hypervigilant to possible signs of loss and ruminate about worst-case scenarios. For example, when anxiously attached people discuss major (but not minor) problems with their romantic partners, they become visibly upset, worry that the problem might undermine their relationship and, in their frustration, behave in a more hostile and caustic manner toward their partners (Simpson *et al.*, 1996).

When avoidantly attached individuals feel threatened, they are distressed at a physiological level, but they are not typically consciously aware of it (see Chapter 2). To keep their attachment systems turned off, avoidant individuals inhibit and control their emotions by disregarding, downplaying, or diverting their attention away from the source of distress. For instance, when they hear distressing information (e.g. someone discussing the recent death of a close friend), avoidantly attached people turn their attention away from the source of distress, think about other things, or downplay the negative impact of the event on those involved (Fraley and Brumbaugh, 2007; Fraley *et al.*, 2000).

These three modes of coping are also associated with different interpersonal goals (see Chapter 2). Securely attached individuals want to build greater intimacy with their partners, so try to forge more closeness with their partners when they can. Anxiously attached individuals crave greater felt security, so they cling to their partners both psychologically and emotionally in the hope of eventually feeling more secure. Avoidant individuals strive to be psychologically and emotionally independent and in control of interpersonal events, so they work to maintain a safe emotional and psychological distance from their partners.

Although these attachment styles are fairly stable over time, they can change when people enter new relationships or encounter experiences that contradict their expectations (Simpson *et al.*, 2003). People who start out being secure, for example, can become insecure if they are suddenly jilted or betrayed by a trusted partner. Likewise, insecure people can become more secure if they meet someone who unconditionally loves and accepts them, warts and all. Bowlby (1973) likened social development as being similar to a railway system in which people set out on one developmental track early in life, but then encounter multiple branch points as they meet new people and have new experiences. If some of these experiences run counter to their expectations, their working models and attachment styles should gradually begin to change. Indeed, as we shall see, the quality of early caregiving by significant others plays a significant role in determining not only which developmental track an individual starts out on, but whether or not she or he continues to move down a particular developmental track across time (Fraley and Brumbaugh, 2004).

Early adult attachment research investigated five main questions: (i) how each attachment style is correlated with the quality and functioning of romantic relationships; (ii) how individuals regulate their emotions and cope with stressful events; (iii) how people process social information about their partners and relationships; (iv) how individuals behave in attachment-relevant situations (such as giving and receiving support and resolving conflicts with partners); and (v) how well individuals fare in terms of mental health outcomes. To date, more than 1500 published studies have examined these kinds of questions. Thus, we can highlight only a few of the most important findings and studies, which we have divided into normative and individual difference-based processes and outcomes.

Normative processes and outcomes in adulthood

Recall that, according to Bowlby, most of the normative attachment stages and behaviors that characterize children also apply to adults, although in somewhat different behavioral and emotional forms. For example, similar to children, adults pass through the same three stages following separation from their attachment figures (protest, despair, and detachment). Attachment figures also serve the same basic attachment functions (proximity maintenance, safe haven, and secure base) in adults as they do in children. The way in which these needs are signaled and satisfied, however, is less visible in adults. This is hardly surprising given the ability of adults to construct mental representations of their attachment figures and to use those representations to comfort themselves when distressed (Mikulincer and Shaver, 2003). Partners who display more secure base behaviors toward their mates – such as availability, non-interference, and encouragement – have partners who are more likely to explore and seek out new opportunities (Feeney and Thrush, 2010).

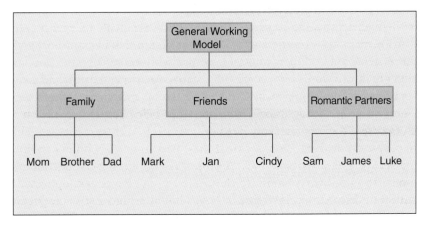

Figure 5.6   Hierarchical model of adult attachment
Source: Adapted from Collins & Read, 1994

As children move through adolescence and into adulthood, they gradually transfer the three attachment functions from their parents to their close adolescent friends and then to their mates (Hazan & Zeifman, 1999), with proximity maintenance usually being the first function that is transferred from parents to peers and secure base being the final one. Thus, during the early teenage years, adolescents actively seek out same-aged friends instead of their parents when they feel upset or worried about something. As time passes, they begin to use their close friends and eventually their romantic partners as emotional refuges and finally as sources of inspiration to help them explore new challenges and possibilities in life.

Research also suggests that adults have internal working models that are hierarchically organized (Collins and Read, 1994). As shown in Figure 5.6, general representations of attachment reside at the top of the hierarchy (e.g. general levels of attachment security), domain-specific representations of attachment with parents, romantic partners, and close friends are in the middle, and representations of specific people (e.g. one's mother, father, or current romantic partner, best friend) exist at the bedrock level of the hierarchy (Overall *et al.*, 2003; see Chapter 2). Attachment working models measured across these three levels tend to be correlated, but these links leave room for differences in attachment across specific people and domains. Returning to the case study we started the chapter with, Claire is insecurely attached to her mother and probably has been with many of her short-lived boyfriends, but she had some secure relationships with close friends early in life. Thus, to understand Claire's attachment history, her relationships with different individuals across different domains must be taken into account (e.g. parents, romantic partners, and close friends).

Domain-specific working models (for example, models of your mother) that are activated in a particular situation often guide how people think, feel, and behave, especially when they are distressed (Mikulincer and Shaver, 2003; Simpson and Rholes,

1994). Indeed, threatening events that induce the feeling of being ill, fatigued, afraid, or overwhelmed activate the attachment system in nearly all adults, which automatically elicits mental representations of attachment figures that can ameliorate distress (Mikulincer *et al.*, 2002). When adults are primed with secure concepts (for example, when they are shown words associated with security, such as love, trust, and care), they report more empathy for normally disliked out-group members (Mikulincer *et al.*, 2001). This suggests that insecurely attached people can experience a sense of felt security, even if it is temporary and fleeting.

Individual differences and outcomes in adulthood

A great deal of research has investigated how adult attachment styles influence how people think, feel, and behave, especially in romantic relationships. Securely attached adults (who score low in both anxiety and avoidance) have positive views of themselves and their partners, which help them maintain optimistic, benevolent, and positive views of their partners and relationships (Hazan and Shaver, 1994). As we have seen, secure people are also strongly motivated to build and broaden closeness and intimacy in their relationships (Mikulincer, 1998), and they often behave in ways that facilitate these goals. For example, when their partners are upset, secure people offer more support to their partners (Simpson *et al.*, 1992). And, when they try to resolve major conflicts with their partners, secure people use more constructive conflict resolution tactics that are more likely to solve the problem and make their partners feel better (Simpson *et al.*, 1996). Thus, it should come as no surprise that secure people tend to have significantly happier, better functioning, and more stable romantic relationships than insecure people (Feeney, 2008).

Anxiously attached adults (who score high on anxiety) have negative self-views and cautious but hopeful views that their partners might, at some point, be there for them. These mixed perceptions lead anxious persons to doubt their worth as relationship partners, resent past attachment figures, worry about relationship loss or abandonment in the future, and remain hypervigilant to even the slightest signs that their partners might be withdrawing from them either psychologically or emotionally (Cassidy and Berlin, 1994). The overpowering goal of anxious individuals is to achieve greater felt security (Mikulincer, 1998), which, ironically, leads them to smother and often scare away their partners. When anxious people try to resolve major relationship conflicts, they get upset quickly and resort to dysfunctional conflict resolution tactics that not only limit the likelihood of solving the problem, but often make the problem worse and the relationship less stable (Simpson *et al.*, 1996). Not surprisingly, the romantic relationships of anxiously attached people tend to be low in satisfaction, poorly adjusted, and rocky (Feeney, 2008).

One of the first studies to document the hallmark *behavioral* features of attachment security and avoidance was conducted by Simpson *et al.* (1992). In this study, female dating partners were told they would be exposed to a set of experimental procedures that caused considerable anxiety and stress in most people. Each woman was then led to a dark, padlocked isolation chamber that appeared to contain shock equipment.

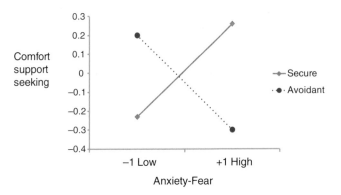

Figure 5.7 When do attachment styles influence behavior?
Source: From Simpson *et al.*, 1992; © 1992 American Psychological Association, Inc.

They were told the equipment was not fully set up, and were then led back to wait with their male dating partner, who knew nothing about the impending stressful task (which never actually occurred). Each couple's subsequent interaction (which was the real study) was unobtrusively videotaped for 5 minutes, and observers later rated how distressed they were, how much support they sought, and how much support male partners offered. As anticipated by attachment theory, the degree to which attachment avoidance predicted behavior depended on the level of distress that the female partners experienced and displayed. For example, if a woman was both distressed and avoidant (measured by a prior questionnaire), she tended to withdraw physically from her male partner and was less likely to seek verbal reassurance and support from him (these results are shown in Figure 5.7). And if the male partner was avoidant and his female partner appeared upset, he was actually less likely to reassure and support her. However, if the male or the female partner was securely attached, the opposite tendencies were observed.

This study is one of many that has confirmed Bowlby's core hypothesis that the attachment system is kicked into action when people are placed under stress or when they are distressed. When relationships are going well, attachment working models tend to stay in the background, exerting few effects. However, when problems arise and one of both partners is under stress, attachment working models blaze into action (see Chapter 11), for good or for ill.

This body of work is also consistent with some recent brain-imaging research. Omri Gillath and his colleagues (2005) asked 20 women who were being scanned via fMRI to first think about and then stop thinking about relationship situations, such as having a heated argument with their husband. When thinking about negative situations (compared to neutral contexts such as driving along a road), highly anxious women experienced greater activity in areas of the brain associated with the pain of rejection, which turns out to be the same part of the brain involved in perceptions of actual physical pain (Kross *et al.*, 2011), and more activity in a brain region associated with sadness and negative emotions. In contrast, more anxious women had less activity in a brain region associated with emotion regulation (the **orbital frontal cortex**, OFC; see Chapter 4). The correlations between self-reports of anxious attachment and the amount of activity in these brain regions were truly remarkable (ranging from .57 to .66), although this study did not control for levels of relationship satisfaction, which might be an issue. The results for avoidant attachment were not as clear cut, but the authors reported that they had difficulty getting strongly avoidant individuals into the study. Not surprisingly, avoidant people are resistant to having the insides of their brains examined while they answer questions about their relationships!

Viewed together, these studies help to explain how and why anxious or avoidant individuals regulate their emotions in intimate relationships.

Life History Models of Social Development

Attachment theory was developed to explain personality and social development from the cradle to the grave. According to the theory, social development is similar to a ball that follows different paths (trajectories) as it encounters different events (social forces) over time. Figure 5.8 shows this model. The ball at the top represents the specific life pathways (valleys) that an individual follows as s/he develops (i.e. as s/he moves down the hill of life over time), which depends on the unique experiences that s/he has at different branch points of life. The earliest branch points, for example, concern the type and quality of parenting that an individual received as an infant and young child. As we shall see, good parenting is a major social experience that can lead people down the lighted (more positive) pathway, whereas poor or negligent parenting may shunt individuals down the darker (less positive) pathway.

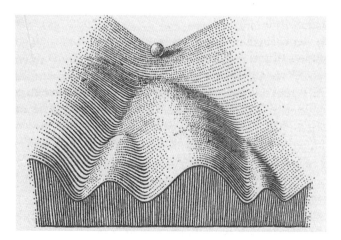

Figure 5.8   Waddington model of development
Source: © 1957 Allen and Unwin

Attachment theory says relatively little about how and especially why certain experiences early in life are related to specific experiences and events that occur later in life. This is where life history theory enters the picture. Life history theory introduces a key idea – that developmental processes themselves have evolved according to the forces of natural and sexual selection.

In Chapter 2, we described life history theory, which helps to explain how and why humans are unique in the animal world, with our large brains, our use of language, and our elaborate cultures. We noted that a cornerstone construct in life history theory is that important developmental switch points often involve tradeoffs. For example, should an individual pour energy and time into growing big and strong (and delay reproduction), or grow rapidly and reproduce early in life? Alternately, should an individual focus on the quantity or the quality of his/her offspring? We also argued that one key to understanding the most curious features of human nature (and our life histories) involve how our intimate relationships work. Not surprisingly, life history theory is also relevant to understanding how and why individual differences in attachment exist. In the next section, we review a pioneering model developed by Jay Belsky and his colleagues in 1991. We then discuss recent qualifications of this model along with some criticisms and controversies about the approach.

The development of individual differences in attachment and mating strategies

Jay Belsky and his colleagues (Belsky *et al.*, 1991) developed one of the first life history models of human social development. Their model is based on the standard assumption that one central evolutionary purpose of early social experience is to prepare children for the social and physical environments they are likely to inhabit as adults. Their evolutionary model of social development addresses how people make decisions about offspring quantity (e.g. having many children and investing less in each one) versus offspring quality (e.g. investing more in a smaller number of children). The information gained from early environments arguably should lead individuals to adopt an appropriate reproductive strategy in adulthood, one that on average increases reproductive fitness the most in future environments, given the cards that people are dealt in their social and physical environments.

As shown in Figure 5.9, Belsky *et al.*'s (1991) model has five stages, the first two comprising (A) specific events in a child's family of origin, such as the level of stress, parental relationship harmony, and financial resources affect, and (B) the quality of early child-rearing experiences, such as the amount of sensitive, supportive, and responsive care the child receives. These experiences in turn affect (C) the child's psychological and behavioral development, particularly attachment styles and internal working models, which then impact (D) the child's rate of physical development (e.g. how quickly sexual maturity is reached relative to his/her peers), and ultimately (E) the specific reproductive strategy adopted in adulthood.

This model suggests that two primary developmental pathways culminate in two unique **mating strategies** in adulthood, which should be familiar by now. One strategy

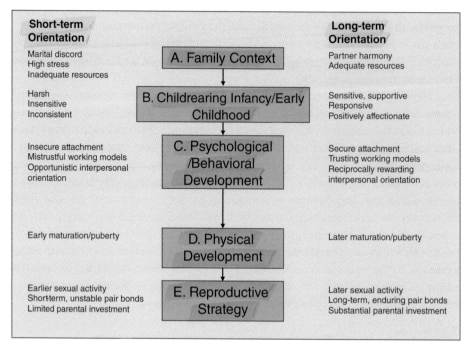

Figure 5.9   Evolutionary model of social development
Source: Adapted from Belsky *et al.*, 1991; © 1991 by the Society for Research in Child Development, Inc. Wiley-Blackwell Publishers)

reflects a short-term, opportunistic orientation toward relationships, especially mating and parenting. Short-term individuals become sexually active earlier in life, their romantic pair bonds are shorter, less satisfying, and less stable, and they devote less time and effort to parenting. In evolutionary history, a short-term orientation would have increased the relative quantity (total number) of children a person had. The second strategy reflects a long-term, investing orientation toward relationships in which sexual activity begins somewhat later in life, pair bonds are stronger, happier, and more enduring, and more time and effort are invested in parenting. A long-term orientation typically should have increased offspring quality (e.g. health and vitality) in evolutionary history.

Research supports most parts of this model (Ellis, 2004). For example, greater socio-emotional stress in families strongly predicts more insensitive, harsh, rejecting, inconsistent, and unpredictable parenting practices (A → B in Figure 5.9). Additionally, economic hardship (Burgess and Draper, 1989), occupational stress (Bronfenbrenner and Crouter, 1982), marital discord (Emery, 1988), and psychological distress (McLoyd, 1990) all predict more hostile and less involved parenting styles. On the flip side, more social support and economic resources are associated with warmer and more sensitive child-rearing practices (Lempers *et al.*, 1989), partly because less burdened parents are more patient with and tolerant of their children (Belsky, 1984).

The connection between parenting sensitivity and attachment in children is also well documented (B → C in Figure 5.9). Insensitive and unresponsive caregiving during the first year of life resulting in the development of insecure attachment (de Wolff and van Ijzendoorn, 1997), which predicts multiple behavior problems later in development. Insecurely attached two-year-olds, for example, are less tolerant and more demanding when they are frustrated (Matas et al., 1978). They also are more socially withdrawn (Waters et al., 1979), less sympathetic when their friends get upset (Waters et al., 1979), and are less well-liked by their classmates (LaFreniere and Sroufe, 1985). When they enter elementary school, insecure children also have more behavior problems, especially difficulties with aggression toward classmates and disobedience toward teachers (Erickson et al., 1985). Each of these behaviors is guided by insecure working models, which in some sense prepare insecure children for the negative, competitive, and less communal relationships they are likely to encounter later in life.

A unique prediction from this model is that the quality of early rearing experiences ought to influence the age at which individuals reach puberty (C → D in Figure 5.9). That is, puberty should occur earlier in life among individuals who develop along the short-term pathway than among those who develop along the long-term pathway. Recent studies have confirmed that greater parent–child warmth and sensitive parenting actually delays pubertal development (D in Figure 5.7) (e.g. Ellis et al., 1999). On the flip side, greater parent–child conflict and coercion speeds up puberty (e.g. Moffitt et al., 1992). On average, the warmth/sensitivity of early caregiving also appears to influence when **menarche** occurs (i.e. first menstruation) by almost a year in many girls. These stunning findings suggest that early interaction and attachment relationships have biological as well as psychological consequences.

Consider a pioneering study by Bruce Ellis and his colleagues (Ellis et al., 1999). They tracked relationships between parents and their children across eight years, starting when children were four to five years old. The biological changes associated with puberty in girls (the appearance of pubic hair, breast development, and menarche) occurred earlier if the parents had a poor romantic relationship, and especially if the father (if he was present in the home) had a less warm and less affectionate relationship with his daughter. The effects were large. For example, the extent to which fathers had a warm/affectionate relationship with their daughters correlated highly (−.43) with delayed pubertal development measured eight years later. Thus, being a "daddy's girl" delays the timing of puberty.

It is important to note that these findings hold only for girls, not for boys. This could be a measurement issue. The marker of puberty in girls (menstruation) is, of course, much easier to identify and measure than is the case for boys (growth spurts and voice changes). Nevertheless, in studies that have examined boys, pubertal timing effects typically have not been found (Ellis, 2004). One reason for this might be that men must accrue more skills, knowledge, status, and resources than women before they can attract and successfully compete for mates (see Chapter 4). If so, selection pressures during evolutionary history might not have acted on pubertal timing in males the same way that they seem to have in females.

Evidence for the final stage of the model (D → E) has also been confirmed. People who report being more securely attached have less promiscuous sexual attitudes and are less likely to have multiple sexual affairs (Brennan and Shaver, 1995). In fact, most securely attached adults claim they ideally would like to have only one sexual partner (mate) during the next 30 years (Miller and Fishkin, 1997). Secure women tend to have sexual intercourse for the first time at a later age than insecure women (Bogaert and Sadava, 2002), and secure men and women report greater satisfaction in their romantic relationships (Simpson, 1990). When trying to resolve difficult problems with their romantic partners, secure adults express less negative affect and display more constructive conflict resolution tactics (Simpson *et al.*, 1996). Attachment security is also associated with better communication in romantic relationships, including greater self-disclosure and more responsivity to self-disclosures by partners (Kobak and Hazan, 1991; Mikulincer and Nachshon, 1991). Not surprisingly, secure adults are also less likely to separate from their partners (Kirkpatrick and Hazan, 1994), they have romantic relationships that usually last longer (Kirkpatrick and Davis, 1994), and they are more committed to their partners (Brennan and Shaver, 1995).

Finally, consistent with the model, many individuals are prescient about how they will fare in later life as parents. Less secure college students, for instance, believe they will be more easily aggravated by their young children if/when they become parents. They expect to be stricter disciplinarians, believe they will behave less warmly toward their children, and are less confident about their ability to relate well to their children (Rholes *et al.*, 1997). Furthermore, avoidant college students believe they will derive less satisfaction from caring for their young children, and they express less interest in having them. Once they do have children, new parents who are avoidant do feel less emotionally close to their newborns as soon as two weeks after birth (Wilson *et al.*, 2007). Later in development, avoidant mothers are less emotionally supportive of their preschool children, and they have a more detached, controlling, and task-focused style of relating to them (Crowell and Feldman, 1988; Rholes *et al.*, 1995). In short, what people say about themselves and their attitudes predicts their actual behavior when it comes to children and parenting. If a potential romantic partner says that he or she does not like children and will not be good with them, these claims should be taken seriously.

To summarize, the evolutionary model of social development has had a remarkable track record of success. But, as is the way with science, controversies remain. We discuss some of these after dealing with some recent refinements of the model.

Variations on a theme

Belsky *et al.* (1991) viewed early father absence as one of several indicators of stress within the family of origin. Ellis and his colleagues, however, believe that fathers play a special role in the development of girls' mating strategies; namely, father absence or stepfather presence provides a particularly clear signal concerning how much girls can trust men in later life to provide good, stable levels of investment in them and their family (Ellis, 2004). Indeed, father absence does predict earlier pubertal development in most girls when they are followed from childhood into adolescence and adulthood (Ellis, 2004). For reasons that remain unclear, similar effects have not been found in

*"I too want companionship, intimacy, someone
to grow old with, but not 24/7."*

Figure 5.10
Source: © 2012 Barbara Smaller

African-American girls (Rowe, 2000). Additional research indicates that the earlier father absence occurs in a child's life (especially within the first 5 years), the stronger the effect it has on how quickly girls reach puberty (Quinlan, 2003; Surbey, 1990). Stepfather presence also affects pubertal timing. For example, greater conflict between mothers and stepfathers, combined with earlier stepfather presence in the home, predicts especially fast pubertal development in girls (Ellis and Garber, 2000).

Recently, Ellis *et al.* (2009) have developed a more nuanced life history model. According to their **environmental risk model**, the degree of harshness/difficulty of the local environment combined with its level of unpredictability determines which reproductive strategy (fast or slow) individuals will adopt in adulthood. Their model predicts, for example, that a harsh environment (e.g. difficulty getting enough food to eat, working long hours for low wages, walking long distances to get fresh water every day, and so forth) will lead to a slow reproductive strategy (i.e. reaching puberty later, delaying marriage and having children, having fewer children), but only if the environment is predictable. If the environment is both harsh and unpredictable, this produces a fast strategy.

This novel element of their theory is vividly illustrated by Barack Obama (2004) in his book *Dreams from my Father*. In the book, Obama compares life in Jakarta, Indonesia (where he spent time as a child) with life in a Chicago ghetto (near where he lived with his wife and daughters while he was a political activist in Chicago):

> I saw those Jakarta markets for what they were: fragile, precious things. The people who sold their goods there might have been poor, poorer even than the folks in Altgeld [Chicago]. They hauled 50 pounds of firewood on their back every day, they ate little, they died young. And yet for all that poverty, there remained in their lives a discernable order, a tapestry of trading routes and middle men, bribes to pay, and customs to observe, the habits of a generation played out every day. It was the absence of such coherence that made a place like Altgeld so desperate, I thought to myself; it was the loss of order." (p. 183).

According to the environmental risk model, the Jakarta situation is likely to push parents into having fewer children, maintaining stable marriages, and keeping the extended family together. Altgeld, on the other hand, with its relatively harsh and unpredictable/hazardous social environment, should push men and women into the fast reproductive lane. Recent research has confirmed that people who are raised in unpredictable environments in childhood (e.g. when their parents move a lot, change jobs, or change romantic partners) engage in riskier sexual and interpersonal behaviors later in life (Belsky *et al.*, 2012), especially if there is a great deal of unpredictability during the first few years of life (Simpson *et al.*, 2012).

Controversies

As we have seen, a life history approach views the attachment system as relatively open-ended, designed to produce the best reproductive outcomes available given the social and physical circumstances. This approach has its critics, however. Some scholars, notably Cindy Hazan, argue that the primary function of attachment in adulthood is to bond adults together (to fall in love) so that children can be raised with greater success (Hazan and Zeifman, 1999; Zeifman and Hazan, 1997). According to this view, evolutionary processes have simply lifted a pre-existing system that was originally designed to promote bonding between mothers and their children, to facilitate bonding between adult romantic partners. There is good evidence supporting this thesis, which we discuss in Chapters 3, 7, and 10. However, this approach implies that the normative evolutionary function of infant and adult attachment is the secure style. The other styles, in other words, represent pathological outcomes or aberrant deviations from modal security. Indeed, as we have seen, being more securely attached in childhood and adulthood is linked to positive outcomes, including longer lives, better health, and happier romantic relationships.

One problem with this thesis is that the occurrence of insecure attachment styles in both children and adults is high. Approximately 40% of people are classified as insecurely attached in many countries. Evolutionary adaptations are never perfect, so they can produce variation around an ideal outcome. However, the sheer number of people who are insecurely attached seems too large to support the claim that evolution generated only secure romantic models. For example, compare this figure (40% insecure) with the likely much lower percentage of adults who have no sex drive, who fail to develop theory of mind abilities (e.g. autistic individuals), or who never develop spoken language. Some adults do fall into these categories, but the numbers are small (probably less than 5%). This suggests that insecure attachments might have evolved as adaptations designed to make the best of the environments and social experiences that people face.

Models assuming that the secure style is normative also imply an implausible view of family life in ancestral environments, given what we know of family life as it exists in contemporary cultures, including hunter-gatherer societies, and what we know from the archeological record. Cross-cultural research indicates that parental investment in children (both emotional and practical) is highly variable. The quality of child-rearing is adversely affected if effective birth control is unavailable, if the genetic father has left and is replaced by a stepfather, if there are few social supports or supportive grandparents, if the birth-spacing is too short, if the family is large, if infants are ill or weak, and if there is poverty and hardship (Hrdy, 1999). These contingencies are hardly rare around the world. And, when such conditions exist, children are sometimes abandoned, abused, or even killed. There is no reason to believe that such factors were rare in ancestral environments; indeed, there is every reason to believe that they were commonplace. For example, there is evidence of infanticide or abandonment of newborn babies in many cultures, including hunter-gatherer cultures (Hrdy, 1999). It is noteworthy however, when babies are abandoned to die or are killed by their mothers, it is almost always done within the first 72 hours, which is true for both humans and other primates (Hrdy, 1999). To do otherwise would allow the inexorable biological and psychological attachment systems to take hold and make separation from the infant almost unbearable.

However, another way of analyzing the empirical data suggests the argument against a thorough-going life history approach still has some steam left. Returning to the two-dimensional model shown in Figure 5.4, we have paid little attention to those individuals defined by the bottom right of the two dimensions – the so-called fearful group (high on both avoidance and anxiety). Research by Mary Main and Judith Soloman (1986) using the "strange situation" found that a number of infants could not easily be classified in terms of Ainsworth's original tripartite categories. These infants – possessing **disorganized attachment** styles – exhibit an incoherent assortment of inconsistent behaviors (anger, aggression, withdrawal, crying, laughing), often in rapid succession. A good deal of research on this group of children has revealed they are often abused or frightened by their parents or are subject to extreme forms of neglect (Solomon and George, 2011). The similarity between fearful and disorganized attachment categories has often been pointed out (Simpson and Rholes, 2002). Moreover, the dire list of outcomes for infants later in life classified with disorganized attachment looks remarkably similar to those catalogued by researchers investigating the correlates of adult fearful attachment in intimate relationships, up to and including clinical depression, sexual offending, child abuse, intimate violence, bipolar disorder, criminal violence, poor mind-reading, and drug abuse (Riggs, 2010).

Our take on this phenomenon is that the disorganized (or fearful) attachment style represents a collapse of the evolved attachment system, a failure to develop a coherent attachment working model. About 80% of individuals from populations of high risk or abuse have been classified with disorganized attachment. More worryingly, up to 15% of samples from middle-class families have also been classified as disorganized (Solomon and George, 2011). This attachment category certainly seems like a pathological failure of the evolved attachment system, rather than a functional outcome linked to short-term versus long-term mating orientations, and its prevalence may be one important limiting condition to a life history approach.

Summary and Conclusions

We opened this chapter discussing the life of Claire, who encountered difficult and stressful experiences early in her social development. It is now possible to understand – from the standpoint of both attachment theory and life history theory – why Claire grew up the way she did.

Recall that Claire was born to a single mother who was well-intentioned, but also had money and relationship problems. Very early in life, Claire and her mother experienced abandonment, the arrest and death of her father, and several other significant hardships. Because Claire was insecurely attached to her mother from nearly the start of her life, she had problems relating to her peers in early childhood. As an adolescent, she started engaging in risky and sometimes dangerous activities, eventually dropping out of school altogether. Claire felt she could not trust people and, as a result, she had a difficult time committing to or becoming emotionally close to any of her many boyfriends. This led to a string of short-term sexual relationships with men who may also have been reluctant to form a long-term bond. Claire, of course, is a prototypic example of someone who enacts a short-term, opportunistic reproductive strategy, one that should have increased her reproductive fitness in difficult and unpredictable environments in our ancestral past. Although her life course and life outcomes are unpleasant ones, they are adaptive when one considers the difficult, stressful, and unpredictable environment in which Claire grew up. She is simply making the best of a tough life situation.

It is important to remember that people do not deliberately decide to enact a short-term or a long-term reproductive strategy. Rather, specific cues or experiences in their early environments lead people to selectively prefer, pay attention to, choose, and behave in ways that facilitate the enactment of a short-term or a long-term strategy. The take-home message is that we are all born to bond, but in different ways depending in part on our early social experience. However, as we have discussed, people can and do change strategies during the life course as events and features of their environments change. Attachment working models are relatively stable over time, but are also malleable and exquisitely attuned to relationship experiences across the life span.

Selecting Mates 6

What people want in a mate – the nature of mating standards – the origins of mate standards – within-gender differences – gender differences and mating strategies – explaining gender differences – mate preferences and the self – explaining within-gender differences – mate preferences and behavior – summary and conclusions

Someday he'll come along
The man I love
And he'll be big and strong
The man I love
And when he comes along
I'll do my best to make him stay

George and Ira Gershwin

In classes we teach on the science of intimate relationships, some of us use a demonstration developed by Bruce Ellis and Harold Kelley (1999). The students in the class are randomly given cards with numbers on them, ranging from 1 to 10, which represent their assigned mating value. These cards are held to their foreheads in such a way that others can see them, but remain out of sight for the card-bearer (so that each individual does not know his or her own mate value). The aim of the game is to get together with the individual with the highest mate value possible (gender is ignored). Once a mate selection is made, the initiator indicates his or her selection by attempting to shake hands. If the individual approached spurns the handshake, then the initiator must look elsewhere. When a couple is formed, indicated by a handshake, then each individual first guesses his or her own mate value number, before taking a peek at the

The Science of Intimate Relationships, First Edition. Garth Fletcher, Jeffry A. Simpson, Lorne Campbell, and Nickola C. Overall.
© 2013 Garth Fletcher, Jeffry A. Simpson, Lorne Campbell, and Nickola C. Overall.
Published 2013 by Blackwell Publishing Ltd.

assigned value. As the class members mill about, individuals pair off, until a small and disconsolate group is left standing in the middle of the room. Inevitably, this group represents the dregs of the mating market, but they too finally pair off in a crestfallen sort of way.

The numbers are then crunched on a laptop, and reported back to the class. The results typically reveal that the mating values of the paired-up partners are highly correlated (about .70 or so), but also that individuals are very accurate at guessing their own mate value after pairing off (with correlations also around .70 between the predicted self-mating values and the actual numbers assigned). This demonstration suggests two important features about choosing potential mates. First, merely utilizing the heuristic – get the best deal possible – is enough to produce **assortative mating** (i.e. mating in which people match highly on given characteristics) in situations where both parties exercise choice. Second, the process of assortative mating provides feedback allowing people to accurately and rapidly assess their own mate value.

Of course, such a classroom exercise is limited and leaves many questions unanswered. Do individuals deliberately choose others who are similar to them? Are people rated according to a simple mate value dimension (good versus bad)? Do people carry round general ratings of their own mate value in their heads, or are such judgments more complex and variegated? For example, does a man who is good-looking, but cold, offer the same overall mate value as a man who is homely and warm? Are there gender differences in what people seek in a mate? And, finally, what are the origins of mate ideals? Evolutionary and social psychologists have devoted much attention to such questions, and a more complete picture of how mate selection works in humans is beginning to emerge.

In this chapter we explore the nature of interpersonal attraction and mate selection. The first topics we deal with concern what men and women around the world look for in a mate and the thorny question of why humans adopt the standards they do. We then discuss both the nature of within-gender differences and across-gender differences in mating strategies, and then why such differences exist. Some of the fascinating ways in which self perceptions and presentations of self are linked to mate selection processes are described. Finally, we analyze the extent to which preferences, perceptions, and desires are related to behavior in this domain.

Searching for a Mate: What do People Want?

In New Zealand, Canada, the United States, Pacific Islands, African hunter-gatherer cultures, and around the world, people focus on more or less the same qualities in evaluating potential mates: traits related to intelligence, warmth and trustworthiness; a second set related to physical attractiveness; and a third set related to status and resources or the ability to achieve them. Moreover, although there are characteristic gender differences in the importance attached to such categories (more on this later), there is also good agreement across both gender and cultures concerning which factors are most important in selecting mates for long-term relationships: The winner is intelligence, warmth, and trustworthiness, with physical attractiveness and the ability to obtain status and resources typically running a close second.

The evidence supporting this generalization comes in various forms. David Buss (1989; Buss *et al.*, 1990) carried out the first systematic analysis in which men and women ranked a range of factors on their importance for selecting mates across 37 cultures. He found that traits like kind, understanding, and intelligence trumped earning power and attractiveness in both genders. A more recent study (Lippa, 2007) using an internet survey asked respondents to choose the most important three traits from a list of 23 items. Over 100 000 responses from 53 nations later, the top 9 items were the same for men and women, and featured familiar items like intelligence, kindness, and good looks. However, all the research on mate preferences discussed to this point shares a similar limitation; namely, the traits presented to participants were based on the hunches or theories of the experimenters. This approach could easily overlook important mate categories.

To deal with this thorny methodological issue, and to develop some valid and reliable scales to measure individual differences in mate ideals, Fletcher *et al.* (1999) initially had groups of women and men write down items that described their own ideal mates for long-term relationships. The hundreds of items that were generated were placed into categories, and any item that was cited by less than 5% of the sample was deleted, which left a total of 49 items. A different sample of students then rated how much importance they placed on each ideal in the context of sexual or romantic relationships. By using a statistical technique known as **factor analysis**, this research unearthed the general way in which people grouped the items together. The items fell neatly into the tripartite mate preference structure that has previously postulated: warmth/trustworthiness (with items like understanding, supportive, considerate, kind, a good listener, and sensitive); attractiveness/vitality (with items like adventurous, nice body, outgoing, sexy, attractive, good lover); and status/resources (with items like good job, financially secure, nice house or apartment, successful, and dresses well). These results proved to be the same regardless of whether the samples comprised men or women, or whether or not individuals were involved in sexual relationships.

What this brand of data analysis (factor analysis) shows is that people differ in terms of which sorts of mate characteristics they think are important, but that these differences occur across the three categories rather than within the sets of specific items that are included within each general ideal category. That is, people do not just set high or low ideal partner standards – individuals set high or low standards in ways that vary in a relatively independent fashion across the three kinds of mate characteristics.

Why do people not want it all? Why is Jane's preferred partner not incredibly kind, highly intelligent, handsome, tall – and rich? First, such people might be plentiful in TV soap operas, but in real life they are remarkably thin on the ground. Second, even when Jane meets such a male paragon he will probably not be interested in Jane (who is not a perfect ten in every category). Third, even if Jane succeeds in striking up a relationship with such a catch, he may be difficult to retain, and Jane may find she needs to invest an exhausting amount of time and resources in maintaining the relationship. Different people favor different tradeoffs and, hence, should differentially weight associated mating criteria – and they do. We shall explain later why different people favor different tradeoffs in these criteria when actually choosing mates.

Reflecting a major theme in this book, what people want in a mate will also vary as a function of their goals. It is true that people want more or less the same things when looking for uncommitted sex or a short-term fling, compared to looking for a long-term partner in terms of the big three (kindness, good looks, and money). However, not surprisingly, well replicated findings show that both men and women report substantially lowering their standards in these domains for short-term compared to long-term relationships. Importantly, there is one exception to this pattern – physical attractiveness – which maintains its importance across mating contexts for both men and women (Fletcher *et al.*, 2004). This result is explicable in terms of **parental investment theory** (see Chapter 2) – the genes of the man or woman flitting through town are all that the other individual can gain (in reproductive terms), given that investment in a long-term relationship is not on offer.

A different way of conceptualizing mating criteria is in terms of the minimum standards required for a romantic relationship to be even considered. In a scene from "Sex in the City" (the TV series) four professional women in their mid-30s are sitting

"I wonder which will fade first—your tan or your animal magnetism."

Figure 6.1   *Source:* © 2008 Liza Donnelly

in a New York bar, bemoaning the lack of men in New York. But there are good-looking men everywhere in the bar – barmen, busboys, valets, and so forth. These men are invisible to Samantha's friends (in mate selection terms) because they are young and possess limited status and wealth; thus, they fail to surpass their minimum standards. Kenrick *et al.* (1993) asked participants to specify minimum criteria for a relationship for a mate differing in level of commitment, including a single date, a one-night stand, sexual relations, steady dating, and marriage. As expected, men and women had similar minimum standards, particularly for traits such as emotional stability, agreeableness, and intellect. Similarly, the minimum standards of both men and women increased as the type of relationship being sought increased in the level of investment required.

The Nature of Mating Standards

Personality traits, status, and resources

There is a wealth of cross-cultural evidence that people everywhere categorize people in terms of personality categories such as warmth, loyalty, and trustworthiness (Church and Lonner, 1998). In contrast, although increased status and resources elevates mating value everywhere, the fashion in which this is done is hugely variable. Living in New Zealand, Canada or the United States, men can gain status by dressing expensively, driving a Porsche, hanging around cafes talking on a cell phone, playing in a band, flashing money around, playing basketball on a winning team, successfully winning a drinking contest at a local dive, being a successful local politician, living in a fabulous house with a view, or even winning an air guitar competition, and the list could go on and on. The key seems to be to provide evidence of the sort of ambition, drive, and ability that signals the probability that one is, or may become, a wealthy man, or perhaps someone who can forge social connections and win respect from the group.

In human ancestral environments, men who wished to establish their status and resource-gathering credentials did not have cafes, cars, or cell phones. Moreover, in hunter-gatherer cultures, it is not easy to accumulate much in the way of resources, given the life-style and the need to travel light. No matter. Political savvy, hunting prowess or fighting ability are respected and confer status in almost every culture. One obvious (evolutionary) explanation for the value placed on hunting ability is that the man will be able to supply more food to his own family. However, in contemporary hunter-gatherer cultures, anthropological research has found that the best male hunters often give away most of the food to friends and others in the tribe (Hawkes, 1991; Smith and Bird, 2000). Such displays of generosity are effective advertisements of status and prowess – "Look at me, I am a great hunter." They also increase the chances of others in the group rallying around and supplying food and support in times of illness or hardship – what goes around comes around (Gurven *et al.*, 2000).

The human desire for status and respect (especially for men) is one of the most powerful, yet most general, human traits. The evolutionary reason is almost certainly

because women (and perhaps men) find related characteristics – ambition, intelligence, resources – so attractive in potential mates, or more accurately, did so during
our ancestral past.

Physical attractiveness

In contrast to status and resources, physical attractiveness is judged in much the same
way both across and within cultures (Berry, 2000). It is commonly, but wrongly,
believed that physical beauty is judged in wildly different and unpredictable ways
across cultures. The reason may reside in our exposure in western cultures to photographs and documentaries featuring men and women from traditional cultures who
look anything but attractive to western eyes. Male members (forgive the pun) of the
Ketengban tribe in New Guinea who wear enormous penis sheaths, or Maori men from
New Zealand with heavily tattooed faces, may not appeal to the average woman living
in the United States. In the same vein, women from the Mursi (a Southern Ethiopian
tribe) who wear enormous discs to push out their lower lips, or women from the
Paduang (in Burma) who wear multiple brass coils around their necks, which length-
ens them to the point where they can die from suffocation if they are removed, may
look grotesque to the average US man.

But this sort of experience is misleading, as it mixes up fashion with the more basic
bodily features associated with physical beauty. True, individuals in western and other
cultures differ (to some extent) in whom they find attractive. Popular magazines
sometimes feature stories that exploit this idea with men varying in terms of whether
they get turned on most by women's legs or breasts, and women arguing over whether
size matters, and to what extent big muscles are attractive. However, the research evidence shows that differences of opinion within western cultures in standards of beauty
and sex appeal are no greater than the differences across cultures. Beautiful or homely
faces are perceived the world over in much the same way. Michael Cunningham and
others (Cunningham et al., 1995) had Asian, Hispanic, Taiwanese, and black and white
Americans rate the attractiveness of faces from all the same ethnic groups. Individuals
from the different ethnic groups overwhelmingly agreed with one another about who
was more physically attractive (with correlations reported over .90!). Such results have
also been replicated with other cultural and ethnic groups (Cunningham et al., 1997).

The universally attractive female face (for men) has a relatively child-like appearance, with wide-set, large eyes, a small nose and chin, prominent cheekbones, high
eyebrows, large pupils, and a warm smile (Cunningham, 1986). The story with men's
faces is more complicated. Michael Cunningham and his colleagues have found that
the universally attractive male face (compared to a woman's face) has a relatively
angular appearance, wide-set eyes, and a large chin – but combined with baby-face
features, including large eyes, and an expressive smile (Cunningham et al., 1990).

One of the major tools that researchers can now exploit is programs that can morph
individual digital photographs in systematic ways, or generate composite photographs
based on hundreds of individual photographs. Using this technique, Gillian Rhodes
created different human facial images based originally on an average female and an

average male face (using both European and Chinese faces). Some of the images created represented exaggerated versions of stereotypical human female and male faces, while others became feminized male faces or masculinized female faces. The results (for both Chinese and European faces) showed that the superfemale faces were rated as most attractive by all the raters, whereas for the male faces the feminized versions were the clear winners (Rhodes *et al.*, 2000). If you are a woman and look like Lindsay Lohan you seem to be on to a winner; if you are a man, then it looks like a compromise between Lewis Hamilton and David Coulthard (Grand Prix drivers) or Hugh Jackman and Leonardo DiCaprio (actors) may be the best bet (although the story becomes more complicated as we shall see).

The development of preferences for attractive faces also requires little or no learning. Infants from 14 hours to 6 months old prefer looking at faces that are attractive rather than unattractive (as defined according to adult preferences) (Slater *et al.*, 1998). Thus, preferences for attractive faces are not only universal, but seem to be hard-wired and present at birth (see Zebrowitz and Rhodes, 2002).

What goes for faces also goes for bodies; namely, particular body prototypes are universally held to be attractive. Perhaps the most widely studied physical trait to date is the female **waist–hip ratio**. Body shape in humans is largely determined by the distribution of body fat rather than the total amount of body fat, and body fat distribution is regulated by sex hormones, as described in Chapter 4. The end result is that women have a much curvier appearance than men, and women's curves have not escaped the attention of both men and researchers. It is true that fashion models tend toward thinness, sometimes to the point that they seem quite emaciated. However, when ordinary men (not fashion mavens) are asked to rate body shapes, fashion-model thinness is not judged as physically attractive (Singh, 1994). Devandra Singh (1993) conducted the first large scale research project focusing on the ideal female body shape. In a creative move, Singh first obtained body measurements from *Playboy* centerfolds between the years 1955–1965 and 1976–1990, as well as from Miss America winners from 1923–1987.

Two trends emerged from Singh's research. First, *Playboy* models and Miss America winners were slimmer in later compared to earlier years. Second, the waist–hip ratio of all women regardless of the year, or their weight, hovered around .70. A waist–hip ratio of .70 means that the waist is 70% the size of the hips, representing a perfect hourglass shape. Moving to the laboratory, Singh next showed a series of drawings representing a woman with waist–hip ratios ranging from .70 to 1.0, depicted as being overweight, underweight, or of normal weight to a large number of participants. Everyone in the sample agreed that the woman with a .70 waist-hip ratio was the most attractive (see Figure 6.2). Recent research using naked body images of real women reveals a similar pattern of effects, with men preferring a waist–hip ratio of around .70, and women of average weight (Perilloux *et al.*, 2010).

Turning to men, those who are muscular, athletic, and tall are sexier than flabby, short men worldwide (Langlois *et al*, 2000; Singh and Luis, 1995). Short, out-of-condition, middle-aged men with potbellies can still do surprisingly well in the mating stakes, if they hold power and prestige, or have other qualities such as high intelligence.

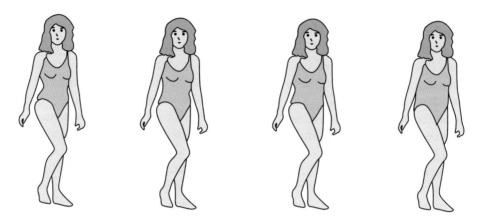

Figure 6.2   Stimulus figures from Singh (1993) depicting different waist–hip ratios, from left to right: .70, .80, .90 and 1.0
Source: © 1993 American Psychological Association, Inc.

Indeed, if there is a famine in the land, then being overweight could be a draw card, given that it may signal the presence of status and wealth. However, excessive corpulence is not regarded as sexy anywhere and what is perceived as universally sexy in women (by men) is the classic hourglass shape with rounded, firm breasts and smooth skin (Singh and Luis, 1995).

Summary

Thus far we have established that both men and women are looking for similar qualities in a potential mate – personality qualities like warmth and trustworthiness, physical attractiveness, and the possession of status and resources or the drive and ambition to gain them. Moreover, these standards and even the way they are embodied or expressed (with the possible exception of possessing status) are close to universal around the world. But why are they universal? We turn to this question next.

The Origins of Mate Standards

Clearly, culture plays a pivotal role in any origin account of ideal mate standards. Within western cultures, for example, individuals are incessantly exposed to theorizing about the nature and functions of relationships from birth, emanating from parents, teachers, friends, the media, books, plays, TV, magazines, songs, and so forth. Such theorizing is certainly not totally coherent, but by the time people enter puberty they have become thoroughly psychologically conditioned with beliefs and expectations about romantic relationships.

However, an answer in terms of a shared cultural heritage only goes so far. One could adopt a relativist approach and claim that cultures develop such theories in some sort of random fashion, or completely tied to historical accident and contingencies. However, such an account is hardly plausible, given the available evidence documented in this book. One commonly accepted answer to this question is that humans have evolved instincts to search out mates according to these criteria, because possessing them enhanced reproductive success in our ancestral environments and probably continues to do so. Steven Gangestad and Jeffry Simpson (2000) argue that mate value is enhanced according to two general but different kinds of criteria: the possession of **good genes** and/or **good investment**. Let's consider the mating criteria we have discussed thus far in terms of this distinction.

Being attentive to a partner's capacity for intimacy and commitment should increase an individual's chances of finding a cooperative, committed partner who would be a devoted mate and parent (good investment). By focusing on attractiveness and health, an individual would be more likely to acquire a mate who was younger, healthier, and more fertile – this is the primary good genes factor. And, by considering a partner's resources and status, an individual should have been more likely to obtain a mate who could ascend social hierarchies and form coalitions with other people who had – or could acquire – valued social status or resources. This last category is likely to represent a mixture of both good genes and the ability to invest in the relationship and the children. If an evolutionary approach is on the mark, then the possession of such traits should hold the promise of higher reproductive success. What evidence is there for this proposition?

Good investment

In humans, as we have noted, offspring require a great deal of intensive parental care over a long period of time to survive, much longer than other primate species. In Chapter 2 we also posited that the role of the family was likely to have been critical in the evolution of humans and their unique abilities and attributes, up to and including the development of culture. In this context two parents are better than one, and men should therefore play an important role in the rearing of their children.

A thorough review of the literature on paternal investment in children by Geary (2000) supports this claim. For instance, father investment in offspring has been linked in pre-industrial times with increased infant health and decreased infant mortality (e.g. Hed, 1987). Paternal investment is also related to improved social competitiveness for children, such as higher socio-economic status in adulthood (e.g. Kaplan *et al.*, 1998) and increased educational achievement for adolescents (e.g. Amato and Keith, 1991). Children born and raised within pair bonds were also more likely to survive to reproductive age in the past, and to be more socially competitive later in life when they attempted to attract mates (Geary, 2000) (also see Chapter 7).

Good genes

It is perhaps obvious why an individual loaded with warmth and trustworthiness, along with high status and wealth, should make an effective mate and parent. After all, such individuals have both the motivation (being kind and considerate), and the means (possessing status and wealth) to be effective and devoted partners and parents. But why should attractiveness be associated with good genes? Human faces and bodies are so routinely perceived as inherently attractive and beautiful (or the opposite) that it is difficult to step back and ask why particular arrangements of the human body are so forcefully and automatically perceived as either beautiful or homely. **Sexual selection** theory provides the most plausible explanation; namely, such features were associated in human ancestral environments with reproductive fitness. Remember the peacock and his gorgeous tail. The most popular explanation for why peahens are so fixated on this feature, when selecting mates, is in terms of the **handicap principle**. That is, large and gorgeously colored tails represent honest advertisements that indicate good health, a robust body, and high fertility (good genes). For humans, the same kind of explanation entails that beautiful people with great bodies were healthier, more fertile, and bore healthier children in the past than those who were less attractive (for both men and women). But is this true and, if so, what are the causal mechanisms involved?

Devandra Singh (1993) argued that a physical feature should only be perceived as beautiful in women when that feature is reliably linked to relative youth, health, and the ability to conceive and sustain a pregnancy. In women, **estrogen** levels are low before puberty and following menopause, but are relatively high between these two periods of life. Women will therefore have the curviest appearance during the most fertile period of their lives, meaning that a low waist–hip ratio is an indicator of fertility in women. A lower waist–hip ratio is also associated with greater overall health in women, with health problems being more prevalent in women with higher waist–hip ratios (Singh and Luis, 1995; Zaadstra et al., 1993). A lower waist–hip ratio, near the .70 level, is also associated with increased fertility in women, whereas a higher waist–hip ratio well over the .70 level is an indicator of decreased fertility (Jasieńska et al., 2004; Singh, 2002).

In a similar vein, women who have more feminine facial features also tend to be more fertile, partly because they have more estrogen (Law Smith et al., 2006). Women who have more masculine facial features, such as a more prominent chin and larger eyebrow ridges, tend to have less estrogen and more testosterone, and are more likely to report experiencing health problems (Thornhill and Gangestad, 2006). More masculine facial features in women are also associated with having more sexual partners and having a less restricted attitude toward having sex in less committed relationships (Campbell et al., 2009), characteristics that men tend to find less appealing in long-term romantic partners (Kenrick et al., 2001).

Another marker of good genes, linked to physical attractiveness, is termed fluctuating asymmetry. Imagine the human body split vertically down the middle from head to toe – highly symmetrical individuals have faces and bodies that are similar across the left and right sides. Individuals who have lopsided faces, with different-sized ears, different looking eyes, and so forth, have high levels of fluctuating asymmetry, as do those with legs, feet, arms and hands that are different shapes and lengths. The word "fluctuating" refers to the way in which asymmetry varies across populations, rather than over short periods of time within individuals.

Fluctuating asymmetry should be a marker of good genes for at least three reasons. First, greater asymmetry is associated with lower survival rates, slower growth rates, and lower rates of reproduction in many different species (Leung and Forbes, 1996; Moller, 1997; Moller and Thornhill, 1998; Thornhill and Moller, 1997). Second, fluctuating asymmetry is partly heritable, meaning that the offspring of more symmetrical people are likely to also be more symmetrical (Moller and Thornhill, 1997). Third, the development of symmetry is more likely to be sustained when individuals have efficient immune systems capable of warding off pathogens, which can cause asymmetry (Moller and Swaddle, 1997). Thus, adults who are symmetrical should have fewer genetic abnormalities, and also possess a hardy and healthy constitution that enables them to remain relatively unaffected by serious disease or illness throughout the course of their development.

Overall, research with humans has shown that men (but not women) with more symmetrical bodies are rated as more physically attractive (Thornhill and Gangestad, 1994). More symmetrical men are also more physical (e.g. more muscular, robust, and vigorous), and less readily dominated by other men (Gangestad and Thornhill, 1997). More symmetrical men also report engaging in physical fights more often with other men (Furlow et al., 1998). Finally, men who are more symmetrical tend to have more lifetime sexual partners (Thornhill and Gangestad, 1994), partly because they are more socially dominant. However, once again, tradeoffs are at work here. More symmetrical men may be better at attracting women, but in relationship contexts they provide fewer material benefits to their romantic partners, and they give them less time and attention than less symmetrical men (Gangestad and Thornhill, 1997).

Higher **testosterone** levels in men are linked to having greater interest in sex (Tuiten et al., 2006) and the likelihood of having more sexual partners (van Anders et al., 2007). However, high circulating levels of testosterone can be harmful to the body if the person is not genetically robust. For example, testosterone can suppress the immune system (Alonso-Alvarez et al., 2007). These facts have led to the controversial proposal that testosterone plays a similar role to the peacock's tail, which handicaps the male peacock and thus is an honest advertisement for good genes. In the same vein it has been argued that only men who can afford these costs can maintain a high level of circulating testosterone; therefore, a high level of testosterone should be a marker of good genes. It is certainly the case that the development of a number of physical traits is partly guided by the sex hormone testosterone, such as facial masculinity, a deep voice, muscular bodies, and masculine behavioral displays (e.g. Penton-Voak and Chen, 2004; Roney and Maestripieri, 2004; Swaddle and Reierson, 2002). Thus, such physical features may indeed constitute honest advertisements of testosterone levels (and perhaps virility) in humans.

Within-gender Differences in Mating Strategies

Sociosexuality and mating strategies

A **mating strategy** is a coordinated set of tactics and behaviors that a person uses, often unconsciously, to attract and retain mates. There are two general types of mating strategies: (i) short-term mating strategies, in which people develop an interest in sex and mating at a relatively young age, have sex earlier in life, and tend to have more sex partners in adulthood; and (ii) long-term mating strategies, in which people develop an interest in sex and mating when they are older, have sex later in development, and have fewer sex partners in adulthood. **Unrestricted** people usually adopt short-term mating strategies, and **restricted** people typically adopt long-term ones, especially in casual dating situations. As described in detail later in Chapter 10, the **sociosexuality scale** developed by Simpson and Gangestad (1991) is a good measure of this mating strategy dimension (see Table 10.1 in that chapter to gain an idea of what this scale measures).

Although there are gender differences in these mating strategies (which we canvas later), there are also large within-gender differences. Restricted and unrestricted individuals are attracted to different kinds of romantic partners. Simpson and Gangestad (1992) found that unrestricted individuals rate a potential mate's physical attractiveness and sex appeal as more important than restricted individuals (also see Wilbur and Campbell, 2010). Restricted people, on the other hand, place more weight on good personal and parenting qualities (e.g. being kind, responsible, and faithful) than unrestricted individuals. Moreover, unrestricted people end up with dating partners who are more extroverted and sexier, whereas restricted people have partners who are more committed to the relationship and are more affectionate, responsible, and faithful (Simpson and Gangestad, 1992). Similar mate preference patterns were found by Herold and Milhausen (1999), who focused on differences in women's perceptions of nice guys (those you take home to mom) versus bad boys (those you don't). Women who had more restricted tendencies preferred nice guys over bad boys. The bad boys, as might be expected, were more preferred by unrestricted women, who perceived the nice guys as dull and boring.

How do bad boys and nice guys present themselves when trying to attract romantic partners? To answer this question, Simpson *et al.* (1999) had single heterosexual men come to the lab and be interviewed for a potential lunch date by a very attractive woman (actually a trained experimental assistant who had been videotaped). Each man thought that she would choose either him or another man (a competitor) for the date. All of the interviews were videotaped and then rated by trained observers. In these spontaneous relationship initiation interviews, unrestricted men were more likely to use competitive tactics associated with short-term mating, such as bragging about past accomplishments, and putting down their male competitor. Restricted men took a different approach. They emphasized their positive personal qualities, suitable for long-term relationships, such as kindness and an easy-going nature.

During initial interactions, a great deal of information is conveyed by nonverbal expressions and gestures. How do men and women signal their interest in short-term versus long-term relationships nonverbally? Simpson, Gangestad, and Biek (1993) had single heterosexual women and men participate in a lab version of the "Dating Game" in which they were interviewed for a possible date by a very attractive opposite-gender person (a trained male or female experimental assistant who had been videotaped). Each interview was once again videotaped and rated by trained observers. During these interviews, unrestricted men were more likely to smile, display flirtatious glances and tilt their heads (a sign of immediate romantic interest), and laugh. Unrestricted men also acted in a more socially engaging, dominant, and slightly arrogant manner non-verbally. Unrestricted women were more likely to lean forward and tilt their heads during the interview, both of which are also expressions of immediate romantic interest (Eibl-Eibesfeldt, 1989). Moreover, strangers viewing these kinds of nonverbal behaviors can accurately detect the degree to which women are sexually restricted to a remarkable degree (Stillman and Maner, 2009).

In summary, people who have a restricted sociosexual orientation prefer mates who, like themselves, value intimacy and commitment and are affectionate, trustworthy, and faithful. To attract these mates, restricted men accentuate their good personal qualities, especially those that will be valued by women who also want long-term relationships. These characteristics reflect long-term mating tactics. On the other hand, people who have an unrestricted sociosexual orientation prefer physically attractive and socially visible mates, and they are more likely to cheat (or at least think about cheating) on their partners (Seal et al., 1994). When attracting mates, unrestricted men use direct competitive tactics and both unrestricted men and women display more openness to sexual contact (e.g. smiles, flirtatious glances, head tilts) when they first meet attractive opposite-gender people.

The menstrual cycle and mate preferences

Intriguingly, not only are some women more into short-term mating strategies than others, but female mating preferences vary within the same women across the menstrual cycle. Human females are fertile (capable of conceiving) for only a brief time during each **menstrual cycle**, from several days prior to the day of ovulation up until the day of ovulation itself (Wilcox et al., 1995). This window of fertility is called the **follicular phase** of the menstrual cycle, and the remainder of the cycle when conception risk is low or non-existent is called the **luteal phase** (see Figure 6.3). A large body of research shows that women's mate preferences, particularly for short-term sexual liaisons, shift dramatically across these two phases of the menstrual cycle, but only for women not taking any form of hormonal birth control (Alvergne and Lummaa, 2009;

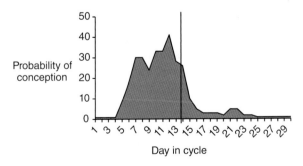

Figure 6.3   Conception and the reproductive cycle

Gangestad and Thornhill, 2008). The birth control pill regulates the flow of androgens, including testosterone, and thus probably evens out women's sex drive across the reproductive cycle.

For example, in one of the first studies of its kind, Steven Gangestad and Randy Thornhill (1998) provided men with a new white t-shirt, which they wore for two nights while sleeping. They were also provided non-scented soap to wash their sheets prior to sleeping in their shirt, and were instructed to shower using a non-scented soap, and not to eat spicy food, drink alcohol, consume other drugs, smoke, have sex with another person, or sleep with another person. After wearing the shirt for two nights, men were asked to place the shirt in a sealed plastic bag and return it to the researchers. The bodily symmetry of each man was measured across ten different body parts (e.g. foot width, finger length) using special calipers. Next, a large number of women arrived at the laboratory and were asked to open each bag and smell the t-shirt inside. After getting a good whiff of the shirt, the women were asked to rate the degree to which each shirt had a pleasant and sexy scent.

For women that were not currently ovulating, or were in the luteal phase of their cycle, their ratings did not correlate at all with the bodily symmetry of the men. However, women that were currently ovulating, or in the follicular phase, rated the scent of symmetrical men's shirts more favorably than the scent of asymmetrical men's shirts (Gangestad and Thornhill, 1998). Moreover, it was not merely that women who were ovulating found the smelly t-shirts less nauseating – they rated the t-shirts worn by the symmetrical men as smelling nicer than fresh t-shirts. The ratings of women taking hormonal birth control, however, did not correlate with the symmetry of the men regardless of the menstrual phase of the women, which suggests that normal hormonal fluctuations (which are suppressed by the pill) are causing this phenomenon. An identical pattern of results has emerged in three other studies (Rikowski and Grammer, 1999; Thornhill and Gangestad, 1999; Thornhill et al., 2003). Women are only more attracted to more symmetrical men, therefore, when they are fertile and potentially able to conceive.

Research has also documented that when women are in the follicular phase of their cycle, compared to when they are in the luteal phase, they are more attracted to masculine facial features (Penton-Voak and Perrett, 2000; Penton-Voak et al., 1999; Scarbrough and Johnston, 2005), more masculine, lower pitched voices (Puts, 2005), masculine body odor (Grammer, 1993), the scent of men who are socially dominant (Havlicek et al., 2005), socially dominant interpersonal behavior (Gangestad et al., 2004, 2007), and more muscular bodies (Gangestad et al., 2007). Again, this pattern of effects is only found for women not taking hormonal birth control.

Tellingly, women's preferences for men as sexual short-term partners shift across the menstrual cycle, whereas their preferences for men as long-term highly investing partners remain stable (e.g. Gangestad et al., 2004, 2007; Penton-Voak et al., 1999). The compelling results of the Gangestad et al. 2004 study are depicted in Figure 6.4. Notice how preferences for more socially dominant and competitive men spike in the follicular phase when women consider men as a short-term sexual partner, but evaluations of the man as a long-term relationship partner do not change across the menstrual

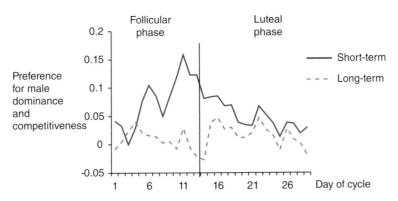

Figure 6.4 Female preferences for male behavioral displays of dominance as a function of day of cycle and mating goal
Source: From Gangestad *et al.*, 2004; © 2004 American Psychological Society

cycle. Since good genes are the only certain benefits that can arise from short-term sexual relationships, and men with good genes tend to invest less time and resources in relationship partners, it is not surprising that women are more attracted to men displaying such cues to good genes (e.g. symmetry, testosterone, social dominance) when they are ovulating.

In addition to women's preferences for short-term sexual partners changing across the menstrual cycle, there are noticeable changes in their actual physical attractiveness and interpersonal behaviors. In the follicular (compared to luteal) phase of the menstrual cycle, women's scent is more attractive to men (e.g. Havlicek *et al.*, 2006; Singh and Bronstad, 2001). The pitch of women's voices also becomes somewhat higher in the follicular phase, a shift that is attractive to men (Bryant and Haselton, 2009; Pipitone and Gallup, 2008). Women also report feeling more attractive during the follicular phase (Haselton and Gangestad, 2006), and are more likely to dress in particularly attractive and revealing clothing (Durante *et al.*, 2008; Haselton *et al.*, 2007). In one clever field study, Miller *et al.* (2007) tracked the tips made by 18 professional lap dancers over a 60-day period, seven of whom reported using hormonal birth control. The results were striking. Dancers on hormonal birth control received a similar amount of tips per day from club patrons regardless of whether they were in the follicular or luteal phase of their cycle. Normally ovulating dancers, on the other hand, earned over $100 more per day in tips when they were in the follicular compared to luteal phase of their cycle (see Figure 6.5).

Gender Differences, Mating Strategies, and Short-Term versus Long-term Liaisons

Not only are there individual differences within men and women in terms of mating strategies but there are, on average, characteristic gender differences; namely, men are

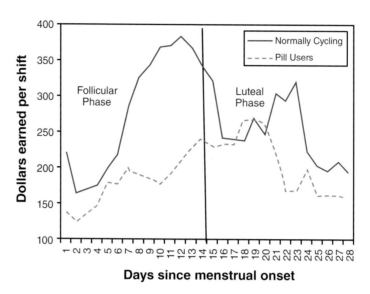

Figure 6.5   Tips earned per shift by lap dancers across the menstrual cycle
Source: From Miller *et al.*, 2007; © 2007 Elsevier

Well-replicated Gender Differences in Mate Selection

Men
- Give more importance to attractiveness (in partners)
- Give less importance to status and resources (in partners)
- Are more interested in sexual variety
- Are more interested in younger women
- Are more interested in casual sex
- Stress their own levels of status and resources in mate selection contexts

Women
- Give less importance to attractiveness (in partners)
- Give more importance to status and resources (in partners)
- Are less interested in sexual variety
- Are more interested in older men
- Are less interested in casual sex
- Stress their own levels of attractiveness in mate selection contexts

---

Figure 6.6   Gender and mate selection

more likely to adopt short-term strategies whereas women focus more on long-term mating strategies. This generalization can be cashed out in several ways, which we describe next (see a summary in Figure 6.6).

Physical attractiveness, age, status, resources, and personality traits

The classic gender difference replicated repeatedly across cultures and studies is that men give more importance to physical attractiveness and relative youthfulness than women, whereas women give more importance to status and resources (or the ability to acquire them) (for reviews, see Feingold, 1992; Fletcher, 2002; Geary, 2010). These differences have been reported across many cultures (Buss, 1989; Kenrick and Keefe, 1992), in large national samples from the US (Sprecher et al., 1994), and in analyses of what people are looking for in studies of personal advertisements (Wiederman, 1993). In studies of on-line dating, women also tend to give more weight to income and physical characteristics than men when deciding who to contact via email (Hitsch et al., 2010).

However, as we indicated previously, in the real world where there are few if any perfect tens, individuals need to trade off mating characteristics against one another, and gender differences may come and go depending on the context and the goals. In the earliest attempt to test the impact of tradeoffs, Norman Li and colleagues (Li et al., 2002) had men and women create their ideal romantic partner using either a limited budget ($20) or a more generous budget ($60), assigning the available money to a list of 10 specific traits. The findings for four of these traits are shown in Figure 6.7 and Figure 6.8. When the budget was limited, this accentuated the classic sex differences. For example, men spent more than twice as much on physical attractiveness than women, whereas women spent far more on yearly income. However, when the budget was generous, the gender differences were attenuated, with both men and women going for a more rounded profile.

Fletcher et al. (2004) found a similar pattern of results when participants were forced to choose between pairs of potential partners who were presented as having a good side and a bad side (e.g. wealthy and cold versus warm but poor). In this study the classic gender differences were strongest when the goal was presented as having a short-term sexual fling, with women emphasizing status and resources and men physical attractiveness when making their choices between the two flawed candidates. However,

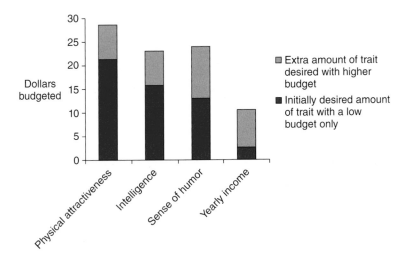

Figure 6.7 Designing a mate by men with a limited or generous budget
Source: Adapted from Li *et al.*, 2002

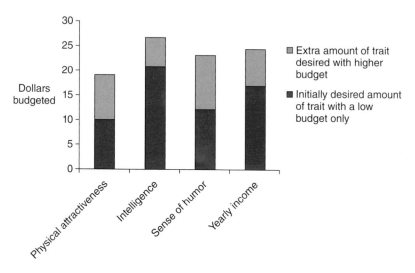

Figure 6.8   Designing a mate by women with a limited or generous budget
Source: Adapted from Li *et al.*, 2002

when considering a long-term relationship, possessing a warm, trustworthy personality more or less trumped being gorgeous or wealthy, although residual gender differences remained. Of course, the choices in the real world will not often be as stark as in this study – participants in the Fletcher *et al.* research could not opt out of making a mate choice (nor in the Li studies could participants save all their money for a relationship rainy day). However, this research does show that contexts count.

Sexual variety

Men are more interested in sexual variety than women. An amusing (possibly apocryphal) story about President and Mrs Coolidge in the 1920s illustrates this hypothesis. While visiting a poultry farm the President and his wife were taken on separate tours. During the tour Mrs Coolidge noticed that the farm had very few roosters but a lot of hens, and she asked the farmer how it was that so many eggs could be fertilized by so few roosters. The farmer replied that the roosters could perform their duty dozens of times per day. Impressed, Mrs Coolidge suggested this fact be pointed out to the President. Upon hearing about this exchange, President Coolidge asked if each rooster performed his duty with the same hen each time. On hearing the answer – the rooster fertilizes the eggs of many different hens each day – the President suggested this fact be pointed out to Mrs Coolidge! To this day, the **Coolidge effect** refers to the tendency for males to be particularly sexually responsive when a new potential sexual partner is introduced. Documenting this effect in rats, for example, Beach and Jordan (1956) found that male rats would mate with female rats in estrus repeatedly

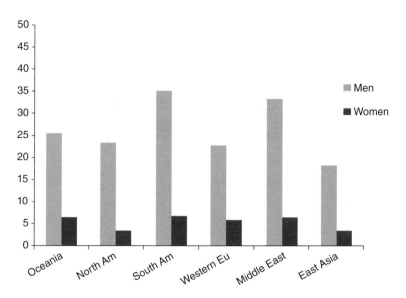

Figure 6.9 Percentages of people who desired more than one sexual partner in the next month from six world regions
Source: From Schmitt *et al.*, 2003; © 2003 American Psychological Association, Inc.

until eventually becoming exhausted, but would begin mating again immediately if new female rats in estrus were placed in their enclosure.

Testing the Coolidge hypothesis in humans, David Schmitt and colleagues (Schmitt *et al.*, 2003) collected a sample of over 16 000 participants across 10 major world regions, including North America, South America, Western Europe, Eastern Europe, Southern Europe, Middle East, Africa, Oceania, South/Southeast Asia, and East Asia. Among other questions, participants were asked how many sexual partners they would ideally like to have in the near and distant future, and the likelihood they would consent to have sex after knowing someone for one month, In every major world region assessed, men reported a greater desire for sexual variety compared to women, as illustrated in Figure 6.9, and a higher chance of consenting to sex after knowing someone briefly (see Figure 6.10). These results make an important point; namely, that overall attitudes to short-term sexual liaisons are strongly influenced by cultural contexts, but that, nevertheless, the direction of the gender differences is the same across cultures.

The stereotype (men are open to casual sex) is no mere fiction. In a famous study Russell Clark and Elaine Hatfield had (brave) male and female confederates approach members of the opposite gender on a US university campus (repeated in 1978 and 1982) and asked if they would go to bed with them. The two studies (published in 1989) found that 72% of the men agreed, whereas none of the women did. This difference was not a function of the attractiveness of the person making the request. When

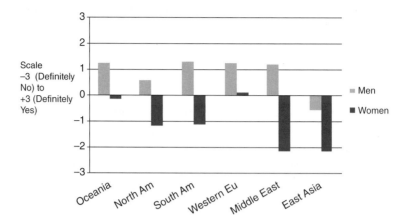

Figure 6.10   Consenting to sex after one month from six world regions
Source: From Schmitt *et al.*, 2003; © 2003 American Psychological Association, Inc.

the same individuals softened the request to going out on a date, 50% of the women and 53% of the men agreed. Oddly, therefore, men were more likely to agree to have sex than to go on a date! Even men who declined the offer of sex apologized, and explained themselves by saying they were married or already involved, whereas women responded with outrage or complaints (e.g. "You've got to be kidding"). One can see the powerful role played by cultural norms here. Overall, however, men are keener on taking advantage of short-term sexual opportunities than women.

Explaining Gender Differences in Mate Selection Strategies

Parental investment theory

Explaining why women and men differ in terms of their preferred mating strategies remains a controversial and hotly debated topic. The standard evolutionary account was initially provided by Robert Trivers in 1972 – parental investment theory. As we outlined in Chapter 2, this theory is couched in terms of differences across sex in the investments made in offspring. In species where the female makes all the investment in raising the offspring, and the male contributes his sperm and nothing else, the females are (sensibly) choosy whereas the males (also sensibly) promiscuously try and mate with as many females as possible regardless of their apparent quality. In bonding species, like *Homo sapiens*, both males and females invest in raising offspring, so both sexes should be choosy. Indeed, as we have seen, men and women are interested in the same qualities in potential mates, and both are picky, especially when seeking long-term relationships. Nevertheless, the gender differences in mating strategies are consistent with gender differences in investment.

When a woman becomes pregnant, she must carry the child for approximately nine months, and may experience serious medical problems during this time. She must endure childbirth, and then lactate for weeks, months, or sometimes years after the baby is born. Men do not experience any of these events. Women are also born with a limited number of ova, which can be fertilized only during a circumscribed period of time, with fertility peaking in the mid-20s and decreasing significantly over time to essentially zero in the late 40s. For men, the minimal amount they need to invest in offspring can involve a single sexual encounter, and men are capable of producing viable sperm from puberty well into old age. Given this stark difference in the minimal amount of parental investment required of men and women, it is perhaps not surprising (so goes the argument) that women should be choosier in different ways than men (as outlined previously), when selecting long-term mates and also generally pickier for short-term sexual liaisons.

Sexual strategies theory

In 1993, David Buss and David Schmitt developed **sexual strategies theory** to explain gender differences in mate selection. The basic idea behind sexual strategies theory is simple; to the extent that women and men faced different adaptive problems associated with mating and reproduction during evolutionary history, they should have enacted different mating strategies, along the lines previously described. However, this theory also identifies certain conditions in which ancestral women might have benefited from engaging in selective short-term mating (Greiling and Buss, 2000). For example, short-term mating strategies could have been successfully used by some women in order to get valuable resources from men, to help women judge a man's prospects as a good long-term mate, or to attract a good long-term mate. Short-term strategies might also have been used by some women to assess a mate's true intentions or actual personal characteristics, including his mate value. In certain situations, short-term mating may also have offered women greater protection, especially if they did not have a stable long-term partner. According to sexual strategy theory, however, women's short-term mating was based on long-term mating motivations and goals. Most women in evolutionary history should have pursued a long-term mating strategy whereas most men should have enacted a short-term mating strategy, and these differences would have shaped how women and men perceive and make decisions about mating and sexual behavior today.

Social structural model

A rival major theory, developed by Alice Eagly and Wendy Wood (1999; Wood and Eagly, 2002), focuses on how culture (social roles and gender role socialization practices) produced the gender differences in sex and mating that are observed. According to the **social structural model**, women and men occupy different social roles in most, if not all, societies. Part of the reason for this is how men and women reproduce. Because women bear, deliver, and nurse young children, women have historically assumed childcare and food-gathering roles in virtually all past and all current cultures.

These social roles have limited the ability of most women to achieve higher levels of status and power within all societies. Men, on the other hand, have historically pursued hunting and other non-childcare roles in all cultures, which have allowed most men to achieve relatively greater status and power in all societies, on average. The origins of gender differences in sex and mating can certainly be traced to differences in the reproductive biology for men and women (Wood and Eagly, 2002), which ultimately has an evolutionary basis. However, from the end of last ice age (11 000 years ago) when populations expanded, people started living in cities, and cultures became politically and economically complex. Thus, it is (plausibly) argued that as men grabbed the levers of power, such gender differences in mating orientations became channeled and magnified by culture.

Resolution

Unlike sexual strategies theory, the social structural model posits that evolutionary forces did not produce psychological adaptations in the mind or brain that direct the way in which women and men make decisions about sex and mating. Thus, sexual selection mainly occurred below the neck. In contrast, sexual strategies theory posits that evolution shaped both the bodies and the minds of women and men when it comes to sex and mating. Differences between these theories have led to some lively exchanges in the literature. Both theories have their limitations, but, given the evidence we have canvassed in this chapter and throughout the book, and the plausibility of the evolutionary account, we believe that sexual selection processes over the long course of evolution was likely to have molded both the body and the mind (or brain) in humans. Although culture certainly plays a major role in influencing sexual strategies (see Chapter 2), biological evolution has left its footprints all over both the intimate relationship body and mind.

Mate Preferences, Self-Presentation, and the Self-Concept

We turn now to a social psychological approach, which stresses the interdependence of partners, and is primarily focused on proximal-level processes. Recent research has examined the way in which men and women shape their mating strategies to cater to the perceived preferences of the opposite gender. Buss (1988b) found that men were more likely to report competing with rivals by displaying tangible resources, showing a high earning potential, flashing a lot of money to impress women, and driving an expensive car. On the other hand, women were more likely to report using tactics that served to display, and improve, physical and behavioral cues that signal youth and physical attractiveness. Other research has focused on how people portray themselves to potential mates by analyzing personal advertisements. In this body of research, men are more likely than women to present their professional status and financial standing, and to mention that they are seeking a physically attractive woman. Women, on the other hand, are more likely than men to highlight their physical appeal, and to mention

that they are seeking a man who possesses relatively high levels of social and professional status (e.g. Campos *et al.*, 2002; Cicerello and Sheehan, 1995; Deaux and Hanna,
1984).

These gender-linked strategies of self-presentation seem to be effective; men who
offer more resources in their personal ads receive more responses from interested
women, whereas women who offer their positive physical features (e.g. slim figure and
youthful age) get more responses from interested suitors (Pawlowski and Koziel, 2002).

The way in which men seek to impress women may be mediated by testosterone
levels. In a clever field experiment, Ronay and von Hippel (2010) had a male experimenter approach young men at a skateboard park and asked them to try an "easy"
trick 10 times, and then try a very difficult trick 10 times (a trick that a good skateboarder lands about 50% of the time). After a short break, the skateboarder did the
same easy and difficult tricks 10 times, either in front of the male experimenter or in
front of a highly attractive female experimenter. While being watched by an attractive
female, the skateboarders took many more risks when attempting the difficult tricks.
Even when they could not land the trick without falling, men being viewed by an
attractive woman attempted it anyway. Attempting more tricks resulted in more failures (i.e. falling down or totally wiping out), but also more successful tricks! These
results are shown in Figure 6.11. Moreover, the risk-taking behavior of these men was
matched by their testosterone levels, having higher levels in their saliva than did skateboarders who were being watched by a man.

People can also enhance their chances in the mating game by making derogatory
remarks about their competitors. Buss and Dedden (1990) asked a large number of
participants to rate how likely they would be to make specific derogatory comments

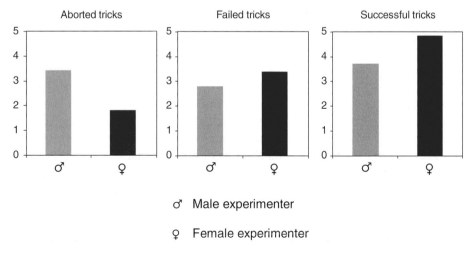

Figure 6.11   Showing off by young men
Source: From Ronay and von Hippel, 2010; © 2010 Ronay and von Hippel. SAGE Publications, Inc.

about rivals when attempting to win the affections of a desirable potential mate. Men reported being more likely to derogate rivals on their resource potential, specifically telling women that their rivals are poor, have no money, lack ambition, and drive cheap cars. Women, on the other hand, were more likely to report saying their rivals were fat, ugly, physically unattractive, and that their bodies have no shape. When faced with rivals for a potential mate, men and women focus their attacks where it really hurts; namely, aspects that are valued highly by the opposite gender.

How the mating game (and the media) shape the self-concept

When people are seeking potential mates, they not only evaluate others, they are also the targets of evaluation. For example, at a nightclub men may be paying attention to the more physically attractive women, but the women are also paying attention to men who appear to have more resources and status. Success in the mating market not only rests on finding people who match one's own criteria, but also on satisfying the criteria of others. Indeed, there is mounting evidence that the self-concepts of men and women correspond to the preferences of the opposite gender (Campbell and Wilbur, 2009). For instance, women are more concerned with their own physical attractiveness than men (Daly et al., 1983), and base their self-worth on their appearance more than men (Crocker et al., 2003). Men, however, are more socially dominant than women, often interrupting and drowning out others in conversations (Frieze and Ramsey, 1976) and thrusting their chin out (Dovidio et al., 1988). The self-esteem of men is also more strongly linked to being independent (Josephs et al., 1992).

Men and women also differ in how they feel about themselves when they compare themselves to same-gender others who are superior on different dimensions. For example, Gutierres et al. (1999) had men and women view a number of profiles of same-sex individuals who varied on attractiveness and ambition. After being exposed to many exceptionally attractive women, the women felt that men would evaluate them more negatively. The ambition level of the women in the profile, however, did not influence how women felt men would perceive them. Men, on the other hand, rated themselves as less desirable mates after being exposed to ambitious, but not physically attractive, profiles of men (also see Buss et al., 2000). Adopting an experimental approach, Roney (2003) had men complete some questions about their personality while in a group setting. This setting, however, was rigged by the experimenter so that the group contained only other men or contained both men and attractive women. Only in the groups where men were exposed to attractive women did they report highly valuing future financial success and material wealth. The presence of potential mates, therefore, led men to personify women's desires to a greater extent.

In Chapter 3, we made the observation that one major way in which modern cultures differ from the ancestral environment is in terms of our current exposure to swarms of images of impossibly attractive and sexy individuals. The cost for people (especially women) of setting the bar rather high can be measured in terms of the surge of eating disorders and the increasing prevalence of cosmetic surgery and breast implants (see Chapter 3). As an aside, if you thought that pictures of fashion models and film stars that regularly adorn fashion and fitness magazines and advertisements are impossibly attractive, you are right. They are impossibly attractive, being routinely digitally altered to remove any imperfections and produce a flawless appearance. Even pictures of ordinary people in magazines are often digitally enhanced. Eric Kee and Hany Farid (2011) recently developed a method of measuring digital enhancement by precisely measuring geometric changes to a person's face and body in photos, such as larger breasts, smaller hips, slimmer necks, as well as color and texture changes, like blurring and sharpening. Comparisons between before and after pictures of 468 people in their study showed just how effective these digital enhancements can be (see Figure 6.12).

Figure 6.12   Examples of published digitally enhanced images and the original versions
Source: Printed with kind permission from Glenn C. Feron. For more images visit: www. glennferon.com

Taken together, this work suggests that men and women evaluate themselves on characteristics that mirror the mating preferences of the opposite sex, with some costs attached, as we have seen. People are only too aware of gender differences in mating strategies and criteria, and model their own behavior accordingly.

Explaining Within-gender Differences in Mating Strategies and Preferences

As we have noted, there exist strong within-gender differences in mating strategies and preferences. What causes people to attach different amounts of importance to different ideal standards within gender? One major factor is self-perceived mate value. If people feel that they have more to offer potential mates, they can then demand more from potential mates (Campbell *et al.*, 2001; Kenrick *et al.*, 1993). For example, individuals who rate themselves as superior in terms of warmth attach more importance to the same ideal standards, those who perceive themselves as more attractive give more weight to the equivalent ideal category, and, finally, those who believe they have more status and resources rate this ideal category as more important (Campbell *et al.*, 2001).

Additionally, when people possess more positive self-evaluations on each ideal mate dimension, they report being less likely to relax their standards, whereas those individuals with less positive self-evaluations report more flexible standards that can more comfortably accommodate sub-optimal potential mates. Regan (1998) has also shown that self-evaluations are linked to expectations for potential mates in both men and women. Accurately assessing one's own mate value, and being able to assess the self relative to the standards of potential mates, allows people to accomplish two important aims. First, it avoids wasting time and energy, and the pain and humiliation of being rejected by people of higher mate value who are not likely to be interested in forming a sexual relationship. Second, it prevents the second kind of mistake by avoiding forming relationships with people of much lower mate value, who may constrain reproductive success (cf. Regan, 1998). In short, people are relatively realistic when choosing mates, and are thus, well aware of some of the nuances (some gender-linked) that we have discussed.

There may also be genetic differences associated with the adoption of long-term versus short-term mating orientations. In two recent studies Hasse Walum and his colleagues have explored the genetic variation on a specific gene (generally termed a **genetic polymorphism**) associated with the expression of oxytocin or vasopressin in the brain. Recall in Chapter 4 we described a body of research showing that these neurotransmitters are involved in the development of long-term bonding and attachment in both voles and humans. Remarkably, in two studies, variability in these genes in humans (**vasopressin** in men and **oxytocin** in women) was associated with the tendency to form successful long-term sexual relationships (Walum *et al.*, 2008; Walum *et al.*, 2012). And, these links were not insignificant. For example, the chances of getting married for men with two copies of an **allele** on this **oxytocin receptor**

gene (in a sample of 552 male twins) were close to double compared to those men not carrying any of these alleles on the same gene (32% versus 17%), and of those who were married the probability of reporting a marital crisis or threat of divorce in the last year was less than half of those with no alleles on the same gene (15% versus 34%). Wow!

Do Mate Preferences Predict Actual Mate Choices?

Most of the research discussed to this point has asked people about their romantic partner preferences, but do preferences map on to the choices people make in the real world? Some recent research has reported that in speed dating contexts mate preferences do not predict actual choices. Eastwick and Finkel (2008) assessed the mate preferences of a number of men and women, and then had them engage in a speed-dating session. Each person had a four-minute "date" with an opposite sex participant, and at the end of the session participants indicated whether they would be interested in meeting each of their "dates" again for a more formal date. Interestingly, the choices people made regarding who they would like to date again were not driven by their stated mate preferences. Kurzban and Weeden (2007) and Todd *et al.* (2007), using a similar speed dating methodology, also reported little evidence for a link between stated mate preferences and the qualities of the people who were selected for future dates.

We cannot conclude from such findings, however, that the gender differences and findings we have previously canvassed based on evolutionary psychology are questionable. Rather, such findings reveal the torturous links that prevail among cognition, affect, and behavior. To understand such linkages, an evolutionary approach (which operates at the distal level) needs to be combined with a social psychological approach (which operates at the proximal level) (see Chapter 2).

In speed dating contexts, based on the prior research we have discussed, both men and women should focus mainly on physical attractiveness. Indeed, in the speed dating research already cited, that is exactly what was found. Based on parental investment theory, women should also be choosier than men. Again, all three speed dating studies cited report that men chose many more individuals they wanted to meet up with again than women. Consistent with this gender difference, Todd *et al.* (2007) found that in speed dating more attractive women demanded males of higher quality across the board to a greater extent than was the case for men – the same gender difference reported by Buss and Shackelford (2008) using a standard self-report methodology.

Consider the task in front of individuals in a speed dating context. From the viewpoint of interdependence theory (Chapter 1), individuals need to assess two things – how interested they are romantically in the other person, and how romantically interested each partner seems to be in them. There is little point in pursuing a relationship if the potential partner appears bored and uninterested, or more blatantly says things like "you are not my type". A study by Place *et al.* (2009) had naïve raters observe videotaped interactions of speed daters. The observers were quite accurate in ascertaining the self-reported levels of romantic interest of the men, but could not tell what the women's romantic inclinations were. This finding is consistent with evolutionary theorizing that women are more selective and coy in expressing romantic interest in mate selection contexts. It also perhaps helps explain why men are less selective than women in such contexts (given the male bias toward not missing out on a mating opportunity).

Finally, it is plausible that the kind of mate standards people (especially men) will use in speed dating contexts are minimal standards rather than ideal standards. However, the research on speed dating has measured ideal standards but not minimal standards, which may partly account for the null findings obtained. On the other hand, Eastwick and Finkel's (2008) argument that ideal standards may be used more strongly as relationships progress past preliminary mate selection stages is also plausible (see Eastwick *et al.*, 2011). Further research is needed to illuminate the links between the mind and behavior in this domain. So stay tuned.

Summary and Conclusions

In this chapter we analyzed how the attributes that men and women look for in a mate are similar in every culture around the world, boiling down to a few general categories: trustworthy, warm, intelligent, attractive, healthy, ambitious, and the possession of status and resources. However, there are also characteristic gender differences in what men and women want in a mate, and these gender differences are also strikingly similar around the world. As summarized in Figure 6.6, men value physical appeal more than women, but are less interested in status and resources. Men are also more into sexual variety than women, and are more likely to accept opportunities coming their way for casual sex.

The universal nature of these mate selection patterns points to an evolutionary explanation. Most evolutionary models start with Triver's parental investment theory; namely, investment in offspring determines how choosy females and males are in the mating game. In bonding species (such as *Homo sapiens*) in which both the males and the females invest a tremendous amount in raising subsequent offspring, both men and women should be on the picky side, as indeed, they are. Thus both men and women are interested in mates who can provide good investment (being kind, intelligent, and wealthy or at least have ambition and drive) and good genes (attractive face and body). However, because women invest more than men in raising offspring, and can have many fewer children than men, women should generally favor long-term mating strategies, and men should be biased toward short-term strategies – which is exactly the pattern seen around the world.

The mating market place is thus different for men and women, and men and women understand this only too well, leading to differences in the way men and women interact and present themselves in mate selection contexts. Women are typically more cautious (than men) in indicating romantic interest, and they pay a lot of attention to their own attractiveness in the mating game. Very attractive women know they have a strong hand and can demand a well-rounded, high-value mate. Men, on the other hand, are more interested in flaunting their status, wealth, and ambitiousness, and are more likely to go for short-term sex if it is on offer.

However, as we have stressed throughout, there also exist strong within-gender differences in mating strategies and standards that are considerably greater in magnitude than between-gender differences. One major cause of such individual differences is simply self-perceptions of mate value. Reflecting the logic of the mating marketplace, those who view themselves as a great catch can afford to be exceptionally picky. As we discussed in Chapter 5, family backgrounds and the social/cultural environment also play a major role in producing short-term versus long-term mating strategies, and provisional evidence suggests genetic factors may also play a role. And, finally, women tend to be more attracted to masculine, assertive men (overflowing with testosterone) when they are ovulating and the chance of pregnancy is greatest, but, tellingly, only when they are considering a short-term sexual fling.

The final take-home message of the research in this area is that human mating strategies are flexible, and both men and women can and do alter their strategies according to their goals, cultural constraints, environmental conditions, and availability of mates. The human mating world would be straightforward if humans displayed their mating values on a 1–10 scale on their foreheads, as is done in the classroom exercise we described at the beginning of the chapter. The real psychological processes, as we have documented, are considerably more convoluted and intriguing.

Part Four

Maintaining Relationships:
the Psychology of Intimacy

Love, Sweet Love 7

Love as a commitment device – the universality of love – biological and behavioral markers of love – romantic relationships are good for you – and they promote reproductive success – facing alluring alternatives – objections to the commitment-device thesis – the nature of love – passionate and companionate love – the maintenance of love – summary and conclusions

See, how she leans her cheek upon her hand!
O that I were a glove upon that hand,
that I might touch that cheek!

William Shakespeare, *Romeo and Juliet*, 2.2

In Verona, a beautiful old city in Italy, a band of volunteers pore over thousands of letters every year seeking solace or advice about their love lives. All the letters are addressed to someone who not only died 450 years ago but was a fictional character to boot; namely, Juliet Capulet, a character made famous in Shakespeare's play about star-crossed lovers, Romeo and Juliet. Both Romeo and Juliet . . . you guessed it . . . lived in Verona. The tradition started in about 1940, when the caretaker of Juliet's (supposed) house and tomb began to answer the letters addressed to Juliet, which had started piling up. Most of the letters are written by women, most seek romantic advice, and all of them receive a handwritten reply.

Seeking advice about love from a fictional character speaks to both the power of romantic love and the power of stories about love. Love and intimate relationships were a central theme in many of Shakespeare's plays and poems. Indeed, love has been

The Science of Intimate Relationships, First Edition. Garth Fletcher, Jeffry A. Simpson, Lorne Campbell, and Nickola C. Overall.
© 2013 Garth Fletcher, Jeffry A. Simpson, Lorne Campbell, and Nickola C. Overall.
Published 2013 by Blackwell Publishing Ltd.

the centerpiece of many stories, plays, songs, and poems since the beginning of recorded history. And there is no sign of this preoccupation with romantic love letting up any time soon. In the United States, for example, romance novels were the most popular literary genre in 2009, capturing 13.2% of all book sales that year ($1.36 billion dollars in sales; Norris and Pawlowski, 2010).

The power and sweetness of romantic love, and its centrality in human affairs, lend it an air of mystery that we suspect is behind the common view that it is hard to measure or define, and perhaps even beyond scientific treatment. In reality, as this chapter will attest to, concerted attempts by scientists from many disciplines and vantage points have converged to reveal a good understanding of both the nature and functions of love. In the first section, we canvass the evidence for the evolutionary explanation for love as a commitment device, and discuss some objections to the thesis. Next, we discuss the nature of love, arguing that it can be basically divided into two kinds – passionate love and companionate love – before discussing some alternative theories that posit more than two kinds of love. Finally, we analyze the role of interpersonal trust before moving to a brief account of how love and intimacy can be maintained over the long haul.

Love as a Commitment Device: Pair Bonding in Humans

The standard evolutionary explanation for the origin of (romantic) love is that it evolved as a commitment device to keep parents of children together long enough to help infants survive to reproductive age. This line of reasoning begins with the fact that, in all sexually reproducing species, ensuring the survival of offspring to reproductive age is fundamental to successful reproduction (Buss, 1988a). But, pair bonding is rare among mammals (only 3% or so of mammals pair bond). Why did pair bonding (and love) specifically evolve in humans?

The argument raised in Chapter 2 addresses the way in which the evolution of an unusually large brain in humans is tied to a decidedly odd life history. In a nutshell, our large brain necessitates being born in an exceptionally undeveloped state (to make it through the birth canal). Time spent in childhood is also significantly stretched in humans compared to other species. Human offspring (uniquely among primates) thus rely on others for many years past weaning to obtain enough food to survive, and to learn the skills and cultural rules for living successful lives. In short, the unique abilities of humans could only have evolved in tandem with a lot of the heavy lifting of motherhood being picked up by others in the family, including the father. Without love, it is hard to see how humans could have evolved.

This argument is plausible, but, like all scientific arguments, the evidence needs to be scrupulously examined. We start with examining the body of evidence supporting the thesis that (romantic) love is an evolved adaptation designed to bond partners together. If love is indeed an evolved adaptation, then it should possess certain characteristics. First, it should be universal. Second, it should be associated with specific hormones and biological markers. Third, successful pair bonding should be associated with good health and successful reproduction. Fourth, mate search mechanisms should automatically shut down (to some extent) in the presence of love. We examine each of these in turn before discussing some of the problems or objections to this thesis that are often raised.

The universality of romantic love

It has sometimes been claimed that romantic love is an invention of European culture, with one popular analysis by de Rougemont ([1940] 1983) dating its inception to the twelfth century. However, there is considerable evidence for both the antiquity and the universality of romantic love. One popular pre-European legend of the Te Arawa tribe of Māori in New Zealand recounts the story of Hinemoa and Tutanekai, a tale resembling that of Shakespeare's Romeo and Juliet. Hinemoa and Tutanekai came from different tribes and were forbidden to marry because of the low status of Tutanekai (Young and Uenukukopako, 1995). Every night Hinemoa would hear the haunting sound of Tutanakai's flute across the lake from the island where he resided (Tutanekai was both handsome and a talented musician), but she could not gain access to a canoe as her father had ensured they were pulled well up on the beach. Finally, Hinemoa decided to swim to Tutanekai's island, a hazardous plan, but one she accomplished using calabashes as floats. They finally fell into each other's arms and lived happily ever after (a much nicer fate than that which befell Romeo and Juliet, who both committed suicide).

It turns out that Māori and western cultures are not alone in terms of the presence of romantic love. An analysis by William Jankowiak and Edward Fischer (1992) found good evidence (based on folk tales, ethnographies, evidence of elopement, and so forth) of romantic love existing in 147 of 166 cultures. This is a conservative figure, given that in 18 of the 19 love-absent cultures the ethnographic accounts were uninformative rather than definitive. In only one culture did an ethnographer claim that romantic love did not actually exist.

Biological and behavioral markers of love

Recent research emphasizes proximate emotional and neurological sub-systems that promote the development and maintenance of romantic relationships. Helen Fisher summarizes some of this research in her model of mating, reproduction, and parenting. According to her model, love and mating behaviors are guided by three distinct emotion systems: the lust, attraction, and attachment systems (1998, 2000). Fisher also provides evidence suggesting that the behaviors related to each of these emotion systems are governed by unique sets of neural activities.

For instance, the lust system motivates individuals to search out sexual opportunities (in general terms) and is mainly associated with estrogens and androgens in the brain. The attraction system, however, directs an individual's attention toward specific mates, leads to the craving for emotional union with this person, and is associated with high levels of dopamine and norepinephrine, along with low levels of serotonin in the brain. Consistent with this suggestion, when both men and women who are deeply in love are asked to think of their partners while their brain is being scanned, regions of the brain that are associated with reward become activated (the same regions activated by cocaine), whereas they do not become activated when thinking of an acquaintance (see the analysis and discussion in Chapter 4). Finally, the attachment system is distinguished by the maintenance of close proximity to a loved one, feelings of comfort and security with this person, as well as feelings of emotional dependency. This system is associated with **oxytocin** (for women) and **vasopressin** (for men) (see Chapter 4). Overall, there are likely to be several neural circuits in the brain that function to promote attraction to specific individuals, and to forming and maintaining long-term relationships (see Chapter 4 again).

Fisher's attraction and attachment systems are similar to Bowlby's **attachment theory** (1969; Chapter 5). To briefly reprise this material, Bowlby proposed that the process of evolution by natural selection equipped infants with a repertoire of behaviors (essential for survival) that serve to facilitate proximity to caregivers, particularly in situations when support is required. Bowlby postulated that the bond forged between mother and infant in childhood provides the foundation for later relationships, and that the attachment system serves similar functions in both infants and adults in regulating the way emotions are experienced and expressed. As we discussed in Chapter 5, Zeifman and Hazan (1997; see also Shaver *et al.*, 1988) propose that attachment is one of the psychological mechanisms that has evolved to solve the adaptive problem of keeping parents together to raise offspring. The secure, loving feelings that partners experience in each other's presence, the lonely feelings while they are apart, and the desire to be together after separations are hallmarks of this attachment system, designed to keep people together in committed relationships.

Indeed, consistent with this thesis, adult romantic sexual love looks similar to the love between parent/caregiver and infant. Shaver *et al.* (1988) listed no fewer than 17 similarities between the two kinds of love, 12 of which we have listed in Table 7.1. For example, lovers often slip into **baby talk** when they talk to one another (nauseating though it might be for the casual observer), use favorite nicknames, and slip into singsong cadences. Lovers have a strong need to spend a lot of time together, often caressing and kissing one another. Lovers seem fascinated with each other's physical appearance, and engage in bouts of prolonged eye contact. Lovers often indulge in horse play and play games together. Lovers become distressed if they are parted for prolonged lengths of time, and are exquisitely sensitive to each other's needs. You get the point.

The similarity between the behavioral manifestations of parent–infant love and romantic love is consistent with the role that oxytocin plays in the formation of attachment bonds in both kinds of relationships. Indeed, the comparative evidence, especially the research with voles (see Chapter 4), suggests that evolution simply lifted the ancient bonding mechanisms originally developed in mammals to bond mother and offspring and then applied them to males in some species. That is the way evolution works – tinkering with pre-existent biological structures and processes.

Table 7.1   Similarities between infant attachment and adult romantic love

Infant attachment	Romantic love
Quality of attachment bond depends on caregiver's responsiveness	Love depends on partner's actual or imagined responsiveness
Caregiver provides secure base for infant to feel safe and to explore	Partner support and love promote feelings of safety and confidence
Attachment behaviors include holding, touching, kissing, rocking, smiling, crying	Loving behavior includes holding, touching, kissing, rocking, smiling, crying
When stressed (afraid, sick, threatened) infant seeks physical contact with caregiver	When stressed (afraid, sick, threatened) lovers seek physical contact with each other
Distress at separation, depression if reunion seems impossible	Distress at separation, depression if reunion seems impossible
Infants share games, toys, discoveries with caregivers	Lovers share toys, games, discoveries
Infant and caregiver engage in prolonged eye contact	Lovers engage in prolonged eye contact
Infant and caregiver seem fascinated with each other's physical features	Lovers seem fascinated with each other's physical features
Usually one key attachment relationship	Usually one key attachment relationship
Use baby talk, nicknames, coo	Use baby talk, nicknames, coo
Upon reunion, infants smile, and reach to be picked up	Upon reunion, lovers smile and hug
Caregiver exquisitely sensitive to infant's needs	Lovers exquisitely sensitive to each other's needs

Source: Adapted from Shaver *et al.*, 1988

Gonzaga and colleagues asked both partners of a number of couples to answer some questions about their relationship and to engage in videotaped interactions with their partners in the lab (Gonzaga *et al.*, 2001). They found that individuals reporting more love for their partners also reported desiring their partners more, were relatively happier with their relationships, spent more time in the physical presence of their partners, and engaged in a number of unique activities with their partners. Interestingly, these individuals were also particularly likely to nod their heads in agreement while talking to their partners and exhibit **Duchenne smiles**, which are spontaneous smiles that use the muscles round the eyes and the mouth, and are linked with positive emotions and enjoyment. When an independent group of raters was asked to watch the soundless videotaped interactions between each couple, they were able to accurately determine which individuals felt more love for their partners simply by observing the expression of nonverbal displays of love (i.e. head nods and Duchenne smiles).

Finally, Gonzaga *et al.* (2006) measured the amount of oxytocin in the blood of a number of women after they had recounted positive emotional experiences regarding love or infatuation (study 2). The women in this study were also videotaped while reliving their positive emotional experiences, allowing the researchers to measure the degree to which they spontaneously displayed nonverbal signs of love and affiliation (i.e. head nods and Duchenne smiles) while just thinking of their partner. Consistent with prior research, women reporting more love for their partners displayed more head nods and Duchenne smiles. Moreover, the expression of these behaviors was also associated with higher levels of oxytocin in the blood (but see Chapter 4).

Romantic relationships are good for you (usually) and they promote reproductive success

Not only are pair bonds universal in humans, they are also associated with psychological and physical health (see Chapter 4). For example, when asked what factors make life most meaningful the majority of people first mention satisfying close relationships, particularly romantic relationships (Berscheid, 1985). To recap some of the material covered in Chapter 4, married people in North America and Europe are happier and more satisfied with life compared to individuals who have never married, widowed, or divorced (Gove *et al.*, 1990; Inglehart, 1990; Myers and Diener, 1995). Married individuals also generally experience better health than their non-married counterparts (Case *et al.*, 1992; Goodwin *et al.*, 1987; Gordon and Rosenthal, 1995). For example, broken social ties, or poor relationships, correlate with increased vulnerability to disease. Heart attack victims are more likely to have a recurrent attack when they live alone, and those who enjoy close relationships cope better with various stressors, including bereavement, job loss, and illness. Finally, happily married individuals are less likely to experience depression than unhappily married or unmarried individuals (for a review see Myers, 1999).

In Chapter 5 we reviewed evidence that also supports the benefits of pair bonding in terms of lower infant mortality, improved social competitiveness, later onset of pubertal timing in girls, and increased educational achievement for adolescents. Thus children born and raised within pair bonds were historically more likely to survive to reproductive age and attain success at attracting mates in adulthood (Geary, 2000).

Another major benefit of exclusive pair bonding is the avoidance of sexually transmitted diseases (STDs). At least 50 STDs have been documented, including viruses, bacteria, fungi, protozoa, and ectoparasites (see Centers for Disease Control and Prevention, 2002). The fertility of women in particular is severely compromised from contracting a STD, and often times the disease can spread to the fetus, or to the infant as he or she passes through the birth canal. For example, women with syphilis have a heightened risk of miscarriage, premature delivery, stillbirth, and infant death, and the chances that the fetus will contract the disease are almost 100% if not treated (Schulz *et al.*, 1990). Although many of these STDs have been recently introduced to humans (e.g. HIV) others have been around for centuries; gonorrhea, for example, is mentioned in the Bible.

The strongest predictor of contracting STDs is the number of sexual partners someone has had (e.g. Moore and Cates, 1990), and therefore a good way to limit the risk of contracting a disease is to limit the number of sexual partners. Because women are more susceptible than men to contracting STDs (e.g. Glynn *et al.*, 2001; Moore and Cates, 1990), thus endangering their reproductive success, the presence of such pathogens may have been a selection pressure for long-term pair bonding (Mackey and Immerman, 2000).

Maintaining love in the face of alluring alternatives

Perhaps the biggest threat to the love and commitment people feel toward their current partners is the presence of desirable alternative partners. In modern societies, individuals are exposed to myriad attractive potential partners on a daily basis through a number of mediums, including television, magazines, the internet, and of course in person. There is evidence that this massive exposure to attractive alternatives to a current relationship partner can insidiously undermine feelings of love (see Kenrick *et al.*, 1989).

Nevertheless, there is good evidence that individuals in established relationships tend to perceive attractive opposite sex individuals as less appealing compared to their less committed or single compatriots (see Johnson and Rusbult, 1989). Simpson *et al.* (1990) had samples of dating and single individuals rate people in magazine advertisements in terms of their physical and sexual attractiveness. As shown in Figure 7.1, both men and women involved in dating relationships rated the physical attractiveness of the opposite sex individuals in the advertisements less positively than single participants. Participants in committed relationships were presumably motivated to derogate the appeal of the models in order to maintain their commitment to their relationship.

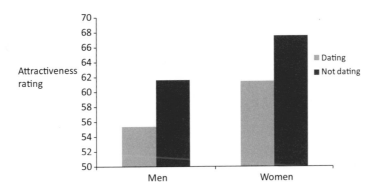

Figure 7.1 Attractiveness ratings of individuals in magazine advertisements as a function of gender and relationship status
Source: Adapted from Simpson *et al.*, 1990

In a more direct fashion, John Lydon and colleagues (Lydon *et al.*, 1999) led participants in committed relationships to believe that an attractive opposite sex individual was attracted to them, thus providing the participants a realistic alternative to their current partner. Those in committed relationships, however, subsequently downplayed the attractiveness of the potential partner, again presumably to defuse the threat posed by having a realistic alternative to their current partner.

Other research suggests that people in established relationships simply pay less attention to attractive opposite sex individuals. In a classic study, participants inspected an array of photographs presented on a screen, including some especially attractive individuals (Miller, 1997). Participants controlled the amount of time they spent viewing each picture with a remote control. Miller found that more committed individuals clicked through the pictures of attractive others more quickly than other photos. Interestingly, spending less time viewing the attractive opposite sex photos also predicted a lower likelihood of the relationship ending at two-month follow-up (also see Gonzaga *et al.*, 2008). Moreover, as described in Chapter 3, research by Jon Maner and colleagues (Maner *et al.*, 2009) showed that this process of blocking a wandering eye over attractive alternative partners for those in loving, committed relationships can occur quite automatically and out of conscious awareness. As the popular song (composed in 1934 and sung by many artists since) intones, "maybe millions of people go by but they all disappear from view, and I only have eyes for you."

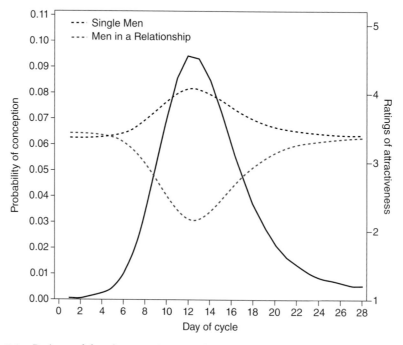

Figure 7.2 Ratings of female attractiveness after interactions as a function of relationship status and reproductive cycle
Source: From Miller and Maner, 2010. 2010 Elsevier Inc.

Finally, in some striking research findings illustrating the power of the automatic system for shutting down mate search, Miller and Maner (2010) asked men and women, working in two-person groups, to complete a number of cooperative tasks. Unbeknownst to the male participants, the woman was a confederate working with the research team. She was not taking any form of hormonal birth control, and the researchers closely tracked her menstrual cycle. Following each interaction, men rated the woman's attractiveness. The results from this study are shown in Figure 7.2. The upside down U (or bell curve) represents the probability of conception (or likelihood of becoming pregnant) across a 28-day menstrual cycle. When the probability of conception of the woman they interacted with was low, both single and partnered men rated her as equally attractive. Single men, however, rated the woman as being more

"Nothing could be better than being here right now with you,
except, possibly, being right over there now with her."

Figure 7.3
Source: 2008 Lisa Donnelly

attractive when the probability of conception of the woman was high, whereas men in relationships rated the same woman as less attractive when her probability of conception was high.

The evidence for the thesis that love is an evolved adaptation in humans may seem compelling at this point. Nevertheless, there are some problems or objections to this proposition that are often raised. First, how does the widespread adoption in many societies of arranged marriages square with the pair bonding thesis? Second, what about the widespread existence of polygyny (one man marrying more than one woman) – is this consistent with treating love as an evolved adaptation for commitment? Third, why do people fall out of love so readily and often separate? In short, is love really powerful enough to fulfill the role ascribed to it by this evolutionary argument? We deal with each these issues in turn.

Arranged marriages

As a thought experiment, ask yourself if you would be willing to marry someone who possesses the interpersonal and physical qualities that you desire in a partner but whom you do not love. Levine *et al.* (1995) asked college students from 11 different countries the same question – only 3.5% of American students said yes, whereas 50% of students from India and Pakistan endorsed this belief.

In collectivist cultures, like India and Pakistan, mate choice has much stronger economic and political implications for the entire family and perhaps the larger community, compared to individualistic cultures like the United States (see Buunk *et al.*, 2010). Indeed, arranged marriages are commonplace in collectivist cultures, such as India, Japan, the Middle East, and China (De Munck, 1996; Gupta, 1976; Hatfield and Rapson, 2006).

Arranged marriages are also common in hunter-gatherer cultures around the world, suggesting that parental influence over mate choice has been a longstanding feature of mate selection in humans. However, in many traditional cultures that practice arranged marriages, brides (and grooms) are typically given some choice in the matter. For example, in arranged marriages in Sri Lanka men and women who like one another (or fall in love) usually let their parents know their choices in advance through indirect channels (de Munck, 1998). Moreover, the criteria that parents and their children use in selecting mates are more or less the same, although parents tend to emphasize the importance of good investment characteristics (e.g. character, status, resources), and perhaps wisely give less weight to attractiveness than do their children (Buunk *et al.*, 2008).

Monogamy and polygyny

A whopping 84% of known cultures allow polygyny, and some men carry harem-building to excess (Fisher, 1992). According to the *Guinness Book of World Records*, the harem champion was an emperor of Morocco, with the unlikely name of Moulay Ismail the Bloodthirsty, who purportedly sired 888 children from his many wives. However, it has been estimated that only about 5 to 10% of men in cultures that allow polygyny actually have more than one wife (Fisher, 1992), the majority of marriages being monogamous. In cultures in which polygyny is illegal it can and does exist in an informal way, with men maintaining a "mistress" to use an old-fashioned term. It is hard to judge the frequency of such arrangements in western countries today, but it is probably quite low.

In cultures that allow polygyny the wives often complain and suffer from bouts of jealousy, and there is evidence that polygynous families are more prone to conflict and intimate violence than monogamous arrangements (see Henrich *et al.*, 2012). Genetically speaking, there is also not much in it for the women. They may certainly attain a share of the status or wealth of their husband, but will probably have to compete for such resources with the other wives. From the male point of view there is the distinct genetic advantage of siring more offspring, but, on the other hand, considerable resources and wealth may be required to maintain more than one wife, and the task of ensuring spousal fidelity may become difficult, if not exhausting. Henrich *et al.* (2012) persuasively argue that the cultural shifts away from polygyny to monogamy over the last few thousand years have occurred because of the interpersonal and social costs exacted by having too many young men hanging around without the realistic chance of developing a long-term sexual relationship.

The existence of **polyandry** (one woman with more than one man) is exceedingly rare, in both humans and other species. The evolutionary reason is obvious. Women can only bear a limited number of offspring, so their reproductive success is not enhanced a great deal. Men are decidedly worse off, reproductively speaking, given that they may not be genetically related to the children they are expending considerable resources in helping to raise. However, in special circumstances polyandry can crop up as an option, such as when women are scarce or when women possess considerable economic power. In summary, the majority of marital relationships – across western, traditional, and hunter-gatherer cultures – are monogamous.

It is also instructive to note what occurs when so-called free love is practiced. The fate of cults in which free love has been attempted dramatically illustrates the point. The Oneida community was started in 1847 by John Noyes, an avant-garde religious zealot. In this community (which at its height had 500 men, women, and children) romantic love was banned, and men and women were expected to copulate with each other – often. Like many cults, Noyes and his immediate family held the whip hand, attempted to rigidly control reproduction (using withdrawal as a means of birth control), and Noyes and his son had first call on the pubescent girls. It did not work. Men and women constantly fell in love and formed clandestine intimate relationships with one another. The ancient love systems have an inexorable logic of their own.

Infidelity and divorce: is love meant to last?

Finally, over the past four decades divorce has been on the rise, whereas marriage seems to be on the decline in many countries, and many now choose to cohabit rather than marry in western countries (see Chapter 12). People continue to fall in love and form committed relationships, but is love meant to last forever?

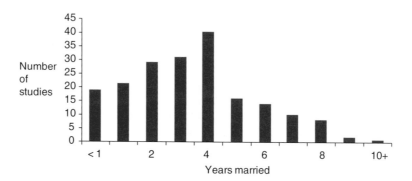

Figure 7.4   Modal years married when divorce occurred from 188 studies and 62 countries
Source: From Fisher, 1992; © 1992 Helen E. Fisher

Helen Fisher (1998) argues that although long-term relationships have obvious reproductive benefits, the fires of romantic love typically last about as long as it takes an infant to make it to about four years old. Perhaps, so goes the argument, romantic love has evolved to meet this limited requirement. In support of this hypothesis, she has shown that the peak period for divorce is about four years across 188 areas, cultures, and ethnic groups from 62 countries (Fisher, 1992; see Figure 7.4). One central problem with this argument is that the majority of married couples in most cultures and countries stay together all their lives (see Chapter 12). Of course, it is hard to know what to make of this point, given the number of factors that may keep couples together, apart from being madly in love, including economic necessity, cultural prohibitions, strongly held values, and so forth. Moreover, one plausible possibility is that (as we will discuss later) the fires of romantic love may be eventually be replaced with a deep form of non-sexual bonding, which may also have evolutionary roots.

As we document later in Chapter 12, one of the major reasons people divorce is linked to extramarital sexual activity, which is common in western countries. Surveys in western countries have produced variable results, but the best surveys using nationally representative surveys in the US show that between 20 and 25% of men and between 10 and 15% of women report having engaged in extramarital sex at some time in their marriage (see Munsch, 2012). Given the different norms and sanctions concerning extramarital sex around the world, however, it is not surprising that there exists a lot of variability across cultures. One study by Careal and associates found that in Guinea Bissau (in Africa) 38% of men and 19% of women reported engaging in infidelity in the previous year, compared with 8% of men and 1% of women in Hong Kong (Carael *et al.*, 1995).

It is not difficult to propose plausible evolutionary arguments for extramarital sexual activity. For males, it looks like a way of having one's cake and eating it too. Males can spread their genes around, with the hope that some progeny will make it to puberty, while also ensuring that their own children are well cared for in the primary relationship. For women, extramarital sex can enable them to obtain some top-quality genes while also perhaps retaining the support of their husbands.

However, extramarital liaisons carry risks and costs. They normally need to be carried out in a clandestine fashion, put the primary relationship at risk, and, if discovered in many cultures can face carry legal penalties or socially sanctioned physical attacks from the sinned-against partner (especially by men against women). Moreover, it is not as if the neurological, hormonal, cognitive, and behavioral "love" systems turn off in extramarital affairs. Thus, sexual activity that goes beyond a one-night stand always carries the risk of developing into full-blooded (and potentially life-wrecking) romantic love. Love is a dangerous emotion.

Summary

In summary, romantic love is likely to have evolved to ensure commitment between partners in order to successfully rear highly dependent offspring. Romantic love exists in the majority of cultures all over the world, and most committed relationships involve only two people. Committed partners are also more likely to downgrade the appeal of potential alternative partners, or not notice them altogether, presumably as a way to maintain the relationship. On its own, romantic love is not enough to make life-long partnership or married bliss a sure bet. However, evolutionary adaptations are never perfect and often possess a jury-rigged quality. Romantic love is no exception, giving a potent motivational push toward the kind of devotion and commitment required for the colossal investment involved in supporting a mate and raising children.

The Nature of Love

Up to this point we have avoided defining love or analyzing its nature in any detail, relying on a shared common-sensical understanding to guide our discussion. However, we now shift toward a discussion of the nature and content of love. If someone says they love another person, what does this mean? Are there different types of love that people can experience? If so, do these different types of love emerge at different stages of the relationship? And, can we really measure something as exotic and labile as love?

In answering these questions, it is important to bear in mind that the study of love in psychology was neglected prior to the 1970s, with the common assumption being made that love is merely a stronger version of liking or attraction. Rubin (1970) challenged this assumption by arguing that love and liking are quite different animals. Rubin conceptualized romantic love as a set of positive thoughts and feelings directed toward opposite-sex peers that could potentially lead to marriage. Liking, in contrast, was defined as having a healthy respect for another person and finding the company of that person rewarding. Indeed, self-reports of liking and loving using Rubin's pioneering scales designed to tap these different sentiments proved to be only moderately correlated.

You might like to conduct another thought experiment at this point. Imagine that you have been involved in a romantic relationship, and you finally tell your partner (sincerely) that you love him or her. What characteristics or properties do you think a relationship or partner must have before deserving such an attribution? Make a list of 5 to 10 items, excluding things that it would be nice to have but are not essential (such as liking the Rolling Stones, or having delicate ears). Our guess (based on getting classes to do this over many years in our teaching) is that your list would include a set of items that speak to the quality of intimacy – such as closeness, trust, respect, warmth, and acceptance – and some items that address the passionate side of love – passion, chemistry, attraction, and sex.

This kind of exercise shows that the glib claim one often hears – love can't be defined – is wrong. Just as well, otherwise individuals would not have the slightest idea of when to use such an attribution or what their partner's declaration of love might mean. Indeed, the division between the two sides of love (what scientists term passionate and companionate love) has informed a good deal of scientific work, suggesting that common sense understandings of love are quite close to the mark.

Passionate love

In 1974, Ellen Berscheid and Elaine Walster (now Hatfield) were asked to write a chapter for a book on interpersonal attraction. They agreed with Rubin (1970) that liking, the primary focus of research on interpersonal attraction, and romantic love were not simply two ends of the same continuum, but were unique entities. Deciding to focus their chapter on love in romantic relationships instead of interpersonal liking, they laid the foundations for the study of passionate love. Passionate love is best described as a state of intense longing for union with another, a feeling that is aroused particularly in the early stages of a romantic relationship. When falling in love, there is a heightened sense of excitement associated with experiencing new and novel activities with a partner. It is also exquisitely pleasurable to be thought of as special, and to be held tightly in the arms of your lover. To add even more spice there is also typically an air of uncertainty in new relationships, along with some daydreaming about the future and a dawning realization that long-held dreams and goals may be fulfilled. Obsessive thinking and passionate desire are basic hallmarks of full-blooded passionate love. Hatfield and Sprecher's (1986) self-report measure of passionate love contains questions that tap into these kinds of feelings associated with passionate love (see Figure 7.5 for some example items).

Self-expansion According to Aron and Aron's (1997) self-expansion model, individuals have a fundamental motivation to grow and expand their sense of self – who they are as a person and how they fit into their social worlds (Aron and Aron, 1986). The process of falling in love provides an excellent opportunity for self-expansion as partners in fledgling relationships engage in novel, exciting, and arousing experiences that produce personal growth and self awareness. Indeed, in the early stages of falling in love Aron *et al.* (1995) found that individuals' self-concept descriptions grew in size

Example items from the Passionate Love Scale and Friendship-based Love Scale	
Passionate Love (Hatfield & Sprecher, 1986)	Friendship-based Love (Grote & Frieze, 1994)
1. I would feel despair if _____ left me.	1. I feel our love is based on a deep and abiding friendship.
2. I yearn to know all about _____.	2. I express my love for my partner through the enjoyment of common activities and mutual interests.
3. I sense my body responding when _____ touches me.	3. My love for my partner involves solid, deep affection.
4. I possess a powerful attraction for _____.	4. My partner is one of the most likable people I know.
5. Sometimes I feel I can't control my thoughts; they are obsessively on _____.	5. The companionship I share with my partner is an important part of my love for him or her.

Figure 7.5 Items from two scales measuring passionate and companionate (friendship-based) love respectively

and diversity over time as they faced new experiences and got to know their partners. Partners also reported higher self-esteem as the relationship progressed. As Chapter 3 discusses, as young lovers spend more time together, their self-concepts begin to overlap as each partner begins to include elements of the partner into their own self-concept (Aron *et al.*, 1991). In essence, "I" becomes "we." Indeed, partners who feel closer to each other literally use the pronoun "we" when discussing their relationship more frequently than "I" (Agnew *et al.*, 1998). Rapid expansion of the self-concept while falling in love can thus be a rewarding experience that enhances feelings of passionate love.

Physical arousal and stress The intense longing associated with passionate love can also be experienced as a state of physical arousal. As we described in Chapter 4, studies using fMRI with individuals in the grip of romantic love show activity in the regions of the brain associated with the release of the neurotransmitters (oxytocin and vasopressin) and elevated levels of dopamine. These substances produce happiness and even euphoria, and trigger the release of hormones linked to sexual arousal (testosterone) and flight or fight stress hormones such as cortisol (Marazziti and Canale, 2004). In a laboratory experiment when individuals experiencing passionate love were asked to think of their partners and relationship in detail (e.g. to recall when they met their partners, and how they fell in love), they exhibited a spike in cortisol that was not observed when asked to think of an opposite sex friend (Loving *et al.*, 2009).

Helen Fisher summarizes it thus:

No wonder lovers talk all night or walk till dawn, write extravagant poetry and self-revealing e-mails, cross continents or oceans to hug for just a weekend, change jobs or lifestyles, even die for one another. Drenched in chemicals that bestow focus, stamina and vigor, and driven by the motivating engine of the brain, lovers succumb to a Herculean mating urge (2004, p. 79).

Does this mean, therefore, that falling in love is detrimental to health? Tim Loving and colleagues (Loving *et al.*, 2009) do not think so. They remind us that starting romantic relationships can be a positive form of stress (Reich and Zautra, 1981). Both positive and negative life events can generate a similar physiological response generally recognized as a stress response (e.g. elevated cortisol levels; Rietveld and van Beest, 2007), but the effects of these events on an individual's health outcomes largely depend on the subjective interpretation of those events. Even though falling in love is physiologically stressful, it may nevertheless be perceived as a positive life event, which should be associated with favorable health outcomes (Brand *et al.*, 2007).

The slow slide in passion Time can be the sword of Damocles hanging over the head of passionate love. Indeed, passionate feelings are more frequent during the early stages of romantic relationships and generally show a pattern of decline thereafter (Acker and Davis, 1992; Baumeister and Bratslavsky, 1999; Sternberg, 1986). As partners get to know each other better, feel more certain about the stability of the relationship, and develop routines of interpersonal behaviors, there is simply reduced opportunity to experience the thrill of novelty and expand the self-concept. In one longitudinal study, it was found that passionate love significantly declined over the course of one year (Hatfield *et al.*, 2008).

Behaviorally, the decline in passionate love over time is captured by the decline in frequency of sexual intercourse. A large body of convergent evidence, starting with the work of Kinsey and colleagues (Kinsey *et al.*, 1948; Kinsey *et al.*, 1953), indicates that the frequency of sexual intercourse among married couples is highest during the early stages of marriage, but declines as time progresses (Call *et al.*, 1995; Marsiglio and Donnelly, 1991). This decline is multiply determined by factors including age-related reductions in sexual capacity (Greenblat, 1983; Kinsey *et al.*, 1953; Lindau *et al.*, 2007), decreased interest in sex with a long term partner (i.e. habituation effects; Huston and Vangelisti, 1991; James, 1981), and major life events such as childbirth/infant care (Call *et al.*, 1995). In the words of a well-known blues song, after the initial excitement of passionate love winds down, *the thrill is gone.*

Companionate love

In contrast to passionate love, **companionate love** is experienced less intensely. It combines feelings of intimacy, commitment, and deep attachment toward others, romantic or otherwise, who occupy an important part of our lives (Walster and Walster, 1978). If you ask individuals to list all the types of love that come to mind, companionate types of love will dominate the list (Fehr and Russell, 1991). For example, maternal love, parental love, friendship, and sisterly love were rated as the top four best examples of love by a large sample of University students in Fehr and Russell's research.

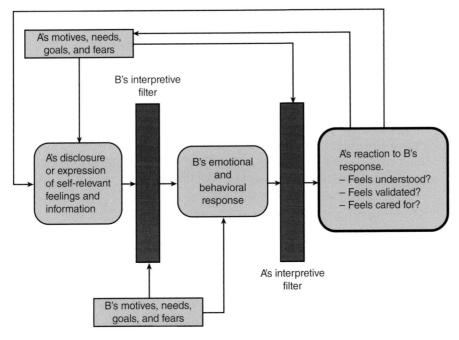

Figure 7.6 Interpersonal process model of intimacy
Source: From Reis and Shaver, 1988. © 1988 John Wiley & Sons

Romantic love, or love between people who are not family members or friends, came in as the fifth best example of love. Friendship-based love therefore develops across a wide spectrum of important relationships in our lives, and is rooted in trust, caring, mutual affection, supportiveness, and friendship (Fehr, 1988). Grote and Frieze (1994) have developed a friendship based love scale incorporating these qualities (see Figure 7.5).

Reis and Shaver's (1988) interpersonal process model of intimacy focuses on the role of self-disclosure, or sharing personal information with another person, and how interaction partners respond to such self-disclosures, during the development and maintenance of intimacy (see Figure 7.6). According to this perspective, self-disclosure alone is not sufficient for intimacy to grow. An additional process – crucial to building intimacy – is the perception that the relationship partner reacts to self-disclosure with warm and sympathetic responses. This, in turn, should make the discloser feel validated, understood, and cared for, setting the stage for increasing levels of connectedness and intimacy to develop within the relationship. In other words, feeling close and intimate with someone is based at least in part on how close and intimate you perceive that person feels toward you (see also Reis *et al.*, 2004; Reis, 2007).

In one longitudinal study testing these ideas, Laurenceau *et al.* (1998) asked individuals to report on interactions lasting more than 10 minutes they had with others each day for a one- or two-week period. Consistent with Reis and Shaver's model, participants felt closer and more intimate with interaction partners when the interaction involved more self- and partner disclosure, and when the participants felt that his or her interaction partner responded positively to his or her self-disclosures.

Links between Passionate and Companionate Love

Take a moment to think of the people in your life you consider as your close friends. If you are in a romantic relationship, you probably feel that your partner is one of your best friends, someone with whom you share a close intimate bond. When participants in a study conducted by Hendrick and Hendrick (1993) were asked to list the name of their closest friend, almost half of them wrote down the name of their partner. The links between companionate and passionate love were also probed in a study that asked people to write down the names of people they love, the names of people they were currently *in* love with, and names of people they were sexually attracted to (Meyers and Berscheid, 1997). They found that individuals generally felt love for people whom they were *in* love with, but were typically not in love with people whom they felt love toward (see Figure 7.7). Additionally, as Figure 7.7 shows, participants generally reported being sexually attracted to people they were in love with, but said they were in love with only about half of the people they were sexually attracted to. Clearly, telling someone you are *in* love with them may convey a very different meaning than simply telling them that you love them.

Romantic relationships typically contain a mix of both passionate and companionate love, but the absence of companionate love in particular can spell trouble for the long-term stability of a relationship. For example, in samples of both older married couples and dating couples recruited from a University population, Grote and Frieze (1994) observed that relationship satisfaction in both samples was more strongly related to perceptions of companionate than passionate love. John Gottman's work led him to conclude that a solid friendship between spouses is the strongest possible foun-

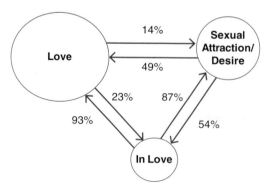

Figure 7.7   Links among love, being in love, and sexual attraction
Source: Adapted from Hendrick and Hendrick, 1993

dation for successful marriages (1999). Therefore, even though sexuality is an integral part of most romantic relationships, and societal norms emphasize that sex should occur within committed relationships (Sprecher *et al.*, 2006), developing a strong friendship with a romantic partner may ultimately be more important for the long-term success of the relationship (see also Chapter 12).

Baumeister and Bratslavsky (1999) (see also Vohs and Baumeister, 2004) intriguingly proposed that the link between companionate love and passion can be caused by changes in intimacy over time. Thus, when intimacy shows relatively large and rapid increases, levels of passion will surge higher. Likewise, when intimacy levels remain unchanged over long periods of time, passion should dip lower. In the early stages of relationships, when partners are falling in love and passion at its apex, there are often frequent escalations of intimacy as partners get to know each other and participate in novel activities. As relationship partners gain an understanding of each other's inner-most thoughts and feelings over time, the rate of intimacy growth typically tapers off as they have less and less to learn about each other. The rate of engagement in novel relationship activities also diminishes, as individuals return to lying on the couch, watching TV, reading books, or surfing the web.

Some research has demonstrated that perceived increases and decreases in perceived intimacy with a romantic partner are linked to positive and negative emotions in a manner suggested by Baumeister and Bratslavsky's model (Laurenceau *et al.*, 2005). More directly testing Baumeister and Bratslavsky's model, Rubin and Campbell (2012) tracked romantic couples over a 21-day period and found that day-to-day increases in intimacy were indeed associated with heightened feelings of passion and sexual activity over time.

Love styles

Around the same time that theory and research were beginning to explore the nature of passionate and companionate types of love, John Alan Lee (1977) developed a typology of six different love styles characteristic of a diversity of relationships. Even in 1977, Lee clearly shared Berscheid's (2010) recent concern over the broad use of the word "love," beginning his paper as follows: "Perhaps the reader will expect me to begin by defining my terms. What do I mean by 'love' or 'loving'? There's the rub! The fictional and non-fictional literature of the western world for twenty centuries is strewn with conflicting definitions of love." (p. 173). A primary goal of Lee's typology, therefore, was to derive a coherent system of classifying different types of love believed to exist.

Lee's typology of love contains three primary styles of love: eros, ludus, and storge. Eros, or erotic love, involves a lover who has a clear and inflexible ideal image of the physical form his or her partner should conform to. This type of lover develops strong feelings for others quickly, and prefers rapid self-disclosure and the quick escalation of intimacy. With a ludus style of love, the ludic lover does not have a fixed image of an ideal partner, and prefers not to commit to any one relationship. While remaining emotionally distant from partners, the ludic lover feels comfortable ending relationships, often after having already formed another, when it no longer suits his or her interests. Storge, compared to the first two styles of love, seems more mature and stable. A storgic lover is attracted to individuals who share common interests and are affectionate rather to individuals who conform to a physical ideal. Storgic lovers are very trusting and not overly needy or dependent, and are comfortable with the slow development of sexual intimacy.

The typology also contains three secondary styles of love: mania, pragma, and agape. Manic love is a combination of eros and ludus, meaning a manic lover has the desire to act on his or her intense feelings for a love object, but simultaneously does not want to commit emotionally to the partner. The result is a type of love characterized by an obsessive preoccupation with the beloved, with little expectation that the relationship will last. Pragma, or pragmatic love, involves a combination of ludus and storge. The pragmatic lover searches for a partner who is a sensible choice, someone that would likely make a good friend. It is hoped that from friendship, love will bloom with time. Lastly, the love style agape is characterized by a sense of duty and selflessness. Love is not governed by feelings of attraction, but by the will, and can be given to anyone regardless of his or her appearance or personal qualities.

A scale developed to measure individual differences in the endorsement of each of Lee's loves styles was created by Hendrick *et al.* (1998). Research using these scales has found that men tend to report higher levels of ludus compared to women, whereas women tend to report higher levels of storge and pragma (Hendrick and Hendrick, 2003). Empirical research directly focusing on Lee's typology is relatively limited, but many of the themes highlighted in his typology are captured by other approaches to the study of love.

Sternberg's triangular model of love

According to Sternberg (1986, 1987), love has three fundamental components: intimacy, passion, and commitment. Intimacy includes feelings of closeness or connection to another person, and is considered an affective (or emotional) component of love. Passion includes physical attraction and a drive for sexual expression with another person, and is largely a motivational component of love. Lastly, commitment encompasses the decision to remain in the relationship over both the short and long term, and is largely a cognitive component of love. The type of love that exists in a relationship is determined by how much intimacy, passion, and commitment individuals feel toward their partners. Sternberg invokes a visual representation of love, with the three components of love forming one side of a triangle (see Figure 7.8). The shape of the triangle therefore changes as the relative amount of each component increases or shrinks. Different shapes therefore represent unique experiences of love. In his influential model, Sternberg discusses eight distinct types of love.

Nonlove Nonlove reflects the complete absence of intimacy, passion, and commitment. This type of (non) love applies to casual acquaintances, or people we have superficial relationships with (e.g. someone we met and casually talk to at the gym). We may like

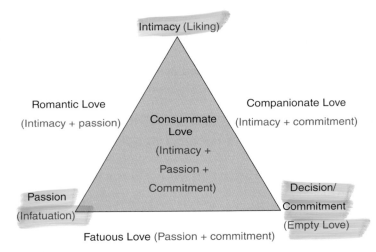

Figure 7.8 Sternberg's (1986) triangular model of love

these people and enjoy our conversations with them, but a true relationship with them does not exist.

Liking The presence of a high degree of intimacy coupled with the absence of passion or commitment results in liking. Liking, or the feelings of closeness and warmth, are typically experienced in friendships.

Infatuation When strong feelings of passion exist, but without intimacy or commitment, **infatuation** is the product. Infatuation is often experienced as "love at first sight," and is linked with strong feelings of passionate arousal for someone that can arise spontaneously and almost instantaneously (e.g. increased heartbeat, sexual arousal).

Empty love Being committed to a relationship partner, but lacking any feelings of intimacy or passion, results in empty love. **Empty love** is not uncommon in relationships that have lasted for many years and have become something of a yawn, but can also be present in abusive relationships where one partner has few perceived options to staying in the relationship. Individuals may also experience empty love in the initial stages of arranged marriages, where there is pressure for the partners to be committed to the marriage but intimacy and passion have not yet had the opportunity to take root and flourish.

Romantic love Romantic love, according this model, results from the combination of high levels of intimacy and passion, but not necessarily commitment. With this type of love, individuals have both a physical and emotional bond, but are not yet completely committed to each other or the relationship. Holiday romances or extra-marital flings may fit this pattern. However, from an evolutionary angle, we (the authors) believe this is a difficult state of affairs to maintain. Once the sexual activity and oxytocin are flowing liberally, pressure will build to make more long-term arrangements. Short-term sexual flings can all too easily and unexpectedly turn into full-blooded love.

Companionate love The combination of intimacy and commitment toward a partner with low levels of passion is known as companionate love.

Fatuous love Marriages that begin in Las Vegas may be based on **fatuous love**; that is, a high degree of passion and commitment in the absence of intimacy. In a whirlwind courtship, partners probably base their commitment to each other on the high degree of passion they experience in the early stages of the relationship. The problem with this type of love is that the passion can taper off as quickly as it soared, not leaving enough time for intimacy to develop. Relationships built on fatuous love (as the name implies) can have a short life.

Commitment and (frustrated) passion can also attain astronomical levels, even in the total absence of behavioral interaction, such as in the (usually painful) cases of **unrequited love.** In one infamous case of unrequited love, John Hinkley shot President Ronald Reagan in 1981 in an attempt to impress Jodie Foster. In a bizarre twist, Jodie Foster had starred in a movie (*Taxi Driver*) in which an older male (played by Robert De Niro) planned an assassination attempt on a local political figure to impress the figure played by Foster in the movie. Hinkley became obsessed with both the movie (which he reputedly watched more than a dozen times) and also the actress Jodie Foster whom he stalked for some time. He scrawled the following letter 2 hours before he shot Ronald Reagan (Caplan, 1984, pp. 46–48):

> Dear Jodie,
>
> There is a definite possibility that I will be killed in my attempt to get Reagan. It is for this very reason I am writing you this letter now.
>
> As you well know by now I love you very much. Over the past seven months I've left you dozens of poems, letters and love messages in the faint hope that you could develop an interest in me. Although we talked on the phone a couple of times I never had the nerve to simply approach you and introduce myself. Besides my shyness, I honestly did not wish to bother you with my constant presence. I know the many messages left at your door and in your mailbox were a nuisance, but I felt that it was the most painless way for me to express my love for you . . .
>
> Jodie, I would abandon this idea of getting Reagan in a second if I could only win your heart and live out the rest of my life with you, whether it be in total obscurity or whatever.
>
> I will admit to you that the reason I'm going ahead with this attempt now is because I just cannot wait any longer to impress you. I've got to do something now to make you understand, in no uncertain terms, that I am doing all of this for your sake! By sacrificing my freedom and possibly my life, I hope to change your mind about me. This letter is being written only an hour before I leave for the Hilton Hotel. Jodie, I'm asking to please look into your heart and at least give me the chance, with this historical deed, to gain your respect and love.
>
> I love you forever.
>
> John Hinkley

Hinkley's letter illustrates the yearning and frustrated passion that can accompany a virtual relationship. It also embodies the timeworn strategy of attaining status through some intrepid act and, thus, attracting the attention (and perhaps love) of the desired person. The only real madness in Hinkley's case was his decision to attempt an assassination of the president, in order to demonstrate his love and prowess. If the plan of assassinating Ronald Reagan was replaced (in the above letter) with joining the foreign legion or becoming a missionary, then the letter might strike one as foolishly romantic rather than insane.

Consummate love Sternberg suggested that **consummate love** results when lovers feel a high degree of intimacy, passion, and commitment for each other. Consummate love represents the pinnacle of an ideal love.

One important aspect of Sternberg's model concerns the way in which the three components vary in the way they develop. As we have already discussed, intimacy often starts slowly and builds over time, then levels off. Passion, in contrast, may often start with a hiss and a roar, but tapers off as intimacy (and perhaps commitment) grow. The tendency for passion to fade is not only true in western cultures, but is probably widespread across cultures. While watching a recently married couple from the !Kung culture horsing about together, another !Kung man commented spontaneously to the anthropologist Marjorie Shostak, "When two people are first together, their hearts are on fire and their passion is very great. After a while the fire cools and that's how it stays . . . They continue to love each other but it's in a different way – warm and dependable." (Shostak, 1981, p. 268).

The Maintenance of Love and Intimacy

> From the moment in which a man and a woman have pronounced together these sweet words: *I love you*, they unconsciously become the priests of a temple in which they must guard the sacred fire of desire. To keep it alive is the great secret of loving eternally.
>
> Paulo Mantegazza (1894, p. 319)

Any fire, even the sacred fire of desire referred to by Mantegazza, requires fuel to continue burning. Perhaps that is why intimate partners, after having been together for a long period of time, wonder aloud how to keep the spark in their relationship, or even maintain intimacy and warmth. How do couples keep the magic alive?

One answer is in terms of maintaining interpersonal trust, which a key ingredient of love and for the maintenance of successful relationships (Fehr, 1988; Simpson, 2007). Trust captures the degree to which individuals can count on current partners to meet fundamental needs and to facilitate important goals. Will my partner arrive on time to pick me up from work? Will my partner comfort me when something bad happens? Will my partner be faithful while I am away at a conference? Someone who trusts their partner would answer "yes" to these questions, whereas someone who does not trust their partner would answer "no" or "not sure."

The cardinal features of trust center on a partner's dependability (i.e. being able to count on the partner for comfort and support during difficult times) and faith in the partner (i.e. being confident that the partner will always be available and supportive in the future). Trust is a complex construct, however, in that it involves three components: person A trusts person B to engage in behavior X (Simpson, 2007). The development of trust in a relationship therefore involves the personalities of both partners (i.e. the general inclination of each partner to trust others), as well as the shared experiences between partners (i.e. partners demonstrating that they are trustworthy).

Holmes and Rempel (1989) argue that relationships suffer when individuals are uncertain about trusting their partners. During daily interactions with their partners, individuals with uncertain levels of trust look closely for cues of possible rejection and acceptance from their partner. These individuals may also actually create situations to test for evidence of their partners' love and commitment (Simpson, 2007). Individuals with uncertain levels of trust experience more extreme emotional highs and lows over time in their relationships, partly because they evaluate their partners and relationships based on daily cues of perceived rejection and acceptance (Campbell *et al.*, 2010).

In addition, individuals who report higher levels of trust hold more optimistic and benevolent expectations about their partner's motives, make more positive attributions about their partner's behaviors, and have more integrated and well-balanced perceptions of their partners that remain open to assimilating new information (Simpson, 2007). More trusting individuals also disregard or downplay what could be construed as negative relationship actions by their partners, minimizing the potential negative impact of minor partner indiscretions (Rempel *et al.*, 2001). When attempting to resolve relationship conflicts, more trusting individuals report that they display more positive and less negative affect (Holmes and Rempel, 1989), and their evaluations of their partners and relationships are less strongly tied to the emotions they experience during these discussions. More trusting individuals also view their partners more positively, especially when they think of negative (yes, negative) relationship experiences (Holmes and Rempel, 1989). That is, when more trusting individuals ponder relationship-threatening events, they step back and consider their partner's positive qualities and if anything feel more confident about the long-term success of their relationship (Holmes, 1991).

When individuals are uncertain about whether they can trust their partners, however, they can become trapped in approach/avoidance conflict situations in which positive partner behaviors are viewed as hopeful signs of possible relationship improvement, but any hint of negative behavior is taken as clear evidence that relationship difficulties are imminent. This hypervigilance can lead to self-fulfilling prophecies; namely, their angst-ridden perceptions may create the very relationship outcomes they wish to avoid (cf. Mikulincer, 1998; Murray *et al.*, 2006). Moreover, when such persons recall positive relationship events, they claim to judge their partner's behavior charitably, yet make cynical attributions regarding their partner's hidden motives (Holmes and Rempel, 1989; Rempel *et al.*, 2001; also see Chapter 3).

Another way of maintaining love is provided by Arthur Aron and colleagues, who suggest that relationship partners should participate together in novel and arousing activities (Aron *et al.*, 2000). In one of their experiments, couples were escorted to a large room where gymnasium mats had been set up to create a large soft surface. Couples were randomly assigned to complete a mundane task or a novel and arousing activity. The mundane task involved some boring repetitive ball rolling. For the novel and arousing condition, partners were bound together with Velcro straps at the wrist and ankle and asked to complete some challenging timed problem-solving tasks involving barriers and pillows. As predicted, the fun-filled, novel task led to a surge of positive evaluations of the relationship, but no change in relationship satisfaction for those completing the boring task.

The explanation for these findings, according to Aron and colleagues, is that engaging in novel and arousing experiences with a partner essentially recreates experiences more typical of the early stages of relationships where intimacy grows fairly rapidly. Breaking out of a routine by doing something new and different with a partner therefore provides the opportunity for increasing intimacy with your partner. Stoking the sacred fire of desire can potentially be as simple as making an effort to seek out new and exciting adventures with your partner.

Berscheid's (1983) emotion model also helps explain why people report heightened feelings of relationship satisfaction after experiencing novel activities with their partner. According to her model, both positive and negative emotions are experienced when individuals are faced with disruptions to their normal routines. As relationships mature, partners tend to develop routines for their daily interactions. For instance, George may always be the first to wake up in the morning to make coffee, let the dog out, and get the paper from the doorway. His partner Mary, on the other hand, may always select some clothes for George to wear to work and make his lunch. Their behaviors are helpful to each other, but they are also stereotyped, mundane, and unexciting.

According to Berscheid's model, George and Mary should feel relatively low levels of intimacy in their relationship over time as they play out this routine morning after morning. If George forgets to make coffee, or if Mary does not do laundry, however, the routine is interrupted in such a way to arouse negative feelings. If George wakes up early to buy Mary a specialty coffee from her favorite coffee shop, or if Mary lays out a new outfit she bought for George's big presentation at work, the routine is interrupted in a positive manner that is likely to arouse positive feelings. Only when the routine is interrupted in a positive manner will couples feel a boost of positive emotions, and thus increased intimacy in their relationships. In Aron and colleagues' research discussed above, it is likely the case that each couple's routines were interrupted in a positive manner (i.e. they did something together that was new and slightly weird), resulting in a boost to their relationship satisfaction.

Shelly Gable and colleagues (Gable *et al.*, 2004) provide another simple suggestion for how to maintain love and intimacy in relationships – when good things happen, share the positive news with your partner. They call this process **capitalization**. But why should capitalization foster relationship wellbeing? Sharing positive experiences with partners requires self-disclosure and open communication, creating both an opportunity for reliving the event as well as for partners to respond joyfully to each other's positive disclosures, thus enhancing perceptions of the partner's responsiveness. In a series of studies testing the positive effects of capitalization attempts in relationships, Gable *et al.* (2004) found that individuals felt uplifted when they shared positive events with their partners. Additionally, close relationships in which partners respond to capitalization attempts enthusiastically (e.g. being genuinely joyful for the partner's success rather than jealous or indifferent) are more likely to experience high levels of relationship wellbeing (e.g. more intimacy and higher levels of daily relationship satisfaction).

Finally, in a similar vein, recent research suggests that the expression of gratitude to relationship partners can provide booster shots for the relationship (Algoe *et al.*, 2010). Tracking couples over a short period of time, Algoe and colleagues asked partners if they expressed gratitude toward their partner each day (e.g. planning a celebratory meal for a partner's recent success, or doing something with the kids so the other partner has some quiet time), and they asked partners how satisfied they were with their relationship each day. Expressing gratitude toward a partner predicted increases in relationship connection and satisfaction the following day, for both recipient and benefactor. A little gratitude, expressed often, may go a long way toward maintaining love and affection in relationships.

Summary and Conclusions

In this chapter we reviewed evidence for the evolutionary thesis that romantic love is a commitment device to keep parents together long enough to help infants survive to reproductive age. The evidence can be concisely summed up. First, romantic love is a universal. Second, it has a distinct suite of behavioral and biological signatures (characteristic of specific evolutionary adaptations) that have a shared evolutionary history with other species. Third, long-term pair bonded relationships promote reproductive success. Fourth, romantic love shuts down or dilutes the search for mates.

We also examined some challenges to the commitment-device thesis raised by the common existence across cultures of arranged marriages, divorce or separation, and polygyny. We argued they do not do serious damage, but they do suggest that romantic love is a non-perfect, jury-rigged solution to a problem, but one that nevertheless gives a potent motivational push to provide the massive investment involved needed to support a mate and raise children. A caveat – we are not arguing that pair bonding love is necessarily enough on its own to provide the sufficient resources and care needed for the successful raising of children over the stretched childhood of large-brained humans. This daunting task also typically involves the family (siblings, grandmothers, fathers, uncles, and aunts), and even non-kin in the village, band, or local community.

In the next section of the chapter we analyzed the nature of love, arguing that it comes in two main forms – passionate love and companionate love. Passionate love usually comes first in a romantic relationship and – as the term implies – is passionate. Lots of sexual activity (or frustrated sexual activity) and obsessional thinking, along with liberal excretions of the arousal and cuddle hormones, characterize this phase. Generally, however, there is a slow slide into a less frenetic relationship phase characterized by commitment and a deep form of affection – companionate love. Alas, in both forms, love often fades, and many sexual relationships eventually cease to be. Keeping long-term sexual relationships ticking over nicely, we argued requires the maintenance of trust, and perhaps also finding ways of introducing some novelty and excitement from time to time (we go into considerably more detail on the causes of relationship dissolution in Chapter 12 and return to relationship maintenance strategies in both Chapter 9 and Chapter 12).

As a supremely astute observer of human nature, Shakespeare understood the power and subtleties of romantic love, as revealed in his plays and sonnets, including Romeo and Juliet. However, as this chapter indicates, over the past few decades science has gone much further than any lay psychologist could possibly go in explaining why and how romantic love wields such influence over human affairs.

8 Reading Minds, Partners, and Relationships

Reality versus illusions – looking through the eyes of love – resolving the paradox of love – causes and consequences of bias and accuracy in relationship judgments – reading relationship minds – summary and conclusions

Love sees not with the eyes, but with the mind;
And therefore is wing'd Cupid painted blind.

William Shakespeare

In a scene from Woody Allen's classic movie *Annie Hall* (one of the great relationship movies, released in 1977), Alvy and Annie, having just met during an arranged tennis game, are having a conversation over a glass of wine in Annie's apartment. Alvy is played by Woody Allen and Annie is played by Diane Keaton. Intriguingly, both actors had a sexual relationship in real life prior to the movie and many aspects of the story line and their characters are borrowed from real-life (although Woody Allen denied the movie was biographical). In the movie, having just met, their private real thoughts and feelings suddenly appear as subtitles on the screen, as they carry on small-talk banalities (thoughts are in parentheses):

ALVY: So, did you do those photographs in there, or what?
ANNIE: Yeah, yeah, I sort of dabble around, you know. (*I dabble? Listen to me. What a jerk.*)
ALVY: They're wonderful. They have a quality . . . (*You are a great-looking girl.*)
ANNIE: Well, I would like to take a serious photography course. (*He probably thinks I'm a yo-yo.*)

The Science of Intimate Relationships, First Edition. Garth Fletcher, Jeffry A. Simpson, Lorne Campbell, and Nickola C. Overall.
© 2013 Garth Fletcher, Jeffry A. Simpson, Lorne Campbell, and Nickola C. Overall.
Published 2013 by Blackwell Publishing Ltd.

ALVY: Photography's interesting because, you know, it's a new form, and a set of aesthetic criteria have not emerged yet. (*I wonder what she looks like naked.*)

ANNIE: You mean whether it's a good photo or not. (*I'm not smart enough for him. Hang
in there.*)

ALVY: The medium enters in as a condition of the art form itself. (*I don't know what
I'm saying – she senses I'm shallow.*)

ANNIE: Well to me, it's all instinctive. You know, I mean, I just try to feel it. You know,
I try to get a sense of it and not think about it so much. (*God, I hope he doesn't
turn out to be a schmuck like the others.*)

ALVY: Still, you need a set of aesthetic guidelines to put it in social perspective, I think.
(*Christ, I sound like FM radio. Relax.*)

Although this is a movie script (and deliberately amusing) it illustrates some important themes about intimate relationship cognition, some of which we have already discussed. First, the thoughts and feelings are quite different to the verbal behavior. Second, both Alvy and Annie are not merely concerned with what the other person is like, but with how they are coming across and how they are perceived by the other person (that is, they are making a lot of **interpersonal attributions**). Third, the classic gender differences we have noted in mate selection (see Chapter 6) are alive and well, and they are both doing a lot of mind-reading, most of which is (apparently) wide of the mark.

In this chapter we examine the research that has investigated the kind of **mind-reading** exemplified in the example from *Annie Hall*, along with the personality and many other judgments people make of their partners at every stage of the relationship. We start with the question – is love blind? We then discuss some important issues that bear on the nature of bias and accuracy of relationship judgments. Next, we outline some of the causes and consequences of accuracy and bias in partner and relationship judgments. Finally, we return to mind-reading and finish with a few conclusions about the power and limitations of the social mind of perceiving reality in intimate relationships.

Looking through the Eyes of Love: Reality versus Illusion in Intimate Relationships

Romantic love is often characterized as loaded with illusions and driven by strong emotions and wishful thinking, a theme captured in the quote from Shakespeare at the beginning of the chapter. This thesis is theoretically plausible. From an evolutionary standpoint, romantic love is typically viewed as a commitment device designed to lead men and women to substantially invest for long periods of time in one another, and accordingly support any resultant offspring (see Chapter 7). The leap of faith required for long-term romantic commitments is thus likely to be powered by strong biologically based attachment emotions, which in turn predispose individuals to put a charitable spin on judgments of their partners and relationships.

The theoretical credibility of this thesis is supported by a wealth of empirical evidence. For example, people routinely rate the chances of their own marriages failing as considerably lower than their perceptions of the population base-rates (Fowers *et al.*, 2001), and they keep their relationship doubts at bay by restructuring judgments or rewriting their relationship stories (see Murray, 2001). And, as love prospers and grows more intense, individuals increasingly exaggerate the similarity with their partners (Murray *et al.*, 2002), the extent to which their relationships have improved over time (Karney and Frye, 2002), and how much their real-life partners resemble archetypal ideals (Murray *et al.*, 1996a, 1996b). In short, judgments of partners and relationships seem to be systematically biased in a positive direction.

There are, however, strong arguments against the "love is blind" hypothesis. The simple fact that many long-term romantic relationships dissolve suggests that the motivating power of love to promote positive bias has its limitations. In addition, the use of evolutionary psychology to support this thesis is a double-edged sword. Evolutionary psychology rests on the Darwinian assumption that mate selection criteria in species (including humans), and their associated attributes, evolved according to natural and sexual selection. The force of **sexual selection** to produce the cumbersome, dazzling tail of the peacock relies on the ability of the peahen to accurately perceive the size and quality of the peacock's tail. What typically goes unnoticed is that this Darwinian assumption entails that human judgments of important attributes in the mating game, such as attractiveness, status, and kindness or trustworthiness, are assessed with reasonable accuracy. If instead, such judgments of potential or actual partners are (or were in our ancestral environment) hopelessly awry, then their use in making judgments of potential romantic partners could not have evolved (see Chapter 6). Thus, the "love is blind" thesis, taken to extremes, undercuts a key assumption in evolutionary psychology.

Moreover, a broad array of empirical evidence suggests that lay judgments of partners and relationships are firmly tied to reality. For example, relationship evaluations quite strongly predict both interactive behavior (e.g. Fletcher and Thomas, 2000) and relationship dissolution (see Karney and Bradbury, 1995). Further, studies using a range of external criteria or benchmarks (including self-reports of the partner, observer ratings of interactive behavior, and the predicted future or recalled past states of the relationship) reveal quite good levels of accuracy in relationship and partner judgments (for a recent review see Fletcher and Kerr, 2010).

Thus, we are left with an apparent paradox – love is both blind and firmly rooted in the real world. Resolving the paradox has turned out to be quite complicated, turning on a considerable amount of research and theorizing that goes well beyond intimate relationships. And the answers remain controversial. In particular, defining and analyzing the concepts of bias and accuracy for any kind of judgment are not as straightforward as they might appear. We discuss three major questions that scientists have struggled with. It turns out that answering these questions goes a long way toward resolving this puzzle. In short order these questions are:

- Can bias can be rational?
- Can judgments be biased and accurate at the same time?
- Are people aware of bias and accuracy in their relationship judgments?

Can bias be rational?

The short answer is yes.

Research case study Consider a classic study by Sandra Murray and John Holmes (1993). In this study, participants initially either completed short exercises designed to buttress perceptions of the relationships with their partners as rarely initiating disagreement or as being very similar to the self, respectively. They were then persuaded to think (by reading bogus *Psychology Today* articles) that either open disagreement (Study 1) or recognizing differences between partners (Study 2) were crucial to the development of intimacy in romantic relationships (the exact opposite of their manipulated perceptions of their partners). The results convincingly showed how participants (relative to controls) resolved their freshly minted doubts by trying to resolve the contradiction between their beliefs and their perceptions. They did this either by embellishing the presence of open disagreement or couple differences, or by emphasizing or reinterpreting other aspects of their relationship to counter the suddenly apparent weakness.

For example, one participant in an experimental condition reported that "On many occasions, I could tell that a problem existed, but she refused to talk about it, almost afraid of an argument . . . on the other hand, she is very receptive to my needs, and willing to adapt if necessary. This is beneficial to our relationship." Another said "My partner never really starts an argument but knows that if something bothers me enough, I will bring it up. However, my partner has come to realize in the past few months that the development of intimacy is important to me and he seems to be more willing to negotiate problems that occur."

In short, as these authors concluded, the participants seemed to crush doubt and maintain their rose-tinted views by simply rewriting history and altering some key relationship perceptions. This process looks, at face value, as anything but scientific or rational. However, other interpretations are possible. Note that this study cleverly engineered a loss of fit between beliefs drawn from **local relationship theories** (e.g. "my relationship is great and free of open disagreement and conflict") and **general relationship theories** (e.g. "open disagreement and conflict are important for producing successful relationships") (see Chapter 3).

The results highlighted by Murray and Holmes (1993) showed that participants commonly responded by rewriting some detailed components of their local relationship accounts (as described above). However, other results (that were not the primary focus of the study) suggested that some participants actually developed more negative relationship evaluations, that some rejected the experimenter-supplied general theory completely, and that the manipulation (not surprisingly) did not work for participants who possessed prior local and relationship theories that were close to the manipulated versions. Thus, the participants overall seemed to have been principally motivated to maintain consistency between their local theories, their general theories, and their relationship judgments (see Chapter 3). And, this looks like a much more scientific and rational process than routinely rewriting history to retain positive views of the relationship.

Projection Another much-studied kind of bias is what is termed **projection** or **assumed similarity**. A lot of research has shown that individuals make judgments of their partner by projecting judgments of the self onto their partner (for a review see Fletcher and Kerr, 2010). But, this does not necessarily mean that projection leads to falsehood or inaccuracy. Consistent with our prior discussion, there is considerable evidence that individuals who perceive more similarity between themselves and their partners are indeed happier with their relationships (Montoya *et al.*, 2008). However, as we know from the **assortative mating** literature, couples are quite often similar in many domains. Schul and Vinokur (2000) found that actual similarity across a wide range of domains (e.g. health, job stress, family life) was high (ranging from correlations of .40 to .72), and that individuals who project more are also more similar ($r = .33$). Thus, individuals may attain accuracy in their judgments by the judicious use of projection.

Indeed, examination of the results produced by Kenny and Acitelli (2001) and Schul and Vinokur (2000) confirms this suggestion, with projection reaching substantial proportions for attributions like closeness, enjoying sex, family life events, relationship satisfaction, and financial strain. It is difficult to thoroughly enjoy sex if your partner hates it, or to be deliriously happy if your partner is miserable. Thus, these kinds of things are likely to be (and are) very similar across partners. However, for those aspects likely to be independent across partners – health, job satisfaction, hours spent at work – projection in these studies was (sensibly) weak.

In general terms, it is clear that using lay theories to interpret and weight incoming information about the partner and relationship is a perfectly rational and scientific procedure, and can help produce accurate judgments. Bias is beginning to sound like a friend of accuracy rather an enemy. However, as you are doubtlessly beginning to discover, the concept of bias is a slippery customer. A different and commonly used way of defining judgmental bias is in terms of overshooting or undershooting a target criterion. We turn next to this aspect of judgmental bias, which we term **directional bias**.

Can judgments be biased and accurate at the same time?

Yes.

Two kinds of accuracy We can initially define the accuracy of judgments simply in terms of their correspondence with reality. But, as psychologists have long known, the empirical investigation of accuracy quickly turns such an apparently straightforward definition into a sea of complexity. A fundamental beginning point is to distinguish between two kinds of accuracy: **directional bias** and **tracking accuracy**. Consider the following example (adapted from Fletcher and Kerr, 2010) as shown in Figure 8.1.

As shown in Figure 8.1, imagine that for a group of four couples, each man rates his female partner on the trait of warmth, and that we have gold standard criteria showing that, in reality, Mary is 5 on warmth, Joane 4, Iris 4, and Anne 3 (all on seven-point scales). If we take the top left graph, it can be seen that all four male partners score a direct hit. You can't be more accurate than this. Thus, the sample overall would produce no directional bias and attain perfect tracking accuracy. Now imagine we

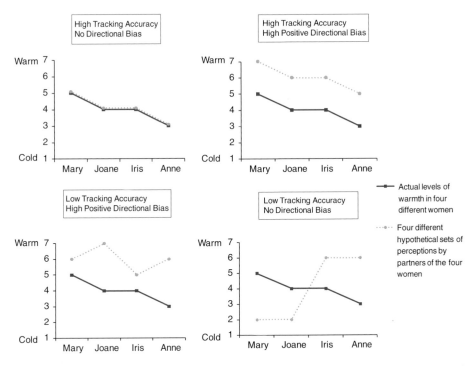

Figure 8.1 Four hypothetical samples comparing judgments with benchmarks showing why directional bias and tracking accuracy are independent

obtained the pattern of results on the top right graph. This hypothetical pattern of male ratings shows an elevated pattern of positive directional bias, but because each man rates his female partner at exactly two units above her actual level of kindness, the sample shows perfect tracking accuracy. The graph on the bottom left shows low tracking accuracy and high positive directional bias, and the bottom right graph shows the remaining pattern of low tracking accuracy but no overall directional bias.

In terms of evaluating the overarching levels of accuracy attained by the sample, both directional bias (positive or absolute) and tracking accuracy can be interpreted as components of overall levels of accuracy. Indeed, as the example just given shows, the logic seems unassailable on this point. Maximum overall accuracy in Figure 8.1 is attained in the unbiased and accurate tracking condition, with the other three exemplars illustrating various degrees of inaccuracy. Statistically speaking, in the two graphs showing high tracking accuracy the judgments and benchmarks are correlated perfectly (1.0), and in the two graphs showing positive directional bias the means of the judgments are higher than the means of the target benchmarks. But these are storybook examples. In real-life relationships, how biased and accurate are people's judgments?

To answer this question, Garth Fletcher and Patrick Kerr (2010) recently reviewed all the published research reporting directional bias or tracking accuracy in intimate relationships. Their survey suggested that researchers measured six different kinds of judgments: personality traits or characteristics of the partner, reflected appraisals or traits that were interactional in nature that were either positive (e.g. forgiveness, love) or negative (e.g., aggression, hostility), mind-reading judgments (like the example we started the chapter with), memories of prior levels of love or relationship events, and predictions (such as likelihood of breakups and future relationship violence). The objective benchmark criteria used to assess bias and accuracy included self-perceptions of the target, behavioral ratings, prior reports of the relationship, relationship dissolution, and so forth.

The results showed that across 98 studies and 27 064 individuals, the tracking accuracy obtained was reliable and substantial (mean effect size $r = .47$). The overall amount of positive directional bias was lower, but was also reliable across 48 studies and 9393 individuals (mean effect size $r = .09$). Thirty-eight of the studies reported findings for both directional bias and tracking accuracy, allowing the two effect sizes to be correlated across studies. The two effect sizes were in fact unrelated ($r = .00$), showing that the two kinds of judgmental accuracy are empirically independent, consistent with our prior discussion. This means that people can (and do) have their cake and eat it too – they can be both positively biased about their partner and accurate.

Research case study To illustrate some of these findings, consider some recent research on the so-called **affective forecasting error** in relationship contexts by Paul Eastwick and colleagues (Eastwick *et al.*, 2008). Prior evidence has indicated a robust tendency in non-relationship contexts for people to predict greater levels of negative or positive affect, following negative or positive events, than actually eventuate (an example of directional bias). The longitudinal research by Eastwick and colleagues found the same effect when individuals first predicted and then experienced the affective outcomes associated with a dating relationship breakup; people experienced significantly less distress than they predicted concerning the relationship breakup (effect size $r = .66$). However, they also evinced significant tracking accuracy of their emotional reactions ($r = .44$). And, the forecasting directional bias almost disappeared for those who were not in love with their partners, those who indicated that it was likely they would start a new romantic relationship a few weeks prior to the breakup, or those who initiated the breakup (see Figure 8.2). In short, only individuals who were significantly invested in the relationship predicted more distress than they experienced when the relationship actually dissolved. It is hard to resist the interpretation that this particular bias has a functional basis, given that it should motivate individuals who have much at stake to maintain and improve their romantic relationship, and perhaps retain their mates.

Are people aware of bias and accuracy in their relationship judgments?

Yes . . . and no.

A puzzle and an explanation William Swann and Michael Gill (1997) found that people were more confident of the tracking accuracy of their judgments (using questions

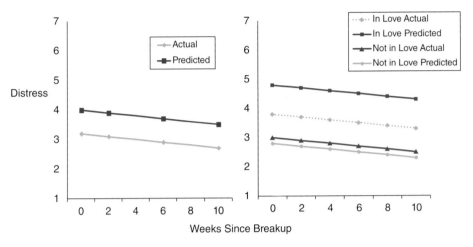

Figure 8.2 Directional bias in predicting the future of relationships
Source: From Eastwick *et al.*, 2008; © 2007 Elsevier Inc.

assessing a wide range of attitudes and behaviors) if their relationships were longer and the lay theories of their partners were more complex and integrated. Unfortunately, there was a minimal link between confidence ratings and accuracy. In a similar vein, Thomas *et al.* (1997) reported that there was no significant association between the accuracy of mind-reading attained during problem-solving interactions and the confidence expressed in the attributions.

In contrast, there is evidence that people can accurately gauge the amounts of directional bias in their relationships. Barelds-Dijkstra and Barelds (2008) reported the familiar findings of individuals believing their partners were more attractive than their partners' self perceptions of attractiveness (positive directional bias). However, when participants were asked to judge how attractive other people found their partner, the positive directional bias significantly dropped, suggesting that individuals were aware to some extent of the bias inherent in their own perceptions. More directly, Boyes and Fletcher (2007) found that men and women in romantic relationships exhibited the standard findings of judging their partners as more warm and attractive than their partners perceived themselves. However, in this study, the researchers also asked the participants how positively biased they thought these judgments were. The results showed that people were quite good at assessing how biased they were. Moreover, these effects were not a function of relationship satisfaction or self-esteem, and so were unlikely to be driven simply by halo effects.

Given the sparse research on this topic, caution should be exercised in drawing firm conclusions. However, the results do raise the question of why individuals may possess better meta-cognition about directional bias than tracking accuracy. Boyes and Fletcher (2007) argue there are two conditions for meta-accuracy of such judgments to flourish. First, there needs to exist a familiar, accessible, and relevant lay theory, such as (in this case) the notion that "love is blind." Second, the existence of such biased judgments needs to be expressed and observable during behavioral interactions. Indeed, there is good evidence that partners in intimate relationships often try to change each other on central relationship dimensions such as warmth, attractiveness, and status (Overall *et al.*, 2006, 2009), and couples will often work collaboratively to improve themselves, for example, by going on a diet or joining a gym together to lose weight. And, it seems likely that individuals in romantic relationships may often communicate their respective (positively or negatively biased) views to each other verbally and nonverbally. If Mary asks George if she looks fat in her new dress, George's reply will be diagnostic about his (biased) perceptions of Mary's attractiveness. Thus, individuals in relationships typically should have abundant evidence available to help judge the amounts of directional bias inherent in partner judgments of specific, relationship-central traits.

In contrast, developing accurate meta-perceptions of the tracking accuracy of mind-reading or personality traits may be more intractable, and perhaps beyond the cognitive resources of many individuals, because of the relative difficulty of the task. For example, with respect to mind-reading, the quality of feedback may be poor (partly because individuals often mask their own emotions and cognitions), the processes involved are often rapid, fleeting, and unconscious, and, finally, unlike directional bias, the perceiver is not making relatively simple, relative assessments between a judgment and a benchmark of some kind (see Ickes, 1993).

Causes and Consequences of Accuracy and Bias in Partner and Relationship Judgments

Having clarified some of the ambiguity about the concept of accuracy, and answered some fundamental questions, we are now in a position to discuss the causes of accuracy and bias and the consequences for the individual and the relationship. Figure 8.3 shows that goals comprise the fundamental causes of judgmental accuracy, which in turn influence two crucial outcomes – the maintenance or erosion of relationship commitment or satisfaction and making important relationship decisions (e.g. do I stay or do I go?). However, which goals are primed and activated should also be a function of moderating variables – relationship stage, individual differences, context, and judgment category. Finally, in this section we review research that examines the extent to which individuals welcome biased or accurate judgments emanating from their partners, and how they respond to them.

Links between accuracy and relationship quality

Let's consider the links between directional bias and relationship quality. The meta-analysis findings from Fletcher and Kerr (2010) are unequivocal. Across 14 studies, there was strong evidence that more positive directional bias is associated with higher levels of relationship quality ($r = .36$). Those who are happier tend to exaggerate the extent to which their partners are attractive or trustworthy, or forgive them more for

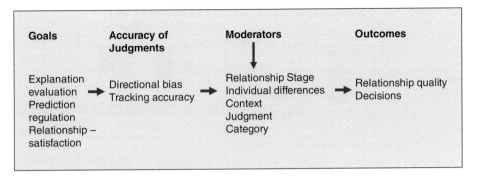

Figure 8.3   Links between accuracy and relationship outcomes

transgressions, or mind-read their intentions as more positive, or recall their relationships as more positive, or predict their relationships will last longer. And, remember that when we say "more," we mean more than the reality benchmarks show is actually the case. Moreover, longitudinal research by Sandra Murray and her colleagues has shown that such positive directional bias also predicts real improvements in satisfaction over time (Murray *et al.*, 2002), and serves to improve the levels of self-esteem of the partner over time (Murray *et al.*, 1996a).

There is also evidence that individuals want their partners to see them in positively biased ways (Boyes and Fletcher, 2007; Swann *et al.*, 2002). Presumably being the target of positive bias satisfies the esteem needs of individuals (i.e. to feel positive and optimistic about the future of their relationship) by fostering a sense of unconditional positive regard, and allowing people to feel that their partner accepts them in spite of their faults or imperfections (see Chapter 9). This state of felt security is a critical factor for the development of relationship satisfaction and stability (Chapters 9 and 12).

On the other hand, if you believe your partner sees you as far more intelligent and worldly wise than you think you are, this may well prove to be a burden. Individuals want their partners to see them in an authentic fashion, more or less as they see themselves. This apparent contradiction is resolved by our prior distinction between tracking accuracy and directional bias. Partner feedback can both verify your self-concept (possess high tracking accuracy) and provide a boost to your self-esteem (being more positive overall than your self-perceptions). Lackenbauer *et al.* (2010) tested this idea by first having both members of dating couples privately provide self and partner ratings on 10 interpersonal traits (e.g. kind, trustworthy). Each person was then provided a graph plotting their own self-ratings, across the 10 traits, against the appraisals supposedly provided by their partners (which were actually fabricated by the experimenters). Thus, in this experiment, participants received feedback that systematically manipulated directional bias (positive or neutral) and tracking accuracy (high or low). Participants receiving feedback that was a combination of positive directional bias and high tracking accuracy reported the most positive relationship evaluations.

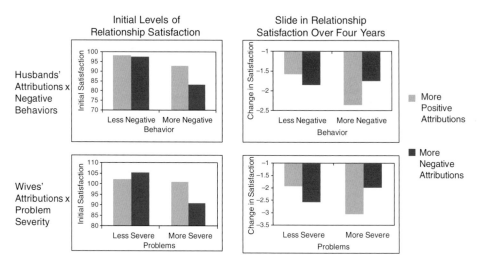

Figure 8.4   Wearing rose-tinted glasses does not always work in relationships
Source: From McNulty *et al.*, 2008; © 2008 American Psychological Association

Before getting too carried away with the power of positive thinking, however, we need to consider other research suggesting that more positive directional bias does not always produce beneficial consequences for the relationship. Steadfastly maintaining sunny partner and relationship judgments works well when the problems are mild and both participants are socially skilled and committed. However, when relationships are in serious trouble, people seem to do better over time when a more negative and realistic stance is adopted, according to research by James McNulty and his colleagues (McNulty and Karney, 2004; McNulty *et al.*, 2008) (also see Chapter 9). In one study of newly married couples, for example, McNulty *et al.* (2008) reported that at the beginning of married life, couples facing difficult problems were happier when they adopted more positive attributions (see Chapter 3). However, when tracked over the next four years, couples who faced serious problems and adopted sunny, optimistic attributions became unhappier, whereas the less optimistic couples did (relatively) better over time (see Figure 8.4).

In stark contrast to the findings concerning directional bias, the meta-analysis by Fletcher and Kerr (2010) showed that the link between tracking accuracy and relationship quality across 27 studies, either positive or negative, was virtually zero ($r = .03$). This finding flies in the face of many predictions that researchers have made over the years. However, as we shall see research has shown that under certain conditions, tracking accuracy is linked to relationship satisfaction and outcomes (but not always positively!). Taken together, these particular research findings yet again illustrate the point that common sense ideas about relationships do not always hold up under the scientific spotlight.

Relationship stage

First meetings If the list of goals shown in Figure 8.3 is examined, one might reasonably guess that at a first meeting with a potential partner, the goals of evaluation (e.g. what is this person like?, do they meet my standards?, is he or she interested in me?) and prediction (e.g. would a first date work out?) would be paramount. Surprisingly, the research in this area is sparse; very little work has examined the directional bias or tracking accuracy of judgments at this very early relationship stage.

However, it is known that in this early scoping-out phase of mate choice people pay a lot of attention to aspects that are generally easily observable (attractiveness, age, ethnicity) or can be assessed with a simple question (what do you do for a job?) (see Chapter 6). And, happily, a lot of research has examined the tracking accuracy of judgments among strangers in non-romantic contexts, especially of personality traits. This research suggests that straightforward personality judgments such as extroversion, conscientiousness, or agreeableness can be assessed with surprising levels of accuracy by strangers (using the self ratings of the targets as the benchmark criterion) after observing an individual for a brief period of time interacting with another, or even just reading their name and address out loud (see Beer and Watson, 2008, for a recent review). However, the best replicated finding across studies concerns the moderate ability of people to judge extroversion under conditions of minimal acquaintance (Beer and Watson, 2008), which is often explained according to the greater observability of this trait compared to other personality traits (Funder and Dobroth, 1987).

From an evolutionary angle (as previously noted) it is important to know how accurate people are in assessing attributes that are pivotal in mate selection contexts, such as physical attractiveness. If people are lousy at judging physical attractiveness in strangers this would throw considerable doubt on an evolutionary approach to human mate selection, because the qualities associated with male and female beauty could not have evolved through sexual selection processes. Fortunately, there is good evidence that such judgments are quite accurate based on minimal observations or interactions (although this research is not explicitly carried out in mate selection contexts). For example, David Marcus and Rowland Miller (2003) had participants rate their own physical attractiveness and that of other men and women who were sitting together in small groups, using a round robin design (i.e. everyone rates everyone else). There was good consensus on the level of attractiveness for specific targets, and targets' self-perceptions generally matched well with how they were perceived (correlations ranging from 0.28 to 0.53). Moreover, individuals' meta-perceptions of how they were perceived generally by others were accurate (with correlations ranging from 0.26 to 0.49). These results are shown in Figure 8.5. As the authors conclude, "we know who is handsome or pretty, and those who are attractive know it as well" (p. 344).

On-going relationships Simply being in a happy, romantic relationship seems to automatically generate a positive directional bias, as we have noted. Moreover, there is good evidence that when passion and romantic love bloom this pushes judgments well into

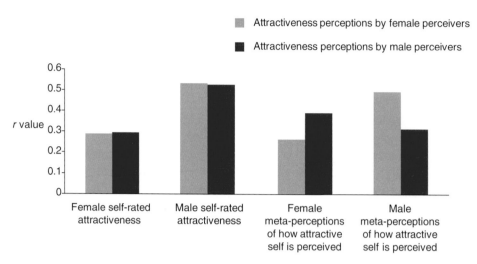

Figure 8.5 Attractiveness is accurately perceived and attractive people know (within bounds) how others perceive them
Source: Adapted from Marcus and Miller, 2003

the rose-tinted realm (see Fletcher and Kerr, 2010). This interpretation is consistent with an evolutionary account of romantic love as a device to encourage long-term bonding in mates (see Chapter 7). However, as romantic love and obsession cools and changes to a companionate form of love marked by contentment and commitment, the motivation that produces positive directional bias also seems to weaken.

Evidence for this latter claim comes from the meta-analysis carried out by Fletcher and Kerr (2010). They found 13 studies that reported the correlation between relationship satisfaction and the amount of positive directional bias. These 13 samples also varied a lot in terms of relationship length from means of 1.77 years to 43.88 years. Figure 8.6 shows that when the effect size produced from each study (indexing the size of the correlation between relationship satisfaction and positive directional bias) was regressed on the length of the relationship (transformed to logs), a significant negative slope was produced. Thus, as the relationships became longer, relationship satisfaction seemed to lose its motivational punch in driving positive directional bias.

Certain stages of the relationship might also prime the need for more accurate predictions of the future of the relationship. Fletcher and Thomas (1996) originally proposed that the goals of producing realistic (minimal positive bias) and accurate (good tracking accuracy) predictions and evaluations concerning the relationship might be especially salient when important decisions regarding changes in commitment are made, such as, for example, when people are deciding whether to leave the relationship, move in together, and get married. In this pre-decisional stage, the levels of commitment should not be such a motivational force producing positive bias, since the amount of investment in the relationship is precisely what is up for grabs. Thus, in this specific context, people may lose their rose-colored glasses and evaluate their

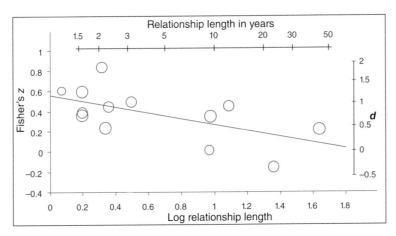

Figure 8.6 Links between relationship satisfaction and positive directional bias as a function of relationship length
Source: Adapted from Fletcher and Kerr, 2010. © 2010 American Psychological Association

relationship in a more brutally frank fashion. In contrast, once important decisions have been made concerning relationship investment (both emotionally and practically), the costs of reversing the decision may (quite rationally) loom large. In this post-decisional stage the goal of maintaining relationship satisfaction should again dominate, leading to positively biased processing once again taking center stage.

Testing these ideas, Faby Gagné and John Lydon (2001) assessed the impact that such post-decisional or pre-decisional mind-sets had on the accuracy of predicting relationship breakup in dating samples in a series of longitudinal studies. Across three studies (two correlational and one experimental) Gagné and Lydon found that individuals who were either encouraged to think, or were already thinking, in an even-handed, pre-decisional fashion (e.g. considering the pros and cons of moving in with their partner or applying for medical school) were quite accurate in predicting the long-term demise of their relationship ($r = .67$). In contrast, those who were pushed away from the goals of prediction and truth-seeking by virtue of being in a post-decisional mental set (e.g. thinking about how they could persuade their partner to move in with them, or how they could get into medical school) were not very accurate in their predictions ($r = .19$). Thus, in terms of our model in Figure 8.3, the demands of the social context seem to have the capacity to push people toward or away from goals like prediction or truth that may then influence tracking accuracy.

Individual differences and context

Self-esteem and stress Possessing low self-esteem seems to limit the operation of positive directional bias in intimate relationships. Murray and her colleagues have shown that lower self-esteem is associated with more negative mean-level bias by

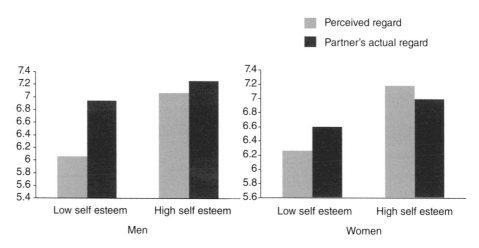

Figure 8.7 Low self-esteem leads individuals to underplay how positively their partners see them
Source: Adapted from Murray *et al.*, 2000

underplaying the amounts of love and satisfaction actually reported by the partner (Murray *et al.*, 2000). These results are shown in Figure 8.7. Recent diary studies by Murray and others also document the subtle and dynamic nature of these processes over short periods of time (typically 3 weeks) in romantic relationships (Murray *et al.*, 2000, 2003a, 2003b, 2006). These studies suggest that when the partner is perceived as being insensitive or transgressing in some way, low self-esteem motivates withdrawal from the relationship, the production of uncharitable attributions, and a slide in relationship satisfaction.

These results suggest that contextual stress, such as the partner behaving badly, interacts with self-esteem to differentially prime the goals of evaluation and avoidance, which, in turn, produces a more negative local relationship theory, and more negative directional bias associated with specific judgments. Crucially, the same studies show evidence of self-fulfilling prophecy effects so that the partners of such folk tend also to become disillusioned over time. We say crucially, because these particular results could only be obtained if the partners of the low self-esteem folk were (to some extent) accurately tracking behavior reflecting the dissatisfaction of their partners.

Security and stress Another example of how individual differences interact with stressful contexts is the research on attachment (see Chapter 5). For example, Collins and Feeney (2004) used an experimental paradigm that manipulated messages of support by romantic partners prior to participants performing a stressful task (preparing and giving a speech that would purportedly be videotaped and rated by other students). Even when controlling for the actual quality of the support given, more anxiously attached adults were more biased toward perceiving their partners as less helpful and well-intended.

Simpson and colleagues designed a methodology in which individuals mind-read the thoughts and feelings of their partners in a threatening context by observing their partners rate the desirability of highly attractive opposite-sex individuals from a local dating pool (Simpson *et al.*, 1995; Simpson *et al.*, 1999). Using a paradigm we describe fully later on, which involves assessing the actual thoughts and feelings of the targets, they found that those who were in closer and more intimate relationships were motivated to produce more *inaccurate* judgments of what their partners were thinking and feeling. Moreover, more anxiously attached individuals were also *more accurate* in their mind-readings, were correspondingly more distressed by the experience, and tended to suffer a greater loss of confidence in their relationships.

A recent study by Overall *et al.* (2012) reveals the same theme. In this study, heterosexual couples had discussions of features they wanted to change about one another, then later recorded perceptions of both their actual regard for their partner and judgments of their partner's regard for them (at each 30-second interval). In this stressful context, women who were more secure in how their partners viewed them showed more positive directional bias and less tracking accuracy. In contrast, women who were less secure in their partners' regard showed more negative directional bias but higher tracking accuracy.

These studies suggest that stress (a moderating variable) interacts with security with the partner or general attachment working models to differentially prime goals such as evaluation and the need to protect the self. Specifically, for individuals with anxious working models, or low security in a specific relationships, this increases monitoring, engages the resources of local stored relationship theories, and thus both simultaneously increases negative directional bias and the levels of tracking accuracy.

Generally, this research illustrates the exquisitely fine-grained way in which partners depend on and influence each other in romantic relationships. This research also shows that relationship interactions are both shaped by, and have behavioral consequences as a function of, the directional bias and tracking accuracy attendant in relationship and partner judgments.

Judgment category

To begin with, there is some evidence that positive bias is more marked when judgments are being made that are especially relevant to mate selection and the kind of standards that people use in assessing their partners and romantic relationships (Boyes and Fletcher, 2007; Swann *et al.*, 2002). Thus, judgments of attractiveness, warmth, and status are influenced by the tendency to idealize partners and relationships. In contrast, judgments of traits like artistic ability and extroversion are less likely to be positively biased, presumably because these categories are not normally used as standards to determine mate value or relationship success, thus they don't matter so much in relationship contexts.

Returning to the meta-analysis by Fletcher and Kerr (2010) reviewing published research reporting directional bias or tracking accuracy in intimate relationships, as previously noted they categorized the kinds of judgments into six categories:

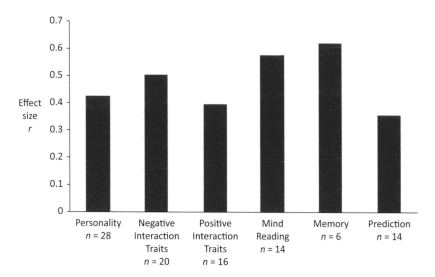

Figure 8.8   Meta-analysis: tracking accuracy in intimate relationships (*n* shows number of studies producing each effect size)
Source: Adapted from Fletcher and Kerr, 2010

personality traits (e.g. kind), **reflected appraisals** or traits that were interactional in nature and were either positive (e.g. trust) or negative (e.g., aggression), mind-reading judgments (like the example we started with chapter with), memories of previous levels of love or relationship events, and predictions (such as breakups and relationship violence). Figures 8.8 and 8.9 show the results, separately for each category. Regarding tracking accuracy, it can be seen that people attain impressive levels of tracking accuracy, regardless of the category. However, perhaps not surprisingly, they are better at remembering the past than predicting the future.

An anomaly and an explanation   The results across categories for directional bias reveal a puzzling anomaly; namely, they show mean levels of positive bias for all categories except for the **interactional** categories. For the negative interactional traits (e.g. criticism and aggressiveness directed to the partner), and for the positive interactional traits (e.g. love and forgiveness for the partner), the default directional bias at the sample level is negative. This means, for example, that individuals are likely to perceive their partners as being more critical of them, and loving them less, than their partners actually report. What gives?

A plausible explanation for these apparently odd finding is in terms of an evolutionary-based theory by Martie Haselton and David Buss termed **error management theory** (Haselton and Buss, 2000). This theory suggests an explanation in terms of the primacy of the goal of maintaining a successful relationship; namely, the relationship costs involved in holding prior positive versus negative biases, which may differ according to the kind of judgment being made. To take the example used by

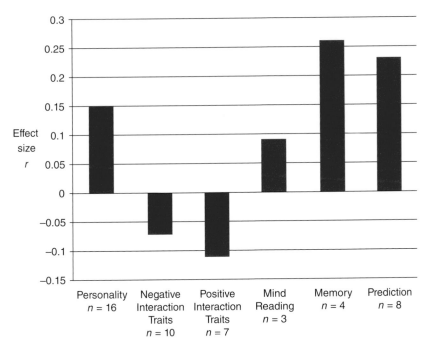

Figure 8.9 Meta-analysis: directional bias in intimate relationships (*n* shows number of studies producing each effect size)
Source: Adapted from Fletcher and Kerr, 2010

Haselton and Buss, an effective smoke fire alarm is designed to be sensitive to small amounts of smoke and heat, which produces many false alarms, as shown in Figure 8.10. In this context, a false negative (an alarm not going off when a fire is present) is more harmful than a false positive (a false alarm). They have gathered evidence for this theory by showing that men tend to over-perceive sexual interest in a potential female partner, whereas women under-perceive commitment in potential male partners. This pattern is linked to standard gender differences previously described (see Chapter 6); namely, men are more interested in short-term sex than women, whereas women are more interested in building long-term relationships. Thus, the costs for men of missing a mating opportunity are higher than for women, whereas the costs for women choosing a partner who is not into commitment are higher than for men.

Now, when a partner judgment consists of an interaction trait that is focused on the connection between the self and the partner (like relationship violence, or forgiveness, or love), it seems plausible that the default bias will be set on the negative side. If one overestimates the forgiveness, trust, or love of a partner for the self, this might lead to complacency, and lack of effort in building a more secure relationship. In contrast, positive biases like perceiving one's partner as more attractive, kind, and ambitious than he or she really is, seem to have fewer obvious downsides. Such individual-level attributions refer to general traits that may have strong implications for relationships,

False Negative Fire alarm does not go off when a fire is present. Cost = High	**Hit** Fire alarm goes off and a fire is present.
Correct Rejection Fire alarm does not go off and no fire is present.	**False Positive** Fire alarm goes off when no fire is present. Cost = Low

Figure 8.10   A fire alarm example showing why bias can have good (or bad) consequences
Source: Haselton and Buss, 2000

but nevertheless are not focused specifically on dyadic interaction. Thus, ironically, adopting a default negative bias for interaction traits may well be motivated by the goal of maintaining and protecting relationship satisfaction (see Figure 8.3).

Summary

Let's summarize our prior analysis before addressing mind-reading in greater detail. Previously in this chapter we laid out a conundrum in the science of relationships; namely, love seems to be both blind and firmly rooted in the real world. The research and our analyses here go some way toward solving this puzzle, establishing that people can apparently be cheerleaders and seekers of the truth simultaneously – that is individuals can be (and often are) both biased and accurate in judging their partners and relationships.

The evidence is consistent with evolutionary approaches to romantic relationships. It supports the existence of Darwinian sexual selection in humans, because people attain good levels of tracking accuracy on traits that are central to mate selection and retention. It is consistent with the argument that biases in relationship perception are adaptive, because such biases seem to be linked to differences in the costs and rewards involved in different outcomes. And, it squares elegantly with the proposal that romantic love is an evolved commitment device designed to lead men and women to substantially invest for long periods of time in one another and their offspring. The optimistic spin that individuals put on their relationship judgments is, on this account, a product of ancient, evolved adaptations.

The research literature also supports a standard social psychological approach in which lay people strive to achieve balance between their relationship theories and their judgments, and in which (relationship-level) **affect**, behavior, and cognition are profoundly interdependent. Lay intimate relationship theories and judgments are typically not castles in the air, remote from partners and the consequences. Rather, such theories and judgments develop in small and intense groups (dyads) in which participants' fates are intertwined. In intimate relationships reality and illusion go hand in hand in the furtherance of goals that have a long evolutionary history, and where the outcomes, for good or ill, have profound personal consequences.

Back to Reading Minds

Methods

How on earth do psychologists study the accuracy with which people read minds? Well, they use several methods. In 1970, Malcolm Kahn published the first study of mind-reading in relationships. Kahn pioneered a technique in which married partners read statements out to one another (e.g., "Didn't we have chicken for dinner a few nights ago") with instructions to use nonverbal cues to indicate either negative (irritation), neutral (curiosity), or positive (elation) emotional reactions. The task for the perceiver is to assess the intention behind the nonverbal behaviors associated with the statements; thus, accuracy can be assessed.

More recently, a commonly used technique, pioneered by William Ickes and colleagues (1990), involves couples in intimate heterosexual relationships being taped having short discussions of important problems in their relationships. Then, each partner independently replays the tape with a remote control, pausing it when he or she can recall experiencing a thought or emotion, and then writing it down. Most people stop the tape between 10 and 20 times, during a typical 10-minute discussion. These times are then swapped, and each partner goes through the tape again, except this time they give their best guess as to what the partner was thinking and feeling at the time points indicated. Using pairs of raters to assess the similarity between the pairs of statements, it is possible to derive scores that represent his or her accuracy in judging the partner. For example, if Mary said she was angry at a given point on the video and George thought she was thinking what a nice fellow he was, then that would be counted as a complete miss. If George thought she was feeling bad, that would be a ballpark hit. To score a bull's-eye, George would have to report that his partner was angry.

Research findings

Research on mind-reading suggests that the treatment provided in the example from the movie *Annie Hall* described at the beginning of the chapter is uncannily accurate in some ways. First, the research shows that people's thoughts and feelings are quite different from their verbal behavior, especially when discussing relationship problems. The content of the private cognitive flow is considerably more pessimistic and negatively charged than the observable behavior, which tends to be sunnier and more positive (Fletcher and Thomas, 2000; Thomas and Fletcher, 2003; Thomas *et al.*, 1997). The typical pattern conjoins a slight furrowing of the brow, a subtle shift in the seat, and maybe a slight edge to the tone of voice, combined with a thought like "He always does that – it is so incredibly annoying." Second, the content of people's thoughts and feelings shows they are explicitly doing a lot of mind-reading of each other and also what might be termed relationship-reading – how they are communicating, how similar they are, what the portents might be for the future of the relationship, and so forth.

However, the overall accuracy of mind-reading is a lot higher than suggested by the movie example, although admittedly this research has been carried out with samples in long-standing relationships. The meta-analysis by Fletcher and Kerr (2010) revealed that the 14 studies published on mind-reading in intimate relationships produced a mean effect size that is equivalent to a correct hit rate of 65% across studies (correcting for chance agreement). This may not seem high, but accurately mind-reading your partner's thoughts and feelings (even someone you know well) is an exceptionally difficult task, as most of us know.

One way of getting a handle on the average level of expertise developed in mind-reading others in relationships is via comparison with activities like music, chess, or tennis. In the study of expertise, it is generally reckoned that one needs about 10 000 hours of practice to become a true expert in a complex and difficult skill. This is why starting young in music, or chess playing, or tennis is generally considered as a prerequisite for becoming an international expert. Humans have intense and prolonged social relationships and they sure start young in developing their expertise in mind-reading and attributional judgments, alongside their burgeoning language skills. Thus, most humans will hit 10 000 hours of the practice tipping point in mind-reading well before adulthood, and are on the way to becoming experts at a complex and difficult cognitive activity.

Researchers have also begun to examine what is happening in the brain when mind-reading and the possible roles of **neurotransmitters** such as **oxytocin**, which, as we explored in Chapter 4, enhance bonding and intimacy. In one study (Domes *et al.*, 2007) puffing oxytocin up the nose improved performance on a standardized test that assessed the accuracy of reading emotions based on looking at pictures of eye regions. In another study by Zaki and colleagues (2009), a version of the technique described in the prior section was used to assess the mind-reading tracking accuracy of stranger's thoughts and feelings while they were discussing autobiographical events. The twist was that participants completed the task while in an **fMRI** machine. The results showed that participants who were more accurate had more activity going in both (i) regions in the **prefrontal cortex** involved in making attributions of mental states (see Chapter 4), and (ii) components of the **mirror neuron system** thought to be involved when people are automatically copying, imitating, or empathizing with others.

Our take on the results of both studies is that they reflect the role played by motivation in the process of accurately reading the minds of strangers (which may often be a desultory affair). More motivation should normally produce both more cognitive effort and higher levels of accuracy, although as we have already noted, in the context of close, sexual relationships, more motivation can be a double-edged sword simultaneously producing more tracking accuracy and more directional bias in partner judgments.

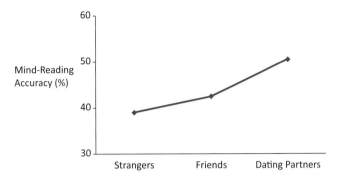

Figure 8.11   Mind-reading accuracy is partly a function of the relationship with the target
Source: Adapted from Thomas and Fletcher, 2003

Individual differences in mind-reading

Humans are remarkably good at mind-reading, but some people are better than others. What predicts differences in ability and performance? Partly it depends on how well you know your partner. Geoff Thomas and Garth Fletcher (2003) found that partners in dating relationships averaged close to a 50% accuracy hit rate in assessing what their partners were thinking and feeling. In contrast, friends of the dating partners who viewed the tapes of the discussions were less accurate than partners in their mind-readings (41%) and strangers who watched the tapes were the least accurate (39%) (see Figure 8.11).

In this same study (Thomas and Fletcher, 2003), the researchers had additional observers rate the extent to which the private thoughts and feelings were clearly expressed in their verbal and nonverbal behavior. Consider two of the related findings together. First, individuals who were strangers to the couples they were mind-reading relied on the targets expressing their thoughts and feelings clearly in their verbal and nonverbal behavior, in order to obtain good levels of accuracy. Second, in stark contrast, the mind-reading accuracy of the dating partners was completely unrelated to how clearly the targets expressed their innermost thoughts and feelings in their verbal and nonverbal behavior.

These two findings are exactly what one would expect *if* the insiders' judgments were theory-driven by their local, specific theories and knowledge about the partner and the relationship (see Chapter 3). This does not mean that relationship insiders use extra-sensory perception to do their mind-reading. Of necessity, they rely on behavioral cues to make their judgments. However, when individuals know other people well, they become aware of idiosyncratic but diagnostic behaviors that outside observers are likely to miss. For example, a slight lowering of the eyes or a vein throbbing in a temple might reliably give their partner a good idea of when they are about to blow, or are especially angry. In long-term relationships a private and idiosyncratic message

Figure 8.12   *Source:* © 2003 Randy Glasbergern

system (mainly nonverbal) is likely to develop that is inscrutable to outsiders. Strangers observe the same behavior but are likely to miss its diagnostic value.

Now, there are limits to the benefits of knowledge and intimacy in romantic relation-ships. Indeed, consistent with the cartoon shown in Figure 8.12, there is evidence that after couples have been together for many years, their mind-reading performance starts to deteriorate (Thomas *et al.*, 1997). The most plausible explanation for this finding is simply that after many years together couples more or less assume (perhaps wrongly) that they know what their partner is thinking and feeling. They also (understandably) seem to lack the motivation to put a lot of mental effort into tracking the verbal and nonverbal behavior of their partners (see Thomas *et al.*, 1997).

Thus, the nature and length of the relationship itself partly determines mind-reading accuracy. But are some people simply better mind-readers than others (before they even get into a given relationship)? There is a long history of research in social psychology investigating the existence and nature of individual differences in the ability to judge others in terms of personality traits (a component of social intelli-gence), dating back to the 1950s. However, the body of research across both relation-ship and non-relationship contexts has produced a hotchpotch of conflicting findings, with some scientists even concluding that individual differences in mind-reading abilities and the like (often termed **social intelligence**) does not even exist (Kenny, 1994). We believe such judgments are premature.

There are several reasons for the failure to find compelling evidence for the existence of social intelligence as an individual difference variable. First, there is no point using designs that have been popular in social psychology, in which strangers make judgments based on observing thin slices of behavior. This kind of design means that the behavior of the target is almost certain to be the major factor in influencing subsequent judgments. Second, researchers ideally should get research participants to make judgments of more than one person, so they can assess their levels of consistency across targets. Third, it is advisable to make the task difficult and prolonged (but not impossible) rather than overly easy and assessed in a one-shot fashion. If chess-playing ability were being assessed, then a researcher would not get a sample of chess players to solve one simple chess problem (most of this sample would do very well) or one impossibly difficult problem (most would fail). Instead, the players would be presented with several chess problems varying from moderately to extremely difficult. These three features have rarely been present in prior research on social intelligence. Hence, it is perhaps not surprising that evidence of individual differences in social intelligence has been hard to come by.

One thing we do know is that it is a waste of time asking people to report how good they are at judging others. Such self-reports of ability have a terrible track record at predicting the accuracy of social judgments – the average correlation between self-report measures and actual performance is close to zero (Davis and Kraus, 1997). So, if you have the sneaking feeling (as do the authors) that people who confess that they have a special ability at reading and judging others are probably not the Einsteins of the social world, then trust your intuitions.

Why this should be so is an interesting puzzle. We suspect the answer is along the lines we have already advanced. First, there are so many factors in determining the accuracy of social judgments that it makes it difficult to isolate and pull out the role that one's own ability has as a causal variable. Mary may know that she has produced accurate judgments of George, but is this because George is easy to read, she has a good relationship with George, or she is a terrific mind-reader. It is hard to say. Second, people make judgments of one another all day, every day, yet receive little substantive, detailed feedback as to how well they are really doing. Third, such judgments are often not communicated to the target, thereby preventing the possibility of feedback. Fourth, people who are genuinely exceptionally high in social intelligence probably understand only too well the difficulty and subtlety of reading others. Accordingly, they may not rate themselves as fantastically good on self-report scales. And, finally, many judgments made of others, and a lot of the underlying psychological processes, are automatic and unconscious.

However, there is some evidence in the relationship domain that, although self-reports may do a poor job at measuring social intelligence, stable individual differences in social intelligence nevertheless exist. In the prior study described by Thomas and Fletcher (2003), for example, individuals who were better at mind-reading someone they knew (partner or friend) were also better at mind-reading couples they did not know (with correlations across the mind-reading tasks of .32 to .73). This finding suggests that some people are simply better at mind-reading than others, supporting the existence of a social intelligence factor. Determining what exactly makes some people better mind-readers, however, remains a work in progress. There is evidence that better mind-readers are better educated, are more likely to be women than men, have higher IQs, and are more cognitively complex (see Fletcher, 2002; Ickes, 1993). On the other hand, as our analysis shows, it is clear that both situational factors and motivation levels powerfully influence both directional bias and tracking accuracy.

Summary and Conclusions

In this chapter we started with a conundrum – based on research and on plausible theoretical grounds, love seems to be both blind and planted in reality. We discussed three ways of resolving this puzzle. First, biased judgments can still be rational. Second, the accuracy of judgments can be assessed in two independent ways (directional bias and tracking accuracy); thus, perceivers can be both positively biased and accurate. Third, people can be aware of directional bias and welcome it (if it is positive!).

Having prepared the groundwork, we then examined the causes and consequences of both directional bias and tracking accuracy of judgments, looking at the roles of the relationship stage, individual differences, judgment category, and context. We concluded that the research literature supports both evolutionary and social psychological approaches. Finally, we analyzed the research on mind-reading, concluding that people in relationships do remarkably well given the sheer difficulty of the task. However, there are strong individual differences in mind-reading ability for reasons that are not understood well at the present time.

Social psychologists have often commented on the flawed or inaccurate nature of lay social judgments. But consider, for a moment, how many hurdles have to be clambered over in making accurate judgments of other people's personality traits, or of their ongoing emotions and cognitions, in intimate relationship contexts (see Funder, 1995). The awkward conversation (and associated private thoughts and feelings) between Alvy and Annie Hall described at the beginning of the chapter exemplifies the severe difficulties involved. First, behavioral information has to be available (which it often is not). Second, the information (when available) needs to be a reliable, diagnostic indicator of the trait or mental item in question, which is not always the case. People are hard to read – they often feign emotions or opinions in order to curry favor, elicit sympathy, avoid (or advance) sexual activity, and so forth. Third, receivers have to pick up and appropriately use the information. Given that such information is often fleeting and comes packaged among a swarm of related behaviors, this is no easy task. To be effective, this final stage often relies on the perceiver having special local knowledge of the target and/or possessing reasonably high levels of social intelligence.

In short, we are struck not by the inaccuracy of adult human social judgments, but by their accuracy in relationship contexts. The glass can be viewed as either half full or half empty. We view the accuracy glass as half full, given the apparently mundane yet almost miraculous ability of humans to make judgments of intimate others based on a welter of information (or virtually no information at all) while automatically accessing elaborate and complex mental stores of information and theories, often during the course of complicated social interactions. The ability of humans to make such social judgments is, however, not a miracle, but an understandable outcome of an animal that has a powerful brain kitted out by evolutionary forces to function effectively within an intensely social and intimate human landscape.

Referring back to the quote at the beginning of the chapter, it is virtually inconceivable that Shakespeare could be completely wrong about anything. But he was not infallible. Love is in the mind, but it is not always painted blind.

9 Communication and Interaction

Couple communication during conflict – moving beyond conflict – good "negative behaviors" and bad "negative behaviors" – when honest communication is healthy and good management fails – providing and communicating support – can partners be too supportive? – summary and conclusions

> The terms *communication* and *relationship*, although not synonymous, are so entangled that it is difficult to talk about one concept without presuming the other.
>
> Sillars and Vangelisti (2006, p. 331).

Think of the top five factors that cause intimate relationships to be successful. If you are like the students we teach, one of those causes would be "good communication." Indeed, it would be hard to conceive of any perceived cause of successful intimate relationships that has more consensus or seems more obvious. Yet, the extensive scientific investigation has revealed a more puzzling and convoluted account than is captured by the conventional wisdom. To help us begin the scientific journey, imagine a couple who have been married for one year after dating each other for three years:

> George and Mary think they are a great match for each other – they both enjoy outdoor activities, films and traveling, they share similar goals like saving for a house, and they both have close relationships with their family. Lately, however, they have fallen into bickering and arguing. George wants more one-on-one time with Mary who spends a lot of time at work and going out with friends. Mary thinks George should be more understanding and help out more with the household chores, particularly given that she contributes more financially.

The Science of Intimate Relationships, First Edition. Garth Fletcher, Jeffry A. Simpson, Lorne Campbell, and Nickola C. Overall.
© 2013 Garth Fletcher, Jeffry A. Simpson, Lorne Campbell, and Nickola C. Overall.
Published 2013 by Blackwell Publishing Ltd.

The kinds of problems George and Mary face are a reflection of the profound **interdependence** that exists within close relationships (see Chapter 1). George's desires, goals, happiness, and behavior toward Mary depend on Mary's desires, goals, happiness, and behavior (and vice versa). Situations will inevitably arise when George and Mary's interests and desires conflict, such as Mary wanting to dine with friends when George fancies a romantic night together. George might not live up to relationship norms and expectations, such as failing to compensate for Mary's work pressure by helping more at home. George and Mary will also disagree at times and behave hurtfully.

These situations have a powerful influence on relationship satisfaction, mainly because they provide diagnostic information about how partners evaluate each other. If Mary chooses George's invitation of a romantic dinner over going out with her friends, this signals trustworthiness and regard. Conversely, if Mary blithely goes out with her friends then George will be left at home feeling resentful and unvalued. If this latter kind of incident becomes commonplace, George's feelings are likely to be communicated both verbally (e.g. making critical comments) and nonverbally (e.g. reacting with a stony silence to Mary's account of the night's festivities). Their relationship may also begin the slow slide into unhappiness that so often leads to dissolution (see Chapter 12).

Couples confront a variety of problems throughout their relationship, including the amount and quality of time spent together, disputes over money, division of domestic responsibilities, and jealousy, not to mention fraught topics like sex, drugs, and alcohol (Storaasli and Markman, 1990). Not surprisingly, couples who face more frequent relationship problems and conflict are more likely to experience declines in relationship satisfaction and are more likely to break up (Kluwer and Johnson, 2007; Murray *et al.*, 1996; Orbuch *et al.*, 2002). Relationship conflict is also bad news on other fronts. More relationship conflict, for example, is linked to greater depression (Beach *et al.*, 1998) and poorer health (Burman and Margolin, 1992; Kiecolt-Glaser and Newton, 2001; see Chapter 4).

Thus, the way couples negotiate relationship problems has major implications for personal and relationship wellbeing. Indeed, communication difficulties comprise one of the most common and pressing problems couples identify in intimate relationships (Broderick, 1981; Storaasli and Markman, 1990). Relationship therapists also report that dysfunctional communication is the most common complaint they deal with, and is the most damaging and difficult to treat (Geiss and O'Leary, 1981). The difficulty for therapists, and everyone else, is that figuring out what constitutes good versus bad communication is not as easy as it sounds. Indeed, it is the basis for a lot of argument in the scientific field. Consider our fictional couple Mary and George again:

> Mary tries to talk to George about their problems and frankly expresses her thoughts and emotions, even when they are negative. Mary's philosophy is that conflict needs to be dealt with openly and honestly. George, on the other hand, tries hard not to retaliate. He believes that the best way to communicate is to suppress angry thoughts and feelings, compromise, and discuss things in a calm, logical, and positive manner. If you do get angry, best to do something else like go for a run.

George and Mary's styles of communication seem like oil and water when put together. Their different approaches to conflict reflect two competing theoretical explanations postulated by scientists as the best way of communicating when experiencing relationship problems: the **honest communication model** versus the **good management model.**

The honest communication model suggests that couples should openly express their negative feelings and cognitions (albeit in a diplomatic fashion), deal with conflict directly, and never leave problems unresolved. If problems are not dealt with, so goes the common belief, then they will continue to simmer and eventually corrode the relationship.

The good management model, in contrast, posits that the regular and open expression of negative thoughts and feelings has caustic effects on relationships, and that exercising good communication skills involves compromise, restraint, and accommodation. Instead of obsessively rehashing the same problems, couples should understand that some issues cannot be resolved and need to be put on the cognitive backburner.

Both models possess intuitive plausibility but also have weaknesses. This chapter evaluates the evidence for each model, describes what happens to relationships when these differing approaches are adopted by individuals, and discusses when, how, and why good communication or good management might be beneficial or harmful for relationships. First, we analyze findings from the study of communication during conflict discussions. Second, we move beyond conflict to examine the links between communication and cognition, and explore how people manage communication during everyday life. We then discuss how (paradoxically) ostensibly good behaviors can have bad consequences and bad behaviors can have good consequences, and we

*"Since we're both working on the same marriage, I thought
it would be a good idea to get together and compare notes."*

Figure 9.1   *Source:* © 2009 Liza Donnelly and Michael Maslin

look at contexts in which good management fails. Finally, the links between communication and supportive behavior are analyzed.

Couple Communication during Conflict

How do couples manage to maintain satisfying relationships in the face of conflict? One major idea that scientists have run with is that relationship stability and satisfaction is primarily determined by how partners respond to the inevitable conflict and disagreement that emerges over time in many relationship. Thus, clinical researchers in the 1970s began to systematically observe how married couples communicate when discussing relationship problems in the laboratory (Gottman, 1979; Weis & Heyman, 1997). Their goal was to document how unhappy and happy married couples differ in handling communication when difficult problems are discussed, and thus be able to predict which couples are on a trajectory to divorce.

What do communication behaviors predict?

As can be seen in Table 9.1, the simple dichotomy between positive and negative communication behaviors devolves into quite a lot of different kinds of behaviors. Compared to couples who are happy with their relationship, unhappy couples are more likely to criticize and put down their partner, interrupt and invalidate their partner's opinions, and either emotionally or physically withdraw. Unhappy couples are also less likely to propose positive solutions, are less affectionate and attentive, and less likely to express positive affect like humor (for reviews see Gottman, 1998 and Weiss and Heyman, 1997).

This initial work was quickly expanded by employing longitudinal designs to test whether negative communication patterns predict declines in relationship satisfaction or divorce. Longitudinal research is important in determining whether communication patterns cause relationship distress or whether simply being dissatisfied in a relationship causes negative interaction behavior (although, of course, causality could flow in both directions). Karney and Bradbury (1995) conducted a meta-analytic review of 115 longitudinal studies and found that the presence of negative interaction behavior (like hostility, invalidation, and withdrawal) was consistently linked to greater probability of divorce and reduced satisfaction of both partners over time. In contrast, more positive interaction behavior (like constructive problem solving, affection, and humor) predicted higher satisfaction and an increased probability of staying together. Specific studies since this review also report similar findings, but with some important qualifications that we discuss below.

In summary, this body of research supports the intuitions of the pioneers such as John Gottman and Robert Weiss – engaging in critical or demanding communication behavior is associated with dysfunctional relationships, whereas expressing positive affect to soften conflict interactions promotes relationship quality. The standard explanation for the destructive impact of negative communication is that hostile communication undermines problem-solving by eliciting destructive affective and

Table 9.1 Communication behaviors often observed in discussions of relationship problems

Type of communication	Specific behaviors	Behavior description
Hostility	*Put-down:*	A comment intended to hurt, demean, or embarrass the partner
	Criticize:	Hostile statement of unambiguous dislike or disapproval of a specific behavior of the partner
	Mind-read negative:	Statement that infers or assumes a negative attitude or feeling on the part of the other
	Turn off:	Nonverbal gestures that communicate disgust, displeasure, disapproval or disagreement (e.g. rolling eyes, screwing up face, shaking head)
Invalidation	*Disagree:*	Statement of disagreement with partner's opinion
	Deny responsibility:	A statement which conveys "I" or "we" are not responsible for the problem
	Excuse:	Any reason for not performing a behavior
	Non-comply:	Failure to fulfill a request
	Interrupt:	Listener breaks in and disrupts the flow of the other's speech
Constructive problem-solving	*Problem description:*	Describing problem using neutral or friendly tone of voice
	Solution:	Proposing the initiation or increase of a behavior or the termination or reduction in frequency of behavior
	Compromise:	A negotiation of mutually exchanged behaviors
Validation	*Agree:*	Statement of agreement with one's partner
	Approve:	Respondent favors partner's or couple's attributes, actions, or statements
	Accept responsibility:	A statement which conveys "I" or "we" are responsible for this problem
	Comply:	Fulfills request
Facilitation	*Assent:*	Listener says "yeah," nods head to indicate "I'm listening" or to facilitate conversation
	Humor:	Light-hearted humor, not sarcasm
	Mind-read positive:	Statements that infer or assume a positive attitude or feeling on the part of the other
	Positive physical touch:	Affectionate touch, hug
	Attention:	Listener maintains eye contact for at least three seconds
Withdrawal	*Avoid:*	Avoiding or closing off to the other
	No response:	Not responding or contributing to the discussion
	No eye contact:	No or glazed eye contact
	Increasing physical distance:	Moving away from partner, erecting physical barriers (e.g. crossing arms)

Source: These categories and descriptions are derived from those used in the Marital Interaction Coding Scheme, originally developed by Weiss and Summers (1983)

behavioral reactions from the partner, which filter through to future interactions and erode relationship quality. Positive conflict behavior is typically assumed to have the opposite effect by fostering an empathic and rewarding relationship atmosphere (Bradbury and Fincham, 1991; Jacobson and Margolin, 1979). Two central patterns that play a central role in the harmful effects of negative communication support this explanation: **negative reciprocity and demand–withdraw.** We briefly examine these two patterns next.

Destructive patterns of communication

An invidious dyadic pattern discovered by John Gottman and colleagues (Gottman, 1994) is negative reciprocity – when negative behavior by one partner is met with intensified negative behavior by the other. Mary cuttingly remarks that if George cooked more he might also be able to lose some weight. George reciprocates negativity when he retorts "speak for yourself, fatso." A full-blown argument ensues with name-calling and invective liberally sprinkled around.

There are several reasons why negativity spirals upwards during distressed couples' interactions. First, dissatisfied partners are likely to interpret comments as intentionally hurtful (discussed further below). Second, even when George tries to defuse the situation his wounded feelings are likely to leak through into his responses nonverbally, Mary is then likely to attend to the underlying angry tone in George's response, and then continue to respond with hostility. This pattern is consistent with the model of the intimate relationship mind depicted and discussed in Chapter 3. Third, because partners get wrapped up in their own hurt feelings and anger, they find it hard to accept each other's attempts to repair the interaction, such as when one partner apologizes. And, because couples have difficulty exiting the cycle, they get locked into a negative tit-for-tat exchange that stifles problem resolution (see Gottman, 1998).

A second destructive pattern of interaction occurs when critical and demanding communication from the person who wants change is responded to with defensive withdrawal. Research has shown that this demand–withdraw pattern predicts poorer problem resolution and reduced relationship satisfaction over time (see Christensen and Heavey, 1990; Heavey et al., 1995; Heavey et al., 1993). Like our example (Mary demands and George withdraws), early investigations of heterosexual couples suggested that women tend to do more of the demanding and men are more likely to withdraw. This stereotypical pattern also appears across cultures, such as Brazil, Italy, Taiwan, and the United States (Christensen et al., 2006) and is strongly associated with declines in marital satisfaction.

However, the kind of problems discussed in laboratory settings, and perhaps those in daily relationship life, are often those that women want action on . . . now! If male issues are discussed, it turns out the roles are reversed; men demand and women withdraw (Klinetob and Smith, 1996). Furthermore, when husbands are more demanding, their wives (oddly) experience a relative increase in satisfaction over time, perhaps because they interpret their husband's engagement in the discussion as a sign of greater commitment (Heavey et al., 1993, 1995). Withdrawal, on the other hand, is consistently associated with declines in relationship satisfaction in both US and European samples (e.g. Bodenmann *et al.*, 1998).

The negative-reciprocity and demand–withdrawal communication patterns capture dyadic processes – how couples respond to each other – and illustrate why negative behaviors like hostility, invalidation, and withdrawal lead to declines in satisfaction. Criticizing, blaming, and pressuring the partner to change evoke both hostile reactions and defensive withdrawal from the partner. These cyclical exchanges impede problem resolution and spread like a virus to interactions more broadly, undermining intimacy, closeness, and, ultimately, the stability of the relationship.

What implications do these findings have for evaluating Mary's honest communication and George's good management approach to conflict? Generally, if Mary's open, direct method is accompanied by hostility and criticism it is likely to be corrosive for the relationship, although women seem to be happier when they are on the receiving end of honest communication than men. When George's good management approach involves avoidance and withdrawal, this turns out to be not so salubrious – withdrawal is one of the strongest predictors of dissatisfaction and dissolution. Furthermore, initial cross-cultural evidence suggests that these outcomes will occur regardless of whether George and Mary are from the United States, Australia, Canada, New Zealand, Europe, Asia, or South America. Nevertheless, the findings highlight the point that the impact of negative (or positive) communication will depend on how that behavior is responded to by the partner, including how the partner interprets the meaning of that behavior – a topic we turn to next.

Moving beyond Conflict

In the 1990s scientists expanded the study of communication beyond conflict resolution. First, attention moved toward the study of cognition in communication (see Chapter 3). Second, it became apparent that communication matters a lot when couples are faced with a variety of relationship-threatening events (e.g. illness, stress, work problems) and not just in situations of overt conflict. We discuss each aspect in turn.

The links between communication behavior and cognition

As we described in Chapter 3, the explanations individuals generate for relationship events, including their relationship problems, are linked to relationship satisfaction. To review the standard finding, less satisfied intimates tend to attribute negative partner behavior to undesirable personality traits and intentions (e.g. he is uncaring and selfish), but write off positive partner behavior to unstable external factors (e.g. he is having a rare good day). Thus, George is likely to explain Mary's late arrival to dinner as yet another indication that he is unimportant to her, yet attribute her early arrival to her desire to be with her friends (and not him). Moreover, George's tendency to jump to negative conclusions about Mary's intentions is likely to produce a decline in their relationship quality (see Karney and Bradbury, 2000).

Cognition and communication are intertwined. It is, of course, quite natural to blame your partner in the course of a heated discussion (covertly or overtly). However, consistently blaming your partner turns out to be one of the most pernicious attributions it is possible to make, promoting negative trains of thought and destructive communication patterns (Fletcher and Thomas, 2000). Moreover, because of the way attributions work, your partner's attempts to be positive will be undercut if you are already unhappy. Dissatisfied intimates tend not to notice their partner's positive messages (Waldinger and Schulz, 2006), and, if they do register, they are often written off in a negative fashion via attributions as we described above.

In a nutshell, negative mind-reading lies at the heart of negative reciprocity. People who are unhappy with their relationships tend to blame their partners for relationship problems, which leads to snide remarks and hostility. Hostility does not have to be verbal. Rolling one's eyes or staring stonily into the distance present powerful non-verbal signals. Hostile communication, in turn, often elicits defensive reactions from the partner, which are readily interpreted as intentionally nasty, escalating into anger and blame, and perhaps kicking off a vicious cycle that is hard to break. In contrast, even when discussing relationship problems, happy couples are more likely to ignore their partner's negative behavior or to respond to it in a benign fashion. They prevent mudslinging interactions from occurring by soothing one another, and they use humor to defuse situations. And one of the principal reasons happy couples can do this is because they are less likely to interpret insensitive or unkind comments about specific problems as a personal attack.

Exploring the links between cognition and behavior has also provided insight into how personality dispositions influence communication and interaction. For example, as outlined in Chapter 5, people high in attachment anxiety obsess about acceptance and half expect they will be rejected. Because they are constantly on the lookout for rejection, anxious intimates are more likely to perceive their partner's actions, such as failure to reciprocate a cuddle, as intentionally rejecting. Furthermore, this attribution bias leads anxious individuals to react with greater hostility and anger during problem-solving discussions (Simpson *et al.*, 1996) and these destructive reactions escalate conflict during daily life (Campbell *et al.*, 2005). And, consistent with the above communication patterns, hostile and defensive behavior arising from expectations of rejection evoke anger and dissatisfaction in the partner (Downey *et al.*, 1998). This anxiety trap is shown in Figure 9.2, with Mary's behavior inducing anger and

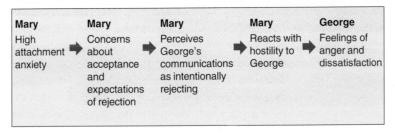

Figure 9.2   Mary, George, and attachment anxiety

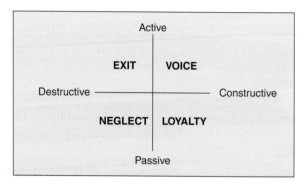

Figure 9.3   The exit-voice-loyalty-neglect typology
Source: From Rusbult *et al.*, 1986a; © 1986 American Psychological Association, Inc.

dissatisfaction in her partner George, which then confirms Mary's expectations about acceptance and rejection. In short, insecure attachment in only one partner can undermine relationship satisfaction and stability in both partners (also see below). Interdependence is assuredly a mixed blessing in intimate relationships.

Responding to relationship threats: accommodation and risk regulation

In an influential model of relationship functioning, Caryl Rusbult and colleagues (Rusbult *et al.*, 1982) laid out four typical responses that people have when feeling dissatisfied in their relationship. As shown in Figure 9.3, these responses fall along two dimensions: whether they are destructive or constructive for the relationship and whether they are active or passive.

Exit includes active responses that are destructive for the relationship, such as ending or threatening to terminate the relationship, and abusing, criticizing, or derogating the partner (e.g. "When my partner behaves in an unpleasant or thoughtless manner, I do something equally unpleasant in return").

Voice incorporates constructive and active responses such as attempting to improve conditions, discussing problems and suggesting solutions, and engaging in efforts to alter problematic self or partner behavior (e.g. "When my partner is upset and says something mean, I try to patch things up and solve the problem").

Loyalty consists of pro-relationship responses such as passively waiting and hoping for improvement, forgiving and forgetting partner offenses, and supporting and maintaining faith in the partner in the face of hurtful actions ("When my partner is angry with me, I hang in there and wait for my partner's mood to change").

Neglect involves passive destructive responses such as allowing the relationship to deteriorate by ignoring or spending less time with the partner, avoiding discussing any problems, and criticizing the partner regarding unrelated issues ("When my partner is rude or inconsiderate, I ignore the whole thing and try to spend less time with my partner").

As evident in these descriptions, this typology captures many of the overt communication behaviors examined in couples' conflict discussions described above. However, the typology also describes behavior that might circumvent overt conflict, such as loyally holding one's tongue to minimize tension and forgiving and forgetting. Such loyal behavior is frequent in everyday life but difficult to measure in the laboratory. Even withdrawal and discussion avoidance – reactions that have been reliably assessed in recorded interactions and linked to important relationship outcomes – are likely to be more prevalent in everyday life than in the laboratory where couples are specifically instructed to discuss their problems.

Nevertheless, the results from research using this typology measuring what happens in everyday life are consistent with laboratory-based approaches (Rusbult *et al.*, 1986a, 1986b; Rusbult *et al.*, 1991). For example, to examine the responses that occur naturally in everyday life, Drigotas *et al.* (1995) asked 28 couples to complete a diary for two weeks during which they recorded every dissatisfying incident that occurred in their relationships. For each dissatisfying event, participants ticked off on a checklist how they and their partner responded. The items on the checklist assessed voice (e.g. talked about problem), exit (e.g. said/did something hurtful), neglect (e.g. ignored partner or problem), and loyalty (e.g. forgave partner, forgot about it). For each behavior, participants also indicated the degree to which their own and their partner's responses were destructive versus constructive for the problem and the relationship. Drigotas *et al.* (1995) found that exit and neglect responses had negative consequences, whereas voice responses were perceived as constructive.

Exit, voice, loyalty, and neglect are often combined to assess a pattern of positive responding that represents the opposite of the negative reciprocity and demand–withdraw patterns identified in the laboratory – a construct termed **accommodation**. Accommodation is the tendency to inhibit destructive exit and neglect responses when faced with negative partner behavior and instead react constructively with voice and loyalty. Thus, in conflict situations, and when partners behave badly, intimates are faced with a dilemma – do you reduce vulnerability by attacking your partner or distancing yourself from the relationship, or do you advance the longer-term motive of protecting and sustaining the relationship (see Rusbult and Van Lange, 2003)?

Accommodation is frankly hard to do in the face of (apparently) hurtful partner behavior (see Chapter 3). You may need to count to 10, crush the immediate response, up to and including physical retribution, and respond in a way that transforms your initial protective impulse into a more controlled effort to sustain the relationship. Perhaps not surprisingly, strong self-control, and the ability to override self-protection concerns are likely to lead to accommodation in response to negative partner actions (Finkel and Campbell, 2001).

Regulating risk Sandra Murray and John Holmes have extended this important framework by outlining how and when self protection versus relationship promotion goals might be managed. Their **risk regulation model** (Murray *et al.*, 2006), and a stack of supporting evidence, suggest that accommodation poses substantial risks. Despite the costs to the relationship, devaluing and withdrawing from the partner (exit and neglect) allows intimates to minimize the risks of the partner continuing to hurt the self. However, accommodating with loyalty and voice may intensify subsequent hurt and rejection if the partner is not receptive to (or does not even notice) such valiant repair attempts. Thus, when George withdraws, Mary can no longer hurl biting comments at him. On the other hand, if George tries to reduce conflict by being affectionate and Mary continues to criticize him, George's hurt becomes accentuated.

Because of these risks, relationship promotion goals more or less require individuals to be sure that their partner will be responsive to accommodative efforts. Those who retain little confidence in their partner's responsiveness are likely to engage in self-protective derogation and withdrawal, whereas those who solidly believe in their partner's commitment and regard will feel safe to enact relationship promotion goals. Examining couples' daily interactions over a three-week period, Murray *et al.* (2003a) found that intimates who were insecure about how much their partners valued them were more likely to behave negatively on days following reported conflict and poor partner behavior. In contrast, individuals who trusted in the continued regard of their partner responded to feelings of rejection by increasing their closeness to their partner the following day.

Murray *et al.* (2006) identified self-esteem as a key variable accounting for the tendency to self-protect within conflict-related interactions. Based on repeated experiences of interpersonal rejection, individuals who have chronic feelings of low self-worth possess pessimistic views regarding the likelihood that others will accept and value the self (Leary and Baumeister, 2000). Accordingly, people with low self-esteem perceive that their romantic partners and family members evaluate them more negatively than they actually do (DeHart *et al.*, 2003; Murray *et al.*, 2000). These chronic insecurities cause individuals to adopt a blanket self-protective mode. Not believing that their partners will be responsive, low self-esteem individuals respond more destructively to their partner's criticism, or when they believe their partner perceives a problem in their relationship (Bellavia and Murray, 2003; Murray *et al.*, 2008). For the same reasons, individuals who are sensitive to rejection and high in attachment anxiety also react to problematic relationship interactions with greater hostility and withdrawal (Overall and Sibley, 2009a, 2009b; see Chapter 5).

These dynamics provide yet another illustration of how cognition and behavior are intricately intertwined. The basic processes are shown in Figure 9.4. First, people enter relationship interactions with beliefs regarding whether their partner will be accepting versus rejecting – beliefs at the core of self-esteem and attachment security. These expectations are activated and guide responses in threatening interactions. As shown in the top half of the figure, when insecurities lead intimates to expect their partners will be generally rejecting and hurtful, the goal of self-protection wins out. This goal incorporates cognitive strategies, such as devaluing the partner and the relationship, and behavioral strategies such as exit and neglect. Those who trust in their partner's continued acceptance and regard, however, are more able to adopt relationship-promotion goals that motivate connection and closeness with the partner and more accommodating behavioral responses (see the bottom half of figure).

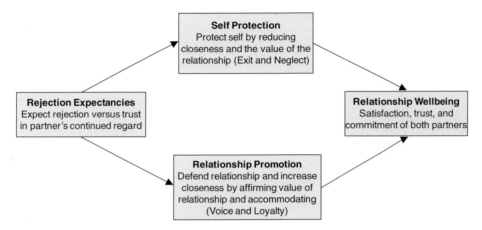

Figure 9.4 Risk regulation and accommodation in response to threatening relationship events
Source: Adapted from Murray *et al.*, 2006 and Murray and Holmes, 2009; © 2006, 2009 American Psychological Association

These different pathways lead to different relationship outcomes (see right side of Figure 9.4). More accommodation is positively associated with concurrent measures of relationship satisfaction (e.g. Rusbult *et al.*, 1991) and forecasts greater satisfaction and stability across time (Rusbult *et al.*, 1998). In addition, scientists have begun to identify mechanisms through which relationships are enhanced by accommodative behavior. For example, accommodation eases problematic interactions by maintaining feelings of acceptance and intimacy (Overall and Sibley, 2008). And, because it communicates loyalty to the relationship instead of ducking for cover and protecting the self, accommodation predicts increases in the partner's trust and relationship commitment over time (Wieselquist *et al.*, 1999). In contrast, as surveyed above, self-protective exit and neglect tend to do the opposite.

Regulating partners As relationships develop, your partner's behavior and characteristics inevitably start to grate on you, from squeezing the toothpaste tube at the wrong end to insensitivity. As previously discussed, people will sometimes swallow hard and try to ignore the behavior (accommodate), but they also often attempt to change the partner. One study reported that 98% of individuals recalled trying to change their partner in some way in the prior six months (Overall *et al.*, 2006).

Consistent with our analysis in Chapter 3, an innovative set of studies by Overall *et al.* (2006) found that the extent to which people worked on their partners to change their ways was motivated by the extent to which they perceived their partners as matching their own ideal standards – the more that individuals perceived their partners as failing to live up their own expectations, the more they tried to influence their partner. By and large, however, individuals reported disappointing results in their attempts to

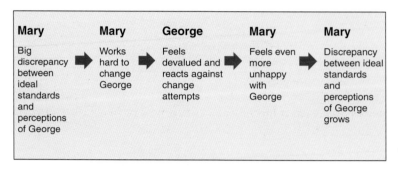

Figure 9.5   Mary, George, and the regulation trap

change their partners. Moreover, the harder people worked to change their partners, the more the discrepancy between their perceptions and their standards grew, and the more dissatisfied people became (especially if the attempts were seen as dismal failures). Picking up another theme explored in Chapters 2 and 3, this research found evidence that the cause of these ill effects was the powerful message sent by such regulation attempts that the approval and acceptance of the partner was waning. Trying to regulate your partner to improve your relationship can become a negative trap. This regulation trap is shown in Figure 9.5.

Summary

To summarize, the **exit-voice-neglect-loyalty** typology and associated research have extended our understanding in several ways. By examining the competing goals underlying communication behavior – do you protect the self from rejection or proactively maintain the relationship – we can now explain why some people (e.g. those low in self-esteem and high in attachment anxiety) behave destructively within conflict situations. We can also tentatively explain why communication influences relationship wellbeing, including the fostering or waning of trust and commitment. Finally, it is clear that the way individuals respond to one another is central to understanding how communication is linked to relationship functioning.

Generally, the work on accommodation seems to support a good management approach to communication. It looks as though George might be right – the best way to respond to conflict is to compromise, talk about the problem, give the partner the benefit of the doubt, and maintain inner confidence that the relationship can only get better. However, the story is not this simple, and we take a lurch into non-intuitive territory.

Good "Negative" Behaviors and Bad "Negative" Behaviors

Let's start with a puzzle. A handful of studies have found that negative communication predicts relative increases in relationship satisfaction across time (e.g. Cohan and

Bradbury, 1997; Gottman and Krokoff, 1989; Heavey *et al.*, 1993, 1995; Karney and Bradbury, 1997); yes we said *increases*, the reverse of the standard finding that negative communication is destructive. For example, as described above, Heavey *et al.* (1993) found that when husbands blamed their partners and pressured them for change, wives reported greater satisfaction one year later. Similarly, over a four-year period, Karney and Bradbury (1997) found that, although satisfaction generally declined across time, greater hostility and criticism by the female partner predicted by with more positive trajectories of relationship satisfaction for both couple members. What is going on here?

The key to deciphering these non-intuitive findings is provided by the distinction between active and passive strategies in the exit-voice-loyalty-neglect typology (see Figure 9.3). Both voice and exit involve the individual actively addressing and attempting to solve the problem, whereas loyalty and neglect are both passive responses. Notably, these odd effects described above have been found when examining negative behaviors that are active and direct, such as criticism, hostility, and blame. Other research has shown that passive behavior even though it is positive, like using humor to minimize conflict or being loyal and waiting for things to improve, is associated with decreasing relationship satisfaction over time (Cohan and Bradbury, 1997; Gottman and Krokoff, 1989), and is less effective at solving the problem than active voice-type responses (Drigotas *et al.*, 1995; Overall *et al.*, 2010). Thus, active can trump passive, even when active is "negative" and passive is "positive."

One explanation for these perplexing findings is that expressing anger and hostility clearly communicates the nature and severity of the problem, motivates partners to bring about change, and, therefore, leads to more successful problem resolution. Positive loyal responses, in contrast, may reduce conflict in the short term, but leave the problem unaddressed (Holmes and Murray, 1996). Supporting this explanation, recent research has found that being demanding and derogating the partner is likely to generate partner change over time (Overall *et al.*, 2009). Moreover, in this research, active constructive behavior, such as directly discussing causes and solutions, was associated with greater change in targeted problems over time, whereas loyalty-type responses, such as using positive affect to soften conflict, failed to produce the desired changes.

Loyal responses might have limited payoff because the targeted partners remain blithely unaware of any problem. Returning to the diary study described above, Drigotas *et al.* (1995) found that, compared to voice, exit, and neglect, loyal acts often went unnoticed by the partner. This is not surprising given that loyalty involves unobservable cognitive effort (e.g. forgiving and forgetting) and restraining overt responses (e.g. resisting self-interested or retaliatory impulses and letting the partner have his/her way). However, because it often goes unnoticed, passive constructive behavior will often have limited impact on the problem, unfortunately leaving loyal intimates feeling even more undervalued and disconnected from their partner (Overall *et al.*, 2010).

Do these findings then suggest that honest communication, no matter how delivered, is the best way to go? Not really. While a critical blaming approach might prompt greater change in the partner, the well-established patterns of negative reciprocity and demand–withdraw suggest that this approach will nevertheless elicit hostility and defensive reactions in the partner. These destructive effects are unlikely to be fleeting,

and the positive changes that are produced by active communication may counterbal-
ance – but not necessarily reverse – the negative impact of these behaviors. Thus, the
most productive way of managing relationship problems may involve using active
strategies that also communicate care and regard, such as directly discussing problems
and suggesting solutions, as long as the message is not gift-wrapped to the point that
it appears as if the communicator does not greatly care whether the problem is fixed
or not (see Overall *et al.*, 2009).

The inconsistencies in the literature, and the fact that all communicative strategies
have their costs and benefits, have produced a sea change in this research area. Instead
of focusing on what behaviors are bad (or good), scientists are increasingly examining
how communication influences relationship satisfaction and stability, such as by motivating the partner to change or reducing trust and felt regard. Similarly, the costs and
benefits of honest communication and good management are likely to depend on other
demands that partners are struggling with, and the type and severity of the problems
couples are dealing with. Indeed, groundbreaking work shows the best communication
approach to adopt will often depend on these types of contextual variables, as we shall
see in the next section.

When Honest Communication is Healthy and Good Management Fails

Stress is . . . well, stressful

Karney and Bradbury's (1995) vulnerability model suggests that enduring vulnerabilities, like low self-esteem and attachment insecurity, and stressful events external to the
relationship, such as work-related difficulties, will influence (i) how individuals react
to relationship problems, and (ii) how different patterns of communication influence
relationship quality. For example, diary studies examining daily stress levels have found
that couples' interactions are more likely to be negative on days when one partner is
experiencing greater stress, such as having arguments in the workplace (Bolger *et al.*,
1989; Halford *et al.*, 1992). Thus, stress limits the ability to negotiate conflict in a
constructive manner, in part because it depletes the resources necessary to control
hostile affect and behavior (Finkel and Campbell, 2001). Moreover, partners who are
more stressed perceive more problems in their relationship, blame their partner more
for problems, and evaluate their relationship less positively (Neff and Karney, 2004;
Tesser and Beach, 1998).

As we noted in Chapter 4, when faced with a stressful event, the brain and the body
work in concert using what is termed the **hypothalamic–pituitary–adrenal (HPA)**
axis to generate fight or flight hormones like **cortisol**, which is similar to **epinephrine**,
but has much longer-term effects. Indeed, for this reason, it is a principal marker of
long-term stress in intimate relationships. Not surprisingly, therefore, more negative
communication patterns when resolving conflict are linked to the production of higher
levels of cortisol as measured in saliva (Powers *et al.*, 2006).

The impact of different communication behaviors is also modified by the additional burdens with which intimates are contending. When Mary is under work pressure she is more likely to blame George for their problems and is less able to accommodate. Moreover, both Mary and George's relationship evaluations might be more negatively affected by hostile and defensive reactions to conflict. Neff and Karney (2009), for example, found that when individuals were experiencing greater stress their global relationship evaluations were more affected by dissatisfying relationship events, such as the way disagreements were resolved, time spent together, or low partner support. Alternatively, echoing the positive implications of honest communication presented above, perhaps it is exactly when partners are taxed and confront severe problems that conflict engagement is most helpful. Supporting this idea, Cohan and Bradbury (1997) found that, when faced with aversive life stressors, wives' expression of anger during problem-solving discussions predicted greater relationship satisfaction 18 months later, whereas more humor by husbands predicted greater probability of divorce.

Why Adopting One Default Strategy is Not a Good Idea

These latter findings highlight the importance of contextual factors in determining when honest communication will be beneficial and good management might fail. In the context of high external demands it becomes more important to resolve relationship difficulties and, thus, employ direct communication that produces change, even if this means expressing negative affect like anger. Soft positive strategies, like humor, can deflect the problem but hinder resolution and, when enacted by the partner, might convey that he or she is not invested in the relationship (but see Campbell et al., 2008). The same outcome is likely when the relationship problem itself is serious and therefore resolution is critical – an assertion supported by a series of recent studies conducted by James McNulty, which we discuss next.

As argued above, hostile communication might lead to positive outcomes because it motivates the partner to change and therefore helps resolve relationship issues. However, this should be particularly true for couples who face severe problems that need a tough love approach, but not true for those couples whose minor difficulties do not warrant a sledgehammer approach. Consistently, McNulty and Russell (2010) have found that blaming, commanding, and rejecting the partner during problem-solving discussions predicted more stable and satisfying relationships for those couples who were initially dealing with more serious problems. We present their findings in Figure 9.6, which plots changes in relationship satisfaction across 1.5 years for more or less negative behavior within problem-solving discussions, depending on whether the problems couples were facing were less versus more serious (adapted from McNulty, 2010). You will notice that regardless of negativity and problem severity, couples generally reported declines in satisfaction. Unfortunately, this is a standard finding – relationship satisfaction tends to wane over time. The amount of decline in this study, however, depended on a combination of negativity and problem severity.

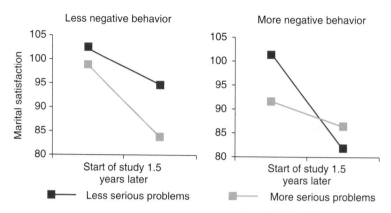

Figure 9.6 The impact of negative behavior and problem seriousness on marital happiness
Source: Adapted from McNulty, 2010; © 2010 J. McNulty. SAGE Publications, Inc.

Consider the change in satisfaction for couples who exhibited low levels of negative behavior in their discussion (see left panel of Figure 9.6). The steepest decline in relationship satisfaction was for those couples who had very serious problems. Further analyses revealed that this was because they experienced growing problems over time. In contrast, when examining couples who had severe problems but engaged in high levels of negative behavior (see the right panel), these couples had more stable levels of relationship satisfaction, and this was because their problems did not worsen over time. In contrast, couples who engaged in more blame and criticism, but were not threatened by severe problems, suffered growing problems and, in turn, declines in satisfaction across time. In sum, negative behaviors that specifically represent direct efforts to get the problem changed are good for relationships, but only when something really problematic needs to be addressed.

Likewise, a positive approach, such as generating positive and benign attributions and forgiving each other, should only be beneficial if partners cease their problematic behavior and problems are resolved. Indeed, McNulty and colleagues (2008) demonstrated that the positive attribution pattern typically associated with happy couples (described above) led to relative increases in satisfaction only when couples were dealing with relatively minor problems. When couples were facing severe problems, positive attributions actually predicted greater declines in satisfaction precisely because problems continued to worsen over time. Similarly, McNulty (2008) found that forgiveness maintained satisfaction only when partners seemed to deserve it. When intimates were more forgiving to partners who often behaved negatively, relationship problems continued to grow and satisfaction persistently declined (also see McNulty and Karney, 2004, and Chapter 12).

This groundbreaking research indicates that it is the ability to adjust communication strategies and behaviors to the contextual demands that is crucial for maintaining close and successful relationships. Partners who adopt either the honest communication or the good management approach as a consistent default strategy, regardless of the situation are likely to (i) do irreparable damage to their relationship when honest and heated communication is disproportionate to the severity of the issue, or (ii) fail to overcome relationship hurdles because smothering negative feelings and actions means the issues are not addressed.

The analysis so far illustrates the complexity and subtlety of the process and concept of communication. Almost everybody in relationships routinely, and often automatically, controls the expression of negative emotions and cognitions, up to and including ruthlessly repressing them (as we indicated in Chapter 3). This seems to be fine and dandy when relationships are running smoothly, but it may stunt improvement when the relationship needs work. The trick is how and when to control this process. When couples need to be in conflict-resolution mode, the expression of anger (within bounds) appears to be beneficial. In this context, anger communicates to the partner that "I am not a doormat;" "this is important to me, so listen to what I am saying;" "I care enough about the relationship to bother exhibiting my concerns;" and "will you PLEASE alter your behavior!" The result: partners and problems are more likely to change for the better.

On the other hand, the expression of even mild anger and irritation in contexts when the partner needs support is corrosive. Consider, for example, how you might react if you were desperately and obviously tired, you had an important and difficult meeting the next day, and your partner exhibited irritation (rather than sympathy or support) when you asked him or her for some advice. In this context, the expression of any negative affect communicates that "I don't care for you," "I do not love you," and "I cannot be counted on when the chips are down." We now turn to the link between communication and interaction within these kinds of situations – situations that may play a crucial role in the way relationships wax and wane over time.

Providing and Communicating Support

Support buffers individuals from the impact of negative events on their mental and physical health. For example, greater spousal support is associated with lower depression in response to a range of stressful life events, including financial problems, illness, work issues, and the transition to parenthood (see Gardner and Cutrona, 2004). Indeed, marital partners are the primary and most important source of support for most individuals (e.g. Beach *et al.*1993; Wan *et al.*, 1996). And, people across gender and cultures expect that their intimate partners will be supportive when needed and they (reasonably) view this support as a critical function of relationships (Burleson, 2003; Cutrona, 1996).

Just like the work we described earlier on communication, researchers initially studied and catalogued how people support one another in intimate relationships. To accomplish this task, couples typically have two conversations: each person playing the role of the support recipient in one discussion (discussing their own personal issue) and the role of support provider in the other (discussing their partner's issue or difficulty). Table 9.2 describes the typical kinds of behaviors displayed by support providers during such interactions.

These support behaviors can be categorized into two broad types. **Nurturant support** captures efforts to comfort or console, without direct efforts to solve the problem, including expressing care, love, and concern (emotional support), validating

Table 9.2 Common communication behaviors in discussions of personal problems

Type of support	*Support behaviors*
nurturant	
Emotional support	• Expresses love and affection • Provides reassurance and comfort • Expresses sorrow or regret for the partner's distress • Communicates understanding and empathy of the situation
Esteem support	• Compliments and emphasizes the partner's abilities • Provides encouragement and comments positively regarding efforts and progress in coping with the issue • Expresses agreement with the partner's perspective on the situation • Tries to alleviate the partner's negative feelings by highlighting barriers to change, external causes of problem, and difficulties in resolving problems to reduce self-blame, derogation, and feelings of failure
Action-facilitating	
Information support	• Offers advice, ideas and suggests actions • Asks questions, searches for causes, and generates solutions or options • Provides detailed information, facts, or news about the situation or about skills needed to deal with the situation • Provides perspective and clarifies the situation to positively reframe, offers alternative courses of action, and provides insight
Tangible support	• Offers or agrees to join in action to reduce stress/problem • Offers or agrees to perform a task or do something that will help • Offers or agrees to take over one or more of the partner's responsibilities while the partner is under stress • Expresses willingness to help
Negative	• Criticizes or blames the partner • Expresses negative affect (e.g. anger, irritation, displeasure, frustration) • Rejects and invalidates partner's point of view • Insists or demands that the partner adopt his/her approach to situation • Minimizes or maximizes the scope of the problem • Is inattentive or uninterested in the problem

Source: Adapted from Overall *et al.* (2010)

the partner, and encouraging confidence that the partner can cope with the problem (esteem support). **Action-facilitating support** is intended to directly assist, including offering information and advice about how to manage the problem (informational support) and providing resources and engaging in activities to help the individual manage the stressful event (tangible support).

Of course, partners can also respond negatively when their partners need support, such as criticizing and blaming the partner, minimizing the problem, and demanding the adoption of their approach to the problem. Thus, the behaviors listed in Table 9.2 can be helpful or distinctly unhelpful. A word of caution here – even the positive forms of support may not work as intended.

Relationship satisfaction and support

In general, intimates who are more satisfied provide more positive forms of support – the nurturant and action-facilitating kind – and exhibit fewer negative behaviors when discussing an issue their partner is facing (e.g. Lawrence *et al.*, 2008; Pasch and Bradbury, 1998; Saitzyk *et al.*, 1997). Longitudinal studies also indicate that support behavior produces changes in relationship functioning. Pasch and Bradbury (1998) and Cobb *et al.* (2001) found that when women behaved negatively within support-related discussions, relationships were less satisfying and more likely to end one to two years later.

Importantly, studies that have examined couples' communication during both conflict and support discussions have found that the way couples support each other influences relationship wellbeing above and beyond how couples interact during conflict (Julien *et al.*, 2003; Pasch and Bradbury, 1998). Furthermore, a recent study measuring support and conflict behavior across time revealed that poor support in laboratory discussions predicted more negative conflict interactions one year later, but not vice versa (Sullivan *et al.*, 2010). Thus, support interactions are not just a function of how couples deal with relationship problems, but are important in their own right and can promote or undermine conflict resolution.

Support behaviors should positively influence relationship wellbeing because they comfort or help solve the recipient's dilemma. Indeed, many studies have examined what types of support determine the extent to which recipients feel genuinely helped and supported during or after an interaction. Greater levels of both nurturant and action-facilitating support have been associated with greater perceived support, whereas the more negative variety of support attempts (e.g. "for heaven's sake pull your socks up") is, not surprisingly, associated with the partner being perceived as unhelpful and unsupportive (Collins and Feeney, 2000; Cutrona and Suhr, 1992; Overall *et al.*, 2010; Verhofstadt *et al.*, 2005). Feeling supported during observed interactions also leads to more positive outcomes for recipients, such as improved mood and self-esteem (Collins and Feeney, 2000; Feeney, 2004) and greater relationship quality (Overall *et al.*, 2010). Moreover, by tracking couples at multiple times over a three-year period, Conger *et al.* (1999) found that more positive support behavior predicted less emotional distress in the recipients over time.

What recipients of support do, think, and feel counts

Importantly, partners who need support are not passive recipients, but are active participants in the interaction process (Barbee and Cunningham, 1995). For example, the degree to which partners provide support depends on how they are approached. Intimates who directly seek support in a constructive fashion are likely to garner greater and more positive forms of support from their partner. In contrast, indirect negative appeals, such as sulking or hinting, or direct appeals laced with accusations or the nonverbal equivalent of "you are a jerk," not surprisingly, tend to elicit distinctively unhelpful responses (Collins and Feeney, 2000; Pasch et al., 1997). Consequently, negative forms of seeking support lead to lower feelings of support and predict more relationship distress over time (Overall et al., 2010; Pasch and Bradbury, 1998; Pasch et al., 1997).

The needs of the support recipient also play a role. Cutrona et al. (2007) found that partners and relationships were evaluated more positively when support was well matched to the recipient's prior behavior. Specifically, when disclosing emotional reactions to a stressor (e.g. "I feel so upset, and it just seems so unfair"), recipients were more satisfied and judged their partner's support as more effective when emotional support, like reassurance and empathy, was provided. In contrast, support that failed to match such an expression of need, such as providing information and advice, led to negative evaluations of the partner and the relationship.

Providing effective support for one's partner is also difficult because people differ in their appreciation of different types of support (e.g. Cutrona et al., 1997; Dehle and Landers, 2005). Taking an innovative approach, Simpson et al. (2007) compared the degree to which securely attached versus avoidant intimates were soothed in response to nurturant and action-facilitating support (see Chapter 5). Secure participants, whose developmental histories involve sensitive and emotionally responsive support from caregivers, were more visibly calmed when their partners provided greater emotional support. In contrast, intimates high in attachment avoidance, whose rejection experiences in childhood automatically produce discomfort with emotional closeness and support, were more calmed by instrumental support.

Reflecting a theme, that by now is sounding commonplace, people's reactions to different types of support also depend on their global relationship evaluations (see Chapter 3). People who are more satisfied in their relationship perceive their partner to be more supportive and helpful, regardless of the type and amount of support provided (Collins and Feeney, 2000; Dehle and Landers, 2005; Julien et al., 2003). Presumably, more satisfied intimates trust that their partner is intending to be helpful, regardless of whether they are actually helping. Furthermore, when people are happy in their relationship they are likely to disregard negative unsupportive behavior as unintentional and driven by external elements of the situation. In contrast, negative behaviors fit the schemas of those who are unhappy in their relationships. Demonstrating this exact pattern, Frazier et al. (2003) found that kidney transplant patients whose partners were unsupportive, for example, refusing to talk and showing little concern about the situation, were more depressed one year post-transplant. This was true, however, only for those patients who started off with low relationship satisfaction. Patients who were initially satisfied with their relationship were not as badly affected by their partners' failure to provide support.

In sum, the evidence indicates that nurturant and action-facilitating support have both immediate and long-term benefits for the individual and the relationship. In addition, this finding is similar across cultures (Burleson, 2003). However, specific types of positive behavior will not always be supportive or lead to benefits for the recipient. Instead, as with communication in conflict situations, the impact of specific types of support communication will depend on the context, including the type and amount of support the recipient desires and the general atmosphere of the relationship.

Can partners be too supportive?

Thus far, the evidence we have canvassed assumes that the more nurturant or action-facilitating support dispensed, the more supported recipients will feel. But, more is not always better. Cutrona (1996), for example, compared recipients' reports of the support they generally received from their partner with the support their partner actually enacted during a standard laboratory interaction. Not surprisingly, intimates were not very enthused when their partner provided less support than they expected. However, recipients also reported dissatisfaction when their partner provided more support than they expected. Indeed, Brock and Lawrence (2009) found that receiving more emotional, informational, or tangible support than desired was more detrimental to relationship wellbeing than receiving less support than desired.

Why is getting too much support a bad thing? Several explanations are plausible. Perhaps it reduces self-esteem because it weakens the recipients' belief that they have the ability to cope with their problems (Fisher et al., 1982). Or, perhaps it increases feelings of dependence and indebtedness (Newsom, 1999), which subsequently increases perceptions of inequity. In support of this last possibility, Gleason et al.(2003) found that intimates reported greater depression, anxiety, and anger on days when they received support but did not reciprocate by providing support for their partner.

Overall, then, supportive communication can produce unintended personal costs, including drops in competence and self-esteem and feelings of inequity. Because of these costs, Bolger et al. (2000) imaginatively hypothesized that the best type of support might be invisible to the recipient. Bolger and colleagues postulated two types of **invisible support**. One form is when the support is outside the recipient's awareness, such as George taking care of unexpected domestic chores without telling Mary. A second form is when the support offered is not interpreted as overt support by the recipient, such as when George tries to help by talking about his own difficulties in similar situations. In both cases, George's behavior may well help Mary cope, but because it is not recognized by Mary as support *per se*, it should not incur the costs of Mary feeling inadequate or that the relationship is inequitable.

To assess whether invisible support circumvents the costs of receiving support, Bolger et al. (2000) examined daily levels of support given and received during a

35-day period when one partner was preparing to take the New York State Bar Examination. Stressed intimates reported greater levels of depression and anxiety when they reported receiving emotional support from their partners. In contrast, recipients coped relatively well when their partners reported providing support but the support was simply not recorded by the recipient as occurring – that is, when the partner's support seemed to be invisible.

Invisible support seems like it is a tough act to pull off. However, recent research by Howland and Simpson (2010) identified specific types of behaviors in laboratory discussions that were supportive and helpful but more or less invisible. They counted indirect, conversation-like support that draws the focus away from the recipient's problem and distress, by using one's own or other people's experiences, as examples of invisible support. Figure 9.7 illustrates their general findings using such practical support and recipients' post-discussion levels of anxiety (controlling for their initial levels of anxiety going in to the discussion). Recipients reported the highest levels of anxiety when they perceived they did not receive support from their partners and independent coders rated their partners' invisible support as low – no surprises here. Demonstrating the benefits of invisible support, however, recipients were the least anxious when they perceived low levels of support, but their partners were rated as providing high levels of invisible support.

How can we reconcile the benefits of invisible support with the prior research showing that observable, direct support (in the laboratory) is linked with higher relationship satisfaction? The discrepancy exists in the focus of the dependent variable: personal versus relationship outcomes. While visible support incurs costs for the individual, research focusing on relationship outcomes suggests (with a few qualifiers outlined above) that visible nurturant and action-facilitating support promotes relationship wellbeing because recipients feel loved and cared for. In contrast, invisible support may bolster coping but also incur relationship costs. For example, if partners

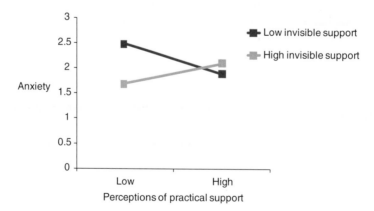

Figure 9.7   The role of invisible support in reducing anxiety
Source: From Howland and Simpson, 2010; © 2010 M. Howland and J. A. Simpson. SAGE Publications, Inc.

are too expert at camouflaging their support, then recipients are likely to feel unsupported and dispirited. Further research on this intriguing topic has confirmed these suggestions (Gleason *et al.*, 2008; Maisel and Gable, 2009). Thus, in the process of providing support there are tradeoffs to be made.

It is clear that providing support that protects the recipients' self-esteem and relationship satisfaction is not a straightforward undertaking. Partners who demonstrate more accurate insight into the recipients' thoughts and feelings, for example, are better support providers (Verhofstadt *et al.*, 2008). Probably because they tend to have greater empathic accuracy, women also adjust the support to their partner's needs more effectively (Neff and Karney, 2005; also see Chapter 8). Similarly, people who have received responsive care in their relationship past (such as those with a secure attachment orientation) are sensitive to their partners' support needs, offering more support when their partners directly seek support, and providing less support when their partners' anxiety levels are low and they do not seek support (e.g. Simpson *et al.*, 2002). More secure women, therefore, might also be more adept at delivering effective invisible support.

Conclusions

Several conclusions can be advanced. First, the way couples communicate and interact when one partner needs support influences relationship satisfaction, regardless of what happens in conflict situations. Second, there are a variety of ways that partners can provide support to each other, including communicating empathy and understanding or offering advice and tangible aid. Third, whether support will be helpful and appreciated requires a reasonably accurate understanding of the type and amount of support the individual desires. Fourth, although support plays an important role in maintaining connection and intimacy, these benefits can come with personal costs to the recipient. Providing more support than is needed or support that is direct and visible might increase the salience of the person's difficulty, resulting in feelings of incompetence, depressed mood, and indebtedness. Fifth, the recipe for effective support seems to reside in being simultaneously responsive to the recipient's needs for closeness and connection by demonstrating care and understanding, while also being sensitive to autonomy and efficacy needs by supplying an appropriate level and form of support.

At this point, you may feel that communication is a minefield, especially when your partner needs help. And you would be right. However, it is not impossible. To return to the opening of this chapter, the crux of the difficulty is that communication in intimate relationships is intensely interdependent. Thus, good communication requires the ability of both partners to ascertain, and be responsive to, the changing needs and demands specific to particular partners and interactions.

Summary and Conclusions

Every couple inevitably confronts problems in their relationship. Our examination of how couples communicate when managing dissatisfaction and conflict has been extensive, yet there is no simple answer as to how couples should best communicate during conflict. Negative responses to conflict fall into the general categories of critical hostility, reciprocating negativity, and defensive withdrawal. However, the link between negative communication and poor relationship outcomes is not straightforward. Instead, highlighting the truly dyadic nature of behavior in close relationships, the impact of specific communications depends on how the partner responds, including whether he/she attacks, retreats, or accommodates.

People instinctively try to protect themselves from criticism and hurtful comments. Indeed, partners often respond to hostility with anger and withdrawal, thus escalating conflict and possibly entering into spiraling cycles of blame and hostility. Committed partners can, however, overcome these self-protective impulses and accommodate in response to negative communication, in the process building trust and commitment. Intimates who feel insecure or dissatisfied in their relationships, in contrast, are more likely to read hurtful intent into their partner's communications and react accordingly.

Moreover, the same communication behaviors can have different, and sometimes opposing, consequences. Hostile and demanding communication, for example, generates dark thoughts and negative emotions in the partner but is also more likely to promote change. Similarly, a soft, positive approach may maintain satisfaction in the short term but yield little improvement because the partner remains blithely unaware of the problem or dismisses its importance. Stepping up the complexity still further, the costs and benefits of particular communication styles depend on how important it is to resolve the problem. When problems are serious, the change brought about from harsh and hostile communication may outweigh the costs of short-term dissatisfaction, whereas a forgiving loyal approach that fails to bring about needed change may erode relationship happiness over time. When problems are mild, however, a direct, aggressive approach is inappropriate, whereas positive, affectionate communication will keep the relationship on an even keel.

Another topic discussed in this chapter concerned how couples communicate when one partner needs support. Positive forms of support include either providing nurturance by expressing care, empathy, and validation to bolster the partner's esteem or by giving information, advice, and tangible aid. Although both types of supportive communication (nurturant versus instrumental) predict good outcomes, not all "positive" social support is perceived as helpful or welcomed. Partners commonly provide more support than is needed or wanted, running the risk of leaving recipients feeling misunderstood, indebted, and/or incompetent. Moreover, to be effective, the specific type of support offered needs to meet the demands of the situation and take into account the desires of the individual. Some people want emotional support, others are more comfortable with information and tangible help, and others don't want support at all. Everyone, however, benefits from feeling understood and cared for, which requires support that is attuned and responsive to the needs of the individual.

In summary, whether trying to resolve a relationship problem or support one's partner through a stressful time, one type of communication does not fit all. The resounding message from this research is that the ability to flexibly adjust communication to the unique needs of the problem, the partner, the relationship, and the wider context is central to maintaining close, satisfying relationships. The fact that many, if not most, intimate relationships are reasonably successful at meeting this apparently daunting task (see Chapter 12) highlights the point that humans are gifted – via evolution and culturally mediated learning – with an extraordinary ability for monitoring and negotiating the intense social landscapes of close, interpersonal relationships.

10 Sex and Passion

Kinsey's first studies of sex – the biology of sex – origins of sexual orientation– gender differences in sex and sexuality – sexual jealousy – sex and relationship satisfaction – sociosexuality – summary and conclusions

> and then I asked him with my eyes to ask again yes and then he asked me would I yes to say yes my mountain flower and first I put my arms around him yes and drew him down to me so he could feel my breasts all perfume yes and his heart was going like mad and yes I said yes I will Yes.
>
> James Joyce, *Ulysses*

In the summer of 1938, the world's leading expert on the American gall wasp, Alfred Kinsey, began teaching a course on marriage at Indiana University. Kinsey's decision to teach this course, which was requested by students, would fundamentally change how people view human sexuality. Kinsey was trained as a dyed-in-the-wool biologist. He realized, however, that in order to teach a course on marriage well, he had to know something about what made marriages unique; including what took place "between the sheets." Being the consummate scientist, Kinsey began reading everything on human sex and sexuality he could get his hands on. After reviewing the entire body of science on sex, he was stunned at how little was known about human sexuality, and he was appalled by the many inaccuracies and over-simplifications about humans as sexual animals.

Realizing that more data were needed, Kinsey started giving his marriage students questionnaires about their sex lives, a decision that did not sit well with many of their parents. This fact, along with the realization that more detailed information could be

The Science of Intimate Relationships, First Edition. Garth Fletcher, Jeffry A. Simpson, Lorne Campbell, and Nickola C. Overall.

Figure 10.1   Alfred Kinsey (1894–1956)
Source: The Kinsey Institute

obtained from interviews with older and more sexually experienced people, led Kinsey to start interviewing people in the community about the most intimate aspects their sex lives – how many sexual partners they had, the various things they liked to do while engaging in foreplay and sexual intercourse, their sexual fantasies and personal fetishes, and many other even more risqué topics.

Conducting these interviews became an obsession for Kinsey. Years later, Kinsey's wife lamented that she rarely spent time at night with her famous husband "since he took up sex" (Halberstam, 1994). During his career as the world's leading expert on human sexuality, Kinsey conducted thousands of lengthy interviews in participants' homes, in restaurants and bars, in parks, and sometimes even in parked cars. He and his colleagues published two landmark books, both of which became bestsellers on the *New York Times* book list: Kinsey *et al.*, 1948, which focused on the sexuality of men, and Kinsey *et al.*, 1953, which focused on the sexuality of women.

In their 1948 book, Kinsey and his colleagues reported that premarital and extramarital sex were considerably more prevalent in men than most people realized, that nearly all males masturbated at least occasionally (with no apparent ill effects), and that more than 25% of men had at least one sexual encounter with another male during their lives. These claims both shocked and intrigued the general public and they made Kinsey a target of heated criticism from conservative political and religious groups. The second book caused an even greater uproar. Kinsey *et al.* reported that women experienced much lower rates of frigidity (low sex drive) than was presumed, women engaged in more premarital and extramarital sex than many people believed, and they experienced surprisingly strong responses to erotic stimuli.

Kinsey also took strong exception to Freud's influential view that clitoral orgasms represented an adolescent phenomenon, and that vaginal orgasms produced by penile thrusting, without clitoral stimulation, constituted the appropriate mature female form. In contrast, Kinsey found few women reporting vagina-centered orgasms, and he thought the clitoris was the main center of sexual responses. Notably, arguments about clitoral versus vaginal orgasms continue today (Colson, 2010), along with dubious claims about the existence of a G-spot (purportedly a sensitive area on the anterior of the vagina) (Kilchevsky *et al.*, 2012).

Kinsey's second book rapidly outsold the first. The famed evangelist Billy Graham claimed that the book would do considerable damage to the already deteriorating morals of American society (Halberstam, 1994), and Kinsey came under increasing attack. Some even accused him of being a communist. In 1954, under political pressure, he lost his primary source of funding. But, by the time of his death in 1956, Kinsey had forever changed the study and understanding of sex and passion in humans. Sex was now more acceptable to study using scientific methods.

We begin by presenting some detail over and above that contained in Chapter 4 concerning the biology of sex and reproduction. Following this, we examine the origins of sexual orientation and discuss some of the most pronounced gender differences in sex and sexuality. We then review what is known about sexual jealousy in women and men, and how the quality and frequency of sex is associated with relationship satisfaction over time. And, finally, we turn to individual differences in sociosexuality – the degree to which individuals feel comfortable engaging in sex without love, closeness, or commitment.

The Biology of Sex

In Chapter 4 we discussed in some detail the nature and functions of the human genitalia and the reproductive systems. We go into some preliminary detail here to complete the biological picture.

The average length of the erect human penis is just under 6 inches (15.23 cm) and it is about 5 inches (12.69 cm) in circumference (Bogaert and Hershberger, 1999), if the self-reports of men can be trusted! All the apes possess a penis bone, which helps in maintaining an erection, with one exception – *Homo sapiens*. The human penis relies completely on maintaining an erection after it becomes engorged with blood, by using the muscles in the shaft of the penis to compress the veins, trapping blood so it can remain hard.

The center of women's sexual enjoyment is the clitoris, which is similar in structure to the penis, having both a shaft and glans. The clitoris, however, is much smaller, typically being about two-thirds of an inch (1.6 cm) in length at rest, but swelling with blood to twice that length during sexual arousal. Compared to the penis, the clitoris is springy in its erect state, primarily because it does not have a muscular mechanism for remaining stiff. Once men experience an orgasm, they typically cannot have another one for at least an hour or two. Women, on the other hand, can have multiple orgasms within short time-periods. The greater capacity for sexual enjoyment by women, however, comes at the cost of lower reliability, as we shall see. Most men have little if any difficulty reaching orgasm during sex as long as they can sustain an erection. Male human sexuality is rather simple and direct. Women, in contrast, are more complex and variable when it comes to sex and sexuality.

Sexual Orientation

How many gay and lesbian people do you think there are in western countries? You might guess 10%, because this is the figure commonly reported by the media. This percentage is derived from the Kinsey surveys, which we discussed at the beginning of the chapter. In his research Kinsey used a seven-point scale anchored by exclusively heterosexual at one end and exclusively homosexual at the other end (men or women). To his credit, Kinsey cautioned that answers to sexual orientation questions vary depending on how a person taking any survey defines the term "sexual orientation." Recent estimates from the 1994 Chicago sex survey (Michael *et al.*, 1994) suggest that 1.4% of women in North America consider themselves to be lesbians or bisexuals, and 2.8% of men in North America self-identify as being gay. However, an additional 6% of men and 4% of women also claimed that they have been sexually attracted to same-sex persons on occasion. Among college students, 1% of both women and men say they are attracted to only same-sex people, but another 12% report having been romantically attracted to at least one same-sex person during their lives (Ellis *et al.*, 2005). According to recent US census statistics, 8.8 million people aged 18–45 in the USA are gay, lesbian, or bisexual, which translates to 4.1% of the total US population (US Census Bureau, 2007).

The origins of sexual orientation

Homosexuality has been with us for as long as recorded history. Same-sex sexual relationships are mentioned, for example, in early Greek writings. The existence of gay men and male–male sexual activity has also been documented in numerous non-western cultures (Muscarella, 2000). When cultural conditions have permitted it, lesbian relationships have also openly existed in many cultures. Take, for example, the flourishing of lesbian relationships in China almost 200 years ago. At the start of the nineteenth century, most marriages in China were arranged by parents or village elders. Many of these arranged marriages were exceptionally restrictive and unhappy ones for young female brides. During the 1800s, however, employment in silk factories in China allowed some women to become financially independent. As a consequence, thousands of Chinese women joined sisterhoods, living together in large cooperative housing units. Long-term sexual relationships flourished in these cooperatives, to the point where the Communist Party outlawed sisterhoods when it came to power in 1949. Similar intimate sexual relationships between women have also been noted in cultures in Africa (e.g. the Lesotho and the Azande tribes) and in South America (e.g. the Suriname tribe; Peplau, 2001).

Why are some people sexually attracted to members of the same gender? The answer is complicated, partly because the sexual orientation pathways appear to be different for women and men (Diamond, 2003; Peplau and Garnets, 2000). Growing evidence suggests that genes and biology play a stronger role in determining sexual orientation for men than for women. Indeed, there is good evidence that male homosexuality has a genetic basis. Male homosexuality tends to run in families, with gay men having about 15% more homosexual brothers than heterosexual men (LeVay, 2009). Compared to heterosexual men, gay men are also more likely to have expressed feminine traits and behaviors during childhood, such as playing with dolls or choosing to be the caring mother figure in pretend-family games. Most studies have asked adults (or their parents) to recall the childhood behavior of gay men. A few studies, however, have identified and then followed young boys who exhibit cross-gender behavior in childhood all the way into adulthood. This research reveals that feminine young boys have close to a 50% chance of becoming gay men (Bailey and Zucker, 1995).

For women, the data tell a different story. Roughly 10% of lesbian women have lesbian sisters (LeVay, 2009), and approximately 6% of girls who act like boys during childhood (extreme tomboys) become lesbians in adulthood (Bailey and Zucker, 1995). However, even though a fairly large percentage of women report they were tomboys during their youth (about 50%), few become lesbians (Peplau, 2001).

When the psychological profiles of gay and lesbian adults are compared, gay men turn out to be more different from heterosexual men than lesbian women are different from heterosexual women. Gay men tend to have more feminine personalities, they are more interested in stereotypical feminine pursuits, and they prefer stereotypical female occupations compared to heterosexual men (Fletcher, 2002). Lesbians, on the other hand, typically cannot be distinguished from heterosexual women in terms of their personalities, physical appearance, and behavior (Lippa and Arad, 1997; Peplau, 2001). One study, however, has found that lesbians tend to be more interested in male-stereotypical hobbies and jobs than the average heterosexual woman (Lippa, 2000).

Aside from their sexual preferences, gays and lesbians are also not much different from their heterosexual counterparts in terms of sexual behavior. Many of the same gender differences that exist between heterosexual men and heterosexual women are also apparent when lesbian women and gay men are compared (Fletcher, 2002). Heterosexual men, for example, tend to have stronger sex drives than heterosexual women and gay men tend to have stronger sex drives than lesbians. Correspondingly, the mean levels of **testosterone** are the same comparing heterosexual to gay men, and also comparing heterosexual to lesbian women.

A well known study by Michael Bailey and his colleagues (1994) compared homosexual and heterosexual men and women on different aspects of mating, such as being interested in uncommitted sex, the frequency of engaging in casual sex, and the importance of physical attractiveness, youth, and status in a sex partner. Gender differences were found in all of the measures, with men (regardless of sexual orientation) being more drawn than women to uncommitted sex, casual sex, and mates who were younger and more physically attractive. Women, on the other hand, placed more weight on the social status of their sex partners, again regardless of sexual orientation.

In summary, in many ways, gays and lesbians are indistinguishable from their heterosexual counterparts. If one wants to understand gays and lesbians, a good place to start may be looking at heterosexual men and women (or, indeed, vice-versa).

Hormones, brain development, and congenital adrenal hyperplasia (CAH) One of the most influential biological theories of sexual orientation proposes that gay men have feminized brains and that lesbian women have masculinized brains, at least to some degree. These processes are thought to occur when fetuses in the womb are exposed to different amounts of testosterone, which can masculinize the brain with regard to sexual preferences and later sexual behavior (Bailey, 1995; Peplau *et al.*, 1999). The **hypothalamus** most likely plays a key role in this process. The hypothalamus regulates emotions, sex hormones, and related sexual behavior in all mammals, including humans. Well-controlled lab experiments have demonstrated that if male rat fetuses are deprived of testosterone during a critical period early in development, certain regions of the hypothalamus remain small, and rats engage in homosexual behavior as adults. Conversely, if female rat fetuses are given high doses of testosterone artificially, the same regions of the hypothalamus increase in size, and female rats display homosexual behaviors when they are adults (LeVay, 2009).

Needless to say, humans are not rats, and experiments that manipulate testosterone in the womb cannot be conducted on humans for ethical reasons. However, a rare genetic condition known as **congenital adrenal hyperplasia** (CAH), which afflicts only women, has provided us with a natural experiment. CAH generates excessive production of testosterone in the womb for chromosomal women, resulting in the masculinization of their genitals (Meyer-Bahlburg, 2001). In fact, some women who have CAH have even been misidentified and raised as males because they appear to have penises.

Today, nearly all women in western countries who have CAH are correctly classified as chromosomal girls right from birth, and they usually receive surgery and hormonal therapy to prevent the excessive development of male physical characteristics, such as body hair growth and deep voices. These women, however, still prefer stereotypically male activities during childhood and adulthood, and they are somewhat more likely to become lesbians or bisexual as adults (Peplau, 2001). However, the majority of adult women who have CAH report being heterosexual in adulthood (Bailey, 1995).

This leads us to an important implication of CAH. If exposure to hormones before birth causes brains to become more versus less masculine (or more versus less feminine), the brains of gay men should be different from those of heterosexual men, especially the hypothalamus. And they are different. Simon LeVay (1991) performed brain autopsies on 18 homosexual men and compared them to 16 men and 6 women who were heterosexual. He focused on specific areas of the hypothalamus that previous research had indicated were much larger in men than women. LeVay showed that one area (the INAH3 area) was two to three times larger in heterosexual men than in gay men, and the size of these regions in gay men and heterosexual women were very similar.

Critics have pointed out that LeVay's findings were not conclusive because these areas of the hypothalamus could have become larger in heterosexual men as a consequence of their sexual experiences when they were alive (Fletcher, 2002). Still, the evidence is consistent with large twin studies in Sweden (Långström *et al.*, 2010) and Australia (Bailey *et al.*, 2000) documenting that sexual orientation has much stronger genetic roots for men than for women, based on comparisons of **monozygotic** (identical) and **dizygotic** (non-identical) twins.

Genes and homosexuality in men This brings us to a longstanding scientific puzzle. If homosexuality has a genetic basis (at least in men), how could it have evolved if most gay men did not have children and, therefore, left few if any descendants who carried copies of their genes? Perhaps in response to social norms and pressures, many gay men during evolutionary history may simply have had children and families, engaging in homosexual affairs privately on the side. But even if gay men did not have their own biological children, they still could have helped their biological relatives – parents, brothers, and sisters – raise their children. This hypothesis is derived from **inclusive fitness theory** (see Chapter 2). If correct, this process would have ensured that the genes of gay men were carried forward into future generations. Other explanations can also be proffered.

Consider the gene for **sickle cell anemia**, which is common in Africa and among African Americans today. It turns out that carrying one copy of the gene, although mildly harmful, just happens to confer resistance to malaria. If one is unlucky enough to inherit two copies of the gene (one from each parent) it is frequently fatal. The net outcome is that in malaria-infested regions (where the gene is most common) people are more likely to survive if they carry the sickle cell gene and will, thus, be more likely to successfully reproduce. In an analogous fashion, if, over eons of time, women had preferred mates who were sensitive, kind, and empathic as long-term mates and fathers, then this process should have selected for genes that conferred such qualities onto their offspring. If the genes involved (there is almost certainly no sole homosexual gene) occasionally produce men with a homosexual orientation, this does not harm an evolutionary explanation, as long as the net outcome (in terms of reproductive success) has been positive for most men and women.

In 1993, Dean Hamer and his colleagues reported a sensational discovery that they had found a set of homosexual genes on the tip of the **X chromosome**. Genes on the X chromosome are inherited from only mothers. Hamer *et al.* (1993) decided to test this possibility after noticing that homosexuality tends to run along the female line in most families. In other words, if a man was gay, it was more likely that his mother's brother was gay, but not his father or his father's brother. Other researchers, however, failed to replicate these initial findings (e.g. Rice *et al.*, 1999), and the search for gay genes continues.

Another discovery suggests yet another genetic possibility. Men who have more older male siblings are slightly more likely to be gay. Each additional male brother increases the odds of being gay by 30% to 40% (Blanchard *et al.*, 2000; Bogaert, 1998; Whitam *et al.*, 1998). These increased probabilities, of course, remain small. For example, having an older brother might increase the chance of being homosexual from 3% to about 4%. In contrast, having a larger number of older sisters has no effect on the probability of male homosexuality, and the probability of a woman becoming a lesbian is not affected by how many older brothers or sisters she has.

One possible explanation for why this effect is confined in this fashion is linked to genes on the **Y chromosome**, which only men have. Three of these H-Y genes produce antigens in the fetus, which in turn create an immune response from the mother, whose body perceives her unborn child as a foreign object. Blanchard and Bogaert

(1996) believe that the H-Y genes masculinize certain parts of the brain. However, the immune response of the mother limits the extent to which the fetus becomes a male, psychologically speaking. If a mother's immune response is too strong, her sons are more likely to become homosexual.

To summarize, male homosexuality may partly reflect a long-standing genetic battle of the sexes, with the genes of women pushing male biology toward the type of male that would increase the mother's reproductive fitness – men who are virile and strong, but are also warm, communal, and loyal. This tug-of-war could have produced a genetic compromise that occasionally produces gay men (Miller, 2000).

Sexual plasticity in women In many species, including humans, females are more flexible than males in terms of their sexual orientation (Diamond, 2003). Roy Baumeister (2000) reviews a considerable body of evidence that supports this view. For example, about 80% of lesbian women report they have had sexual intercourse with one or more men during their lives, whereas only 50% of gay men report ever having sex with a woman. Women are also more likely to fluctuate over time in being attracted to women versus men, and they switch between the two more easily (Diamond, 2000, 2008). When sexual arousal is measured physiologically, most men are aroused by sexual images of just women, but many women are aroused by images of both men and women (Chivers *et al.*, 2004). Women are also more likely to report being bisexual or potentially interested in such a lifestyle (Diamond, 2003).

In addition, women are more likely to claim they became a lesbian for social or political reasons, such as wanting to support women's causes or issues. Men, in contrast, rarely report they became gay for social or political reasons. Accounts of mate-swapping illustrate the same point. Among couples that temporarily exchange mates, heterosexual women are more likely to have and enjoy sex with other women. Mate-swapping heterosexual men, in contrast, are less likely to relish the idea of having sex with other men (Baumeister, 2000).

Cross-cultural evidence reveals the same basic story – more variability in sexuality for women than for men (see Baumeister, 2000; Diamond, 2003). In some cultures women are not believed to experience orgasms. Descriptions of sexual intercourse in cultures as something that men want, but women endure, appear frequently in the anthropological literature (Davenport, 1997). In other societies, however, women expect to have orgasms, and apparently do so with some regularity. In a similar vein, some cultures view sexual behavior and intercourse as ugly and shameful, whereas others view it as erotic and beautiful. For the Gusii of southwest Kenya, coitus is seen as inherently hostile and with disgust by women. Sexual intercourse in this culture has been described by anthropologists as resembling a form of ritualized rape – it is a battleground, in which men physically overcome the women, in the process causing them pain and humiliation (Davenport, 1997).

In contrast, pre-European Pacific cultures, such as that of Hawaii, were famous for their open and positive attitudes to sexuality. In Mangai, one of the Cook Islands in the South Pacific, young men were given extensive education in lovemaking techniques by other men, and also given practical exercises in sexual intercourse by older women.

Women Tend to have More Flexible Sexual Systems than Men

- Women show more swings in sexual activity over long periods of time than men.
- Education and religious experiences influence women's sexuality more than men.
- Women are more likely to engage in homosexual acts in jail than men.
- Women are more likely to change sexual orientations than men.
- Sexual activity is more variable across cultures for women than men.
- Sexual orientation for women appears to be less genetically determined than for men.
- Women are more likely to engage in homosexual acts in orgy or swinging contexts than men.

Figure 10.2 Gender and flexibility of sexual systems
Source: From Baumeister, 2000

Sexual intercourse was supposed to be enjoyable for both men and women, and a man's reputation could be ruined if he was not a good lover and his partner did not regularly experience orgasms (Davenport, 1997).

These results, summarized in Figure 10.2, do not imply that men's sexual behavior is impervious to situational or cultural forces. For instance, 30 to 45% of men in prison, most of whom are heterosexual, engage in consensual homosexual acts. Consistent with the erotic plasticity argument, however, the rates of lesbian activity are about 50% in prison (higher than the rate for men) (Gagnon and Simon, 1968). Cultural norms, beliefs, and practices can also exert powerful influences on the sexual behavior of men. In some Melanesian cultures, such as in the Sambia in Papua New Guinea, the adolescent boys are required to carry out oral sex with adult bachelors as part of initiation into manhood. Such practices are based on the belief that swallowing the semen of older men helps in the development of bravery and other masculine traits in adulthood. Gilbert Herdt (1981) in his classic treatise on the Sambia, describes how young adolescent males were coached and persuaded into such behavior. Interestingly, Herdt claims that the incidence of homosexuality (as a lifestyle choice in later life) was no higher in Sambian culture than western culture, and that the majority of men married and lived heterosexual lives (marrying normally signals the end of homosexual behavior for the Sambia).

Gender Differences in Sex and Sexuality

The notion that most men have a stronger sex drive than most women has, until recently, sharply divided academics and scientists. However, after exhaustively reviewing the evidence, Roy Baumeister and colleagues (Baumeister *et al.*, 2001) concluded

"Not tonight. The cat is in my lap."

Figure 10.3 *Source:* © 2009 Liza Donnelly and Michael Maslin

that "the combined quantity, quality, diversity, and convergence of the evidence render the conclusion indisputable" (p. 21); namely, that men, indeed, have a higher sex drive than women. Sex drive can be defined as the craving or desire for sexual activity and sexual pleasure, and it should be distinguished from the concept of sexual capacity. Women, as we have seen, have greater sexual capacity than men in the sense that they can experience multiple orgasms over short time periods. Keeping firmly in mind the caveat that there exists greater within-gender variability in many sex drive measures than between-gender differences, what evidence led Baumeister and his colleagues to conclude that men tend to have stronger sex drives than women? These gender differences are summarized in Figure 10.4. We discuss each one in turn.

Gender differences in sex drive

First, daydreaming about sex is a good measure of sex drive because it is not affected by social pressures, taboos, or norms. One can have sexy daydreams while sitting on a bus, watching TV with friends, or even reading this book! Many studies have confirmed that men think and fantasize about sex much more than women do. The Michael *et al.* (1994) sex survey, for instance, reported that 54% of men think about sex every day, whereas only 19% of women do. Parenthetically, we cite this survey frequently because it remains one of the most authoritative sex surveys published. It used face-to-face interviewing, it carefully selected the sample of 3432 individuals that was representative of the US population, and it achieved a remarkably high success rate in

Men have Stronger Sex Drives than Women
Compared to women:
• Men think about sex more often.
• Men initiate sex more often in relationships.
• Men desire sex more often in relationships.
• Men masturbate more than women.
• Men report fewer problems with low sexual desire.
• Men more often pay money or offer gifts for sex.
• Men more often watch (and pay for) pornography.
• Men have orgasms more reliably and easily than women.
Note: The same gender differences are typically found when comparing lesbian and gays.

Figure 10.4   Gender and sex drive
Source: From Baumeister *et al.*, 2001

obtaining consent – 79% of the original random sample contacted agreed to take part (cutting down on self-selection problems that are endemic with sex surveys).

Second, men experience spontaneous sexual desire at least twice as often as the typical woman does. Men, for example, are more likely to experience sudden and strong sexual thoughts and urges that divert their attention from what they are currently doing.

Third, men initiate and request sex more frequently than women. In heterosexual relationships, for example, men initiate or desire sex nearly twice as often as their female partners. This gender difference is illustrated in Woody Allen's movie *Annie Hall*, in which a psychiatrist asks Alvy how often he has sex. Alvy replies "hardly ever, maybe three times a week." When Annie (Alvy's wife) is posed the same question by her psychiatrist, she answers "constantly, I'd say three times a week." This gender difference is evident in the early dating stages of relationships, and at every stage of marriage, right on through to old age. The major exception is when romance is heated and passionate, when newly established couples often simply cannot get enough of each other (Sternberg, 1986).

An obvious artifact that may dampen sexual desire for women is the fear of pregnancy, which is likely to be stronger than for men. One way to address this factor is to examine sexual desire in same-gender sexual relationships, in which pregnancy is not possible. This analysis also takes account of the possibility that men and women in heterosexual relationships characteristically influence each other in ways that may produce gender differences in sexual desire. For example, if men generally make lousier and more selfish lovers than do women, this could turn women off sex, but lead men to desire sex more frequently than their partners.

The research reveals clear-cut tendencies for gay men to engage in more frequent sexual activity than lesbians, and this is true in both committed relationships and in short-term casual sex outside committed relationships. Philip Blumstein and Pepper Schwartz (1983) reported that two-thirds of their sample of gay men had sex three or more times a week, whereas only one third of the lesbian women had sex at this frequency. After 10 years in a relationship, 11% of the gay men were maintaining this high frequency of sex, whereas only 1% of the lesbian women remained at this level. In summary, neither fear of pregnancy, nor the interaction between heterosexual men and women, appears to be responsible for causing gender differences in sex drive.

Fourth, men report masturbating more than women. This gender difference is large and consistent across all age groups and countries. Estimates from Michael *et al.*'s (1994) sex survey reveal that 60% of men and 40% of women masturbated at least once during the past year, and 40% of men and 10% of women masturbate at least weekly.

As an aside, the cultural history of masturbation in western societies makes interesting reading. Standard medical opinion in the 1700s viewed masturbation as causing a medley of nasty complaints, including neurosis, poor eyesight, epilepsy, memory loss, and tuberculosis. In America, by the middle of the nineteenth century, doctors and self-appointed health experts had jumped on the bandwagon and written bestselling books describing the nasty consequences of masturbation and advising people on how to recognize and prevent it (Michael *et al.*, 1994). In Kellogg's bestseller, published in 1888, he described 39 signs of masturbation to watch for, including rounded shoulders, weak backs, paleness, acne, heart palpitations, epilepsy, bashfulness, boldness (and timidity), mock piety, confusion, smoking, nail-biting, and bed-wetting. Sylvester Graham (the inventor of the Graham cracker) wrote in his 1834 book *A Lecture to Young Men* that masturbation (or what he termed self-pollution) would transform a young boy into "a confirmed and degraded idiot, whose deeply sunken and vacant, glossy eye, and livid, shriveled countenance, and ulcerous, toothless gums, and foetid breath, and feeble, broken voice, and emaciated and dwarfish and crooked body, and almost hairless head – covered perhaps with suppurating blisters and running sores – denote a mature old age! a blighted body – and a ruined soul!" (p. 38).

To curb masturbation, Kellogg recommended a range of solutions including eating his newfangled cornflakes, bandaging the child's genitals, covering the genitals with a cage, tying the hands together, circumcision without an anesthetic, or (for girls) applying carbolic acid to the clitoris. He also strongly advised against anyone consulting a quack to deal with this problem (oddly not including himself in this category!). Graham advised men to eat grain, avoid meat, and sleep on hard wooden beds. Other entrepreneurs developed devices (some patented) including a genital cage that used springs to hold a boy's penis and scrotum in place, or a device that sounded an alarm if the boy had an erection.

By the middle of the twentieth century, medical doctors and psychiatrists had backed away from the ludicrous claims of charlatans like Kellogg, and jettisoned the proposition that masturbation caused blindness or other physical maladies. However, it was still widely believed the practice could cause mental disorders and produce sexual dysfunction, such as impotence and premature ejaculation.

In summary, a reading of western cultural history related to masturbation makes it clear that the bulk of the social pressure and dire warnings were directed against men, not women. In line with this interpretation, a study in 1974 reported that men felt guiltier than women after masturbating, and also considered the practice to be more perverse than did women (Arafat and Cotton, 1974). The upshot is that if culture were all-pervasive, then men should masturbate less than women. The alternative explanation for western cultural history is that the norms and social pressures were mainly focused on men, because it was (correctly) ascertained that men were more likely to masturbate than women if left to their own devices.

Fifth, women report a higher frequency of problems of low sexual desire in relationships than do men. In one study of over 900 clients who were being seen for a variety of sexual dysfunctions, about four times as many women as men were diagnosed as suffering from low sexual desire (Segraves and Segraves, 1991). In relationships and marriages more generally, arguments about the desirable frequency of sex predict higher levels of dissatisfaction. More often than not, as reflected in the Woody Allen movie example given earlier, the man is upset about his partner withholding or showing little interest in sex, whereas the woman is concerned about her husband pressuring her for more sex (Buss, 1989).

Finally, men commonly pay money or present gifts in return for sexual favors, but women almost never do. Men also spend considerably more money than do women on pornography, and spend much more money than do women on magazines, like *Playboy*, that specialize in publishing titillating pictures of nude or semi-nude women in provocative poses. Women, in contrast, spend much more money on romance novels than do men. True, magazines similar to *Playboy*, but designed for women and featuring nude pictures of men, have been floated on the marketplace (such as *Playgirl* and *Viva*). However, such magazines have either folded or shifted their emphasis away from blatant sexual titillation because this approach has proved not to be commercially viable.

Gender differences in desire for multiple sex partners

Numerous studies have asked men and women how many people they ideally would like to have sex with in the future. On average, men report higher numbers than women. One study, for example, found that the typical college male desired eight partners over the next two years, whereas the typical college woman wanted just one partner (Buss and Schmitt, 1993). Another study found that men ideally wanted an average of 64 partners during their lifetime, whereas women wanted only 2.7 partners (Miller and Fishkin, 1997). These data are misleading, however, because these mean differences are driven by a small percentage of men who want incredibly large (and often unrealistic) numbers of mates. When median scores – scores right in the middle of a distribution – are examined, men and women have fairly similar preferences in the number of desired mates. In fact, the median number of desired lifetime partners was one for both men and women in Miller and Fishkin's (1997) study.

Other studies have asked heterosexual individuals to report the total number of sexual partners of the opposite gender (excluding prostitutes) they have had in their lives. Results consistently show that men report having about twice as many sex partners as women report (Buss and Schmitt, 1993; Simpson and Gangestad, 1991). This result, of course, is not logically possible. Since each man has sex with one woman, the mean number of total sex partners must be the same, on average, for each gender. One explanation for this anomaly might be the way in which women and men define sex. Everyone agrees that vaginal intercourse constitutes sex, but that kissing does not. When President Clinton told the American people that he did not have sex with "that" woman (Monica Lewinsky), he later explained himself by claiming that he did not have sexual intercourse with her. It turns out that Clinton is unusual among American men; most men count oral sex as having sex, although women are less inclined to do so (Sanders and Reinisch, 1999).

Other research has suggested that gender differences in estimating the number of sexual partners is caused by men and women using different recall techniques (Brown and Sinclair, 1999) Men tend to estimate a number; then round up (e.g. "It is somewhere between 25 and 30 – let's say 30"). Women think about intimate relationships more than men and possess more elaborate memories of such relationships, even the short-lived ones. Thus, women are more likely to actually recall each one in turn, and count as they go (e.g. "Let's see, my first one was Frank – a lovely boy – then there was Larry, who was absolutely hopeless and didn't last long, and then there was John – huge ego"). This method tends to produce an underestimate as the individual totals mount and sexual encounters may be forgotten. The timeworn stereotype that men who have many sexual partners are "swashbucklers," whereas women who do the same thing are "sluts," also probably still has some currency. Thus, these biases in recall of sexual encounters (men overestimate, women underestimate) may have a motivational element driving them along.

In summary, men generally have a stronger desire for sex and associated sexual pleasure than women do. Nevertheless, there is much more variability on most sexual measures within each gender than there is between men and women (Kinsey *et al.*, 1948, 1953; Simpson and Gangestad, 1991). For this reason, some women have a similar, or even higher, sex drive than their male romantic partners. We will return to the topic of individual differences in sociosexual behaviors near the end of this chapter. Men and women also develop sexually along different trajectories. Women's interest in and desire for sex typically peaks in their 30s, whereas men experience a gradual decline in sex drive from 18–19 years of age onward (Gagnon, 1977; Hunt, 1974). This means that gender differences in sex drive are likely to be at their maximum when men and women are in their late teens, and at their minimum when partners are 30–40 years old (Fletcher, 2002).

Gender differences in negotiating sex in relationships

When romantic relationships begin, men and women tend to agree on when and how much sex to have. As relationships progress, however, women's desire for sex wanes more than men's (Klusmann, 2002). This reflects the different relationship needs and motives that each gender has. For men, intimacy tends to be indexed by the amount and quality of sex; for women, intimacy is more commonly assessed according to the amount and quality of shared emotions and feelings. This may partly explain why men usually initiate sex in relationships, and why women often rebuff their partner's frequent sexual advances (Byers and Heinlein, 1989). As relationships become more established, both genders report becoming more dissatisfied with the sexual component of their relationship, but the connection between sexual behavior and relationship satisfaction tends to be stronger for men than women (Storaasli and Markman, 1990). When men become sexually dissatisfied, they are more likely than women to seek out extramarital relationships (Atkins *et al.*, 2005), usually for sexual rather than emotional gratification (Glass and Wright, 1992).

Sexual Jealousy

Folk wisdom and evolutionary principles suggest that men and women tend to experience jealousy somewhat differently, depending on its source. To test this idea, David Buss and his colleagues (1992) asked heterosexual women and men how they would feel if they learned that their romantic partner engaged in two types of infidelity – sexual infidelity (imagine your partner having passionate sexual intercourse with someone else) versus emotional infidelity (imagine your partner having strong feelings for, and perhaps falling in love with, someone else). In this study, men and women chose which type of infidelity would be the most upsetting. Compared to men, women report they would experience greater jealousy in response to their partner feeling strong emotions for another person than in response to the sexual intercourse scenario. Compared to women, men said they would be more jealous by sexual infidelity than emotional infidelity.

Women of course know they are the genetic mother of their children, whereas men can never be completely sure they are the genetic father of their children. This is termed **paternity uncertainty** in evolutionary psychology. Throughout evolutionary history men could never be 100% certain they were the biological fathers of their mate's children. To complicate matters, women are receptive to mating across the entire 28-day ovulatory cycle (Thornhill and Gangestad, 2008).

This creates a problem for men. How can a man ensure his extensive investments in his mate and children will propagate his own genes, rather than those of another man, into future generations? Sexual jealousy is one answer, according to evolutionary thinking. Jealousy motivates men to guard their mates, to punish interlopers, and to ward off potential rivals. These actions, in turn, should increase the likelihood of paternity certainty. Hence, the realization that another male has had sex with one's romantic partner should be more distressing to men than a partner's mere emotional infidelity.

This evolutionary view has been supported in other studies (e.g. Edlund *et al.*, 2006) and across cultures (e.g. Buunk *et al.*, 1996; see Figure 10.5), but it has also been chal-

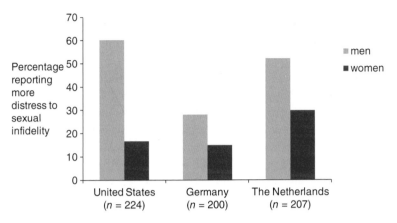

Figure 10.5   Jealousy as function of gender in three western countries
Source: From Buunk *et al.*, 1996; © 1996 American Psychological Society

lenged. David DeSteno and Peter Salovey (1996) have argued that when people think about hypothetical mate infidelities, men and women base their judgments on stereotypes about gender differences, such as "Men have sex without love, but for women, the two go together." Thus, when women are told their partners are having sex with another female, they should not automatically assume that their partners are madly in love with her and their relationships are necessarily threatened. When men are told that their partners are having sex with another male, however, they are also likely to assume that their partners might well be in love with him, which should make men feel threatened. To test this hypothesis, DeSteno and Salovey (1996) investigated the degree to which women and men find each type of infidelity upsetting. When the stereotypical beliefs of men and women were held constant (statistically controlled), the gender differences in sexual jealousy found by Buss and his colleagues disappeared.

However, this evidence does not damage an evolutionary approach. Consider where such stereotypical beliefs come from. The most likely hypothesis is that the stereotypical beliefs in question are derived from lay, everyday observations of people's sexual attitudes and behavior. Such behavioral gender differences, in turn, may very well be rooted in human biology and genes. Thus, the causal chain might work as follows. Genes (in part) cause men and women to behave differently, which in turn generates the development of (correct) related stereotypical beliefs, which in turn initiates sexual jealousy in different doses for men and women, depending on the information they have on hand. This causal model is perfectly consistent with contemporary evolutionary theory, and with the evidence adduced by DeSteno and his colleagues.

In addition, an evolutionary account anticipates that sexual jealousy should exist in all cultures, it should be evoked in specific circumstances, and it should motivate men in particular to guard or punish their mates if they suspect their mates might be having sex with other men. Cross-cultural and anthropological evidence broadly supports these conjectures. Across all known cultures, women who commit adultery are punished more harshly than men who commit the same adulterous acts (Daly *et al.*, 1981). Moreover, sexual jealousy on the part of husbands is a common motive for wife-beating (or worse) in dozens of societies, including hunter-gatherer cultures (Daly *et al.*, 1981).

One exception to the rule that men are strongly motivated to establish paternity and, thus, suffer the tortuous pangs of jealousy when their partners have sex with other men, is a group of hunter-gatherer cultures in South America, including the Ache, the Barí, and the Canela. In these cultures it is believed that babies inherit characteristics from all men who have had sexual intercourse with a woman leading up to her pregnancy. Thus, both the primary father (the husband) and the secondary fathers are expected to provide food and help raise the child. Accordingly, women who discover they are pregnant try to seduce men who are good hunters or have high status in the group. Stephen Beckerman and his colleagues (1998), who have studied the Barí, confirmed that children who have secondary fathers had the best survival rates 15 years after birth (80%), whereas only 60% of children who had only one father survived to 15. A woman's motivation to have sex with secondary fathers in these cultures is therefore not misplaced.

One might wonder whether men in these South American cultures experience intense sexual jealousy. Men in the Ache say they are not jealous, but they often beat their wives for having sex with other men (Hill and Hurtado, 1996). In the Canela, both men and women are expected to have sex freely with others, including group sex, from adolescence onward. Men must have sex with any woman who requests it as a matter of "duty." The obligation for women to engage in sex with men who ask for it is not as strong, but repeated requests that are denied result in charges of "sexual stinginess" and eventual punishment (Crocker and Crocker, 1994). However, Canela husbands experience jealousy, and Canela tribes go to some lengths to teach husbands how to repress and control these powerful feelings. With increasingly more western contact, young Canela husbands began to express their sexual jealousy more directly and often assert ownership of their wives (Crocker and Crocker, 1994). In short, elaborate cultural arrangements designed to quell men's jealousy and control over the sexual behavior of their wives seem fragile and difficult to maintain.

In conclusion, sexual jealousy seems to be rooted in basic biological and evolutionary processes for both genders. However, the principal sources of threat are subtly different for women and men. For women, the main threat is losing the support of investing mates. Men, in contrast, run the risk of investing huge amounts of time, effort, and resources in children to whom they are not genetically related. These gender differences represent yet another variation on a central theme we have encountered before; namely, women have a stronger relationship orientation toward sexuality than men.

Sex and Relationship Satisfaction

One might assume that a host of relationship scientists have been beavering away for years studying the links between sex and intimate relationship evaluations and processes. Oddly, this is not the case. Nevertheless, a few studies have found that greater sexual satisfaction has a stronger effect on marital satisfaction than simply having sex more frequently, and that, over time, changes in sexual functioning in relationships parallel changes in relationship quality (Byers, 2005; Sprecher and Cate, 2004). Two questions can be asked: (i) does good sex result in good relationships?; and (ii) do good relationships lead to better sex? We consider each question in turn, focusing primarily on longitudinal studies, which allow researchers to disentangle which variable – sexual functioning or relationship satisfaction – exerts a causal influence.

Does better sex lead to better relationships?

At least five longitudinal studies suggest that better sexual functioning results in better relationship quality over time. In dating couples, men who report being more sexually satisfied are less likely to break up with their partners a year later (Sprecher, 2002), and men and women who report fewer arguments over sex (e.g. when to have it, how often it should take place) are less likely to experience drops in relationship satisfaction over time (Long et al., 1996). In newlyweds, wives who initiate sex have higher marital satisfaction two years later (Huston and Vangelisti, 1991). Similarly, husbands who report higher quality sex and "sensuality" with their wives tend to be more satisfied with their marriages three years later (Lawrence et al., 2008). And across six months, husbands' reports of how satisfied they are correlate with how frequently they have had sex, although no such relation exists for their wives (McNulty and Fisher, 2008). In sum, the evidence indicates that better sex can improve relationship satisfaction, or at least slow down its gradual decline.

Do better relationships lead to better sex?

What about the flip-side? Does any research reveal that better relationships can improve sex or sexual satisfaction? The answer is a qualified yes. Although some studies have not found a good relationship good sex connection (e.g. Huston and Vangelisti, 1991; Sprecher, 2002), others have. For example, Byers (2005) found that higher marital satisfaction and better marital communication both predicted greater sexual satisfaction 1.5 years later. In another study, Larson et al. (1998) found that marriages in which wives reported more open communication, and husbands reported more empathic communication, resulted in greater sexual satisfaction in wives one year later. In addition, wives' open communication and beliefs that their marriage was stable predicted husbands' sexual satisfaction one year later. Thus, higher quality relationships may improve, or at least hold steady, sexual satisfaction.

In summary, our best guess at this time is that sexual functioning and perceptions of relationship quality are reciprocally linked over time.

Communication may be critical

The quality of communication within relationships may also play a role in understanding the links between sexual and marital satisfaction. In a study of nearly 400 married

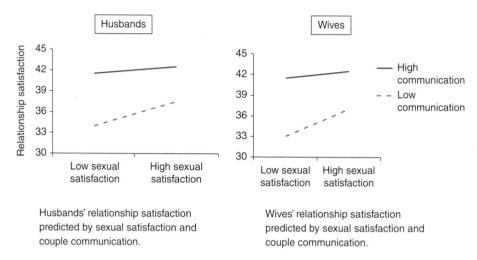

Figure 10.6 Links between relationship satisfaction and sexual satisfaction depend (in part) on communication
Source: From Litzinger and Gordon, 2005; © 2005 Taylor and Francis Inc.

couples, Litzinger and Gordon (2005) found the standard positive correlation between sexual satisfaction and marital satisfaction. However, they also identified a variable that appears to turn on and turn off this effect to some extent for both men and women – the quality of communication within the marriage (as shown in Figure 10.6). When communication is open and good in a marriage, good sex does not increase marital satisfaction very much. But when communication is poor, partners remain reasonably satisfied as long as they also enjoy good sex. And when both communication and sexual satisfaction are low, marital satisfaction hits rock bottom. Thus, high-quality sex may partly make up for poorer communication in many marriages, at least in terms of general marital happiness.

Individual Differences in Sociosexuality

As discussed at the beginning of this chapter, Alfred Kinsey and his colleagues in the 1940s embarked on the most extensive and ambitious study of human sexuality that has ever been conducted, even to this day. Kinsey's main goal was to document population norms –means, standard deviations, and ranges – of all kinds of sexual attitudes, preferences, and behaviors. One of the most striking findings in these data was how different people were on a host of sociosexual attitudes and behaviors (Kinsey *et al.,* 1948, 1953). Over the years, dozens of studies have reconfirmed that people differ widely on many measures of sociosexuality, ranging from wanting many versus few sex partners, to the number of preferred lifetime sex partners, to one's willingness to enter extra-pair relationships (e.g. extramarital affairs), and to attitudes about having and enjoying casual sex (Buss and Schmitt, 1993; Gangestad and Simpson, 2000).

Many of the sociosexual attitudes, preferences, and behaviors that Kinsey and his colleagues identified are correlated, and some of them form a psychological dimension now known as sociosexual orientation (Gangestad and Simpson, 1990; Simpson and Gangestad, 1991). This construct was discussed in Chapter 5. To recap, individuals at one end of this dimension – those who have a more restricted sociosexual orientation – expect more love, commitment, and emotional closeness before having sex with their romantic partners. Restricted individuals, for example, claim they must feel emotionally close to their romantic partners before becoming sexually intimate with them, they have sex with fewer different partners during the past year, and they rarely if ever have short-term hook-ups (Simpson and Gangestad, 1991). Individuals at the other end of the sociosexuality dimension – with a more unrestricted orientation – require less time and emotional connection before having sex. Indeed, unrestricted persons typically report having had several different sexual partners in the past year, and they are more willing to consider hook-ups when such opportunities arise (Simpson and Gangestad, 1991). The items on the original Sociosexual Orientation Inventory (SOI) are shown in Table 10.1.

As we have already seen, some of the variability in sociosexual attitudes and behaviors is associated with gender differences. Compared to the average woman, the typical man holds more permissive attitudes about casual sex, fantasizes more often about having sex with different partners, and is more willing to engage in unrestricted sociosexual acts (Buss and Schmitt, 1993; Eysenck, 1976). Nevertheless, there is four to five times more variability in sociosexual attitudes and behaviors *within* men and *within* women than there is between the average (mean) scores of men and women (Kinsey et al., 1948, 1953; Simpson and Gangestad, 1991). Analyzing data from hundreds of men and women, Gangestad and Simpson (2000) found that mean gender differences explained only 16% of the variance in seeking short-term mates, 9% of the variance in the number of different sex partners desired in a specific time period (e.g. one year), and 20% of the variance in the likelihood of agreeing to have sex with an attractive, opposite-gender person whom one had just met. Overall, gender differences explain about 25% of the variance of the levels of interest in engaging in casual sex (Oliver and Hyde, 1996). In fact, almost 30% of men in the USA have *less* favorable attitudes toward casual sex than the average woman (Gangestad and Simpson, 2000). Similar estimates have been documented in many other countries and regions of the world (Schmitt, 2005; Schmitt et al., 2003).

As noted in Chapter 5, restricted and unrestricted sociosexual orientations reflect long-term and short-term mating strategies, respectively. Schmitt (2005) translated the Sociosexuality Scale into 25 languages and gave it to thousands of people in more than 50 countries. Consistent with the material in this chapter certain things were universal. For example, men were less restricted than women across all cultures. However, the nature of the social and physical environment also influenced the mating strategies adopted across cultures. In cultures where there were more men than women, everyone shifted toward a long-term strategy. In contrast, when there were more women than

Table 10.1   The Sociosexual Orientation Inventory

1. With how many different partners have you had sex (sexual intercourse) within the past year?
2. With how many different partners have you had sex (sexual intercourse) in your lifetime?
3. How many different partners do you foresee yourself having sex with during the next 5 years?
4. With how many different partners have you had sex on one and only one occasion?
5. How often do you fantasize about having sex with someone other than your current dating partner (when you are in a relationship)? (Circle one).

    1) never   5) once a week
    2) once every two or three months   6) a few times each week
    3) once a month   7) nearly every day
    4) once every two weeks   8) at least once a day

6. Sex without love is OK.

                    1   2   3   4   5   6   7   8   9
                    _____

        I strongly disagree   I strongly agree

7. I can imagine myself being comfortable and enjoying "casual" sex with different partners.

                    1   2   3   4   5   6   7   8   9
                    _____

        I strongly disagree   I strongly agree

8. I would have to be closely attached to someone (both emotionally and psychologically) before I could feel comfortable and fully enjoy having sex with him or her.

                    1   2   3   4   5   6   7   8   9
                    _____

        I strongly disagree   I strongly agree

Note: Individuals who have and foresee more sexual partners, fantasize more about having sex with people other than their current partner, and have more positive attitudes toward engaging in casual, uncommitted sex have an "unrestricted" sociosexual orientation. Individuals who report the opposite responses have a "restricted" sociosexual orientation. Men tend to score higher than women on the SOI.
Source: From Simpson and Gangestad (1991). © 1991 American Psychological Association, Inc.

men, the average mating strategy shifted in the other direction toward a short-term strategy. These shifts are explicable in terms of the mating market. When women are in short supply, they can call the shots and demand a long-term strategy from their mates. When men are in short supply, they can call the shots to a greater extent and have more access to short-term sexual encounters. This difference can be seen in Figure 10.7.

In Chapter 5 we discussed a version of life history theory, which hypothesized that when times are tough (but when life remains predictable) people will hunker down and switch to a more serious and stable long-term mating strategy. Indeed, Schmitt (2005) found that when environments were more difficult (e.g. higher rates of teen pregnancy, more child malnutrition, higher levels of infant mortality), this was linked

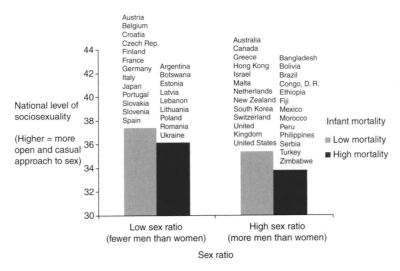

Figure 10.7 Across countries, sociosexuality varies as a function of sex ratios and toughness of the environment
Source: From Schmitt, 2005; © 2005 Cambridge University Press

to stronger long-term mating strategies across cultures. This difference can also be seen in Figure 10.7, in relation to the levels of infant mortality.

Moreover, when life is tough women more than men tend to adjust their sociosexual orientation toward a long-term strategy. This has the effect of increasing the gap between genders, as men more or less stay locked into a short-term orientation. In contrast, in nations that have high levels of equality and enjoy high standards of living (like the USA, Canada, and New Zealand) the gender gap decreases because women are more likely to endorse a short-term mating strategy. These findings are consistent with the proposition advanced previously that women have more flexible sexual systems than men.

Summary and Conclusions

This chapter has revealed some key gender differences in sexuality, which are remarkably consistent with what is known about mate selection and mating strategies (see Chapter 6), and the sex hormones (see Chapter 4). Men have stronger sex drives than women and are prone to keeping the sexual component (of love) separated from commitment and intimacy to a greater extent than are women. Sexuality comprises a more biologically encapsulated system for men than for women, and is thus less permeable to other beliefs and cultural influences. These gender differences are undoubtedly linked to men possessing stronger short-term mating strategies than women in every culture and nation that has been investigated.

Popular wisdom has it that men have less control over their sexual urges than do women. In one sense this is true. Priests sometimes masturbate and have sex with women, even though these are mortal sins in the Catholic Church (Murphy, 1992). American president (Bill Clinton) had casual sex with a young woman in the White House, including sexual play with cigars, even though he was painfully aware of the disastrous and humiliating consequences if (as must have seemed likely) he was found out. In a complementary fashion, sexuality for women is more open-ended and permeable, more responsive to social conditioning, circumstances or context, and more open to the influence of culture than is true for men. In short, women's sexual desires and behavior are less biologically determined than is the case for men.

Reflecting a central theme we have stressed in the book, within-gender differences in sexuality are much greater than between-gender differences. These within-gender differences seem to come under the umbrella of general short-term versus long-term mating strategies, and are influenced by a multitude of factors including cultural-level factors, personal family background, and so forth.

When Alfred Kinsey started asking questions about sexual behaviors in his undergraduate marriage class in 1938, our knowledge of sex and mating was confined to grand theories, such as Freudian psychoanalytic theory, and anecdotal stories. No one really took the scientific study of sex in humans seriously. Kinsey and his colleagues changed this cavalier approach by carefully asking questions, recording answers, and then stepping back to look for patterns in the sexual lives of women and men from all walks of life. Many scientists and government leaders of the day scoffed at Kinsey's early work, viewing him as crackpot, a communist, or a pervert. The public found many of his methods and results shocking and surprising, but at the same time fascinating. Both of Kinsey's books, while panned by many academics, became *New York Times* best sellers.

Understanding human sexuality is a necessary step for understanding the links between human nature and intimate relationships. Thanks in part to Alfred Kinsey scientists are a lot closer to achieving this goal today than in 1938.

Relationship Violence **11**

Gender differences in intimate violence – resolving the apparent paradox – nature and frequency of intimate violence – homicide – intimate violence from different theoretical perspectives – explaining the massive variability in intimate violence – violence prevention – summary and conclusions

> And most of all would I flee from the cruel madness of love, the honey of poison-flowers and all the measureless ills.
>
> Alfred, Lord Tennyson, *Maud*

As this quote from Tennyson illustrates, the same forces that drive the search for love and intimacy also motivate and set the scene for the dark side of human emotions and behavior in intimate relationships – rape, revenge, jealousy, violence, hatred, and even intimate homicide. Moreover, as we shall argue, such emotions and behaviors are not purely a function of pathology nor are they confined to particular cultures – they are built in at the ground level of human nature.

We know much about the prevalence and nature of intimate violence. The existence of competing views in any science, including psychology, is par for the course. However, the vitriolic levels of argument in this arena are legendary, and consensus has been hard to reach. The reasons partly have to do with the serious implications this debate has for public policy and safety, and the associated strongly held and contrasting ideological positions.

When one of the leading researchers in the field, Murray Straus, first presented data at a conference in 1977, suggesting that women were equally as violent as men in relationships, he was roundly booed. In subsequent years, he and his colleagues were

The Science of Intimate Relationships, First Edition. Garth Fletcher, Jeffry A. Simpson, Lorne Campbell, and Nickola C. Overall.
© 2013 Garth Fletcher, Jeffry A. Simpson, Lorne Campbell, and Nickola C. Overall.
Published 2013 by Blackwell Publishing Ltd.

subjected to numerous personal attacks and threats, up to and including death threats (Straus, 1999). Some researchers have also apparently suppressed data from large-scale studies that would have supported the contention that women in intimate relationships are frequently violent toward men (Straus, 1997).

The same kind of attitude is evident in the media. For example, experts interviewed on TV or the radio invariably stress the point that wife-beaters come from all socioeconomic strata, and that wealth and privilege do not protect women from the violent behavior of their partners. Too true. However, what they fail to mention is that, as everyone who is familiar with the research literature knows, there exists a strong link between serious partner abuse and socioeconomic status. Men who have lower incomes, lower-status jobs, or are unemployed are more likely to use physical violence against their partners (Magdol *et al.*, 1997; Straus and Gelles, 1990). The relationship between lower socioeconomic status and intimate homicide is especially marked (Polk, 1994).

So, in this chapter, like all of the topics in this book, it pays to park your prior beliefs before entering, and to examine what the science has to say in an open-minded fashion. We start with the topic already broached concerning gender differences in intimate violence, from pushing a partner to homicide. We then discuss the many factors explaining the massive variability of violence in intimate relationships, both within and across cultures, in the context of different theoretical approaches. Finally, we briefly consider how the scientific work in this area might provide guidance in the prevention and treatment of intimate relationship violence.

Gender Differences in Intimate Violence

Consider the following question. In intimate heterosexual relationships, who are more violent and physically aggressive – men or women? Our guess is you answered "men." Everyone knows that men are generally more aggressive and violent than women. Moreover, a substantial campaign over the last four decades across all western countries has been directed at raising public awareness of the problems of domestic violence and abuse that were previously condoned or hidden. In the process, laws have been changed, police practices have been substantially altered when dealing with domestic abuse, and networks of women's refuges or safe houses have been established.

Numerous campaigns, media interviews, books, and magazine articles in western countries have also painted more or less the same picture of the prototypical violent episode of a marital couple – male partner (probably drunk) comes home, complains about the dinner not being ready, and physically lashes out at his wife in an unprovoked assault. Conversely, the couple has a heated verbal argument, leading to the man attacking the women brutally with his fists. Male violence is almost always portrayed as an attempt to control a female partner or punish her for some imagined or real behavior, and the woman is cast as the helpless and bullied victim.

Indeed, there is a good deal of evidence consistent with this stereotypical view. Women are routinely killed more often than men by their partners (as we document later), and men are much more commonly arrested than women for intimate violence in western cultures (see Dutton and Nicholls, 2005). For example, in the UK, in a snapshot of one month in December, 2006, of the 3100 cases reported, 94% of those charged with assault or criminal damage against their partners or ex-partners were men (UK Crown Prosecution Service, 2007). In the same vein, four large government surveys conducted in the UK, Canada, and USA uniformly found that women report being a victim of criminal assault by their partners more frequently than men. For example, the US National Violence against Women Survey carried out in 1995 to 1996 found that of the 8000 men and 8000 women surveyed, 22.1% of women, but only 7.4% of men, reported having been a victim of physical assault by their partners across their lifetimes (Tjaden and Thoennes, 2000).

Research using the conflict tactics scale

However, when researchers began to measure rates of violence in intimate relationships from the 1970s using self-report scales that were not framed in terms of criminal behavior, and used community samples, the results were sharply at variance with both the conventional wisdom and the evidence just briefly reviewed. Most of this research has used the **conflict tactics scale**, originally developed by Murray Straus and published in 1979. A much longer version of this scale was also developed and published 17 years later (Straus *et al.*, 1996).

This scale asks individuals to report how often they have experienced a range of aggressive events in the past year of their relationship. Some of the items from this scale are shown in Figure 11.1. As can be seen, these events range from verbal violence behaviors such as sulking or stomping out of the room, to minor physical violence such as pushing or slapping, to extreme violence such as beating the partner up or using

Sample Items from the Conflict Tactics Scale (CTS)-assessed in terms of the number of times each event was initiated by the rater or the rater's partner over the past year.		
Verbal aggression	Minor Violence	Severe Violence
Insulted or swore at him/her	Threw something at him/her	Kicked, bit or hit him/her with a fist
Sulked or refused to talk about an issue	Pushed, grabbed, or shoved him/her	Beat him/her up
Stomped out of the room or house or yard	Slapped him/her	Choked him/her
Did or said something to spite him/her		Threatened him/her with knife or gun

Figure 11.1 Items from the conflict tactics scale (CTS)

a knife. Most studies ask people to report both how often they have initiated each activity, and also how often they have been subject to such behavior from their partner in the past year. The scales have together been cited in academic articles over 4000 times (as of October 2012), and have been widely used around the world. In a meta-analysis published in 2000, John Archer analyzed the results of over 70 studies, involving more than 60 000 participants, across many countries, including the USA, Canada, New Zealand, Korea, Israel, and the UK. It has also been used with both married and dating couples and, more recently, with lesbian and gay couples.

The results using the scale have consistently revealed frequencies of aggressive behavior in relationships much higher than the prior evidence from crime victim surveys had suggested. For married couples, about 16% of couples report at least one act of physical violence in the previous year (Straus and Gelles, 1988). For dating and cohabiting couples (who are, of course, younger than samples of married couples) the rate of violence is about double the married rate, the estimates being closer to 30% (see, for example, Hanly and O'Neill, 1997; Magdol et al., 1997). As might be expected, however, the reported rates for minor physical violence are considerably higher (in the 15 to 30% range) than for severe physical violence (in the 5 to 15% range).

The research bombshell Presumably surveys framed in terms of criminal behavior produce under-reporting because of the reluctance of individuals to interpret a push or a slap by their significant other as a criminal assault. However, the real bombshell from this body of research concerns the gender differences obtained, which are in stark contrast to the sex-role stereotype described above of the violent male and the victimized woman. The rates of violent acts (both minor and major) reported by men and women in intimate relationships using the conflict tactics scale are roughly equivalent, although there is a slight tendency for both men and women to report that women are more likely to be initiators of violence than men (Archer, 2000). Moreover, the prevalence and correlates of violence in lesbian and gay relationships is similar to those found in heterosexual relationships, and lesbian relationships are no less violent than gay relationships (Burke and Follingstad, 1999).

These findings of symmetry in intimate violence across gender have been obtained in both dating and married samples, across several countries, and using a variety of sampling and interviewing techniques (e.g. telephone and face-to-face interviewing). Most of this research has been reported in peer-reviewed journals, has used exemplary methodologies, and has included large samples (some in the thousands). In short, these research results are remarkably robust and well replicated. They have also resulted in claims that the incidence of violence of women against men in intimate relationships has been ignored or trivialized, and even that there exists a well-hidden "battered husband syndrome" (Steinmetz and Lucca, 1988). It is not difficult to see why these findings have provoked a storm of controversy.

Can people's intuitions and popular stereotypes really be that wrong? It turns out the answer is yes . . . and no. To begin to unravel the nuances and complexities in the scientific story, we first examine some of the most common criticisms leveled at the body of research using the conflict tactics scale, including those related to:

- the reliability and validity of the scale;
- research that has examined the contexts and motives of partners involved in violent episodes in intimate relationships;
- research that has examined how couples in violent relationships interact when discussing problems;
- the consequences of aggressive acts, including the most severe imaginable – death.

Is the conflict tactics scale reliable and valid?

In response to the counterintuitive results produced by the conflict tactics scale, criticisms have been leveled at both its **reliability** and **validity.** The reliability of a scale is concerned with its consistency. Consistency can be measured in at least two major ways. One method is in terms of the internal consistency of a scale. If a scale purportedly measures one construct (such as the tendency to be aggressive in a specific relationship), then people who complete the scale should be consistent in their responses across the items; that is, if respondents say they sometimes choke their partner, they should also be likely to report that they sometimes push their partner. The second method used is to get the same group of people to complete the same scale at two different points of time, leaving enough time (normally at least three weeks) between the two administrations to remove the possibility that people are simply remembering their prior responses and repeating them. The conflict tactics scale has performed well using either measure of consistency, with good internal reliability being reported (Straus *et al.*, 2006), and also good reliability found over time using overall indices of intimate violence. O'Leary *et al.* (1994), for example, reported correlations of .79 for men and .70 for women over a 12-month period in married couples, which reveals exceptional stability over this period of time.

Evidence of reliable measurement merely shows that the instrument is assessing something other than random noise (e.g. mistakes made by the respondents) or some construct that is inherently wildly variable (such as daily mood). Such evidence does not tell us what construct is actually being measured. The issue of whether a test or scale measures what it is intended to measure is termed its validity. Can we trust the conflict tactics scale to accurately reveal levels of violence and violence in intimate relationships? There are several standard ways of testing the validity of any scale or test. However, they all boil down to the same thing – does the test predict affect, behavior, or cognition in a fashion that is consistent with the underlying theory specifying what the test or scale supposedly measures?

How accurate are self-reports from the conflict tactics scale? It is certainly plausible that people might under-report levels of violence in their own relationships, given the possible shame or discomfort engendered in admitting such behavior to a total stranger.

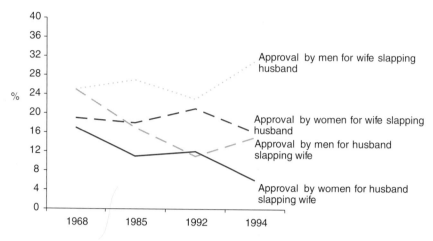

Figure 11.2   Approval of slapping spouse by gender from polls over time
Source: From Straus *et al.*, 1997; © 1997 SAGE Publications, Inc.

Surveys have shown that there exists general disapproval of intimate violence in western countries, and this attitude has strengthened to some extent over the last three decades. One analysis of a series of large surveys from 1968 to 1994 in the USA, by Straus *et al.* (1997), showed that approval by respondents of slapping a wife's face by a husband (under some circumstances) dropped from 20% in 1968 to under 10% (averaging across gender) in 1994, although men were somewhat more approving than women (see Figure 11.2). In the same time span, however, the percentage of respondents approving a wife slapping a husband's face (under some circumstances) increased slightly from 22% to 23% (see Figure 11.2), suggesting that the drop in approval for slapping a spouse was specifically focused on male violence. Interestingly, in the 1968 survey, over 70% of men and women cited being sexually unfaithful as justifying such an action (Strauss *et al.*, 1997).

This kind of asymmetry in approval of violence depending on the gender of the assailant (at least the less severe variety), may be a function of strength and size differences between men and women. A man hitting a woman is never funny, because it resembles bullying, whereas a woman hitting a man can be amusing – witness TV sitcoms where a woman hitting or pushing a man, or pouring beer over his head, is often portrayed to get a laugh.

In the course of a critique of the validity of the conflict tactics scale, Russell Dobash and his colleagues (Dobash *et al.*, 1992) argued that research showing poor agreement between partners who have completed the conflict tactics scale decisively invalidates the scale. Actually, the percentages of agreement across partners for each item are high (around 90%), but this is mainly produced by couples agreeing that no violence occurred in the last year. When the data are examined for couples in which at least one individual reported a violent act, the results show relatively weak levels of agreement, considering each item on the conflict tactics scale separately (Szinovacz and Eagly,

1995). However, given the vicissitudes of memory, response biases, and general noise, this is exactly what should be expected, especially given the inherent difficulty of accurately recalling who did what to whom concerning specific relationship events that occurred up to a year before.

Notice, however, that there is weak evidence of agreement between partners when taking each item on the conflict tactics scale separately. When faced with this situation, good psychometric practice is to sum the different measures of the same construct and then recalculate the relation between the two measures. Aggregating data in this way has the effect of substantially increasing the reliability of the measure, which in turn produces a far more accurate estimate of how this measure relates to other factors. To explain why, imagine assessing the relationship between the ability of a group of baseball batters and some measure of physical hand–eye coordination obtained in the laboratory. If the number of safe hits in a single game was used as a measure of batting ability, the two variables – safe hits and hand–eye coordination – would be related weakly at best. This is simply because there is so much luck and random noise involved in the success of a baseball batter in a single game that performance in one game constitutes an exceptionally unreliable measure of batting ability.

To obtain a more accurate measure, batting performance needs to be summed across many games, say for a whole season. If this expanded measure of batting ability was then correlated with hand–eye coordination, the real association between the two variables would be more accurately assessed. If the actual relationship between batting ability and test performance was high as a matter of empirical reality (say $r = .80$), the test would now reveal this at a lower but still substantial level (assuming that our measure of hand–eye coordination was also reliable and valid). For example, if the reliability of both measures was .90, then the correlation produced would be .65 ($.90 \times .90 \times .80$).

What goes for baseball goes for violence in relationships. Thus, the solution is to combine the individual indices of violence in relationships from the conflict tactics scale and recalculate the amount of agreement across partners. When this has been done, the agreement between partners is quite high (rather than non-existent or weak) with correlations of up to .70 (see Cantos *et al.*, 1994; Lawrence and Bradbury, 2001). These correlations represent more accurate estimates of the extent to which partners agree, and are not simply the inflated results of statistical tricks. Moreover, in a study by Lynn Magdol and colleagues (1997) using a large sample of couples, it was found that the same factors (educational attainment, employment status, and so forth) successfully predicted the incidence of violence – as assessed by the conflict tactics scale – in exactly the same way regardless of whether the rates of violence used came from the individuals' reports of self as protagonist or the reports of their partners as victims. These particular results provide powerful evidence for the validity of the conflict tactics scale.

Finally, there is solid evidence that responses to the conflict tactics scale predict what is often thought of as the gold standard in psychology – behavior. For example, several studies have found that couples who report high levels of severe violence, when matched against couples who are equal in terms of perceived marital quality but low in reported violence, are observed to be more caustic and critical with one another when discussing marital problems (Babcock *et al.*, 1993; Leonard and Roberts, 1998). The scale also predicts divorce with spectacular success. Erika Lawrence and Thomas Bradbury (2001) followed 56 recently wed couples over a four-year period, and found that couples who reported any violence (48% of the sample) sustained a 137% higher risk of separation or divorce than the non-aggressive couples. Couples who reported severe levels of violence (kicking, beating, and so forth) were especially likely to separate – 96% of this group failed to last the four years out (also see Chapter 12).

We have gone into some detail here in order to counter the scoffing that one occasionally hears from experts and laypeople alike concerning the validity of self-reports, especially concerning a charged topic like intimate violence. Of course, it is vital at some point to examine behavior. Self-reports are subject to distortion and bias, and they only go so far as proxies for behavioral events or as guides to personality traits and internal emotions and cognitions (see Chapters 2 and 4). There is also a long history in social psychology documenting the point that the links between what people say and what they do is variable and often uncertain. Nevertheless, the study of both verbal reports and behavior (and the connections between them) is a cornerstone of the science of intimate relationships.

In summary, in spite of claims to the contrary, a dispassionate analysis of the evidence shows that the conflict tactics scale provides reasonable ballpark estimates of the frequency of violence in intimate relationships. However, the critics are a long way short of being done.

What do the results from the conflict tactics scale really mean?

As critics have often pointed out, a problem with the conflict tactics scale is that it is not informative about the context and motives in which intimate violence occurs. It is possible, for example, that women are violent or aggressive mainly in defense of themselves or their children. Evidence from interviews with battered women describes the popular account, already alluded to, of almost anything triggering the man's violence (from wearing the wrong clothes, to being late, to making a critical comment). The eruption of violence from men is subsequently followed by abject apologies and empty promises that it will not happen again. The antecedent typically reported by the women is some sort of challenge to the authority of the partner, and the women claim that they rarely hit first (see for example, Dobash and Dobash, 1984; Walker, 1984).

The main difficulty with this body of research is that it only asks women about male-to-female violent episodes, and it uses self-selected samples of women who were battered by their husbands. It is folly to draw substantive conclusions about the natural ecology and nature of violence in intimate relationships from such work.

One clue about the nature of relationship violence is that one of the most powerful predictors of whether either men or women report being a victim of intimate violence is simply the extent to which they also report being perpetrators of intimate violence. A study by Lynn Magdol and colleagues (1997), with a sample of 861 young adults from New Zealand, found that women who were victims of severe violence from their partners were 10 times more likely to be perpetrators of severe violence, while victimized men were 19 times more likely to be perpetrators. This evidence suggests that intimate violence is typically a two-way street rather than consisting of one individual (man or woman) beating up a hapless victim. Moreover, several studies have found that women report striking the first blow in an argument as often as men (see Straus, 1997).

Various studies have also examined the attributions of the participants, using either general samples or couples seeking marital therapy. Again, these studies show a largely symmetrical pattern of reported explanations for the violence (of self or partner) across gender for both moderate and severe violent episodes, although there is some evidence that women attribute their own violence to self-defense somewhat more than men (Cascardi and Vivian, 1995) and there is reliable evidence that women are more fearful than men when couples are involved in a physical altercation (Cascardi *et al.*, 1999; Vivian and Langhinrichsen-Rohling, 1994). There is little evidence, however, that women are typically violent or aggressive in relationships mainly in response to the threatened or actual physical violence of their partners.

It is certainly the case that the incidence of violence is asymmetrical in some relationships. However, this asymmetry is not always from the male to the female. A study by Dina Vivian and Jennifer Langhinrichsen-Rohling (1994) of couples seeking marital therapy found (to the authors' surprise) that a subgroup of verbally and physically abused husbands emerged, that was as large as the group of abused wives. The largest group, consistent with what I have already outlined, was composed of couples who were equally abusive (albeit at relatively low levels). In short, the emerging evidence shows that a lot of intimate physical violence is dyadic in nature (see Langhinrichsen-Rohling, 2010).

Resolving the paradox

Two main ways have been proffered to resolve the stark inconsistency between the feminist-grounded literature and the criminal statistics, suggesting that men are more violent than women in intimate relationships, and the more general research examining relationship violence using the conflict tactics scale. We examine each of these in turn.

All men are not the same Perhaps both approaches are correct, but are examining different kinds of male samples. Women who escape to refuges, or end up in hospital with injuries, or whose partners are arrested, might be partnered with violent men who use physical violence to intimidate and control their partners. For this kind of sample, severe violence might also be largely asymmetrical with most of the violent behavior directed against women by men. When surveying or studying community-based samples, however, this kind of couple, and associated relationship violence, might fade into the tail in one of the distributions, and become less statistically visible.

The number of women ending up in hospital as a result of assaults from their husbands, in women's refuges, or even killed by their husbands, and the visibility of such events in the media, can make it appear as if such male violence is an epidemic. In fact even a superficial analysis makes it obvious that relatively small numbers of people can and do wreak havoc in society. The same victims (who may also be offenders) also tend to be counted again and again in crime statistics. As an illustration, in a survey of criminal offending with a large randomly selected sample of adults in New Zealand, a mere 0.05% of the sample (both men and women) accounted for a whopping 68% of the total number of times that people reported being physically or sexually assaulted. In short, a small number of people are apparently repeatedly being criminally assaulted, whereas most people are never or seldom assaulted (New Zealand Ministry of Justice report, 1996). The same pattern is true in other western countries.

There are also massive differences across couples and individuals in the propensity toward violence. Perhaps because they are so busy explaining the presence of violence in relationships, psychologists and others sometimes forget that in 50% or so of intimate relationships, at least in western countries, recourse to any sort of physical violence is non-existent or extremely rare. Michael Johnson (1995) in an influential article suggested that there are basically two different kinds of intimate relationship violence: common couple violence and patriarchal terrorism. Common couple violence consists of less severe violence, with both genders being victims and perpetrators. This kind of violence tends to be occasional and is largely a function of normal dyadic social psychological processes. Patriarchal terrorism, in contrast, is carried out by men who systematically use severe forms of violence to intimidate and control their partners – these are the classic wife-beaters whose partners escape to refuges, or end up in hospital, or are sometimes killed.

Johnson received considerable flak for his terminology from opposing camps. Many did not like the term "common" to describe relationship violence with its connotation of normalcy and acceptability. And others had problems with the term "patriarchal terrorism" because of its built-in feminist explanation in terms of societal oppression of women. To avoid such problems, Johnson has altered the terminology to **situational couple violence** versus **intimate terrorism**. In any event, a good deal of research has supported this kind of dichotomy (see Langhinrichsen-Rohling, 2010).

A different kind of equally influential analysis by Amy Holtzworth-Munroe and Gregory Stuart (1994) suggests that at one end of the intimate violence spectrum are men who might occasionally use the less serious forms of violence in their relationships. These men are not especially violent outside the family, have not suffered excessive violence in their childhood, are not particularly impulsive, have secure attachment styles, have reasonable social skills, do not have hostile attitudes toward women, and do not approve of violence generally. At the other end of the spectrum is every woman's nightmare – the prototypical partner-beater. This individual regularly uses severe forms of violence in his relationships, is generally violent outside the family, has suffered from excessive violence in his childhood, is impulsive, has an insecure attachment styles, has poor social skills, has hostile attitudes toward women, and generally approves of violence.

Severity and consequences of physical violence There also exists a well documented and marked asymmetry between male and female intimate violence, which may account for the persistent intuition that men are more violent than women in intimate relationships. Simply put, men are bigger, stronger, and more skilled at inflicting violence than women; hence, acts of violence by men against women are bound to cause more severe injuries and physical damage than the same acts carried out by women against men.

Surveys based on self-reports with large community-based samples have indeed found that the likelihood of intimate assaults by men causing injury is much higher than for women assailants (Straus, 1997). Studies from emergency rooms in hospitals similarly reveal that women are more likely to report being injured by their partners than are men. For example, a national sample of 1.4 million people admitted to hospital departments in 1994 in the USA found that 37% of the women and 5% of the men reported being injured by their partners or ex-partners.

In Archer's meta-analysis (2000), women were close to twice as likely to suffer injuries compared to men. Moreover, in a follow-up analysis focusing on the individual items in the conflict scales, Archer (2002) reported that women were more likely to slap, kick, bite, punch, or hit with an object. Men, on the other hand, were more likely to beat up, choke or strangle. These differences are likely to be function of gender differences and size. Gender differences in strength and size are also apparent in Jocelynne Scutt's (1983, p. 104) descriptions of typical violent episodes in a study of 127 married couples in Australia. Husbands were:

> slapped with an open hand or hit with hands; beaten with fists; kicked, scratched and bitten; had hair pulled; were hit with objects, including a frypan, saucepans, skillet, brooms, mugs, an ashtray and a squeegee mop. Three were threatened with a kitchen knife; two had crockery thrown at them; one was poked with a peeling knife. One was pushed down stairs and one had a pannikin of hot, soapy water from the washing machine thrown over him.

It is perhaps hard to imagine much nastier violence. However, it is informative to read (on the same page) Scutt's list of behaviors that violent men performed that women did not:

> No husband victim was punched about the head and shoulders, or in the stomach. Punches were aimed at the chest. No husband was attacked in the groin. No wife directed punches so injuries would not show; nor did wives say this is what they would do . . . No husband was threatened with a gun or chased with guns, knives, axes, broken bottles or by car. Husbands were not kicked or stamped on with steel-capped boots or heavy work boots; no husband was "driven furiously" in a family car, nor was any tossed out at the traffic lights. None was pushed against a wall or flung across the room; they were not held down in threatening positions, or against the wall unable to move. Strangling and choking were not used. No wife attempted suffocation with a pillow. Husbands were

not locked out, confined to particular areas of the house, or isolated from friends, nor were any given ultimatums about time spent away from home shopping . . . No husband had arms twisted and fingers bent; none was frog marched out to the garden to hose, dig or mow the lawn. None was ordered to weed the garden whilst being kicked from the rear. Nor was any husband dragged out of bed at midnight to change the washer on the kitchen tap.

Many men, because of their strength and size advantage, can use physical violence or the threats of physical violence to coerce, humiliate, and control their partners in a fashion that women are generally unable to emulate (even if they wanted to). This does not mean that women do not also sometimes attempt to control, coerce, and humiliate their male partners, but they will generally not have access to the broad menu of physically violent activities, available to men, in the pursuance of such goals.

Summary

To summarize, the conflict tactics scale is a reliable and valid scale for assessing the frequency of intimate violence. Its widespread use reveals that levels of violence are quite high in many countries around the world, and also shows that men and women initiate about the same number of violent acts in intimate relationships. However, men use more serious forms of physical violence than women and are considerably more likely than women to inflict injuries. This latter gender asymmetry reaches its zenith in the most extreme outcome possible of intimate relationship violence; namely, the death of the partner.

Till Death do us Part: Homicide in Intimate Relationships

In virtually all countries from which data are available, men kill their partners more often than women do (see Figure 11.3). Margo Wilson and Martin Daly (1992) collated data, from the 1930s to the late 1980s, showing that for the total number of intimate homicides men were guilty of 100% of cases in India, 95% across several African cultures, 86% in Denmark, 81% in England/Wales, 76% in Australia and Canada, and 71% in Scotland. The same pattern is true in New Zealand, with 87% of intimate homicides carried out by men from 1993 to 1998 (see Fletcher, 2002). The data from 2000 to 2005 in the USA again show the same pattern, with men killing 7093 female partners or ex-partners, and women killing 2063 partners or ex-partners. As shown in Figure 11.3 this means 77% of the intimate murders were committed by men against their partners (see US Bureau of Justice, 2007).

A few other background facts are useful to help explain and illuminate the different psychological motivations involved for men and women for intimate homicide. In all western countries, including the USA, men kill much more frequently outside the context of intimate relationships than do women. In the USA, for example, from 2000 to 2005, 32% of women homicide victims were killed by a partner or ex-partner,

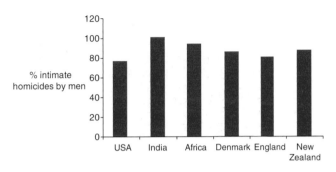

Figure 11.3   Intimate homicide: huge gender differences round the world
Source: Taken from Fletcher 2002; Wilson and Daly, 1992

whereas only 3% of men were killed by an intimate (US Bureau of Justice, 2007). Men much more frequently kill their ex-partners than women (Wilson and Daly, 1992). And finally, men quite frequently commit suicide after killing their wife. Women almost never do. For example, in Block and Christakos' (1995) analysis of Chicago intimate homicides from 1965 to 1990, 25.2% of white men committed suicide after killing their partner, but not a single white female did so. Finally, the number one factor in predicting intimate homicides, for either men or women as victims, is the prior incidence of serious intimate violence (Campbell *et al.*, 2007). We return to these facts later.

Explaining Relationship Violence

Up to now we have concentrated on establishing the broad empirical realities, amid the confusion and clamor of competing views and interpretations. In the course of this next analysis we will describe some of the factors that explain the massive variability of relationship violence both across and within cultures, and we put together an integrated framework that takes both distal and proximal-level factors into account (see Chapter 1).

To help in this task, a general schematic model is shown in Figure 11.4. In this model the **distal** factors comprise the genetic and cultural forces, which are not independent but influence one another over deep time (see Chapter 2). These distal factors feed into the more **proximal-level** factors that we have split into three components – the individual differences that people bring with them into relationships (e.g. **attachment working models**), the relationship-level factors (e.g. relationship communication), and contextual factors (e.g. situational stress).

The three dominant theories that deal with relationship violence – an evolutionary approach, a feminist perspective, and a social psychological view – tend to focus on

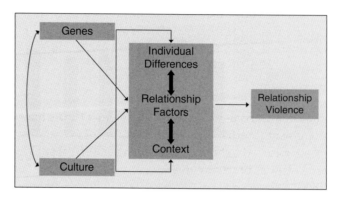

Figure 11.4   A general model of intimate violence

different aspects in Figure 11.4, with evolutionary psychology concentrating on evolutionary **adaptations** (via genes), feminist approaches focusing on the role of culture, and social psychological approaches dealing with the proximal-level determinants. In the following discussion we outline the strengths and weaknesses of each major approach, which will help to build an overarching approach to relationship violence, along with a more inclusive and powerful theory dealing with all the relationship phenomena considered in this book.

An evolutionary approach

At first blush, intimate violence or homicide seems like a tough nut for an evolutionary account to crack, given that such activities seem likely to decrease (not increase) the chances of insemination occurring or of children surviving until adulthood. All the evidence points toward dyadic violence constituting a largely maladaptive way of dealing with conflict (see Chapters 9 and 12). Asymmetric violence, such as wife-beating, is likely to be even more corrosive. The prototypical script for developing hatred in relationships is the suffering of unjustified pain and humiliation at the hands of a partner that the individual is powerless to prevent – a good description of asymmetric intimate violence. Relationship violence in western societies is associated with increased chances of separation, homicide (by both men and women), and male suicide. In short, as a strategy for controlling one's spouse (or partner) it looks downright dysfunctional, viewed either in contemporary terms or in terms of long-term adaptive advantages in our evolutionary past.

However, the way in which biological evolution influences behavior can be convoluted. We draw mainly from the work of Margo Wilson and Martin Daly in the following discussion (Daly and Wilson, 1988; Daly *et al.*, 1981; Wilson and Daly, 1992, 1993, 1996). Their emphasis is on explaining the propensity of men to be violent toward women, leading in its most extreme form to homicide. They do not dismiss the fact that women are sometimes violent and even kill their husbands, but they argue that female intimate violence is usually a reaction to, or a defense against, male violence (we will return to this point later). In the hands of Wilson and Daly, an evolutionary approach to intimate violence is intellectually subtle – so we take some time to expound it.

Their argument is by now a familiar one. It is based on the observations that human males have a problem with establishing paternity, and that female humans are sexually receptive almost constantly. Sexual competition, and the costs of rearing a child fathered by another man, are assumed to be strong selection pressures that have influenced the evolution of psychological processes and structures. The need for men to establish paternity, and the associated long-term effort involved in helping raise one's children to maturity, so the argument goes, have evolved tendencies in men to take a proprietary view of women's sexuality and reproductive capacity – to be "motivated to lay claim to particular women as songbirds lay claim to territories, as lions lay claim to a kill, or as people of both sexes lay claim to valuables" (Wilson and Daly, 1993, p. 276).

The cross-cultural evidence supports the postulation of an evolved male sexual proprietorial tendency, with a set of features that are virtually ubiquitous across cultures; namely, institutions of marriage with rights and obligations, the valuation of female faithfulness, the "protection" of women from outside sexual contacts, the conception of adultery by women as a property violation, and the special case of a wife's unfaithfulness as a "justifiable" provocation for male violence (Wilson and Daly, 1993). The occasional claim by anthropologists that in some cultures sexual activity is a free and easy affair devoid of sexual jealousy or possessiveness is almost certainly without foundation (see Chapter 10).

Women are also possessive of their male mates, and should be powerfully motivated to hold on to their male partners to help raise the children. The difference between the genders is that men are more focused on the sexual aspects than are women. Thus, as described in the previous Chapter 10, men suffer from sexual jealousy primarily as a response to their partners having sex with another person, whereas women are more psychologically attuned to the threat of losing the relationship.

The final step in the argument is that because men have greater physical strength than women, they will be tempted to use this resource to exercise control over their partners and to express their sexual jealousy in physical terms. Hence, there is no suggestion by Daly and Wilson that men have evolved psychological mechanisms to attack and kill their partners and their own children. Rather, the tendency for men to be violent toward women is essentially a byproduct of men's greater physical size and strength, combined with a syndrome of evolved psychological tendencies to view sexual access to their mates as a valuable personal possession to be guarded and protected. On this account, excessive intimate violence by men represents a dysfunctional manifestation of formerly functional adaptations. The tendency of a minority of men to behave in such a dysfunctional fashion does not endanger the evolutionary thesis, provided that the average advantages to fitness have been sustained over evolutionary time by the evolved mechanisms. Evolutionary adaptations often carry costs that are outweighed by the advantages in terms of reproductive fitness.

Such an evolutionary account is theoretically plausible, and is consistent with the evidence from several studies across different countries that sexual jealousy and threats of women leaving (or actually leaving) are common reasons for men murdering their partners or ex-partners (see Campbell *et al.*, 2003a, 2003b; Kaighobadi *et al.*, 2009). Homicide by women, in contrast, is more often motivated by defending themselves or their children against their partner's persistent physical abuse (Polk, 1994; but see Harris, 2003). The partners in question will also often be boyfriends or stepfathers, not the biological father of the children (Campbell *et al.*, 2007).

The strength of an evolutionary account (indeed its main aim) is that it provides causal explanations for human dispositions and proclivities that are widespread across cultures. Thus, Daly and Wilson postulate the existence of evolved tendencies in men to take a proprietary attitude toward their women partners. Excessive violence, such as homicide, is treated as an occasional dysfunctional outcome, as an evolutionary trade-off associated with this evolved male proprietorial attitude to women. This kind of explanation predicts the existence of systematic gender differences in intimate violence across cultures. From the evidence we have reviewed here, extreme forms of violence – leading to injury and death – are indeed mainly perpetrated by men against women across cultures.

Daly and Wilson's evolutionary approach also impressively deals with some of the puzzling findings concerning the factors associated with male homicide, and the differences in the contexts in which homicides are perpetrated by men and women. For example, men often kill their ex-partners, whereas women are less likely to do so, and men quite often commit suicide after intimate homicides whereas women hardly ever do. If men view women in terms of sexual ownership (more than the other way around), then losing such a precious possession for men who perceive they have little else to hang their manhood and status on may be the final straw.

We conclude that an evolutionary approach nicely explains what Michael Johnson has termed intimate terrorism. However, it does not explain, or even deal with, what he has termed situational couple violence. The use of minor to moderate forms of violence is equally prevalent in men and women in western countries, and, hence, requires a different sort of analysis. Moreover, the fact that many intimate relationships in western countries are virtually free of any physical violence should be kept in mind. Theories that explain the presence of intimate violence also need to explain its absence. Evolutionary approaches tend to repeat the error of a feminist approach in that they typically treat all interpersonal violence as something men do to women, rather than in terms of dyadic interactions that often involve women initiating a physically violent interchange.

A feminist perspective

Not all those who argue that violence in intimate relationships is something that men do to women adopt a feminist approach, but feminist approaches do advocate such views. According to this approach, gender is a pivotal social and political structure or principle that pervades and structures society. Thus, the use of violence by men against

Qui aime bien châtie bien.

Figure 11.5 Old French proverb illustrated by Grandville

women in intimate relationships is part of a general societal pattern in which men maintain their power through the subjugation and mistreatment of women. Intimate violence is placed in the same category as rape, sexual harassment, and incest, in which men are inevitably the perpetrators and women are the victims. Intimate violence in relationships is thus caused by men, and is linked to their dominant role in society (see, for example, Kurz, 1997).

Even a superficial knowledge of the history of western society makes it obvious that women have been discriminated against and repressed, especially in marital and sexual relationships, as shown in the illustration of the French proverb – he *who loves well, punishes well* – by J. J. Grandville published in 1845 (see Figure 11.5). The illustration is intended as a satirical comment on the proverb. Nevertheless, physical punishment of both children and wives has been regarded in the past in western cultures as both normal and even desirable, right up to the twentieth century.

Until relatively recently, American women were regarded in law as the property of their husbands, with husbands being legally entitled to confine wives against their will and to use force to obtain their conjugal rights. Adultery by wives was regarded as a basis for seeking financial compensation through the law, and often also as a reasonable defense for killing one's wife. Related laws and legislation have only slowly been dismantled over the last 100 years, and this process continues today. In Texas, for example, if a man killed his wife because she had been unfaithful to him, this constituted a legal defense until 1976.

Feminist approaches to intimate violence often lean toward a postmodernist orientation. Thus, they stress political and practical aims rather than standard scientific goals. Such political aims deal with policy, law, the provision of women's refuges, police practices dealing with rape and intimate violence, and so forth. It is not difficult to see why those adopting a feminist approach to intimate violence reacted against the work of Murray Straus and others using the conflict tactics scale, which suggested intimate violence in heterosexual relationships is a two-way street. A recent example is the response by Jacquelyn White and colleagues (White *et al.*, 2000) to John Archer's (2000) immaculate and detailed review of the literature in intimate violence, in which they argued that Archer should have downplayed the findings because they would undermine efforts to eradicate violence against women.

Not all postmodernists are feminists, however. For example, Paul Heelas (1989) adopting a strong relativist position, argues that Yanamamö wife-beating should not be considered violence because inflicting physical injuries is how a husband shows that he cares for his wife in this culture! The fact that wife-beating among the Yanamamö can cause serious injuries, and even death, and that Yanamamö women try hard to avoid such treatment, are points that seem to have escaped this author (see Chagnon, 1992).

The feminist approach has its strengths. First, it reasonably stresses the link between societal norms and values and what happens within intimate relationships. Second, it correctly identifies the differences in power that men and women have traditionally had in relation to sex, intimate relationships, marriage, and so forth, as central to understanding violence in intimate relationships. However, it also has its weaknesses. First, it has nothing to say about the origins of such societal patterns. Second, it has no explanatory resources to deal with the huge differences across heterosexual relationships. Why are many relationships in western society devoid of violence, and why does the incidence and extent of violence vary so much within and between cultures? Feminist approaches, as a matter of principle, stick to a broad sociological level of analysis and, hence, have relatively little to offer by way of explanation.

A social psychological approach

A social psychological approach deals well with what is termed situational couple violence, which is dyadic and perpetrated by both men and women. It also deals with the proximal-level forces shown in Figure 11.4.

Starting with the impact of individual differences, more violent individuals in relationships are younger (Bookwala *et al.*, 2005; Carrado *et al.*, 1996), less well educated (Magdol *et al.*, 1997), more likely to be unemployed (Magdol *et al.*, 1997), more depressed (Filson *et al.*, 2010; Magdol *et al.*, 1997), have more accepting attitudes to violence against women (Archer, 2006), and tend to have insecure attachment working models (Godbout *et al.*, 2009). Moreover, these kinds of variables not only predict intimate relationship violence within western cultures, but also within non-western cultures, such as India (Martin *et al.*, 1999) and Eastern Uganda (Karamagi *et al.*, 2006; also see Archer, 2006).

Contextual factors that increase the risk of intimate violence include alcohol consumption, which impairs self control and fosters hostile responses, and again this seems to be the case across many countries and cultures (see Graham *et al.*, 2011). Emotions like sexual jealousy and anger can also be powerful triggers of relationship violence (Fitness, 1996). However the role of such factors needs to be located within a dyadic, interpersonal context. In Chapter 2, we outlined three key axioms and associated terms from a key social psychological theory termed interdependence theory – internal standards, mutual influence, and interpersonal attributions.

The research on intimate violence confirms the central role played by these last two of these factors. Specifically, as we noted previously, perhaps the strongest predictor of violence perpetrated by one individual in a relationship is simply how often the other partner initiates violence (see Magdol *et al.*, 1997). Couples who are dissatisfied, experiencing a lot of conflict, and have caustic and critical verbal arguments, also tend to have higher levels of violence (Gottman *et al.*, 1995; Stith *et al.*, 2008). Finally, an imbalance in relationships status in the relationship, specifically with higher levels of socioeconomic status or decision-making power residing with the female partner, is a predictor of intimate violence (Babcock *et al.*, 1993). This last finding is consistent with both an evolutionary and a feminist approach, because it suggests that some men feel threatened when their partners have more power in the relationship.

In the model of the relationship mind shown in Figure 3.1 (Chapter 3), cognitions and emotions comprise the proximal-level causes of relationship behavior, but self-regulation processes typically moderate the way in which these are expressed, often shutting them down completely. A recent study by Eli Finkel and colleagues (Finkel *et al.*, 2009) found that people frequently reported experiencing urges to physically assault their partners when having an argument (51% of the sample), but less than half this figure (21%) reported acting out this urge. In a clever experimental follow-up, these authors devised an analogue measure of intimate violence by measuring how long individuals would ask their partners to sustain painful yoga poses about a drawing they produced. As depicted in Figure 11.6, receiving negative feedback had no effect in the control condition. However, when the cognitive self-regulatory resources of participants were depleted by getting them to do a difficult perceptual task, participants "punished" their partners more after receiving negative feedback about their drawings.

A straight personality account seeks to explain the tendency for intimate violence in both men and women in terms of stored personality characteristics, beliefs, attitudes, and the like. A full-blooded social psychological account (which includes personality) of interpersonal violence goes further, and describes the way in which such stored dispositions interact with cognitive and affective processes, both within individuals and also in terms of interpersonal interchanges. For example, a study by

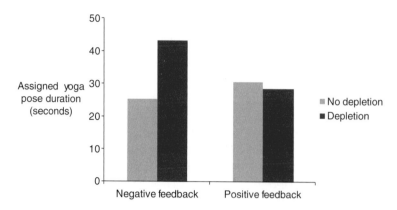

Figure 11.6 Punishing your partner as a function of feedback and cognitive resource depletion
Source: From Finkel *et al.*, 2009; © 2009 American Psychological Association

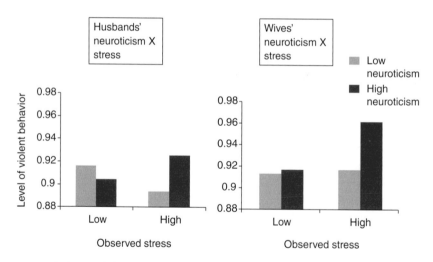

Figure 11.7 Intimate violence as a function of the interaction between neuroticism and stress
Source: From Hellmuth and McNulty, 2008; © 2008 American Psychological Association

Hellmuth and McNulty (2008) tracked 169 couples for the first four years of their marriage. As shown in Figure 11.7, they found that individuals who were neurotic were especially likely to be physically aggressive when they were suffering high levels of stress. However, these negative effects of being neurotic were wiped out when stress levels were low.

The evidence marshaled in this chapter suggests that relationship violence can effectively be interpreted and explained with the focus on the relationship context, rather than simply on one individual using physical violence against a helpless victim. Asymmetric violence happens in relationships to be sure; however, physical violence also frequently occurs in the context of dyadic conflict and argument. At low levels of couple violence, the evidence indicates that women are equally likely to initiate physical violence. As the intensity and lethality of violence rises, however, the dangers for women increase more sharply than for men. However, even when the violence in a relationship is one-way traffic, the nature of the relationship and the participants' relationship cognition and affect remain an important component of a social psychological explanation for the violent behavior.

The major strength of a social psychological account is that it offers a fine-grained explanation of the proximal-level processes involved in the dyadic interchanges that lead to physical violence. Thus, it deals well with the wide individual and couple differences within cultures. However, it has two major lacunae. First, it does not address the ultimate distal causes of dispositional proclivities to violence in men or women, which also means that the causes for fundamental gender differences are not dealt with. Second, it fails to consider the wider cultural contexts that clearly play a role in the explanation of violence in intimate relationships.

Explaining variability in intimate violence within and between cultures

Attempting to integrate the distal and proximal-level causes for intimate violence operating at the distal (evolutionary adaptations and culture) and proximal (individual differences and dyadic relationship) levels, can explain some of the puzzling variability both within and between cultures.

For example, we can take into account the manifold ways in which environmental and cultural factors interact with basic inherited characteristics. Such interactions can combine to produce cultural settings in which a significant minority of women can become almost as violent and lethal as men in intimate relationships (compare the vanishingly small number of men killed by their partners in India, with the substantial number in the USA). Alternately, cultures and sub-cultures currently exist in which the incidence of severe male violence is extremely rare (e.g. wealthy men living in Scandinavia). Such cultural differences point to the power of the culture in shaping human psychology, and provide evidence of the malleability of biological imperatives in humans. However, cultures have to work hard to combat incipient tendencies deriving from our biological inheritance. Perhaps no cultures in the history of humankind have worked harder than western cultures over the last 50 years (impelled, in part, by the women's movement) to develop laws and institutions that address gender-linked inequalities and give women and men a just and level playing field in marriage, divorce settlements, and intimate relationships. Yet, serious intimate violence by men against women continues to be a major problem in western cultures.

A principal challenge for any evolutionary approach is to explain the wide variability, both within and between cultures, in intimate violence. The existence of such differences in intimate violence is typically explained by evolutionary psychologists in terms of the way in which cultural and environmental factors interact with, and either suppress or exaggerate universal biologically inherited dispositions. For example, the tendency for men (but rarely women) to stalk and murder their ex-partners – often accompanied by the chilling vow "if I can't have her no one will" – is an extreme manifestation of a distinct male pattern of possessiveness in romantic liaisons.

The ability to anonymously stalk one's ex-partner in western cultures has been ominously enhanced with the availability of e-mail, the internet, and Facebook – to the point that some states in the USA have passed cyber-stalking laws. The first person to be prosecuted in California under this law, in January 1999, was Gary Dellapenta, who posted messages under his ex-partner's name (with attached phone number and address) in online chat rooms describing her supposed desire to be raped by a stranger. The victim subsequently received dozens of obscene phone calls and terrifying house calls by men in the early hours of the morning. It took some determined computer sleuthing to catch the villain.

However, certain kinds of men are more likely to murder their partners in western countries; namely, men who are highly depressed, suffer psychiatric problems, are of low socioeconomic status, are unemployed, and have drug-related problems (Campbell *et al.*, 2007; Polk, 1994). For such men, the loss of their partners and children may be the final nail in the coffin of their perceived worth and social status. The common tendency of men to commit suicide after such murders is consistent with this account – they have nothing left to live for, and their wives (so they believe) deserve to die along with them. Severe violence, threats of such violence, or death threats, represent final throws of the dice by desperate men, impelled by a potent psychological cocktail of sexual jealousy and the desire not to lose their last precious "possession" – their wife and children.

Another factor that should influence intimate violence is the intensity of intrasexual competition. If there are lots of spare men floating around, this should increase the tendency for men in sexual relationships to more vigilantly guard their mates, be more likely to suffer from sexual jealousy, and hence, to fall back on violence to control their partners. Consistent with this proposal, wife-beating is more common in polygamous societies (that have more spare men hanging around) than in monogamous societies (Levinson, 1989).

Whether marriage is arranged or based on choice is also related to differences in violence across societies. This in no way implies that in cultures that practice arranged marriage romantic love and extramarital affairs are unheard of, or that the normal processes of bonding, love, and intimacy do not develop in arranged marriages (see Chapter 7). However, when arranged marriage is combined with both a dowry arrangement and **patrilocality** (the woman going to live with the husband and his immediate family), this particular combination can place women in a more dangerous position. Prime examples are the well-publicized cases of bride-burning in India. There is also evidence that in India the female in-laws may at times combine with or encourage the husband in the physical abuse of young wives (Fernandez, 1997).

Overall levels of violence and crime in a society perhaps also produce a climate in which violence may come to be regarded as a legitimate form of behavior in the exercise of power, and this may spill over into intimate relationships. An analysis by Wilfred Masumura (1979) of 86 traditional cultures found that higher levels of intimate violence were associated with relatively high rates of personal crime, theft, violence, homicide, and feuding.

However, one should be wary of taking this generalization too far, given that cultures often have disparate social norms that apply to separate domains, and also differ in terms of specific social norms and sanctions against male violence against women either inside or outside marriage. For example, the much lower rate of intimate homicide in the USA among Latinos as opposed to among African-Americans, even though the two groups have similar socioeconomic and crime profiles, can be explained by the strong prohibition of violence against women in Latino culture (Block and Christakos, 1995). This prohibition in Latino culture may be linked to the fact that Latinos are predominantly Catholic, and Catholicism assigns a special status to wives and mothers (exemplified in the deification of the mother of Jesus – the Virgin Mary).

A review and analysis of cross-cultural studies by John Archer (2006) intriguingly found that as gender equality and economic power for women increased across countries, women became more violent in relationships and men became less violent. The existence of sexist attitudes and approval of wife-beating in cultures was also associated with higher rates of violence toward women. These differences across cultures are not subtle. The example given by Archer is Egypt, where gender equality is low. In this country close to 70% of a representative sample agreed that a man was justified in beating his wife for refusing sex or answering him back. By contrast, in New Zealand, which has relatively high levels of gender equality, the approval rates for the same questions were 1%.

Can Relationship Violence be Prevented, and, if so, How?

Our discussion and analysis shows that intimate violence is a product of many factors operating at multiple levels, from genetic distal origins and related gender differences, to the influence of culture, along with personality traits and contextual factors, including the dynamics of the dyadic interaction. This analysis suggests that changing people's violent behavior in intimate relationships is a tall order. Nevertheless, we know that in some cultural contexts, for some couples, intimate sexual relationships are devoid of violence. Indeed, as we noted previously, physical aggression is essentially non-existent in close to 50% of relationships; thus, non-violent relationships are commonplace.

Not much can be done currently about the genetic wellspring of violent or aggressive proclivities, and associated gender differences (although who knows where genetic engineering will take the human species). However, behavior within intimate relationships is strongly influenced by cultural norms, legal systems, socialization, and personal experiences in the family (see Chapter 5). And cultural norms that encourage or discourage family and relationship violence can and do change substantially over time. Thus, social media campaigns against intimate violence (which are commonplace in western countries) may help to change attitudes, and perhaps even behavior, over time.

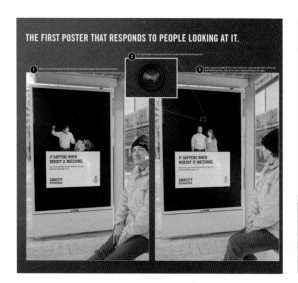 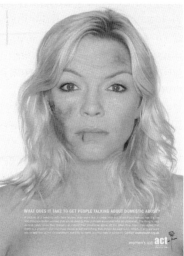

Figure 11.8   Can intimate violence be prevented? Advertising programs
Source: Images (left) Reprinted with permission by advertising agency Jung von Matt. http://
www.jvm.com/en/ ©Jung von Matt/Spree GmbH (right). Reprinted with permission from
Women's Aid Federation of England. © 2007 Women's Aid Federation

Such advertising can get pretty slick. Figure 11.8 shows an example sponsored by
Amnesty International in Hamburg, Germany, of a poster in a bus stop. The bus stop
is installed with a device that tracks eye gaze. When the individual looks at the poster,
it shows a smiling, seemingly happy, couple. When the individual's eyes are averted,
the poster switches to the man punching the woman.

Marital therapy can help couples communicate better and deal with conflict in more
harmonious ways (see Chapter 12). However, the success of treatments for male
violence, usually mandated as part of the sentence for criminal convictions related to
intimate violence, has been poor (Babcock *et al.*, 2004). Jennifer Langhinrichsen-
Rohling (2010) has argued that part of the problem is that existing, state-supported
intervention treatments are overwhelmingly based on a feminist approach, and thus
focus on the male while eschewing approaches which deal with the couple's communication and interaction.

If we are right that intimate violence is, in part, a function of relationship dynamics,
then ignoring the role of female partners, and the relationship more broadly, is bound
to limit the effectiveness of either advertising blitzes or clinical interventions. However,
the role of the relationship, and of women generally, in the incidence of intimate
violence is increasingly gaining recognition by psychologists and others, and promising
interventions have been tested that operate at the dyadic level. For example, Woodin
and O'Leary (2010) first developed a brief two-hour motivational interview that runs
over risk factors, negative outcomes of relationship violence, the role of alcohol, and

the need for change. This feedback is addressed to both members of the couple, not just the men. In testing the effectiveness of the intervention, 50 dating couples (who all previously indicated some physical violence in their relationships) were tracked over nine months – the results showed a surprisingly large reduction of intimate violence for both men and women, compared to a control group.

Summary and Conclusions

We began this chapter with a conundrum. On the one hand there is a good deal of evidence consistent with the conventional wisdom that men are more violent than women in intimate relationships. But, on the other hand, well replicated evidence from many studies using the conflict tactics scale shows that men and women initiate about the same number of violent acts in intimate relationships. Moreover, the conflict tactics scale has turned out to be a reliable and valid measure of relationship violence.

We resolved this puzzle in two ways. First, the kind of violence in relationships can be strikingly different. What Michael Johnston has termed situational couple violence consists of less severe violence, with both genders being victims and perpetrators. This sort of violence tends to be occasional and is largely a function of normal dyadic social psychological processes. Intimate terrorism, in contrast, is carried out by men who systematically use severe forms of violence to intimidate and control their partners – these are the classic partner-beaters whose partners escape to refuges, or end up in hospital, or even dead. The community samples typically accessed using the conflict tactics scale mainly report violence fitting into the situational couple camp. Second, because men are stronger and bigger than women they have the edge in the ability to physically intimidate and threaten, and they also inflict more serious injuries than women. Indeed, men are more likely to kill women than women are to kill men in intimate relationships all over the world.

None of the theoretical approaches we have considered are flat-out wrong, unless they are presented as stand-alone grand theories that attempt to exclude other approaches – which unfortunately is sometimes the case. Both evolutionary approaches and feminist approaches have a lot to offer in terms of the distal causes – be they evolutionary adaptations or cultural structures. And, social psychological approaches offer insight into the proximal-level forces involved in dyadic interaction. Knitted together, they promise a more comprehensive and satisfying explanation of intimate violence. We postpone such a thorough-going integration of such approaches until the final chapter. However, it is already apparent from this chapter why the dark side of human emotions and behavior in intimate relationships – exemplified in relationship violence – can be such a short psychological journey from love and passion.

Part Five

Ending Relationships:
the Causes and Consequences
of Relationship Dissolution

Relationship Dissolution **12**

Predicting relationship dissolution – are the fates of relationships sealed before they begin? – the power and limitations of relationship maintenance strategies – consequences of relationship dissolution – the impact of divorce on children – moving on and letting go – relationship therapy – summary and conclusions

> You've been messing where you shouldn't have been messin', and now someone else is gettin' all your best . . . You keep lying when you ought to be truthin', you keep losing when you ought to not bet, you keep saming when you ought to be changin', now what's right is right but you ain't been right yet . . . These boots are made for walking, and that's just what they'll do. One of these days these boots are gonna walk all over you . . . Are you ready boots, start walking . . .
>
> Nancy Sinatra

You have finally found someone to love. You have traversed the fraught mating market, and invested considerable time and resources in a budding relationship, including integrating your partner into family and friendship networks. You have overcome the inevitable difficulties along the way, such as jealousy of attractive rivals and learning to trust each other, and you are still together and relatively happy a year down the track. This is a feat in itself – around 65% of newly minted dating relationships don't last the year out (Fletcher *et al.*, 2000b). But, you are now ready to take the next big step.

Fifty years ago, that step would have been marriage, but in western cultures the majority of couples now live together before or instead of marriage (Cherlin, 2004), although the rates vary considerably across countries with Scandinavian countries leading the way. To give a few examples, the proportion of those cohabiting prior to

The Science of Intimate Relationships, First Edition. Garth Fletcher, Jeffry A. Simpson, Lorne Campbell, and Nickola C. Overall.
© 2013 Garth Fletcher, Jeffry A. Simpson, Lorne Campbell, and Nickola C. Overall.
Published 2013 by Blackwell Publishing Ltd.

marriage is above 90% in Sweden (Andersson and Philipov, 2002), 78% in Australia (Hayes *et al.*, 2010), and 66% in the USA (National Center for Family and Marriage Research, 2010). Moreover, many cohabitating couples have children. In the US, for example, more than 40% of cohabiting couples have children. In short, **cohabitation** has become a long-term option (replacing marriage) for many people. Regardless of whether the step is to live together "in sin" (as it was quaintly termed in previous generations) or to get married, this decision represents a serious relationship investment for most people.

What are the odds of romantic relationships ending in dissolution? The figure that is bandied around in the zeitgeist for marriage is 50%. Actually, the only countries that even approach this figure are Belgium and the USA (OECD, 2011), and the divorce rate in the US seems to be have been coming down over the last decade or so (Heaton, 2002). The probability of first-time marriages ending in divorce is closer to 35% in other western countries like New Zealand, Australia, Canada, and the UK (Bascand, 2009; Bramlett and Mosher, 2002; Jain, 2007). Countries like Mexico, Italy, Greece, and Turkey, have lower divorce rates again, but, like almost everywhere else, the divorce rates in these countries have also markedly increased since the 1970s (OECD, 2011). The world record for the lowest divorce rate is the Philippines (close to zero), but this is because it is the only country in the world in which divorce remains illegal (with a few exceptions made for Muslims). Some representative figures for different countries are shown in Figure 12.1, using crude divorce rates per 1000 population in 1970, and the increase in 2008.

The odds of successful, lasting cohabitation are even slimmer than those of marriage. Over half of non-married couples who live together break up within two years and about 90% dissolve within five years (Bumpass and Sweet, 1989). The ties that bind couples together when cohabiting are just not as strong as when marital vows are made, although the explanations for this fact are contentious (as will be seen later).

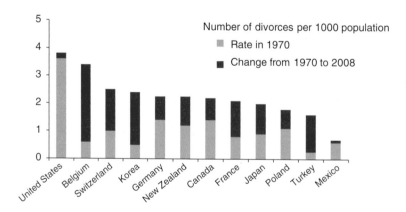

Figure 12.1 The increase in crude divorce rates from 1970 to 2008 across 12 countries
Source: Based on data from chart "SF3.1.E: The increase in crude divorce rates from 1970 to 2008" from OECD (2011), OECD Family Database, OECD, Paris. www.oecd.org/social/family/database

The growth over the last 60 years in divorce rates, cohabitation, and the increasing numbers of sole parents and blended families, have together generated fears that the standard family structure is in tatters, and that traditional values are going the way of the dodo. However, a historical and cross-cultural overview suggests there is nothing unusual about current relationship dissolution and divorce rates around the world. Marriage, in one form or another, with its rights and obligations, is a universal (Fletcher, 2002), and so is divorce or separation (Fisher, 1992; see Chapter 7). Hardly surprising then that separation, divorce, and heartbreak are regular themes in pop songs and the media (illustrated by the lyrics of Nancy Sinatra's 1966 signature hit, at the beginning of the chapter).

The earliest known study of divorce, by the noted Egyptian historian al-Sakhawi in the fifteenth century, reported that for about 500 women in Cairo, 30% of marriages ended in divorce, and women married more than once, with many marrying three times or more (see Rapoport, 2005). During the nineteenth century in Japan, in rural villages divorce and remarriage were commonplace. One analysis of registers in two rural villages in Japan revealed that more than 66% of marriages ended in divorce before individuals reached the age of 50 (Kurosu, 2011). However, women married very early in life in this cultural setting, and as the level of investment in children and the extended family expanded after five or six years of marriage, the probability of divorce sharply reduced. Finally, divorce rates in hunter-gatherer cultures are comparable to those found today in urbanized, industrialized countries. For example, an analysis in 1970 of 331 marriages in the Kung! San, a hunter-gatherer culture living in Southern Africa, found that 39% ended in divorce (Howell, 1979).

In all these cases, much like current-day western societies, these cultures were relatively tolerant of marriage break up, and the social and legal sanctions against divorce were muted. It is, of course, easy to find examples throughout history and today where the divorce rates are much lower, some of which we have already cited. Culture can bend divorce rates and separation strongly both directly (through legal and social sanctions) and indirectly via mating norms and rules, the amount of economic power granted to women, economic conditions, and so forth. However, such analyses do not explain why divorce and relationship dissolution can be so variable within countries and cultures. In this chapter, we examine the predictors of relationship dissolution and divorce primarily within western cultures, for the simple reason that most of the relevant research has been carried out in such countries. On the other side of the coin, we also discuss what pulls couples together and helps maintain long-term relationships. We then turn to the consequences of relationship dissolution for the adults involved and their children. The chapter ends with an examination of the effectiveness of therapeutic approaches to help couples sustain and improve their intimate relationships.

Predicting Relationship Dissolution: What Drives Couples Apart?

We have summarized the factors that research has shown predict relationship dissolution in Table 12.1. This is, of course, a laundry list. It does not tell you the relative

Table 12.1   Predictors of relationship instability and dissolution

Greater risk of relationship dissolution

Socio-demographic variables	*Relationship-level factors*
Younger age	Premarital cohabitation
Unemployment	Perceived lack of similarity in attitudes and values
Low income	Many relationship problems
Low level of education	Infidelity and betrayal
Not religious	Hostile communication
Ethnicity	Stressful conflict interactions
Gender	Aggression and violence
	Poor communication
Relationship history	Poor support
Parental separation	Lack of (or fluctuating) commitment, love, and trust
Parental conflict	Low sexual satisfaction
Children from prior union	Negative illusions
Premarital parenthood	Poor coping with external stress
Prior marriage	
Individual differences	
Accepting attitudes toward divorce	
Neuroticism	
Attachment anxiety and avoidance	

importance of each factor, nor does it tell you how they are linked together in a causal chain. We will build a more detailed picture in this section that explains why and how these variables work together to put couples on a path toward relationship dissolution or longevity.

Socio-demographic variables, relationship history, and individual differences

The factors listed under these three particular headings in Table 12.1 have one thing in common – they are part of the baggage that people bring with them into new relationships. Let's list them briefly. Being married young, with no job, little money, and low levels of education all increase the chances that marriages will end in divorce (Kitson *et al.*, 1985; Kurdek, 1993). Couples who are not religious or differ in their religious orientation are more likely to divorce (Kitson *et al.*, 1985), and in the US, more African American marriages end in divorce compared to other ethnic groups (Bramlett and Mosher, 2002). Childhoods involving parental conflict and divorce predict subsequent divorce in adulthood (Amato, 1996, 2010). Remarriages end in divorce more than first-time marriages, and bearing children prior to marriage increases the risk for divorce (Heaton, 2002). Having more accepting attitudes toward divorce (as a way of solving relationship problems), and being neurotic or having an insecure attachment orientation may also increase the chances of later divorce. Finally, in countries that are relatively egalitarian, and where women have economic power, women tend to make the decision to terminate both married and dating relationships more often than men. In the USA, for example, in 70% of marriages that end women make the decision to divorce (Amato and Previti, 2003; Brinig and Allen, 2000).

Why are these factors associated with divorce or separation, and how are they linked? Remember Claire from Chapter 5. Claire was a participant in a longitudinal study, which has continued to track her and a large sample of other people since the mid-1970s. She is a good illustration of how some of these factors are tied together and why they might predict divorce or separation. Claire was bright, but her troubled and unpredictable family background led to her dropping out of school and having problems sustaining a steady job. She also developed an **anxious** and **avoidant attachment** orientation, and had a succession of short-term sexual relationships from an early age. In short, Claire's kind of background will tend to produce a double whammy in terms of both adopting a short-term mating strategy and a tendency to be at the wrong end of the clutch of socio-demographic factors associated with divorce and separation (being young, unemployed, having low education attainment, and so forth).

Research supports our conclusions about Claire and also suggests why some of the other factors listed above (and in Table 12.1) predict divorce and separation. For example, African Americans are more likely to get divorced than white Americans partly because they have lower incomes, education, occupational status, and more premarital births – all risk factors for divorce (Orbuch et al., 2002). Strong religious beliefs are associated with lower chances of divorce because religious folk (compared to non-religious folk) tend to have stronger moral objections to divorce and more firmly held traditional family values. And, as we documented in Chapter 9, neuroticism and insecure attachment lead to greater dissolution because of the ways in which these individual differences negatively influence the way couples interact and manage their relationships, and erode levels of relationship investment (e.g. Kurdek, 1993).

As we have already noted, children of divorced parents are more likely to divorce as adults. Studies by Matt McGue and his colleagues report that genes are responsible for about 50% of the tendency to get divorced (McGue and Lykken, 1992). Although this estimate likely inflates the actual contribution of genes (see Fletcher, 2002), this work and other research (e.g. D'Onofrio et al., 2007) indicates that genetic inheritance predisposes people to develop negative personality traits, such as neuroticism, thus increasing the probability of marital breakdown. Consistent with our analysis in Chapter 5, children of divorced parents are more likely to develop insecure attachment working models (Crowell et al., 2009), and to experience anger, aggression, and dysfunctional communication in their adult intimate relationships (Crowell et al., 2009). Parental conflict, even in the absence of divorce, also predicts poor efficacy and management of relationship conflict and subsequent drops in satisfaction in both married and dating relationships (Amato and Booth, 2001).

Finally, how do we explain the tendency for women to make the decision to terminate marriages much more frequently than men, at least in cultures that grant them the power and economic clout to make such decisions? Paul Amato and Denise Preveti (2003) argue that this can be explained by women (more than men) monitoring their relationships more closely, initiating discussions about problems, and being more sensitive to problems in the relationship. In short, women are more likely than men to adopt the role of relationship manager.

Are the fates of relationships sealed before they begin?

The bottom line of our analysis is that the distal factors that people bring with them into relationships – such as age, family history, and attachment working models – influence the chances of divorce or separation via the effects they have on proximal-level relationship processes such as communication and relationship evaluations. Which raises the question, how powerful are these distal factors? If you enter a relationship with a deck stacked with negative or positive indicators, is the fate of your relationship already decided?

Benjamin Karney and Thomas Bradbury (1995) analyzed 115 longitudinal studies (representing some 45 000 marriages, mainly in the USA) using a **meta-analysis** to sort out what predicted divorce (a meta-analysis averages the size of the effects across several studies and, thus, increases confidence in the results). Their review showed that although socio-demographic variables, relationship history, and individual differences predicted divorce, the effects were relatively weak, ranging from zero to 18% increased probability of divorce (note we have recalculated the correlations they reported into percentages). Possessing an unstable, neurotic personality had the biggest effect, producing an increased chance of divorce of 16% for men and 18% for women averaged across several studies. However, the effects of other personality variables were quite a lot lower, ranging from zero to 11%.

In contrast to these distal individual-level variables, dyadic factors that capture what is happening inside the relationship – such as perceptions of relationship quality, sexual satisfaction, and communication – proved to be considerably more powerful predictors of divorce. Averaging across studies, for example, lower levels of relationship satisfaction or more negative conflict behavior was associated with a 23% to 30% increased chance of divorce. A recent meta-analytic review of non-marital romantic relationships showed the same pattern, with relationship-level factors being four or five times more powerful predictors of dissolution than individual-level factors such as attachment working models (Le *et al.*, 2010). Figure 12.2 shows the impact of some representative factors, based on multiple studies, on relationship dissolution in non-marital romantic relationships. As can be seen in the figure, the most powerful factor was the absence of positive illusions (see Chapter 8), which was associated with a 23% probability of dissolution (we calculated this figure based on the effect size reported in Le *et al.*, 2010).

Taken together these findings suggest that the baggage people bring into their relationships does not wholly determine the fate of relationships. Although individual-

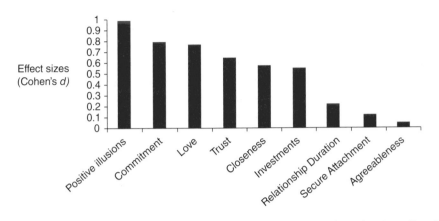

Figure 12.2 Representative examples from Le *et al.*'s (2010) meta-analysis showing effect sizes for predictors of relationship dissolution in non-marital romantic relationships

level distal factors – such as age and personality – shape relationship dynamics and behavior, they leave plenty of room for relationship processes to take over and mold the future course of the relationship. We now move into a discussion of these proximal relationship-level processes.

Relationship-level factors

A term sometimes used to describe pre-marital cohabitation is "trial marriage." Actually, many couples move in together for economic reasons, convenience, or because of an unplanned pregnancy (Sassler, 2010). Still, it remains a plausible hypothesis that couples who live together for a period of time and then marry may lower their chances of divorce or separation. Unfortunately, research has typically found the opposite pattern; namely, that couples who cohabit before they marry are more likely to divorce and have lower relationship satisfaction (Brown and Booth, 1996; Hall and Zhao, 1995; Heaton, 2002).

These findings have sometimes been trumpeted in the media as proving that living together prior to marriage is a bad idea and leads to divorce along with various assorted ills of modern society. However, an alternative plausible explanation is that the two samples in question (those who live together prior to marriage and those who don't) are different. Indeed, research has shown that the two samples are quite different – couples who cohabit prior to marriage are typically less religious, younger, less well-educated, and have lower commitment to the relationship (see Kulu and Boyle, 2010; Soons and Kalmijn, 2009). And, as we have seen, these are all risk factors for divorce. When such factors are controlled for, many studies report that the link between cohabitation and divorce diminishes or disappears (e.g. Kulu and Boyle, 2010).

Some recent research in Australia has even suggested that the link between cohabitation and marriage breakdown is in the process of being reversed for younger couples, with those married in the 1990s being *less* likely to divorce if they cohabit prior to marriage (e.g. Hewitt and de Vaus, 2009). These latter findings highlight the point that the normative and legal structure of sexual relationships has been undergoing rapid change. In many western countries today, cohabitation represents a viable, legally recognized alternative to marriage for both heterosexual and same-sex couples that involves similar benefits, processes, and consequences. Thus, it has been argued that as societal values change, and cohabitation becomes the norm, the advantage that marriage confers on individuals in terms of wellbeing and health, compared to cohabitation, will gradually disappear (see Soons and Kalmijn, 2009).

A good example of a dyadic variable is the extent to which partners possess similar values and attitudes. The belief that higher similarity is good for relationships is a popular one, and there is some evidence that dissimilarity in attitudes is associated with greater probability of divorce (e.g. Karney and Bradbury, 1995; Kurdek, 1993). Other studies have also found greater similarity in personality to be related to higher relationship satisfaction (e.g. Luo *et al.*, 2008). However, overall, the evidence is mixed, and methodologically rigorous approaches to assessing similarity find weak or even non-existent links between similarity in attitudes or personality traits and perceptions of relationship quality (Dyrenforth *et al.*, 2010). A more consistent and well-replicated finding is that couples who *perceive* themselves to be more similar are happier with their relationship (see Chapter 8). Given the existence of the commonly held belief that similarity between partners causes good relationships, perhaps perceptions of relationship quality push around perceptions of similarity, rather than vice-versa.

One of the more obvious relationship-level factors is simply the number and seriousness of problems that couples face. Infidelity, jealousy, drinking, spending money, moodiness, and failure to communicate all increase the risk of divorce and dissolution (Amato and Rogers, 1997). People's own accounts of why they divorce also suggest that infidelity is a major cause, along with violence, drinking and drug use, not getting along, continual disagreements, and, finally, growing apart (e.g. Amato and Previti, 2003). Problems concerning the division of labor have also become commonplace as women in relationships with children have entered the workforce in large numbers and expect more egalitarian sharing of household responsibilities (deGraff and Kalmijn, 2006). And, as we have discussed in other chapters (especially 3 and 9), blaming the partner for the source of such problems is a corrosive attribution that compounds conflict and, as an unfortunate bonus, impedes post-divorce coping and adjustment (Amato and Previti, 2003).

In a nutshell, the inevitable life issues and tribulations that couples encounter take their toll on relationships, particularly if they produce high levels of stress and are managed poorly. Janice Kiecolt-Glaser and colleagues, for example, have shown that greater levels of stress hormones, like epinephrine and norephinephrine, during conflict interactions predict greater dissatisfaction and probability of divorce in newlyweds, as shown in Figure 12.3. (Kiecolt-Glaser *et al.*, 2003; see Chapter 4). Handling conflict and problem-solving interactions is a nuanced and delicate business that can all too easily end up in character assassination and spiraling levels of negativity, aggression, and withdrawal (see Chapters 9 and 11). And, we reiterate the point that such

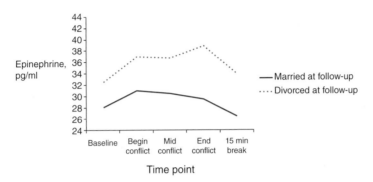

Figure 12.3 Epinephrine production in conflict discussions predicts later divorce
Source: From Kiecolt-Glaser *et al.*, 2003; © 2003 American Psychological Association, Inc.

interdependent responses increase the probability of divorce and break up, well over and above the contribution of the individual differences and socio-demographic factors described previously.

External stress also plays a role. Daily hassles, such as work stress, increase problems and negative interactions within the relationship, undermine satisfaction and intimacy, and sap the resources that people need to deal with relationship problems (see Chapter 9). Low income is therefore (not surprisingly) a solid predictor of relationship dissolution and divorce (Conger *et al.*, 1999). However, if couples can effectively and positively support each other, and successfully cope with such problems, this promotes relationship satisfaction and stability (Sullivan *et al.*, 2010; Chapter 9). Finally, family and friends can be a curse or a blessing for intimate relationships. When close others disapprove of the relationship, and when couples are not embedded within supporting social networks, this increases the likelihood of break up. In contrast, being integrated within a larger supporting network of friends and family promotes relationship wellbeing and provides a stronger base when couples face difficulties (Sprecher *et al.*, 2006).

To summarize, the way couples work together to cope with the inevitable challenges that life throws up determines both relationship evaluations and the longevity of the relationship. Perhaps the most powerful proximal-level determinants, which we have only touched on thus far in this chapter, comprise evaluations and commitment to the relationship. We now turn to discussing this class of factors.

Love and investment

The surge of passionate and romantic love at the beginning of relationships is rarely sustained over time and, in the typical relationship, dwindles over the first few years (Sprecher and Regan, 1988). Companionate love – involving feelings of commitment, intimacy, and deep affection – generally shows slower declines and is critical to keep relationships going over the long term (see Chapter 7). Lower overall levels of love and trust, and higher rates of deterioration across time, independently predict increased chances of relationship dissolution (Kurdek, 1993, 2002; Le *et al.*, 2010). Lower sexual satisfaction also reduces overall relationship wellbeing and longevity in both non-marital (Sprecher, 2002) and marital relationships (Karney and Bradbury, 1995) (see Chapter 10).

These facts will probably not strike anyone as much of a revelation. Indeed, all of the factors we have discussed that predict dissolution also typically influence levels of satisfaction, and drops in satisfaction almost always precede break up, at least for the partner who decides to end the relationship. However, perhaps less obviously, there is one central proximal-level evaluation that trumps relationship satisfaction in predictive power; namely, commitment. People who are committed to their relationship intend to remain in that relationship, are psychologically attached to that relationship, and are oriented toward the future of that relationship (Arriaga and Agnew, 2001). High levels of commitment predict relationship stability over and above satisfaction (Le *et al.*, 2010), suggesting that satisfaction is but one component that influences commitment (Bui *et al.*, 1996).

The principal role of commitment, and the factors that promote or undermine people's motivation to keep their relationship intact, are embodied in the **investment model** developed by Caryl Rusbult (Rusbult, 1983; Rusbult *et al.*, 1998). The investment model is based on interdependence theory and the principle that commitment will be enhanced (and relationships will continue) to the extent that the perceived benefits associated with the relationship outweigh the costs (see Chapter 2). These costs and benefits are captured by three postulated causes of commitment – satisfaction, quality of alternatives, and investment size (as shown in Figure 12.4).

Satisfaction level Satisfaction signals how rewarding the relationship is in comparison to expectations. People are less satisfied when their partner and relationship fall short of their ideals and more satisfied when their relationship compares favorably to their ideals (Chapter 3). And, there is good evidence that satisfaction influences the likelihood of break up because it increases or reduces commitment (Le and Agnew, 2003).

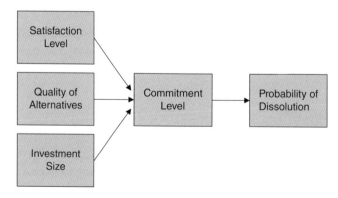

Figure 12.4   Rusbult's investment model
Source: Adapted from Rusbult *et al.*, 1998

When relationship rewards are inconsistent and people's satisfaction fluctuates wildly, this also undermines commitment and can eventually lead to break ups (Arriaga, 2001).

Quality of alternatives Commitment is also shaped by how the relationship compares to the quality of perceived alternatives. Alternatives are usually relationships with other attractive partners. For example, the risk of divorce is greater when the workplace is stacked with eligible members of the opposite gender (Scott *et al.*, 2001). Even people who have stable, happy relationships, and who realize they have a range of high-quality alternatives available, may become less committed and more likely to terminate their relationship (Bui *et al.*, 1996). When people have few alternatives they are more likely to remain committed (something is often better than nothing) . . . that is until the relationship becomes so acrimonious and dissatisfying that not being in a romantic entanglement can seem like Nirvana.

Investment size The amount of time, effort, psychological energy (emotions, identity, etc.), and economic resources invested in long-term relationships are typically huge and thus also influence commitment and likelihood of separation. The formula is simple: the more investment in the relationship, the more people have to lose, and thus commitment is boosted and the probability of separation or divorce decreases (Le and Agnew, 2003; White and Booth, 1991). Consistently, across countries and cultures one of the major determinants of the divorce rate is the economic power possessed by women. Divorce rates are higher in countries where economic interdependence is low and women do not need to rely on marriage for financial security (Barber, 2003).

Why is commitment so important? A strong orientation toward the future of the relationship means that when relationship difficulties are encountered – like conflict and infidelity – people are powerfully motivated to overcome hurt and anger and strive to repair their relationships. Even when the known risk factors that people bring with them into relationships are absent, relationships will nevertheless still falter and break down. And, perfectly happy relationships can all too easily run into trouble. In the next section we change tack and instead of asking what spoils relationships, we ask what sustains happy, well-adjusted relationships. Most of the answers to this question have already been provided in previous chapters. Here, we summarize and integrate this material.

The Power and Limitations of Relationship Maintenance Strategies

The concept of relationship maintenance refers to the volitional and automatic strategies that partners use to preserve and sustain long-term, satisfying relationships. When relationships are jogging along, a web of routine maintenance interactions, that may be close to invisible, help retain intimacy and connection in everyday life. These may be as mundane as talking over the day's activities, hugging or displays of affection,

*"Marry me, Bridget—I want to spend at least a couple of
years of the rest of my life with you."*

Figure 12.5 *Source:* © 2009 Liza Donnelly and Michael Maslin

offers of help, having a good laugh over something, and the micro moments of intimacy and respectful understanding that occur regularly in healthy relationships (Stafford and Canary, 1991; see Chapter 7). The maintenance of relationship engagement and positivity means that when couples are faced with the inevitable conflict or disruption of external events, they have a solid foundation available to help weather the trial.

Of course, even in the most harmonious relationships irritating behaviors occur, and negative perceptions and attributions leak through. This is when the principal role of commitment kicks in. Research stemming from Caryl Rusbult's investment model (see Figure 12.4) has shown that commitment motivates important ways of behaving and thinking that help to maintain relationships over time. These are depicted in Figure 12.6.

When partners are hurtful, for example, it (usually) helps to inhibit the immediate impulse to retaliate with hostility and mean words and instead try to resolve the situation in a calm, forgiving and supportive manner – a process termed **accommodation** (see Chapter 9). Accommodation can be a tough ask. It takes a concerted effort to transform the desire for revenge into looking after the wellbeing of the relationship and it requires a good dose of motivation. Thus, accommodation is strongly predicted by commitment, and it keeps relationships on a positive and even keel (see Chapter 9).

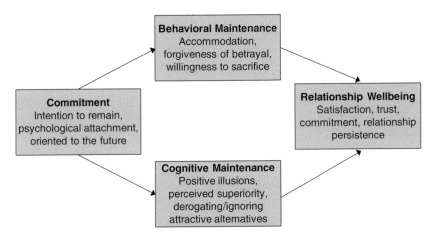

Figure 12.6 Commitment and relationship maintenance
Source: Adapted from Rusbult *et al.*, 2001

Committed intimates are also more likely to overcome the painful emotions and desires for revenge that accompany partner betrayals, and they show more willingness to sacrifice their own desires and goals to benefit the partner. Both forgiveness of betrayal, and the willingness to sacrifice, boost relationship well-being, and thus reduce the risk of dissolution (Bono *et al.*, 2008; Van Lange *et al.*, 1997).

In previous chapters, we have discussed the central role played by relationship cognition. Indeed, the evidence shows that maintaining good, healthy relationships is facilitated by charitable attributions for your partner's questionable behavior (Chapters 2 and 9), and maintaining a sunny and optimistic view of your partner and relationship or what we termed positive illusions (see Chapter 8). Committed partners also tend to perceive their relationship as being superior in relationship quality and future happiness compared to other people's relationships, and this tends to preserve satisfaction and reduce the risk of break up (Rusbult *et al.*, 2000). Finally, as described in Chapter 7, committed intimates downplay the attractiveness of tempting alternatives thus maintaining commitment and satisfaction.

Despite evidence supporting the benefits of these behavioral and cognitive tactics, they can only go so far in the face of a grim reality. In a program of research James McNulty and his colleagues (see McNulty, 2010) have repeatedly shown (using state-of-the-art longitudinal designs tracking newly married couples) that more positive expectations and attributions, and more forgiveness, effectively maintain satisfaction among spouses facing infrequent and minor problems. However, exactly the same optimistic recipe predicts worse outcomes among spouses facing frequent and severe problems. For relationships in trouble it turns out that adopting a grittier but more realistic approach helps acknowledge, address, and resolve problems over time, albeit with some costs attached (see Chapter 9). Holding onto positive expectations when the relationship continues to deteriorate, and forgiving a partner who continues to transgress, exacerbates problems and ultimately undermines self-respect. In short, if partner and relationship judgments stray too far from the cold, hard reality they adversely impact the relationship and the individuals within those relationships (see Chapter 8).

Criticism, scorn, and withdrawal, as we have seen, are relationship killers if they become a regular feature of intimate relationships. But single events can be equally toxic when they represent a betrayal of a central, perhaps assumed, norm about love and intimate relationships. Punching your partner, spending all your partner's money on a gambling addiction, or having a clandestine affair with someone from the office are not good ideas if you want to retain a stable relationship. Not surprisingly, the associated shattering of trust and relationship security also makes forgiveness difficult to say the least.

Can relationships survive such crises? Yes. Some couples manage to traverse the minefield created by such betrayals and find the balance between the perpetrator making amends and the forgiveness of the victim to rebuild relationship satisfaction and personal wellbeing (e.g. Bono *et al.*, 2008; Fincham *et al.*, 2007; Lawler *et al.*, 2003). Often, however, couples are unable or unwilling to climb such a steep mountain. Trust is often never restored, and the relationship slides into separation or divorce. Infidelity, for example, is one of the most commonly cited causes for divorce (Amato and Previti, 2003).

The long-term consequences of a shattering of trust is illustrated in a diary of divorce published in *The Telegraph* (an English newspaper) in 2011 in five parts by Penny Brookes who left her husband after 25 years of marriage and five children (see Brookes, 2011). This first entry starts with an unexpected phone call:

My life changed in a split second one evening in January five years ago . . . "Is that Penny? . . . Why don't you open your eyes? . . . your husband and Anna . . . You have to get a divorce". I recall being propelled back to the age of 12 when my parents had told me they were splitting up. Trembling I rang my husband . . . I bombarded him with questions and – for the first time in 19 years of married life – I shouted at him . . . Then he started on me. It was my fault. We hadn't had sex for years . . . I hadn't shown him any affection . . . I put my work and children before him . . . My weight dropped to under eight stone from nearly nine. I lived on sweet tea . . . Breathing was difficult . . . Meanwhile my husband swore he hadn't seen Anna, but by now I was on red alert. Hating myself, I checked his mobile and rang an unknown number. "Is that Anna?" I bluffed. "No she's at the gym" . . . Shaking, I confronted him. Then he confessed he still had feelings . . . he went outside with his mobile. "What did you say?'" I asked when he came back. "I said I wasn't leaving my wife," he replied. Only then did it sink home this had been a real possibility . . .

It had been nearly four years ago since I had any peace of mind . . . but instead of getting better it was getting worse . . . And, so we carried on . . . I still felt tired and ill. I lost concentration during my weekly tennis game. I forgot things. I had hideous dreams . . . My husband sensed something was up. "What's wrong?" he would ask. I retorted that I still felt upset about his affair. "But that was years ago, can't you forget it?", he said . . . Then one night . . . he asked if I could see any future in the relationship. I took a deep breath and whispered "No" . . . I felt terrible, awful, wicked. But I could not go back. (© Telegraph Media Group Limited 2006.)

This raises an important point, which we have thus far danced around. The tenor of our discussion has been that separation and divorce are bad, and staying together is good. But is staying in a toxic, miserable relationship a "good" outcome, even if it can be managed? Probably not, especially when violence and serious psychological abuse are involved. On the other hand, relationship dissolution is hardly a trouble-free process (as Penny's diary attests to) and it can have devastating effects.

Consequences of Relationship Dissolution

Most of the research examining the consequences of relationship dissolution has focused on divorce. People rate divorce as one of the most stressful life experiences, and, compared to people who remain married, divorced folk are lonelier, more prone to suicide, and less happy. As we noted in Chapter 4, divorced people also suffer more serious health problems and die earlier (Bloom *et al.*, 1978; Kiecolt-Glaser and Newton, 2001; Rogers, 1995; Sbarra and Nietert, 2009). A recent meta-analysis of longitudinal studies by Sbarra *et al.* (2011) found that adults who were divorced at the start of the included studies were 23% more likely to be dead from all causes at a follow-up assessment! In this section we expand on the prior brief treatment of the health consequences of losing a partner or relationship dissolution offered in Chapter 4.

Admittedly, it is difficult to assess to what extent the problems associated with divorce are caused by relationship dissolution *per se*. As we previously noted, poor personal wellbeing is also a precursor of marital dissolution, being associated with ongoing marital problems, stressful life events, and personality factors that influence both psychological and relationship health (Mastekaasa, 1994). Nevertheless, longitudinal studies reveal that psychological wellbeing decreases at separation (e.g. Booth and Amato, 1991) and life satisfaction remains lower three years later (Lucas, 2005). Again, we quote a portion of Penny's diary to give a flavor of the emotional and psychological difficulties that are part and parcel of going through a divorce, but also to show that people can and do recover from the grief of losing a key intimate relationship.

> I had been gone for precisely four weeks, two days. Every morning I woke up at 3am, gripped with fear. What had I done? Then I had to make myself remember what it was like to wake up at 3am on the edge of the bed, next to my husband, feeling totally and utterly trapped . . . The following week, I actually had to check my diary to remember how many days I had been on my own. I joined the local sports club and started swimming on Sunday mornings . . . Finally I slept without a torch in my hand . . . It was finally time to say goodbye to my lovely house. Even though I had left some five months earlier, I was not prepared for the pain of wondering through the empty rooms after my husband had departed with his removal van . . . My friends came in to help me clean for the new people . . . Standing in the hall I said goodbye. Goodbye to my old life. Goodbye to the family I had fought so hard to keep together. Goodbye to false pretences. Hello to being true to myself. Hello to uncertainty. (© Telegraph Media Group Limited 2006.)

Not all relationships end because of divorce. Over 50% of marriages end because one spouse dies. The loss of a spouse through death is traumatic and, not surprisingly, is associated with increased depression and dissatisfaction with life (Lee and DeMaris, 2007) (see Chapter 4). Men, in particular, can become socially isolated, lonely, and depressed, probably because they have fewer intimate relationships to call on outside of their marital relationship (Hatch and Bulcroft, 1992). Relationship quality also partly determines the severity of the loss. People who are more dependent on their relationships suffer more, as do those whose relationships were warmer and more intimate (Carr et al., 2000). People also often continue to have a relationship with their partner beyond death, talking to them on a regular basis even years later (Carnelley et al., 2006). It also seems that the commonplace phrase "dying of a broken heart" is not merely a metaphor – bereavement increases the risk of mortality, particularly within the following six months and particularly for men (Stroebe et al., 2007). Nonetheless, the majority of the bereaved adjust over time and many form new relationships that help to protect them from the poor outcomes associated with relationship loss (Bonanno et al., 2002).

Similarly, despite the distress experienced during divorce, people are generally resilient and as time passes they usually recover (Booth and Amato, 1991). However, people who have low incomes and women, especially those who have not been in the work force, face greater economic hardship and this makes adjustment more difficult (Booth and Amato, 1991; Hanson et al., 1998). The level of distress also depends on the reasons for separation. Infidelity, in particular, seems to exert quite a toll, particularly if the aggrieved party is left by the unfaithful partner (Amato and Previti, 2003; Sweeney and Horowitz, 2001).

There are also protective factors that help people adjust. Those who decide to end the relationship, and possess better pre-existing coping skills and support networks, show better recovery (Amato, 2000). Indeed, because women are more likely to end relationships, and men have fewer intimate support networks, men typically have a tougher time (Braver et al., 2006). Men also tend to have less contact with their children, which exacerbates post-divorce distress. Indeed, divorce is much more fraught across the board when children are involved. One reason is that couples with children typically need to remain in contact to negotiate and manage custodial arrangements. These interactions can be hostile and this kind of unhelpful conflict can last for years (Adamson and Pasley, 2006). Which raises the question of how divorce influences children's wellbeing.

The impact of divorce on children

In response to the high divorce rates, and increasing numbers of single-parent households, concern has been increasingly voiced about the impact that relationship dissolution has on children. Most research has focused on how children from divorced families differ from children in intact families – not surprisingly this body of work shows that divorce negatively impacts on child and adolescent adjustment. Divorce has been linked to poorer academic performance and lower educational attainment, more problematic behaviors like aggression, substance abuse, early sexual activity, lower emotional wellbeing and self-esteem, and higher depression (see Barber and Demo, 2006 for a review).

The reasons why divorce undermines children's wellbeing are varied, and include economic difficulties associated with single-parent families (Barber and Eccles, 1992), difficulties with joint decision-making and parental regulation, especially during the developmental trials of adolescence (Barber and Demo, 2006), and a weakening of the psychological resources needed to parent effectively (Amato, 1993). However, it is generally accepted that the primary causes of children's divorce-related distress (or lack of it) are linked to parental conflict before, during, and after the divorce.

Prior to the divorce, and regardless of the parents' relationships with the children, when the parents' relationship is in bad shape, children experience emotional and social difficulties, including depression, behavioral problems, and poor quality friendships (Davies et al., 2006). Conflict between parents is particularly distressing if the children perceive they are the cause of their parents' disagreement and unhappiness (Stocker et al., 2003). Thus, when conflict in the marriage is nasty and recurring, children are better off if the parents separate (Amato, 1993).

However, and this is a large however, if the marital battleground merely shifts to the post-separation context, especially if the children are used by the parents to get at each other, this does not bode well for the children's wellbeing (e.g. Vanderwater and Landsford, 1998). Thankfully, most couples eventually manage to get past this stage and establish more friendly and routine interactions around their children (Adamson and Pasley, 2006). When they do, this leads to improved outcomes for children, including less depression and fewer behavioral problems. Indeed, meta-analytic studies indicate that the overall negative impact of divorce is relatively small in magnitude, and many children cope surprisingly well (Amato, 2000; Amato and Keith, 1991).

Moving on and letting go

Relationship dissolution can and does have positive consequences. Some relationships are unhealthy, and some are downright dangerous. Getting out of such relationships reduces stress and depression, and provides the opportunity to develop a more rewarding life (Amato and Hohmann-Marriott, 2007). Despite the initial devastation, many people report benefits of divorce (up to 90% in some samples). This is not just because of the relief experienced after deciding to end a relationship which has become toxic. Even unwanted divorce or relationship dissolution can lead to personal growth, improvement in self-efficacy and self-esteem, and developing closer relationships with friends and family. People also often report greater autonomy, new leisure interests, and more success at work (see Tashiro et al., 2006 for a review). Of course, individuals also cope with relationship dissolution via rationalizations and denial, and retrospective reports of growth are probably positively biased. Nonetheless, these shifts in perceptions are an important indicator of recovery and help people move on.

The degree to which people can turn divorce into a positive experience differs across individuals and situations. We have summarized the major factors involved in Figure

Factors Predicting Recovery from Relationship Dissolution
- Secure, optimistic personality
- Financial security
- Good social networks and support
- Acceptance of loss
- Letting go of love and anger toward ex-partner
- Accomplishing identity change
- Managing conflict over children
- Entering new sexual relationship

Figure 12.7   Recovery from relationship dissolution

12.7. Some studies have found that men experience less personal growth in the after-math of divorce, although the effects tend to be inconsistent (Amato, 2000). As noted above, women are more likely to leave relationships and men tend to lack the rich networks of social support that women tend to cultivate. Friends and family play a huge role in coping with stress and grief and help to ameliorate the loss of identity that occurs when a pivotal intimate relationship ends. Those who feel utterly alone after a relationship breakdown, and have no other close relationships to fall back on, face an uncertain and possibly bleak future unless they can replace the lost attachment figure.

An attachment perspective (see Chapter 5) suggests that the process of coping with relationship dissolution is similar to the sequence of reactions to attachment loss in childhood (see Hazan and Shaver, 1992): **protest, despair, and detachment**. After the initial shock of a partner's death, for example, the bereaved typically exhibit protest behavior characterized by high levels of anxiety, rumination, and compulsions to be near the partner, often visiting and talking to the deceased at their favorite places or gravesite. In the aftermath of a relationship break up, individuals often oscillate between withdrawal and contact, sometimes struggling to re-establish the relationship until eventually accepting it is over. When the loss is finally accepted, despair can follow, and may continue until people finally wipe the attachment slate clean, ready for new inti-mate attachments to be forged.

However, there are massive individual differences in the pace at which these stages are traversed. Some feel strongly attached to their ex-spouse for years, even decades, after marriages have ended, along with continued angst and depression (Sbarra and Emery, 2005). The more people hold onto feelings of either love or hurt and anger, the less able they are to adjust over time (Frazier and Cook, 1993; Sbarra and Ferrer, 2006). Not surprisingly, those with an anxious attachment orientation – preoccupation with acceptance and fear of rejection in uneasy concert with a longing for closeness – have the most difficulty letting go (Sbarra, 2006). People who are secure, in contrast, grieve and express their anger and pain, before (relatively) successfully detaching from the prior relationship.

A central component of the recovery process involves identity change. As relation-ships develop, partners are integrated into the individual's self-concept and the self expands (see Chapter 7). When relationships dissolve, the process is slammed into reverse and people are forced to redefine who they are, as "we" returns to "me" (Lewandowski *et al.*, 2006). The subsequent lack of clarity in the self-concept magnifies the pain and sadness associated with relationship loss (Slotter *et al.*, 2010). Nonetheless, as we noted, this period of adjustment also provides opportunities for personal growth and development.

Most people eventually enter new relationships. In the USA, 85% of people eventually remarry. The median length of time between divorce and remarriage is three years, and the likelihood of remarrying or cohabiting within 10 years of divorce is 70% (with estimates for Europe even higher; Ganong *et al.*, 2006). Although a new family situation poses difficulties when children are involved, developing new relationships helps people recover from divorce (Wang and Amato, 2000). New connections, or even the potential for future relationships, seem to be particularly helpful in promoting anxiously attached individuals' detachment from their ex-partners (Spielmann *et al.*, 2009).

In sum, as seen throughout this book, intimate relationships are a central source of psychological and physical wellbeing. When entering relationships, people typically experience euphoria, passion, and self-expansion. Once established, the love that flows from a secure base is a key ingredient in happiness and fulfillment. But, the positive emotions experienced throughout relationship development are matched by the intense distress and turmoil experienced when relationships fail. Although the norm is one of resiliency and eventual recovery, relationship dissolution is often a crushing blow, and predicts poorer psychological and physical health, even for those who bounce back.

Not surprisingly, then, when good relationships go bad, most people do not give up easily and will use a variety of behavioral and cognitive tactics to hold onto what they have. Some couples seek professional help in an attempt to save their marriage or relationship. Indeed, the presenting problems associated with seeking professional help from psychologists are frequently linked to relationship issues, such as depression (Swindle *et al.*, 2000). The common problems that couples bring to relationship therapy involve the familiar ones we have previously discussed, such as communication issues, power struggles, lack of loving feelings and affection, domestic disputes regarding finances and children, infidelity, sex, and violence (Whisman *et al.*, 1997). Moreover, as we document, the most popular approaches to relationship therapy target relationship processes that are critical to relationship functioning and happiness.

Relationship Therapy

One of the founding quacks in the relationship field, Dr James Graham, established a lavish erotic therapy center in London in 1781, advertised as improving sexual relations and fertility. It became a fashionable destination for aristocrats of the day. Believing that sexual attraction was electrical in nature, Graham invented the magneto-electrical celestial bed, which was large, ornate, and decorated with fresh flowers along with a pair of live turtle doves. While the couple had sex, oriental aromas were released, electrical pulses were produced, and music wafted from a hidden organ (no pun intended), matching the increasing intensity of the couple's movements.

You won't be able to find a celestial bed today, but sex and relationship therapy is much bigger business than in Graham's day. A mountain of self-help books advertise recipes for maintaining or repairing relationships, often described in terms of steps or secrets with the numbers ranging anywhere from 3 to 100. There are books for men and for women, for teenagers and for older folks. Many focus on specific themes, such as money, sex, and communication, along with quirky topics such as how to stop pets getting in the way of true love or how to iron a shirt. And, of course, there are always TV shows, with gurus like Dr Phil, to help sort people out. This blizzard of information makes it difficult for the consumer to sort the wheat from the chaff, and avoid the modern-day versions of Dr Graham.

In the following section, we briefly outline some major approaches to relationship therapy, link these to core processes we have considered throughout the book, and evaluate their success. Our treatment is necessarily brief, but it may assist those seeking help for their relationship to make more informed choices.

Traditional behavioral couples therapy

In 1979 Neil Jacobson and Gayla Margolin published a pioneering development of couple therapy, which integrated social exchange principles (such as those outlined by interdependence theory, Chapter 1) with social learning theory. In their account, relationship satisfaction is driven by the balance between rewards and costs in a relationship (social exchange) and relationship dysfunction was thought to occur when partners' behaviors become more punishing than rewarding. A key element of this behavioral approach is understanding how damaging behaviors are rewarded, and rewarding behaviors punished, according to the way they are responded to by the partner (social learning).

This focus on observable behaviors, and dyadic patterns of reward and punishment, were the impetus for the bulk of research examining conflict behavior, which we outlined in Chapter 9. The dyadic interaction patterns described in that chapter illustrate how damaging behaviors can be rewarded. Take the demand–withdrawal pattern. When Mary gets upset and angry, George disengages and leaves the room. However, if George's withdrawal causes Mary to suppress her negative emotions in later interactions (and ask George for forgiveness) in order to preserve closeness, his behavior will be rewarded and so he will be more likely to adopt this tactic in the future. Thus, although withdrawal tends to exacerbate problems, and often leads to dissatisfaction and divorce over the long haul (see Chapter 9), George's dysfunctional behavior is maintained.

Traditional behavioral couples therapy focuses on identifying the specific behaviors that produce dissatisfaction and the ways in which these behaviors are maintained. Problematic interaction patterns are targeted by developing constructive communication skills, such as listening and perspective taking, and then these skills are applied to resolving specific problems. The problem-solving skills targeted for improvement are consistent with those that research suggests are successful in resolving conflict and sustaining relationships; these include directly targeting the problem, reducing blame, generating solutions that incorporate change by both partners, and maintaining positivity (see Chapter 9). Couples are also encouraged to exchange more positive, loving behaviors to enhance closeness and make relationships more rewarding (the type of daily maintenance and intimacy-generating behaviors discussed previously in this chapter and in Chapter 7).

Cognitive behavioral couples therapy

Cognitive behavioral couples therapy extends the traditional behavioral approach by acknowledging to a greater extent the role played by cognition in the initiation, maintenance, and outcome of the behaviors exchanged in a relationship (Baucom and Epstein, 1990; Epstein and Baucom, 2002). In prior chapters (especially 3 and 9), we showed how the appraisal and interpretation of relationship events shape the meaning, response, and ultimate impact of those events. A biting or dismissive remark is more of a mountain than a molehill if the receiving partner attributes it to selfishness rather than a stressful day (attributions), believes that good relationships will always be conflict-free (unrealistic expectations), attends to acidic comments but fails to recognize loving ones (selective attention), or believes that partners should always be cherishing no matter what the circumstances (inflexible standards).

Cognitive behavioral couples therapy targets these unhelpful cognitions and attempts to generate more forgiving attributions, more reasonable expectations, less selective attention, and more positive relationship beliefs. The goal is to make couples more aware of their automatic thoughts and expectations, assess the validity and consequence of those beliefs, and revise maladaptive cognitions through conscious clarification and evaluation. This process builds understanding across partners and, by increasing the veracity and generosity of their perceptions, reduces the degree to which partners react with hurt, bitterness, and hostility. Recognizing that cognition and behavior are entwined, interventions for modifying damaging behavior (as in traditional behavioral couples therapy) are also assumed to generate more positive and adaptive relationship cognitions and emotions.

Integrative behavioral couples therapy

Integrative behavioral couples therapy is further extension of traditional behavioral couples therapy. Based on their clinical and empirical observations, Neil Jacobson and Andrew Christensen (1998) argued that targeting behavior change is not always helpful, particularly for couples who, despite being committed to maintaining their relationship, face irreconcilable differences. Integrative behavioral couples therapy integrates behavioral strategies for change with promotion of acceptance and tolerance of differences in personalities, views, values, and communication styles. It does not encourage acceptance of dissatisfying and harmful behaviors as such, but instead promotes acceptance of personal differences that lead to clashes across partners, such as George's autonomous need to work things out on his own and Mary's desire for connection and collaboration.

The overarching goal of integrative behavioral couples therapy is to help couples accept and understand each other while motivating them to make needed improvements where possible. In addition to communication and problem-solving training, it promotes acceptance by highlighting how specific problems arise from differences between partners, encouraging understanding of the other's perceptions and mutual responsibility (**empathic joining**), and helping couples distance themselves from specific problems by intellectually dissecting the issue without accusation and blame and then tackling the problem together (**unified detachment**). For example, by understanding how their demand–withdraw pattern stems from different autonomy–connection needs and coping strategies, George's withdrawal should become less hurtful and Mary's demanding less threatening. Acceptance and understanding should also reduce the pressure for either George or Mary to dogmatically maintain the correctness of their own approach, fostering a closer connection, and, paradoxically, a more conducive environment for change.

Emotion focused couple therapy

Emotion focused couple therapy draws on attachment theory (see Chapter 6) to understand and treat relationship distress (Johnson, 2004). The therapist's job is seen as providing a secure base for exploring the attachment-related needs and insecurities at the root of the relationship difficulties. The initial focus is on shifting destructive interaction cycles imbued with harsh and angry affect by helping partners recognize and express the vulnerable attachment-related fears that underlie their negative responses. Clarifying that Mary's demands and conciliations are driven by intense separation anxiety, and that George's withdrawal is triggered by feelings of guilt and failure, should help George and Mary understand each other's inner experiences and the cause of their dysfunctional interactions. It is thought that sharing such vulnerabilities should help George and Mary become more emotionally engaged, compassionate, and responsive to each other's needs. The ultimate goal is to generate a healthy, secure attachment bond from which couples can collaboratively approach problems, safely share and regulate their emotions, and trust in each other's love and support.

Does relationship therapy work?

Reviews of controlled trials show that these kinds of therapies produce similar levels of effectiveness in improving targeted domains of relationship functioning, including emotional acceptance, more forgiving and generous cognitions, and more constructive communication (Snyder *et al.*, 2006). The primary marker of success is whether couples become more satisfied. Around 70% of couples demonstrate improvement in levels of satisfaction by the end of treatment compared to control groups who have not received therapy (Shadish and Baldwin, 2003, 2005). That said, if you raise the bar so that success is defined in terms of formerly distressed couples describing their relationship as now positively satisfying, the success rate drops to around 40–50%. And, unfortunately, about a third of these couples do not maintain their improvement over time and eventually divorce (Christensen *et al.*, 2006; Shadish *et al.*, 1993).

So although couples therapy can be effective, it certainly is no cure-all. High levels of initial distress impede improvement, as does lack of commitment and low trust in the partner's regard (two elements that we have shown are critical for relationship success). Unfortunately, of the minority of couples in relationship trouble who actually seek help, most wait until their relationship is all but over and only the remnants of commitment and regard are left to work on (Doss *et al.*, 2004). And, as we have seen, relationship difficulties are also commonly accompanied (and to some extent caused) by problems residing within the individual members of the couples (not the relationship), such as neuroticism, depression, drug and alcohol addiction, unemployment, and so on. Furthermore, the interdependent nature of relationships means that whether a relationship thrives or dives also depends on the unique nature of the relationship between two people. It is not surprising that marital therapy has not proved to be as effective as therapies tailored for individual-level disorders (Seligman, 1995).

We cannot emphasize enough the magnitude of the task facing the couples therapist. Moreover, the simple descriptions we provided do not convey the difficulty or richness of the therapeutic process, or how therapy is typically tailored to the experiences and difficulties of each unique couple. In practice, many therapists draw on a range of perspectives and techniques to fit the specific needs and difficulties of each couple, rather than sticking to one approach. In addition, the existing literature is not yet informative on what techniques are most effective for specific types of couples facing particular problems, or the best ways to prevent relapse to ensure lasting improvement. Finally, keep in mind that it is problematic to necessarily count divorce or separation as a failure. If the process of therapy convinces one or both partners that the best course of action is to leave the relationship, and empowers them to take that course, such an outcome does not seem to us to necessarily constitute a failure.

The challenge of helping couples once they have reached the point of seeking treatment has led to the development of a variety of marital prevention and enhancement programs to help couples acquire core relationship skills before they run into significant difficulties. The most widely evaluated preventive programs are those based on the central therapies outlined above, such as the **premarital relationship enhancement program** (Markman *et al.*, 1994), which focuses on (i) developing constructive communication skills and more realistic expectations so couples are equipped to tackle any future problems; and (ii) building commitment and bonding experiences to ensure couples continue to actively maintain the quality of their relationship. There is good evidence that these types of programs generate more positive communication and enhanced satisfaction, but little is known about long-term effects, such as the longevity of the relationship (Hawkins *et al.*, 2008). Moreover, those who voluntarily seek this type of program might already possess the motivation and wherewithal to cope with relationship and life hurdles; thus, such programs probably miss out on dealing with the high-risk couples who may need it most (see Bradbury and Lavner, 2012).

The need for preventative programs highlights the point that sustaining relationships is more often than not a tough, ongoing task. Humans fall in love, sometimes choose mates badly, and enter relationships with dispositional and historical baggage. They face stressors and demands on their relationship outside of their control, while needing to coordinate different beliefs, expectations, and behavioral styles, and they encounter a variety of potentially devastating events. Given the extraordinary social and technological environment we currently live in, the way in which we are assaulted with glossy images of attractive alternatives, and the freedom in western countries to form and dissolve long-term relationships, the number of marriages that stay the course for life, in our view, is remarkable. Given the difficult and complex nature of the task, the success with which expert therapists can help people make decisions, communicate more effectively, and cope with distress in intimate relationships is equally impressive.

Summary and Conclusions

Since the 1950s the divorce rate in western countries has steadily increased, facilitated by more relaxed social norms concerning divorce, the widespread adoption of no-fault divorce legislation, and the increased economic independence of women. Still, the majority of couples across western countries (from 50 to 75%) who get married stay married, figures that are similar to other cultures round the world including hunter-gather cultures in Africa. These statistics, and our analysis in this chapter, are consistent with a major theme in this book; namely, humans are a bonding species, with a strong drive toward establishing long-term, monogamous sexual relationships.

Of course, human mating patterns are nothing if not flexible, and a long list of factors that people bring with them into long-term sexual relationships increase the probability of break ups including being young, having no job, little money, being neurotic, or having insecure attachment styles. However, the research suggests that these factors exert their causal power by feeding into more proximal-level causes such as communication and relationship management skills, and levels of investment and commitment. In particular, those who have a long-term mating orientation (see Chapter 5) tend to have the required commitment and command of cognitive/emotional and behavioral strategies needed to foster and sustain their relationships, including a charitable and optimistic attitude to the partner, and the ability to adjust levels of honesty and accommodation according to the situation (see Chapter 9).

Even the happiest and best regulated relationships can fall prey to the power of external events, and certain behaviors that humans have a weakness for, especially infidelity, can destroy the foundation stone of any good relationships; namely, trust. And, when long-term relationships end, as scientists have assiduously documented, they typically produce difficulties for both the adults and the offspring, up to and including suicide, depression, and health problems. Fortunately, reflecting the resilience of human nature, most people recover and many eventually forge new and successful intimate relationships.

We also briefly described some of the principal relationship therapies. They are all linked to the empirical work and theories in the broader scientific field, but stress different major elements in the psychology of intimate relationships including dysfunctional interactive behaviors (cognitive behavioral couples therapy), maladaptive cognitions (cognitive behavioral couples therapy), accommodation (integrative behavioral couples therapy), and the power of attachment and emotions (emotion focused couple therapy). The modest success rates attained by these therapies we think are impressive, given the complex and difficult nature of the therapist's task, and the brute facts that humans do not choose their parents or their evolutionary heritage, often choose mates badly, face many temptations in the modern world (from access to pornography to the possibility of extramarital sex), and often endure ongoing demands and stressors more or less outside of their control.

This chapter illustrates the aphorism that there is no free lunch in human nature. The sweetness of love and intimacy carry with them the power (often actualized) to inflict extended pain and grief when relationships end. This is the hand humans have been dealt – as we have seen it is not infrequently handled with both skill and courage.

Part Six

Conclusion

Assembling the Relationship Jigsaw 13

The power of culture and evolution – are humans just another ape? – gender differences – within-gender differences – the future of intimate relationships – science and intimate relationships – conclusion

> Several blind men were presented different parts of the elephant to feel. When asked what sort of a beast it was, the person who felt the tusk said it was like a spear, the individual who felt the trunk said it was like a plough, the one who felt the tail thought it was like a pestle, the man who felt the foot felt it was like a pillar, and so forth. They proceeded to disagree and to quarrel, each insisting that he had the correct model of the elephant, and eventually came to blows.
>
> Indian parable from the Buddhist canon

The parable of the blind men and the elephant illustrates some key themes in this book. Just like the elephant, intimate relationships have an independent reality outside the theories in laypeople's (or scientists') heads. However, because of the complexity of relationships, different scientific disciplines and theories focus on separate components and operate at different levels of analysis. Thus, explanations and interpretations of the data emerging within different disciplines can be misleading about the nature of the overall relationship animal. Like the blind men, scientists (and laypeople) often come to (verbal) blows about the nature of relationship reality. However, simply adopting an ecumenical approach, and declaring everyone a winner, is unhelpful. The vastly more disciplined and difficult project is to figure out how the different components and approaches should be integrated and understood in terms of the causal processes involved. Playing the game this way does produce

The Science of Intimate Relationships, First Edition. Garth Fletcher, Jeffry A. Simpson, Lorne Campbell, and Nickola C. Overall.
© 2013 Garth Fletcher, Jeffry A. Simpson, Lorne Campbell, and Nickola C. Overall.
Published 2013 by Blackwell Publishing Ltd.

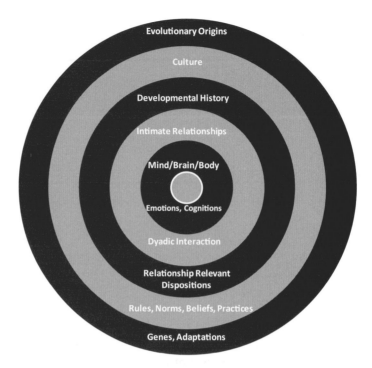

Figure 13.1   From distal (outer circle) to proximal domains (inner circle). Domains are in the top half, and associated units, which do the causal work, are shown in the bottom half of the circle

winners and losers, but it also shows that different theories and approaches are often complementary rather than contradictory.

As shown in Figure 13.1, adopting an interdisciplinary approach involves locating intimate relationships within a large web of causes that range from deep time (in the form of ancient evolutionary adaptations) to processes that currently exist in the minds and social networks of individuals. However, all the factors that make up this **distal–proximal** dimension must be represented at the proximal level in our minds/brains, and bodies; otherwise, it is hard to see how they could exert any influence on partners or relationships. Thus, at the bottom of each segment in Figure 13.1 we have shown the **proximal** units that do the causal work. By adopting this broad and multi-disciplinary approach, we gain a deeper and more valid picture – and understanding – of how and why intimate relationships operate as they do. Indeed, this book is one long argument (with associated evidence) for this proposition.

In this final chapter, we review six themes that tie together different parts of the relationship elephant: (i) the power of culture and evolution and their linkages; (ii) the similarities and differences between humans and other species; (iii) the analysis of gender differences; (iv) the significance of within-gender differences; (v) the future of research on intimate relationships; and (vi) a final look at the scientific study of intimate relationships.

The Power of Culture and Evolution

We have argued throughout that cultural processes and biological adaptations are inextricably intertwined. They have evolved together, and they interact to produce the cognitions, emotions, and behaviors that are part of people's daily relationship lives. This generalization is illustrated in the way different cultures approach romantic love (which we have claimed is an evolutionary adaptation) in the context of specific marital arrangements. Although **monogamous** relationships are the norm in most cultures, **polygynous** marriages are also common, and even **polyandrous** marriages exist, although they are rare. The existence of polyandrous marriages poses a special problem for evolutionary approaches because there seems to be nothing in it for the males, in terms of reproductive success.

Let's analyze an example of a polyandrous marriage system, which exists in Kinnaur, a region high in the Himalayan mountains that is populated by small, isolated villages. In Kinnaur, farming conditions are tough, resources are scarce, and life can be precarious. In such conditions, polyandrous marriage avoids the fragmentation of limited agricultural land, and assists the survival of both offspring and parents by sharing resources, having more than one husband working the land, and reaping the benefits of unmarried female relatives helping with the extended family (Tiwari, 2008). The reduction in reproductive success for the men is also allayed to some extent by the custom in Kinnaur of two or more brothers marrying the same woman (which makes sense in light of **inclusive fitness theory**).

Several aspects of Kinnaur marriages stand out based on a recent detailed ethnography by Geetanjali Tiwari (2008). First, married women claim that these marital arrangements can only be maintained if favoritism is avoided so that jealousy does not erupt between their multiple husbands. As one Kinnaur wife put it, "To be a polyandrous wife is to be mute" (Tiwari, 2008, p. 128). Another wife said: "Honesty is hard, too hard sometimes to keep in polyandrous marriages" (Tiwari, 2008, pp. 133). In these marriages, honesty and open communication is a luxury, and **good management** rules. Although Kinnaur wives frequently complain about husbands who often become jealous and competitive, the husbands also need to cooperate to an unusual degree, which includes negotiating sexual access to the wife they all share. Second, romantic love is alive and well in Kinnaur culture. Many polyandrous marriages start with a romantic entanglement, and the brothers of the loved individual are invited, as per the custom, to join the union. It is also relatively common for men to have affairs outside a marital union and form a monogamous marriage with one wife. Third, the norms and values of the wider community in Kinnaur support polyandrous relationships by stressing the values of practicality, kindness, patience, generosity, equal treatment of children in a family, and maintaining the norms and rules that support these unique marital arrangements. Fourth, as a market economy gathers pace in Kinnaur, and men can afford to start and maintain monogamous marriages, polyandrous unions are losing favor and households are increasingly becoming monogamous (Tiwari, 2008).

This analysis of Kinnaur marital arrangements nicely captures the power of both culture and evolutionary adaptations, and the links between the two. It also illustrates the spectacular ability of humans to monitor and manage their intimate relationships in complicated situations, including the ability to regulate emotions and behavior in the spirit of cooperation, harmony, and group unity.

Are Humans Just Another Ape?

In Chapter 2, we suggested that how humans manage their intimate relationships lies at the heart of human nature, helping to explain the evolution of the unique features of human nature and abilities linked to our large brain and extended childhoods. But how similar are the biology and psychology of intimate relationships to those of other species, especially other primates? We have commented on this issue here and there throughout the book. We now pull all the threads together and draw some more general conclusions.

The famous evolutionary biologist, Theodosius Dobzhansky, once said: "Nothing in biology makes sense except in the light of evolution." If we replace "biology" with "intimate relationships," the quotation remains valid: "Nothing in intimate relationships makes sense except in the light of evolution." There is little if anything unique about the human biological machinery involved in sexual reproduction or adult bonding. The **hormones, neurotransmitters,** and biological design of human reproductive systems reflect designs that go back millions of years and that we share with many other mammals. Moreover, the characteristic features of human genitalia and reproductive systems are similar to other primate species that have monogamous or polygynous mating systems (and are dissimilar to species that have multi-male/multi-female mating systems with sperm competition going full blast). This evidence is consistent with social psychological and anthropological research on romantic love, which has documented that humans bond with specific mates, but may have different mates across the life-course.

The way in which women rear their offspring with the assistance of their partners or extended family is also common across species (especially birds), but it is atypical in mammals. Among the apes, the only species that has similar mating arrangements to humans is the gibbon, which shared a common ancestor with humans about 18 million years ago, and is more distantly related to humans than the **great apes.** Observations of gibbons in the wild have revealed a pattern of mating and caregiving that is eerily similar to humans (Palombit, 1994). Gibbons are monogamous and live in family groups, but both male and female gibbons will leave their mates, especially if other available single gibbons of the opposite sex appear on the scene. Moreover, a new male in the gibbon nuclear family will adopt any unrelated infants and will help care for them (e.g. by carrying and defending them). However, like humans, stepfather gibbons are not as solicitous as genetic parents. Gibbons continuously monitor the quality of their mates while also taking into account the availability of alternative mates. To complete the analogy, Gibbons also have flexible mating arrangements, and (just like the people in Kinnaur), develop polyandrous groups when their ranges are larger and food becomes scarce (Savini *et al.*, 2009).

Nevertheless, humans are unique in several respects among apes and most other primates (including gibbons) in terms of mating and family arrangements. First, humans have relatively short periods of time between pregnancies (three to four years in hunter-gatherer cultures). Second, women live for many years after menopause and significantly contribute to rearing their grandchildren. Third, and perhaps most importantly, individuals living in hunter-gathering and traditional cultures live in relatively large groups comprising several families, which are typically based on either monogamous pair bonds, or a mixture of monogamous and polygynous marital arrangements. None of the other apes, including the gibbon, resemble this complex pattern of family and kin arrangements (Flinn, 2011).

In Chapter 2 we argued that these mating arrangements of **Homo sapiens** were linked to the stretching of human life history, especially in childhood and adolescence, which, in turn, enabled the most truly unique and remarkable feature of the human species to evolve; namely, the development of the **cerebral frontal cortex**, which facilitated our ability to use language, to learn quickly and easily, and to plan into the future. These capacities generated the development of culture and technology, which enabled humans to take a step that no other animal has ever managed – to figure out how sexual reproduction works. Because of the invention and use of contraception, this step has to some extent short-circuited the evolutionary feedback mechanism of reproductive success, which is the lever of biological evolution, while simultaneously allowing cultural forces to play an even greater role in the psychology of intimate relationships.

Moreover, the ability to mind-read, explain, predict, and regulate partner and relationship behavior has reached unprecedented levels in the human species. Studies of communication in intimate relationships have established that typical couples, most of whom are in relatively stable and happy relationships, are exquisitely attuned to each other's moods, needs, interactive behaviors, and attitudes. This fine attunement is as much unconscious as conscious, and although most of the current research has been conducted on western samples, it seems unlikely that such prodigious abilities are due to reading self-help books or watching TV shows of relationship "experts" such as Dr Phil (consistent with our example of relationships in Kinnaur, and other cross-cultural research). This high level of social intelligence, facilitated by the stretching of childhood in human life history, laid the groundwork for the extraordinary levels of cooperation witnessed in humans today (e.g. in corporations, neighborhoods, towns, cities, armies, and nations).

Gender Differences

Humans have evolved in the recent past, at least in evolutionary terms. For this reason, the footprints of our evolutionary past can be readily discerned in the intimate

Table 13.1   Analysis of well-documented gender differences in intimate relationships

- Women are more motivated and expert lay psychologists than men in intimate relationships

  Women are more likely than men to:
  - decide to leave intimate relationships
  - approach conflict and communicate about relationship problems
  - talk openly to their friends about their intimate relationships
  - monitor and think extensively about their intimate relationships
  - be more accurate at mind-reading
  - produce complex explanations for the demise of relationships
  - possess detailed and vivid memories of local relationships

- Men adopt a more proprietorial attitude toward women's sexuality and reproductive behavior, than vice versa

  Men are more likely than women to:
  - become sexually jealous at possible or actual sexual infidelities and react violently
  - kill or seriously injure their partners

- Men possess a stronger and less malleable sex drive, and a stronger orientation toward short-term sexual liaisons, than do women

  Men are more likely than women to:
  - fantasize about sex
  - seek out short-term sexual liaisons
  - masturbate
  - initiate sexual activity
  - maintain one sexual orientation throughout adult life
  - report strong and frequent sexual desires

- Women are more focused on level of investment in intimate relationships than are men

  Women are more likely than men to:
  - perceive physical attractiveness as relatively unimportant in mate selection
  - perceive mate status and resources as important in mate selection

Source: Adapted from Fletcher (2002)

relationship mind, revealing that human nature is subtly different for men and women. Evidence for gender differences in relationships has been scattered throughout the book. Table 13.1 systematically groups the primary gender differences in intimate relationships that have been documented in both western and non-western cultures.

As can be seen, gender differences fall into four coherent patterns: (i) women are more motivated and expert lay psychologists than men, at least in the context of intimate relationships; (ii) men adopt a more proprietorial attitude toward women's sexuality and reproductive behavior; (iii) men have a stronger and less malleable sex drive, and a stronger orientation toward engaging in casual, short-term sexual liaisons than do women; and (iv) women are more focused on the partner's level of investment in relationships than men.

We believe that the most plausible explanation for these systematic gender differences is the existence of gender-linked evolutionary adaptations, some of which have resulted in cultural practices that have effectively sustained these differences. Culture assuredly plays an important role in minimizing or accentuating these gender differences, as can be seen from the anthropological and cross-cultural record, but these gender differences are relatively stable and resistant to change across cultures. There is, however, another powerful counter-argument to consider; namely, that evolutionary psychologists identify supposedly universal gender differences based on data from modern cultures that have only existed in full-blown since the last ice age, which ended about 12 000 years ago (Fisher, 1992; Miller, 2000). In modern cultures, individuals can amass vast resources and food reserves, populations can expand rapidly, most people live in cities, and complex, hierarchical political systems are developed. Humans prior to the last ice age lived in small mobile groups as hunter-gatherers, a very different milieu to that of modern cultures.

As a result, so goes the argument, small biological differences between men and women may well have become amplified during the past 12 000 years into larger gender differences than existed for most of our evolutionary history. In large-scale societies (including western societies), up until recently, men took control of most of the resources and political power, and women were assigned to the status of second-class citizens. Thus, it is perhaps not primarily biology but culture that has produced the gender differences listed in Table 13.1. To test this theory one might examine gender differences in hunter-gatherer cultures, which represent the kind of social environments in which 99% of our species' evolution has taken place during the last million years. And, in hunter-gatherer cultures such as the !Kung in Africa, it has been argued that we indeed find relatively egalitarian social systems with monogamous marriages and women who have considerable power, freedom, and autonomy.

How should this argument be evaluated? Needless to say, culture can and does exert tremendous influences on gender differences and the roles that men and women assume in their cultures and societies (Eagly & Wood, 1999). There is, however, much variability among hunter-gatherer cultures with respect to gender differences and the status of women (Kelly, 1995). Australian aboriginal cultures like the **Tiwi**, for example, look very different from African hunter-gatherer cultures. In addition, ethnographies of relatively egalitarian hunter-gatherer cultures suggest that the most pronounced gender differences parallel the four generalizations shown in Table 13.1 (Kelly, 1995; Lee, 1978; Shostak, 1981). For example, Kung women often have much older husbands who are assigned to them at a young age. If they protest long and loud enough, they can usually separate from their assigned husbands, eventually ending up with the husband of their choice. However, young brides must protest – such rights are not granted to them as a matter of course. In addition, !Kung men physically assail their partners more often than vice versa, especially when they suspect sexual infidelity on the part of their wives.

In sum, even in the most liberal and egalitarian hunter-gatherer cultures, men adopt a more proprietorial attitude toward women's sexuality and reproductive behavior than vice versa. There is also good evidence that all four major gender differences exist even in some of the most egalitarian and emancipated cultures that have ever existed in terms of the economic and political power wielded by women; namely, western cultures such as New Zealand, the USA, Sweden, the UK, Australia, and Canada (which is not to say that such western cultures are perfect on this standard by any means). The fact that some of the worst excesses of gender-linked prejudice and inequality were redressed in western cultures only after prolonged and determined political battles (e.g. the Women's Rights movement of the 1970s) illustrates the power wielded by both cultural norms and practices and our evolutionary heritage.

Evolutionary psychology and feminism are at one in postulating the widespread tendency for men to attempt to control the sexuality of women (although feminism and evolutionary psychology disagree about the origins of this tendency). One naive response to the feminist viewpoint is that women often assume the dominant role in educating and socializing their sons and daughters about the mores and norms of their culture. Female genital mutilation, for example, is usually carried out by women in certain parts of Africa, who wholeheartedly believe in the practice and try to persuade their daughters of its value. We say "naive" because this is the way cultures work – people are socialized from childhood to accept and eventually promote the core values and beliefs of their culture. The fact that women are socialized to accept and act on a set of beliefs and practices that may repress and restrict women attests to the power wielded by human cultures, and does not impugn a feminist approach.

One of the remarkable features of evolutionary answers to the origin of gender differences is their ability to explain some forms of human behavior that appear to pose major problems for evolutionary theories, because they impair the individual's chances of achieving reproductive success. We have discussed several examples of this throughout the book, including men killing their wives and children (and then committing suicide) and the prevalence of homosexuality. The key to solving this conundrum is that such situations are relatively rare, and thus affect few people. The genes that produce the normal range of human behavior have been selected for because they have, *on average*, resulted in more successful mating strategies.

Thus, in our ancestral past, women may have ideally preferred men with slightly more feminine personality qualities, such as sensitivity and kindness, as long-term mates and investing fathers. Similarly, men who adopted a proprietorial view of their female mates most likely prevented sexual infidelities and, thus, sent their own genes into future generations more effectively than did men who were lax about their mate's extracurricular sexual activities. The fact that these evolved tendencies pull in starkly different directions (kindness versus jealousy and aggression) fits human nature perfectly.

Within-gender Differences

As we have repeatedly emphasized, gender differences must be juxtaposed with the tremendous variability in attitudes, emotions, and behavior that exists within each gender. This brings developmental processes into the picture. Explaining how children develop into adults requires an understanding of how genetic templates become intertwined with the social environments in which children develop, which can lead individuals down different developmental tracks as they mature. For example, ambivalent or cold parental care of daughters, combined with extended contact with genetically unrelated males such as the mothers' boyfriends, pushes daughters toward an insecure **attachment style** and an opportunistic **mating strategy** in adulthood that is geared toward early reproduction and lower parental investment. In contrast, a warm and loving relationship with both parents during childhood pushes adolescent girls toward a **secure attachment style** and a penchant for long-term, committed relationships in adulthood, producing the search for romantic partners who are warm, loyal, and devoted fathers.

Some psychologists (most famously Freud) assumed that the social learning process more or less stops during early childhood (e.g. the first five years of life), and that humans are stuck with their psychological legacy from that point onward. Nothing could be further from the truth. The learning process never stops, and humans remain exquisitely attuned to their environments, their intimate relationship experiences, and forces in their wider culture throughout their entire lives. **Attachment working models**, for example, are stable, but can and do change considerably from relationship to relationship and over time in response to how individuals are treated by new attachment figures.

The interplay between the environment and the intimate relationship mind can also be seen in daily relationships. Consider the following question: Is it better to express your anger directly and honestly to your partner, or should you repress your anger and avoid upsetting your partner? The perhaps infuriating answer is "It depends." For example, if George expresses anger in an important problem-solving discussion with his partner, this may turn out to be neutral or even beneficial for solving the problem. In contrast, if George expresses anger when his partner crashes the car (through no fault of her own), this is likely to be corrosive to the relationship.

Consider another question: How does the brain respond if someone holds your hand while you are feeling pain? The answer, again, is "It depends." If someone holds your hand, you will be likely to have reduced neural activity in specific areas of your brain that produce sensations of pain (such as the **ventral anterior cingulate cortex** [VACC] and the **hypothalamus**, which regulates the release of cortisol). However, these soothing effects will be stronger if the hand-holder is your partner, especially if you have a happy relationship.

Finally, there exist key interactions between relationship partners themselves. The intimate relationship mind influences behavior in myriad ways. One core process involves connections between partner expectations, partner ideal standards, and judgments of the partner and relationship. If expectations and desires closely match perceptions of relationship reality, people are happy and committed; if not, happiness and commitment slide, and the relationship is not likely to have a rosy future. However, individuals are not simply free to build castles in the air while ignoring reality. One person's intimate relationship mind is at least partly locked into his or her partner's intimate relationship mind through the conduit of behavior. If George's theory of the relationship becomes divorced from reality (which includes the relationship theories in his partner's head), his partner is likely to deliver a painful correction to George's theory at some point in the relationship.

Humans have wonderfully sophisticated intimate relationship theories for some of the same reasons that scientists have theories – to explain, evaluate, predict, and control events. But such aims, and how they are fulfilled, vary depending on the specific circumstances. If Mary's partner does something negative and unexpected (like forgetting her birthday), Mary is likely to be kicked into conscious attributional overdrive to explain, and perhaps control her partner's errant behavior in the future. On the other hand, if Mary's partner continually repeats a well-rehearsed and expected negative behavior, such as failing to lower the toilet seat after use, Mary may do nothing cognitively, emotionally, or behaviorally, except perhaps to unconsciously attribute the event to the belief that her partner is an airhead around the house.

The Future of Intimate Relationships

One question often asked is "What is the future of intimate relationships?" In contemporary societies, people are constantly bombarded with information about what makes for a good and happy relationship (along with images of beautiful people, their beautiful partners, and their seemingly idyllic relationships). The internet has rendered such information a mere mouse-click away, and internet dating has rapidly become a popular way to quickly meet potential partners and forge new relationships (Finkel *et al.*, 2012).

Online dating, in particular, has become commonplace in many countries. It is not really dating as much as it is a method of contacting and communicating with potential partners – dating really starts when face-to-face-contact occurs. Between 2007 and 2009, a nationally representative survey in the US found that 22% of heterosexual couples had met their current partners through internet dating, and one report estimated that 25 million people accessed an online dating site in one month alone in 2011 (Rosenfeld and Thomas, 2010)! One of the difficulties with using online dating companies is the vast number of profiles that are available for browsing. When choices and options become too numerous, the normal decision-making process of mate selection can freeze up, become impossibly time-consuming, or encourage individuals to push their ideal standards to unrealistically high levels (Finkel *et al.*, 2012).

The advertising claims of many online dating services must be taken with a grain of salt. One of the most successful sites (eHarmony), for example, claims that "Out of all the single people you will meet in your life, only a very few would make a great relationship partner for you . . . by combining the best scientific research with detailed profiling of every member, we screen thousands of single men and women to bring you only the ones that have the potential to be truly right for you" (eHarmony Scientific Match-Making, 2012). The algorisms used by different companies vary, but, like eHarmony, are typically based on the extent to which self-reported personality traits, interests, values, interests, and so forth are similar between specific pairs of potential partners. The problem is that the degree of similarity between partners on these dimensions weakly explains success or stability in romantic relationships (see Chapter 12; Finkel *et al.*, 2012). Thus, even though such websites may be useful in sorting out and contacting potential partners, advertising claims that they offer a scientific, gold-plated way to find your "soul mate" may have little substance.

Our general answer to the question posed – What is the future of intimate relationships? – is two-fold. First, humans are cultural animals, born to live and learn within cultures. Thus, the cultural shifts since the last ice age – from about 12 000 years ago when *Homo sapiens* started the long march from an ancient hunter-gather life style to the contemporary information age – have exerted massive influences on intimate relationships, ranging from why and how we select mates, to why and how we maintain relationships, to why and how we sometimes dissolve relationships. Second, human nature is not just a cultural product but was forged in the evolutionary past, which is why many of the topics we have covered in this book have a universal, timeless quality about them.

Science and Intimate Relationships

This book shows that science is alive and well in the study of intimate relationships, and that relationship science operates in a similar fashion to other domains within the social and behavioral sciences. As we have seen, seemingly ineffable constructs such as love and interdependence can be reliably and validly measured, and we are well on the way toward understanding how they influence everyday relationship functioning. Relationship scientists can also predict important relationship phenomena, such as marital separation and relationship satisfaction, with high levels of accuracy. The evidence for these points belies the common belief that human behavior – especially in intimate relationships – is too complicated and random to be predictable or understood.

Although science often leads to consensus, it also leaves many important questions unanswered and routinely raises intriguing new questions. Moreover, science (including the science of intimate relationships) is a hotbed of controversy, argument, claim, and counter-claim. Consensus in science rarely means 100% agreement. By adopting an interdisciplinary approach, we can analyze the extent to which theories and evidence emanating from different domains fit together, and thus more effectively test theories and hypotheses along with generating new theories and questions.

The links between the science of intimate relationships and conventional wisdom are complex. Sometimes we have suggested that some psychology textbooks are wrong and that common sense is correct (e.g. men do actually have stronger sex drives than women). More often, however, we have argued that common-sense beliefs tend to be overly simplistic, problematic, or even flat-out wrong. Yet even when common sense is totally incorrect, this does not imply that relationship scientists can afford to simply disregard it – common-sense (lay) theories, regardless of their validity, can and do powerfully influence people's daily interpersonal behavior.

We have attempted to focus on the science of intimate relationships, and not to sail into moral, legal, or political waters. We do not mean to downplay the importance of the latter issues, nor imply that a good scientific understanding of intimate relationships is irrelevant to these issues. Sometimes people, including scientists, are motivated to suppress knowledge or advise against discovering how the world really works on the grounds that prejudice and discrimination might be encouraged. It is true that scientific knowledge can be used for good or ill, and it can also be exploited to justify particular moral and political stances. Ignorance, however, is not bliss. Ignorance and closed minds are fertile ground for prejudice, discrimination, and human folly. Used wisely, scientifically based findings can help people understand their own intimate relationships better, allow professionals to develop more effective relationship therapies, and permit the development of more humane and effective public policies.

Conclusion

In conclusion, intimate relationships are a marvelous domain for understanding the complexity and wonder of human nature. In truth, the positive and negatives of intimate relationships are two sides of the same coin. They come as a package deal, just as the needs for intimacy and love bring with them the fear of rejection and the pain of relationship loss. This is part of the human condition that we humans are unique among species in grasping and understanding.

Glossary

accommodation: The tendency to inhibit destructive responses when faced with negative partner behavior, and instead react constructively.

action-facilitating support: Support within relationships intended to directly assist, including offering information and advice about how to manage the problem (informational support), and providing resources and engaging in activities to help the individual manage the stressful event (tangible support).

adaptation: In Darwinian evolutionary theory this concept refers to the way in which a trait (biological, psychological, or behavioral) has evolved enabling the organism to live more successfully in a social or physical environment

adrenal glands: Sitting on top of the kidneys, these two glands are chiefly responsible for releasing hormones in response to stress (e.g. cortisol and epinephrine).

affective forecasting error: A tendency for people to predict greater levels of negative or positive consequences, following negative or positive events, than actually eventuate (an example of directional bias).

allele: Genes have two copies (one from each parent), each copy being termed an allele. It is frequently the case that one of the alleles may be different in certain individuals. When the alleles vary in this way across a population it is termed a genetic polymorphism.

alloparents: Individuals (kin or unrelated) who assist in the child-rearing of offspring of whom they are not the parents.

allostatic load: Refers to the amount of strain produced by repeated changes in physiological responses and heightened activation of biological systems as they respond to stress.

Alzheimer's disease: The most common form of dementia, most often diagnosed in people over 65 years of age.

amygdala: Almond shaped organs deep within the temporal lobe of the brain. Main functions are linked to memory and emotions.

anomie: A term popularized by the French sociologist Emile Durkheim in his influential book *Suicide* (1897). It refers to a breakdown of the social norms linking the individual to the wider community.

The Science of Intimate Relationships, First Edition. Garth Fletcher, Jeffry A. Simpson, Lorne Campbell, and Nickola C. Overall.

anterior: Refers to regions in the front of the brain.

antigens: A substance from either within or outside the body that provokes an immune response via the generation of antibodies.

anxious: Can refer to an attachment style or working model. Anxiously attached adults are uncertain that their attachment figures (partners) will be sufficiently attentive, available, and responsive to their needs. These concerns keep their distress levels high and their attachment systems turned on, leading to hypervigilance, rumination, and the use of emotion-focused coping strategies.

asexual reproduction: A mode of reproduction by which offspring are produced from a single parent, and inherit the genes of that parent only.

assortative mating: Occurs when mated pairs are more similar than would be expected by chance. For example physical attractiveness is moderately strongly correlated across partners in romantic relationships.

assumed similarity: Refers to the degree of similarity within the individual between self-judgments and judgments of the partner; often termed projection.

attachment system: An innate behavioral attachment system that Bowlby postulated was originally shaped by evolution to keep vulnerable infants in close physical proximity to their caregivers, particularly during infancy and young childhood.

attachment theory: A theory originally developed by John Bowlby explaining the operations of an innate attachment system, formed in early childhood but in operation across the life span. The theory has a normative component (explaining typical features of attachment) and an individual-difference component (explaining how and why people with different attachment styles think, feel, and behave).

attribution theory: A general term for a set of theories from social psychology that describe and explain how humans make causal and other attributions for human behavior (the theory explains explaining).

Australopithecus afarensis: An extinct hominid living in Africa from 3 to 4 million years ago, that had features characteristic of both prehistoric apes and the homo line ancestral to modern humans.

avoidant: Can refer to an attachment style or working model. Avoidant individuals strive to avoid intimacy, thus preventing the possibility of rejection and subsequent distress. They avoid giving or receiving support in relationships, and control their negative emotions by downplaying or diverting their attention.

axons: Also known as nerve fibers, they are long, slender projections of neurons that typically conduct electrical impulses to other neurons or parts of the brain.

baby talk: The way that adults often talk to babies (high pitched voice, simplified vocabulary, positive affect, etc.).

basic emotions: A short list of emotions (ranging from 5 to 17) usually considered to be universal, evolved emotions that have specific signatures, including nonverbal behavior, neurological and hormonal elements, associated behaviors, eliciting conditions, and consequential behaviors.

behavior control: Derived from the part of interdependence theory that describes forms of dyadic influence, referring to a situation in which both partners exercise power over a decision or behavioral interaction.

behaviorism: A psychological approach that labels all human psychological activity (affect, behavior, and cognition) as behaviour, and views such behavior as a function of the external environment and contingencies (rather than being internally caused or under the control of the individual). This approach dominated psychology up until the 1960s, when it was largely supplanted by the cognitive revolution.

bilateral activation: Occurs when the same brain region is activated in both hemispheres of the brain.

biological homologue: A byproduct of an evolved adaptation (such as the human male nipple) that serves no special function.

blank slate: A term referring to the view that humans are born without instincts and learn everything from experience, perception, and socialization.

blood–brain barrier: Refers to the separation of circulating blood in the body from the brain fluids in animals. This prevents large molecules like bacteria from entering the brain from the body, while allowing other substances like oxygen, glucose, carbon-dioxide, and some hormones to cross the barrier.

brain hemispheres: Refer to the left and right sides of the human brain.

brain imaging: Refers to a range of techniques developed over the last 50 years which map activity in the brain. Since the 1990s brain mapping has been dominated by functional magnetic resonance mapping (fMRI), because of its low invasiveness, lack of radiation exposure, and relatively wide availability.

capitalization: Communicating positive news to another individual (e.g. a romantic partner).

cardiovascular system: Distributes blood around the body. Main components are the heart, blood, and blood vessels.

cervix: The neck of the womb joining the top of the vagina.

cingulate cortex (CC): A region of the brain resembling a collar formed round the corpus collosum. Serves multiple functions linked to both cognitions and emotions, including the regulation of emotions.

clitoris: The center of women's sexual enjoyment, it is similar in structure to the penis, having both a shaft and glans. It is typically about two-thirds of an inch (1.6 cm) in length at rest, but swells with blood to twice that length during sexual arousal.

cognitive behavioral couples therapy: An approach to relationship therapy that con-centrates on changing unhelpful cognitions (e.g. negative attributions, unrealistic expectations), and generating more positive cognitions.

cohabitation: Living together in a romantic or sexual relationship without being married.

companionate love: In contrast to passionate love, companionate love is experienced less intensely. It combines feelings of intimacy, commitment, and deep attachment toward others, romantic or otherwise.

comparison level (CL): Expectations about what benefits are deserved in a relationship.

comparison level alternatives (Clalt): Perceived quality of available alternative partners or relationships.

confirmatory factor analysis: A type of factor analysis in which prior factor analytic models are tested, using measures of statistical fit.

conflict tactics scale: A commonly used self report scale developed by Murray Straus that measures the frequency of mild to severe forms of intimate violence.

congenital adrenal hyperplasia (CAH): A rare genetic condition, which afflicts only women, generating excessive production of testosterone in the womb resulting in the masculinization of the genitals.

Coolidge effect: The tendency for males in many mammalian species (more than females) to show renewed sexual responses when a new potential sexual partner is introduced, even when sexual interest has waned in prior but still currently available partners.

cooperative breeding: A social system in which either kin or non-kin of the parent(s) assist in the rearing of offspring.

corpus collosum: A fibrous bundle in the brain connecting the left and right hemispheres.

correlational: Research designs examining the associations between variables without experimental manipulation of any of the variables.

cortisol: A steroid hormone released in response to stress. It has the effects of raising blood sugar levels and suppressing immune functions.

cuddle hormones: Oxytocin and vasopressin (often tagged the cuddle hormones) are released both in the bloodstream in the body and as neurotransmitters in the brain. They have multiple functions including the facilitation of bonding in both mother–child relationships, and in romantic relationships between adults (for both men and women).

Darwinian evolutionary theory: Refers to Darwin's theory that simple forms of life slowly evolve into different species as a function of natural selection that determines which variants will survive and successfully reproduce. Often also used to cover Darwin's later theory of sexual selection.

deactivating strategies: A process by which negative emotions are repressed or ignored.

demand–withdraw: A negative pattern of interaction that occurs when critical and demanding communication from one partner is responded to with defensive withdrawal.

diffusion tensor imaging (DTI): A similar technique to fMRI, this technique maps the connecting fibers in the brain by recording the rate at which fluids (mainly water) in the connecting fibers (white matter) diffuse into the surrounding tissue.

directional bias: Produced when an individual or sample systematically rate a target as either more positive or more negative when compared to some benchmark.

dismissive-avoidant: A category of attachment that combines a low anxiety attachment style with a high avoidant style.

disorganized attachment: A form of infant attachment style that is incoherent and inconsistent, and does not readily fit into Ainsworth's original tripartite attachment distinction.

distal: Refers to causes from the past and/or from spatially distant origins (see proximal).

dizygotic: Refers to non-identical twins, who share about 50% of their genes.

DNA: Common acronym for deoxyribonucleic acid, which is a molecule containing the genetic information used in almost all living organisms.

dopamine system: Associated with rewards and punishment, dopamine is a powerful motivating neurotransmitter generated in the mid brain regions, especially the ventral tegmental area (VTA).

dorsal: Refers to regions in the top part of the brain.

dorsolateral prefrontal cortex (DLPFC): A region in the prefrontal cortex mainly involved in controlling and directing behavior.

Duchenne smiles: First noted by the French physician Guillaume Duchenne in the nineteenth century, a Duchenne smile involves both muscles round the eyes and muscles round the mouth, whereas a non-Duchenne smile involves only the major muscles round the mouth.

embodied cognition: A research domain based on the proposition that bodily and perceptual processes and cognition work to influence one another within an integrated biological system.

emotion focused couple therapy: An approach to relationship therapy that focuses on the development of a healthy attachment bond, enabling partners to understand and regulate their attachment-related needs and negative emotions (e.g. anger and fear).

emotion scripts: Story-like concepts that detail the causes and consequences of different emotions, including the responses of partners.

empathic joining: A term used in integrative behavioral couples therapy referring to encouraging the understanding of the other's perceptions and mutual responsibility.

endocrine glands: Glands in the brain and body that create and release hormones.

endocrine system: The system of glands in the body that release and regulate hormones.

environmental risk model: A life history theory developed by Bruce Ellis and colleagues proposing that both the harshness and unpredictability of the local environment (partly) determine mating strategies in adulthood.

epinephrine: Epinephrine (also known as adrenaline) is a major fight-or-flight hormone that increases heart rate, constricts blood vessels, and dilates air passages.

error management theory: Based on evolutionary psychology, this theory by Haselton and Buss argues that perceptual and judgmental biases often have a functional basis linked to survival and reproductive success.

estrogen: A primary female hormone with many functions, but typically involving sex, reproduction, and the development of secondary sex characteristics.

evoked culture: A term coined by Tooby and Cosmides referring to aspects of culture (beliefs, behavior, etc.) that are actually products of evolutionary adaptations evoked by different social or physical environments.

exit–voice–neglect–loyalty typology: This typology by Caryl Rusbult and colleagues specifies four different responses to dissatisfaction in relationships. These responses fall into two dimensions: constructive versus destructive and active versus passive.

experimental: A research method which involves the manipulation of one variable and random assignment to groups.

factor analysis: A statistical technique that analyzes the correlations among a set of variables to ascertain the underlying existence of subsets of variables (termed factors) that correlate highly among themselves but not with variables in other sub-sets.

fallopian tubes: Two tubes about 10 inches (25.4 cm) in length from the ovary to the uterus in humans, which the female ovum passes down.

fate control: Derived from the part of interdependence theory that describes forms of dyadic influence, this term refers to a situation in which influence or power is dominated by one partner.

fearful-avoidant: A category of attachment that combines a high anxiety attachment style with a high avoidant style.

felt security: The desire to maintain psychological proximity, which slowly replaces the desire for physical proximity as children move through the toddler years and into middle childhood.

fight or flight hormones: Hormones, such as epinephrine and cortisol, that prepare the body for action when encountering stress by increasing heart rate, blood pressure, and the availability of glucose.

fluctuating asymmetry: Refers to the extent to which the left and right sides of the body (including the face) are symmetrical.

folk psychology: The corpus of beliefs and theories shared by any given culture concerning human emotions, cognition, and behavior.

follicular phase: The initial phase of the menstrual cycle, in which conception is relatively likely.

functional magnetic resonance imaging (fMRI): A brain imaging method that measures activity in different parts of the brain by assessing changes in blood flow. When specific parts of the brain work hard, they call up increased flows of blood (containing additional oxygen and glucose). The magnetic field generated by the brain imaging machine is able to pick this up because oxygen-rich blood is more affected by magnetic fields than oxygen-thin blood.

game theory: Mathematical modeling of strategies used in interactions that involve conflict and cooperation.

general relationship theory: A lay set of beliefs and expectations concerning how intimate relationships function in general terms (rather than applying to a specific relationship).

genetic polymorphism: In general usage, a gene that allows for different adult forms or behavior to develop, depending on some other cue (such as an environmental trigger).

genome: The entire store of hereditary information in the DNA of an individual or species.

glans: The head of the male penis in humans and other mammals.

good genes: A concept in sexual selection theory postulating that features of the body attractive to the opposite sex are associated with (good) genes that can increase reproductive success.

good management model: A model postulating that instead of openly expressing negative thoughts and feelings, exercising good communication skills involve compromise, restraint, accommodation, and ignoring problems that resist being resolved.

grandmother hypothesis: A theory that the tendency for women to live for many years past menopause (unique among primates) is an evolutionary adaptation based on their contribution to the quality and survival of their grandchildren.

great apes: An evolutionary branch that includes humans, chimpanzees, gorillas, and orangutans.

half-life: In biology this refers to the time that a substance in the body (such as a hormone) takes to reduce its effects by 50%.

handicap principle: In sexual selection contexts this principle holds that males who can afford to maintain exaggerated, costly ornaments or behavior, honestly signal to females that they are healthy specimens with good genes.

hippocampus: Located deep in the middle of the brain, this ancient structure is mainly concerned with emotions and memory.

Homo heidelbergensis: Living from 400 000 to 600 000 years ago in Europe, and earlier in Africa, and often considered to be a direct ancestor of both *Homo sapiens* and Neanderthals.

Homo sapiens: Latin for wise man, this is the taxonomic term for modern humans.

honest communication model: A model postulating that couples should openly express their negative feelings and cognitions (albeit in a diplomatic fashion), deal with conflict directly, and never leave problems unresolved.

hormones: Chemicals released in the body by glands or cells that regulate or control other cells or organs.

hunter-gatherers: Small-scale nomadic bands, living off wild plants and animals. This was the dominant way of life until the development of agriculture from about 10 000 years ago.

hypothalamic–pituitary–adrenal (HPA) axis: A major part of the neuroendocrine system that controls reactions to stress and regulates many body processes, including digestion, the immune system, mood and emotions, sexuality, and energy storage and expenditure.

hypothalamus: Located in the mid-brain, this organ controls the metabolism and the release of hormones from the pituitary gland.

in parallel: Cognitive processes that occur simultaneously.

inclusive fitness: A theory proposed by William Hamilton positing that altruism can evolve by individuals promoting the survival and reproductive success of close relatives (who share the individual's genes).

integrative behavioral couples therapy: An approach to relationship therapy that integrates behavioral strategies for change with the need for partners to accept and tolerate differences in personality, values, and communication styles.

interactional traits: Traits, such as aggression, love, and trust, which work interactively across couples.

interdependence theory: A social psychological theory framed in terms of the rewards that partners perceive they provide each other, and the way they coordinate their behavior in different types of situations.

internal working models: A key component of attachment theory, these refer to the beliefs, expectancies, and attitudes about relationships based on earlier experiences with attachment figures.

interpersonal attributions: A sub-set of interactional traits, which specifically refer to attributions of one partner directed toward the other (e.g. love, trust, regard).

intimate terrorism: A term coined by Michael Johnson to refer to the kind of severe intimate violence used by men to intimidate and control their partners.

investment model: Based on interdependence theory by Caryl Rusbult, this model postulates that commitment is influenced by three causes – satisfaction, quality of alternatives, and investment size.

invisible support: Partner support that is not consciously perceived as support by the recipient.

life history theory: A group of theories seeking to explain the evolutionary roots of differences in developmental pathways across the life span both across and within species.

local relationship theory: A lay theory about a specific intimate relationship.

long-term memory: Memories that are stored in a long-term fashion.

love styles: Based on Greek terms for love, this typology developed by Lee contains three primary styles of love (eros, ludus, and storge), and three secondary styles (mania, pragma, and agape).

luteal phase: The latter half of the menstrual cycle in which the risk of conception is low.

materialism: As a general view holds that only energy and matter exist. As applied to psychology, this thesis rejects mind–body dualism and implies that the mind and the brain refer to the same thing.

mating strategies: Typically divided into short-term (low investment in the partner and parenting) and long-term strategies (high investment in the partner and parenting).

menarche: Refers to the first menstrual cycle experienced in female humans, typically occurring from age 12 to 14.

menopause: Refers to the end of the menstrual periods, signaling the end of the fertile phase of a woman's life. Usually occurs in the late 40s or early 50s.

menstrual cycle: In humans a reproductive cycle regulated by the release of hormones and lasting about 28 days, with ovulation usually taking place in days 13 to 16.

meta-analysis: A method, with associated statistics, that combines results from different studies to assess the average effect size and examine which factors might predict the different effect sizes obtained across or within studies.

mind-reading: The process of attributing mental attributes to others (e.g. emotions, thoughts, attitudes, beliefs).

mind–body dualism: A thesis positing that attributes of the mind and body belong to different realms of reality.

mirror neurons: These neurons fire both when an animal acts and when an animal observes the same action performed by another. Some have argued that mirror neurons may be important in humans for understanding the actions of other people, and for learning new skills by imitation.

modularity: An important assumption of evolutionary psychology as originally formulated by Cosmides and Tooby, holding that the human mind is composed of many independent modules that have evolved to deal with specific problems encountered in the Pleistocene.

monogamy: Mating system involving one male and one female.

monozygotic: Refers to identical twins, who share 100% of their genes.

multi-male/multi-female: Mating system involving multiple sexual encounters between several females and several males.

multiple regression: A statistical multivariate approach analyzing the influence of multiple predictor (independent) variables, while controlling for the shared variance across the predictor variables.

natural experiments: Naturally occurring situations which approximate an experimental design in which participants are randomly assigned to different groups.

Neanderthals: A large-brained hominid species that lived in Europe and elsewhere over the last 600 000 years or so, becoming extinct about 30 000 years ago. Does not appear to be a direct ancestor of *Homo sapiens*, although recent evidence suggests some interbreeding between Neanderthals and humans occurred leaving a residue of Neanderthal genes in modern humans.

negative reciprocity: An interactional pattern occurring when negative behavior by one partner is met with intensified negative behavior by the other, often leading to negative escalation.

neurons: Neurons (nerve cells) comprise a core component of the brain and nervous system. There are about 100 billion neurons in the human brain.

neurotransmitters: Chemicals that regulate communication among neurons in the brain.

new world monkeys: Comprise 53 species of monkey found in Central and South America.

ontogenetic: A term referring to the development of the organism over the life span.

orbital frontal cortex (OFC): A brain region, just above and behind the eyes, involved in regulating and planning behavior specifically linked to rewards and punishments.

ovary: A reproductive organ (in pairs) producing the ovum in human females about once every 28 days.

ovum: The human female egg.

oxytocin: A substance known as a "cuddle" hormone having effects both in the brain and the body on a range of social behaviors in humans including bonding behavior, principally in the female.

oxytocin receptor gene: A gene that allows for the uptake of oxytocin in the brain, found on human chromosome 3p25.

pancreas: A large gland just below the stomach, producing several important hormones and also fluids assisting digestion in the small intestine.

parental investment theory: Developed by Robert Trivers, this influential theory (generally successfully) predicts that the sex making the larger investment in nurturing and protecting offspring will be more discriminating in mating, and that the sex investing less in offspring will compete for access to the higher-investing sex.

paternity uncertainty: Refers to the fact that males do not know with certainty they are the genetic parents of their offspring.

patrilocal: Refers to the widespread practice of the married couple living with or near the husbands' parents.

penis bone: This is found in many mammals and the apes, but not in humans.

phenotype: The observable physical form and behavior of a given species.

pineal gland: A small hormonal gland at the base and center of the brain.

pituitary gland: A small hormonal gland near and connected to the hypothalamus.

Pleistocene: The period from about 2.6 million years ago to 12 000 years ago, during which time the earth experienced repeated cycles of glaciation, and modern humans evolved.

polyandry: Refers to a form of marriage in which a woman has two or more husbands at the same time.

polygyny: Refers to a form of marriage in which a man has two or more wives at the same time.

posterior: Refers to regions in the back part of the brain.

prefrontal cortex: The area in the very front of the brain.

premarital relationship enhancement program: A program for helping couples before they get married focusing on communication skills, realistic expectations, and building commitment.

preoccupied: A category of attachment that combines a high anxiety attachment style with a low avoidant style.

primates: Primates include humans, apes, monkeys, and promisians. There are thought to be about 350 primate species.

projection: The process of making attributions to others based on perceptions, beliefs, or attitudes about the self.

prostate gland: The function of this gland is to secrete a slightly acidic fluid, milky in appearance, that constitutes 20–30% of the volume of the ejaculated semen in humans.

proximal: Close in time and/or distance.

proximity maintenance: In attachment theory refers to staying close to, and resisting separation from, the attachment figure.

psychoanalysis: A form of psychological analysis and therapy developed by Sigmund Freud.

reflected appraisals: Judgments or evaluations of what one partner thinks the other partner thinks of them. For example, the extent to which Mary thinks George loves her.

regulatory genes: Genes that control the expression of one or more other genes.

reliability: The level of consistency in a particular measure of something.

risk regulation model: Developed by Sandra Murray and colleagues, this model explains how people balance the goal of seeking closeness to a romantic partner against the goal of minimizing the likelihood and pain of rejection. The central premise of the model is that confidence in a partner's positive regard and caring allows people to risk seeking dependence and connectedness.

safe haven: In attachment theory this means turning to the attachment figure for comfort and support when distressed.

secure: A category of attachment that combines a low anxiety attachment style with a low avoidant style.

selection: A key concept in evolutionary theory that refers to elements in the social or physical environment that influence survival and reproductive success.

self-esteem: Refers to the positivity of the overall evaluation of the self.

self-expansion model: Developed by Aron and Aron, this theory proposes that humans have a primary motivation to expand the self, and that individuals often achieve self-expansion through intimate relationships in which the other becomes integrated into the self.

seminal fluid: Mainly produced by the prostate and seminal vesicles, seminal fluid contains a diverse array of chemicals to help sperm on their way and counteract the slightly acidic environment of the vagina.

sequence of attachment reactions: Proposed by John Bowlby as the basis for attachment theory, this is a specific sequence of behavior observed in all primates after separation between parent and offspring. Stage 1 is protest, stage 2 is despair, and stage 3 is detachment.

serially: Cognitive processes that occur sequentially, one process at a time.

serotonin: A hormone released in the brain and the body with multiple functions, including the regulation of mood, sleep and appetite.

sex hormones: There are a range of hormones involved in sexual activity, the two main ones being testosterone and estrogen.

sexual dimorphism: Refers to sex differences in species of size, ornamentation, and behavior.

sexual reproduction: In general terms this process involves the creation of a new organism by combining the genetic material from males and females from within the same species.

sexual selection: This theory, originally developed by Darwin, describes which features of the organism have evolved as a function of mate choice by females and/or males.

sexual strategies theory: Proposed by David Buss and David Schmitt to explain gender differences and similarities in mate selection and intimate relationships, this theory is based on classical evolutionary psychology principles.

sickle cell anemia: This is a genetic blood disorder in which the red blood cells assume an abnormal, rigid, sickle shape.

situational couple violence: Developed by Johnson, this category of intimate violence consists of less severe forms of aggression, with both genders often being both victims and perpetrators.

social intelligence: The ability, advanced in humans, to explain, predict, and control oneself and others in social contexts.

social neuroscience: The study of neuronal and bodily processes underlying social behavior and interaction.

social structural model: Developed by Alice Eagly and Wendy Wood, this model focuses on how culture (social roles and gender role socialization practices) produces gender differences, including those found in mate selection and intimate relationships.

sociosexuality: Refers to individual differences in the willingness to have sex in short-term versus long-term relationships.

sperm competition: Consists of competitive strategies among males after insemination to increase the chances of reproductive success.

Sternberg's triangular theory of love: A model of love based on the three components of intimacy, passion, and commitment. The kind of love developed depends on the combinations and levels of each component.

strange situation: A test to measure individual differences in attachment patterns in young children, developed by Mary Ainsworth. Children are stressed by being briefly left alone, then reunited with their caregivers, and their behavior is observed and coded.

subliminal priming: Stimuli that are presented below the threshold of conscious awareness.

synapses: A structure in the brain that permits a neuron to pass an electrical or chemical signal to another neuron. There are about 100 trillion synapses in the human brain.

testes: Gonads in male primates that produce sperm and also hormones such as testosterone.

testosterone: This hormone has a range of functions but is closely linked to sexual arousal, especially in males.

theory of mind: The uniquely human ability to attribute mental states to oneself and to others in the service of explanation, prediction, control, in interpersonal contexts.

third variable: A variable that causes two other variables to attain a correlation that is spurious and does not reflect a causal link. For example, higher depression (a third variable) may cause both poor health and lower relationship quality, producing a spurious correlation between health and relationship quality.

thymus: Located above the heart and behind the sternum, this organ plays a role in the immune system, especially prior to puberty.

thyroid: This gland in the neck controls how quickly the body uses energy, makes proteins, and also controls how sensitive the body is to other hormones.

tracking accuracy: The accuracy with which people's judgments of others track one or more benchmarks in a relative fashion. This is usually indexed using correlations.

traditional behavioral couples therapy: An approach to relationship therapy that focuses on identifying and changing specific interactional behaviors linked to communication and intimacy.

transmitted culture: Aspects of culture (beliefs, behavior, etc.) that are maintained over time because they are communicated across individuals and down generations.

unconscious/automatic processing versus conscious/controlled: An important cognitive dimension. Unconscious/automatic processing is unconscious, automatic, fast, effortless, not readily verbalizable, and undemanding of cognitive capacity. Conscious/controlled processing is conscious, controlled, slow, readily verbalizable, and demanding of cognitive capacity.

unified detachment: A term used in integrative behavioral couples therapy referring to helping couples to distance themselves from specific problems without accusation and blame, and then tackling the problem together.

unrequited love: Love for another that is not reciprocated in any way.

uterus: Also termed the womb, it directs blood flow to the external genitalia during sexual arousal, and is where the fetus develops before birth.

vagina: The tube-shaped part of the reproductive tract in females, connected to the uterus at one end and opening to the outside of the body on the other end.

validity: The two major kinds of validity are construct validity and predictive validity. Construct validity concerns the extent to which a given measure actually assesses a construct. Predictive validity concerns the extent to which a measure predicts other phenomena.

variation: A key element in Darwinian evolutionary theory, variation across individuals allows selection to produce differences in reproductive success, thus providing the engine for evolution to occur over time.

vas deferens: Tubes connecting the testes to the seminal vesicles in many species, including humans.

vasopressin: A closely related hormone to oxytocin, it has effects both in the brain and the body on a range of social behaviors including bonding in humans, principally in the male.

ventral: Refers to regions in the bottom part of the brain.

ventral anterior cingulate cortex (vACC): Bottom part of the cingulate cortex, it has several functions, including the regulation of emotion and motivation.

ventral tegmental area (VTA): Located close to the midline on the floor of the midbrain, the VTA is linked to the dopamine system, rewards, addiction, and emotions related to love.

ventromedial prefrontal cortex (VMPFC): A region in the prefrontal cortex mainly involved in perspective-taking, making attributions to the self or others, and regulating anxiety.

vulva: The external genital organs of women.

waist–hip ratio: The ratio between the waist and hips, generally thought to be most attractive in women when it is close to .70.

working memory: Part of the cognitive system holding consciously accessible information that can be mentally manipulated.

X chromosome: One of two sex-determining chromosomes in many animals, including humans. Women have two copies of the same X chromosome (inherited from their mothers) and men have one copy.

Y chromosome: One of two sex-determining chromosomes in many animals, including humans. Women have no Y chromosome, and men have one Y chromosome (inherited from their fathers).

References

Acevedo, B. P., Aron, A., Fisher, H. E., & Brown, L. L. (2011). Neural correlates of long-term intense romantic love. *Social Cognitive and Affective Neuroscience*. Online publication.

Acker, M., & Davis, M. H. (1992). Intimacy, passion and commitment in adult romantic relationships: a test of the triangular theory of love. *Journal of Social and Personal Relationships, 9,* 21–50.

Adamson, K., & Pasley, K. (2006). Coparenting following divorce and relationship dissolution. In M. A. Fine & J. H. Harvey (Eds), *Handbook of Divorce and Relationship Dissolution* (pp. 241–261). Mahwah, NJ: Lawrence Erlbaum.

Agnew, C. R., Van Lange, P. A. M., Rusbult, C. E., & Langston, C. A. (1998). Cognitive interdependence: commitment and the mental representation of close relationships. *Journal of Personality and Social Psychology, 74,* 939–954.

Ainsworth, M. D. S. (1979). Infant-mother attachment. *American Psychologist, 34,* 932–937.

Ainsworth, M. D. S., Blehar, M. C., Waters, E., & Wall, S. (1978). *Patterns of Attachment: a Psychological Study of the Strange Situation.* Hillsdale, NJ: Erlbaum.

Algoe, S. B., Gable, S. L., & Maisel, N. C. (2010). It's the little things: everyday gratitude as a booster shot for romantic relationships. *Personal Relationships, 17,* 217–233.

Alonso-Alvarez, C., Bertrand, S., Faivre, B., Chastel, O., & Sorci, G. (2007). Testosterone and oxidative stress: the oxidation handicap hypothesis. *Proceedings of the Royal Society B, 274,* 819–825.

Alvergne, A., & Lummaa, V. (2009). Does the contraceptive pill alter mate choice in humans? *Trends in Ecology and Evolution, 25,* 171–179.

Amato, P. R. (1993). Children's adjustment to divorce: theories, hypotheses, and empirical support. *Journal of Marriage and Family, 55,* 23–38.

Amato, P. R. (1996). Explaining the intergenerational transmission of divorce. *Journal of Marriage and Family, 58,* 628–640.

Amato, P. R. (2000). The consequences of divorce for adults and children. *Journal of Marriage and Family, 62,* 1269–1288.

The Science of Intimate Relationships, First Edition. Garth Fletcher, Jeffry A. Simpson, Lorne Campbell, and Nickola C. Overall.
© 2013 Garth Fletcher, Jeffry A. Simpson, Lorne Campbell, and Nickola C. Overall.
Published 2013 by Blackwell Publishing Ltd.

Amato, P. R. (2010). Research on divorce: continuing trends and new developments. *Journal of Marriage and Family, 72,* 650–666.

Amato, P. R., & Booth, A. (2001). The legacy of parents' marital discord: consequences for children's marital quality. *Journal of Personality and Social Psychology, 81,* 627–638.

Amato, P. R., & Hohmann-Marriott, B. (2007). A comparison of high- and low-distress marriages that end in divorce. *Journal of Marriage and Family, 69,* 621–638.

Amato, P. R., & Keith, B. (1991). Parental divorce and the well-being of children: a meta-analysis. *Psychological Bulletin, 110,* 26–46.

Amato, P. R. & Previti, D. (2003). People's reasons for divorcing: gender, social class, the life course, and adjustment. *Journal of Family Issues, 24,* 602–626.

Amato, P. R. & Rogers, S. J. (1997). A longitudinal study of marital problems and subsequent divorce. *Journal of Marriage and Family, 59,* 612–624.

Anderson, S. W., & Jaffe, J. (1972). *The Definition, Detection and Timing of Vocalic Syllables in Speech Signals.* Scientific Report No. 12 of Communication Sciences, New York State, Psychiatric Institute.

Andersson, G. & Philipov, D. (2002). Life-table representations of family dynamics in Sweden, Hungary and 14 other FFS countries: a project of description of demographic behaviour. *Demographic Research, 7,* 67–144.

Anthony, D. B., Holmes, J. G., & Wood, J. V. (2007). Social acceptance and self-esteem: tuning the sociometer to interpersonal value. *Journal of Personality and Social Psychology, 92,* 1024–1039.

Arafat, I. S., & Cotton, W. L. (1974). Masturbation practices of males and females. *Journal of Sex Research, 10,* 293–307.

Archer, J. (2000). Sex differences in aggression between heterosexual partners: a meta-analytic review. *Psychological Bulletin, 126,* 651–680.

Archer, J. (2002). Sex differences in physically aggressive acts between heterosexual partners: a meta-analytic review. *Aggression and Violent Behavior: A Review Journal, 7,* 313–351.

Archer, J. (2006). Cross-cultural differences in physical aggression between partners: a social-role analysis. *Personality and Social Psychology Review, 10,* 113–133.

Aron, A., & Aron, E. N. (1986). *Love and the Expansion of Self: Understanding Attraction and Satisfaction.* New York, NY: Hemisphere Publishing Corp/Harper & Row Publishers.

Aron, A., & Aron, E. N. (1997). Self-expansion motivation and including other in the self. In S. Duck (Ed.), *Handbook of Personal Relationships: Theory, Research and Interventions* (2nd ed., pp. 251–270). Hoboken, NJ: John Wiley & Sons Inc.

Aron, A., Aron, E. N., & Norman, C. (2001). Self-expansion model of motivation and cognition in close relationships and beyond. In G. J. O. Fletcher & M. S. Clark (Eds), *Blackwell Handbook of Social Psychology: Interpersonal Processes* (pp. 478–501). Oxford: Blackwell.

Aron, A., Aron, E. N., & Smollan, D. (1992). Inclusion of other in the self scale and the structure of interpersonal closeness. *Journal of Personality and Social Psychology, 63,* 596–612.

Aron, A., Aron, E. N., Tudor, M., & Nelson, G. (1991). Close relationships as including other in the self. *Journal of Personality and Social Psychology, 60,* 241–253.

Aron, A., Norman, C. C., Aron, E. N., McKenna, C., & Heyman, R. E. (2000). Couples' shared participation in novel and arousing activities and experienced relationship quality. *Journal of Personality and Social Psychology, 78,* 273–284.

Aron, A., Paris, M., & Aron, E. N. (1995). Falling in love: prospective studies of self-concept change. *Journal of Personality and Social Psychology, 69,* 1102–1112.

Arriaga, X. B. (2001). The ups and downs of dating: fluctuations in satisfaction in newly formed romantic relationships. *Journal of Personality and Social Psychology, 80,* 754–765.

Arriaga, X. B., & Agnew, C. R. (2001). Being committed: affective, cognitive, and conative components of relationship commitment. *Personality and Social Psychology Bulletin, 27,* 1190–1203.

Atkins, C. J., Kaplan, R. M., & Toshima, M. T. (1991). Close relationships in the epidemiology of cardiovascular disease. In W. H. Jones & D. Perlman (Eds), *Advances in Personal Relationships* (Vol. 2, pp. 207–231). London: Jessica Kingsley.

Atkins, D. C., Yi, J., Baucom, D. H., & Christensen, A. (2005). Infidelity in couples seeking therapy. *Journal of Family Psychology, 19,* 470–473.

Babcock, J. C., Green, C. E., & Robie, C. (2004). Does batterers' treatment work? A meta-analytic review of domestic violence treatment. *Clinical Psychology Review, 23,* 1023–1053.

Babcock, J. C., Waltz, J., Jacobson, N. S., & Gottman, J. M. (1993). Power and violence: the relationship between communication patterns, power discrepancies, and domestic violence. *Journal of Consulting and Clinical Psychology, 61,* 40–50.

Bagatell, C. J., Herman, J. R., Rivier, J. E., & Bremner, W. J. (1994). Effects of endogenous testosterone and estradiol on sexual behavior in normal young men. *Journal of Clinical Endocrinology and Metabolism, 78,* 711–716.

Bailey, J. M. (1995). Biological perspectives on sexual orientation. In A. R. D'Augelli & C. J. Patterson (Eds), *Lesbian, Gay, and Bisexual Identities over the Lifespan* (pp. 104–135). New York: Oxford University Press.

Bailey, J. M., & Zucker, K. J. (1995). Childhood sex-typed behavior and sexual orientation: a conceptual analysis and quantitative review. *Developmental Psychology, 31,* 43–55.

Bailey, J. M., Dunne, M. P., Martin, N. G. (2000). Genetic and environmental influences on sexual orientation and its corre-

lates in an Australian twin sample. *Journal of Personality and Social Psychology, 78,* 524–536.

Bailey, J. M., Gaulin, S., Agyei, Y. A., & Gladue, B. A. (1994). Effect of gender and sexual orientation on evolutionarily relevant aspects of human mating psychology. *Journal of Personality and Social Psychology, 66,* 1081–1093.

Baker, R. R., & Bellis, M. A. (1995). *Human Sperm Competition: Copulation, masturbation and Infidelity.* London: Chapman & Hall.

Baldwin, M. W., Carrell, S. E., & Lopez, D. F. (1990). Priming relationship schemas: my advisor and the Pope are watching me from the back of my mind. *Journal of Experimental Social Psychology, 26,* 435–454.

Bancroft, J. (2005). The endocrinology of sexual arousal. *Journal of Endocrinology, 186,* 411–427.

Barbee, A. P., & Cunningham, M. R. (1995). An experimental approach to social support communications: interactive coping in close relationships. *Communication Yearbook, 18,* 381–413.

Barber, N. (2003). Divorce and reduced economic and emotional interdependence. *Journal of Divorce and Remarriage, 39,* 113–124.

Barber, B. L., & Demo, D. H. (2006). The kids are alright (at least, most of them): links between divorce and dissolution and child well-being. In M. A. Fine and J. H. Harvey (Eds), *Handbook of Divorce and Relationship Dissolution* (pp. 289–311). Mahwah, NJ: Lawrence Erlbaum.

Barber, B. L., & Eccles, J. S. (1992). Long-term influence of divorce and single parenting on adolescent family- and work-related values, behaviors, and aspirations. *Psychological Bulletin, 111,* 108–126.

Barelds-Dijkstra, P., & Barelds, D. P. H. (2008). Positive illusions about one's partner's physical attractiveness. *Body Image, 5,* 99–108.

Bartels, A., & Zeki, S. (2000). The neural basis of romantic love. *NeuroReport, 11,* 3829–3934.

Bartels, A., & Zeki, S. (2004). The neural correlates of maternal and romantic love. *NeuroImage, 21*, 1155–1166.

Bartholomew, K., & Horowitz, L. M. (1991). Attachment styles among young adults: a test of a four-category model. *Journal of Personality and Social Psychology, 61*, 226–244.

Bascand, G. (2009). Marriages, civil unions, and divorces: year ended December 2009. Retrieved February 1, 2012, from http://www.stats.govt.nz.

Baucom, D. H., & Epstein, N. (1990). *Cognitive-Behavioral Marital Therapy*. New York, NY: Brunner/Mazel.

Baumeister, R. F. (2000). Gender differences in erotic plasticity: the female sex drive as socially flexible and responsive. *Psychological Bulletin, 126*, 347–374.

Baumeister, R. F., & Bratslavsky, E. (1999). Passion, intimacy, and time: passionate love as a function of change in intimacy. *Personality and Social Psychology Review, 3*, 49–67.

Baumeister, R. F., & Leary, M. R. (1995). The need to belong: desire for interpersonal attachments as a fundamental human motivation. *Psychological Bulletin, 117*, 497–529.

Baumeister, R. F., Catanese, K. R., & Vohs, K. D. (2001). Is there a gender difference in strength of sex drive? Theoretical views, conceptual distinctions, and a review of relevant evidence. *Personality and Social Psychology Review, 5*, 242–273.

Beach, F. A., & Jordan, L. (1956). Sexual selection and recovery in the male rat. *The Quarterly Journal of Experimental Psychology, 8*, 121–133.

Beach, S. R. H., Fincham, F. D., & Katz, J. (1998). Marital therapy in the treatment of depression: toward a third generation of therapy and research. *Clinical Psychology Review, 18*, 635–661.

Beach, S. R. H., Martin, J. K., Blum, T. C., & Roman, B. C. (1993). Effects of marital and co-worker relationships on negative affect: testing the central role of marriage. *The American Journal of Family Therapy, 21*, 313–324.

Becker, A. E., Burwell, R. A., Gilman, S. E., Herzog, D. B., & Hamburg, P. (2002) Eating behaviours and attitudes following prolonged exposure to television among ethnic Fijian adolescent girls. *British Journal of Psychiatry, 180*, 509–514.

Beckerman, S., Lizarralde, R., Ballew, C., Schroeder, S., Fingelton, C., Garrison, A., & Smith, H. (1998). The Bari Partible Paternity Project: preliminary results. *Current Anthropology, 39*, 164–167.

Beer, A., & Watson, D. (2008). Personality judgment at zero acquaintance: agreement, assumed similarity, and implicit simplicity. *Journal of Personality Assessment, 90*, 250–260.

Bellavia, G., & Murray, S. (2003). Did I do that? Self-esteem-related differences in reactions to romantic partners' moods. *Personal Relationships, 10*, 77–95.

Belsky, J. (1984). The determinants of parenting: a process model. *Child Development, 55*, 83–96.

Belsky, J. (1997). Attachment, mating, and parenting: an evolutionary interpretation. *Human Nature, 8*, 361–381.

Belsky, J., & Cassidy, J. (1994). Attachment: theory and evidence. In M. Rutter & D. Hay (Eds), *Development through Life: a Handbook for Clinicians* (pp. 373–402). Oxford: Blackwell.

Belsky, J., Rovine, M., & Taylor, D. G. (1984). The Pennsylvania Infant and Family Development Project, III: the origins of individual differences in infant-mother attachment: maternal and infant contributions. *Child Development, 55*, 718–728.

Belsky, J., Schlomer, G. L., & Ellis, B. J. (2012). Beyond cumulative risk: distinguishing harshness and unpredictability as determinants of parenting and early life history strategy. *Developmental Psychology, 48*, 662–673.

Belsky, J., Steinberg, L., & Draper, P. (1991). Childhood experience, interpersonal development, and reproductive strategy: an evolutionary theory of socialization. *Child Development, 62,* 647–670.

Berry, D. S. (2000). Attractiveness, attraction, and sexual selection: evolutionary perspectives on the form and function of physical attractiveness. *Advances in Experimental Social Psychology, 32,* 273–342.

Berscheid, E. (1983). Emotion. In H. H. Kelley, E. Berscheid, A. Christensen, J. Harvey, T. L. Huston, G. Levinger *et al.* (Eds), *Close Relationships* (pp. 110–168).San Francisco, CA: Freeman.

Berscheid, E. (1985). Interpersonal attraction. In G. Lindzey, & E. Aronson (Eds), *The Handbook of Social Psychology* (3rd ed., pp. 110–168). New York, NY: Random House.

Berscheid, E. (2010). Love in the fourth dimension. *Annual Review of Psychology, 61,* 1–25.

Berscheid, E., & Peplau, L. A. (1983). The emerging science of close relationships. In H. H. Kelley, E. Berscheid, A. Christensen, J. H. Harvey, T. L. Huston, G. Levinger *et al.* (Eds), *Close Relationships* (pp. 1–19). San Francisco, CA: Freeman.

Berscheid, E., & Walster, E. H. (1974). A little bit about love. In T. L. Huston (Ed.), *Foundations of Interpersonal Attraction* (pp. 157–215). New York, NY: Academic.

Birkhead, T. (2000). *Promiscuity: An Evolutionary History of Sperm Competition.* Cambridge, MA: Harvard University Press.

Blaicher, W., Gruber, D., Bieglmayer, C., Blaicher, A. M., Knogler, W., & Huber, J. C. (1999). The role of oxytocin in relation to female sexual arousal. *Gynecologic and Obstetric Investigation, 47,* 125–126.

Blanchard, R., Barbaree, H. E., Bogaert, A. F., Dickey, R., Klassen, P., Kuban, M. E., & Zucker, K. J. (2000). Fraternal birth order and sexual orientation in pedophiles. *Archives of Sexual Behavior, 29,* 463–478.

Blanchard, R., & Bogaert, A. F. (1996). Homosexuality in men and a number of older brothers. *American Journal of Psychiatry, 153,* 27–31.

Block, C. R., & Christakos, A. (1995). Intimate partner homicide in Chicago over 29 years. *Crime and Delinquency, 41,* 496–526.

Bloom, B. L., Asher, S. J., & White, S. W. (1978). Marital disruption as a stressor: a review and analysis. *Psychological Bulletin, 85,* 867–894.

Blumstein, P., & Schwartz, P. (1983). *American Couples.* New York, NY: Simon & Schuster.

Bodenmann, G., Kaiser, A., Hahlweg, K., & Fehm-Wolfsdorf, G. (1998). Communication patterns during marital conflict: a cross-cultural replication. *Personal Relationships, 5,* 343–356.

Bogaert, A. F. (1998). Birth order and sibling sex ratio in homosexual and heterosexual non-white men. *Archives of Sexual Behavior, 27,* 467–473.

Bogaert, A. F. & Hershberger, S. (1999). The relation between sexual orientation and penile size. *Archives of Sexual Behavior, 28,* 213–221.

Bogaert, A. F., & Sadava, S. (2002). Adult attachment and sexual behavior. *Personal Relationships, 9,* 191–204.

Bolger, N., DeLongis, A., Kessler, R. C., & Wethington, E. (1989). The contagion of stress across multiple roles. *Journal of Marriage and the Family, 51,* 175–183.

Bolger, N., Zuckerman, A., & Kessler, R. C. (2000). Invisible support and adjustment to stress. *Journal of Personality and Social Psychology, 79,* 953–961.

Bonanno, G. A., Wortman, C. B., Lehman, D. R., Tweed, R. G., Haring, M., Sonnega, J. *et al.* (2002). Resilience to loss and chronic grief: a prospective study from preloss to 18-months postloss. *Journal of Personality and Social Psychology, 83,* 1150–1164.

Bono, G., McCullough, M. E., & Root, L. M. (2008). Forgiveness, feeling connected to others, and well-being: two longitudinal studies. *Personality and Social Psychology Bulletin, 34,* 182–195.

Bookwala, J., Sobin, J., & Zdaniuk, B. (2005). Gender and aggression in marital relationships: a life-span perspective. *Sex Roles, 52,* 797–806.

Booth, A. & Amato, P. (1991). Divorce and psychological stress. *Journal of Health and Social Behavior, 32*, 396–407.

Booth, A., & Dabbs, J. M., Jr. (1993). Testosterone and men's marriages. *Social Forces, 72*, 463–477.

Bowlby, J. (1944). Forty-four juvenile thieves: their characters and home life. *International Journal of Psychoanalysis, 25*, 19–52 and 107–127.

Bowlby, J. (1969). *Attachment and Loss: Vol. 1. Attachment*. New York, NY: Basic Books.

Bowlby, J. (1973). *Attachment and Loss: Vol. 2. Separation: Anxiety and Anger*. New York, NY: Basic Books.

Bowlby, J. (1979). *The Making and Breaking of Affectional Bonds*. London: Tavistock.

Bowlby, J. (1980). *Attachment and Loss: Vol. 3. Loss*. New York, NY: Basic Books.

Bowlby, J. (1982). *Attachment and Loss* (2nd ed). New York, NY: Basic Books.

Boyes, A. D., & Fletcher, G. J. O. (2007). Metaperceptions of bias in intimate relationships. *Journal of Personality and Social Psychology, 92*, 286–306.

Bozarth, M. A., & Wise, R. A. (1996). Toxicity associated with long-term intravenous heroin and cocaine self-administration in the rat. *Journal of the American Medical Association, 254*, 81–83.

Bradbury, T. N., & Fincham, F. D. (1991). A contextual model for advancing the study of marital interaction. In G. J. O. Fletcher & F. D. Fincham (Eds), *Cognition in close relationships* (pp. 127–147). Hillsdale, NJ: Erlbaum.

Bradbury, T. N., & Lavner, J. A. (2012). How can we improve preventive and educational interventions for intimate relationships? *Behavior Therapy, 43*, 113–122.

Bramlett, M. D., & Mosher, W. D. (2002). Cohabitation, marriage, divorce, and remarriage in the United States. *Vital and Health Statistics, Series 23*. Washington, DC: US Government Printing Office.

Brand, S., Luethi, M., von Planta, A., Hatzinger, M., & Holsboer-Trachsler, E. (2007). Romantic love, hypomania, and sleep pattern in adolescents. *Journal of Adolescent Health, 41*, 69–76.

Braungart-Rieker, J. M., Garwood, M. M., Powers, B. P., & Wang, X. (2001). Parental sensitivity, infant affect, and affect regulation: predictors of later attachment. *Child Development, 72*, 252–270.

Braver, S. L., Shapiro, J. R., & Goodman, M. R. (2006). Consequences of divorce for parents. In M. A. Fine & J. H. Harvey (Eds), *Handbook of Divorce and Relationship Dissolution* (pp. 313–337). Mahwah, NJ: Lawrence Erlbaum.

Brennan, K. A., Clark, C. L., & Shaver, P. R. (1998). Self-report measurement of adult attachment: an integrative overview. In J. A. Simpson & W. S. Rholes (Eds), *Attachment Theory and Close Relationships* (pp. 46–76). New York, NY: Guilford Press.

Brennan, K. A., & Shaver, P. R. (1995). Dimensions of adult attachment, affect regulation, and romantic relationship functioning. *Personality and Social Psychology Bulletin, 21*, 267–283.

Brinig, M. F., & Allen, D. W. (2000). "These boots are made for walking": Why most divorce filers are women. *American Law and Economics Review, 2*, 126–169.

Brock, R. & Lawrence, E. (2009). Too much of a good thing: underprovision versus overprovision of partner support. *Journal of Family Psychology, 23*, 181–192.

Broderick, J. E. (1981). A method for derivation of areas of assessment in marital relationships. *The American Journal of Family Therapy, 9*, 25–34.

Bronfenbrenner, U., & Crouter, A. (1982). Work and family through time and space. In S. Kamerman & C. Hayes (Eds), *Families that Work* (pp. 39–83). Washington, DC: National Academy Press.

Brookes, P. (2006, February 20–24). The diary of a divorce: part one to part five. *The Telegraph*. Retrieved September 9, 2011, from http://www.telegraph.co.uk/culture/3650346/The-diary-of-a-divorce-part-one.html.

Brown, N. R., & Sinclair, R. C. (1999). Estimating number of lifetime sexual partners: men and women do it differently. *Journal of Sex Research*, *36*, 292–297.

Brown, S. L., & Booth, A. (1996). Cohabitation versus marriage: a comparison of relationship quality. *Journal of Marriage and the Family*, *58*, 668–678.

Bryant, G. A., & Haselton, M. G. (2009). Vocal cues of ovulation in human females. *Biology Letters*, *5*, 12–15.

Bui, K. T., Peplau, L. A., & Hill, C. T. (1996). Testing the Rusbult model of relationship commitment and stability in a 15-year study of heterosexual couples. *Personality and Social Psychology Bulletin*, *22*, 1244–1257.

Bumpass, L. L., & Sweet, J. A. (1989). National estimates of cohabitation. *Demography*, *26*, 615–625.

Burgess, R., & Draper, P. (1989). The explanation of family violence: the role of biological behavioral and cultural selection. In L. Ohlin & M. Tonry (Eds), *Family Violence* (pp. 59–116). Chicago, IL: University of Chicago Press.

Burkart, J. M., & van Schaik, C. P. (2010). Cognitive consequences of cooperative breeding in primates? *Animal Cognition*, *13*, 1–19.

Burke, L. K., & Follingstad, D. R. (1999). Violence in lesbian and gay relationships: theory, prevalence, and correlational factors. *Clinical Psychology Review*, *19*, 487–512.

Burleson, B. R. (2003). The experience and effects of emotional support: what the study of cultural and gender differences can tell us about close relationships, emotion, and interpersonal communication. *Personal Relationships*, *10*, 1–23.

Burman, B., & Margolin, G. (1992). Analysis of the association between marital relationships and health problems: an interactional perspective. *Psychological Bulletin*, *112*, 39–63.

Buss, D. M. (1988a). Love acts: the evolutionary biology of love. In R. J. Sternberg & M. L. Barnes (Eds), *The Psychology of Love* (pp. 100–118). New Haven, CT: Yale University Press.

Buss, D. M. (1988b). The evolution of human intrasexual competition: tactics of mate attraction. *Journal of Personality and Social Psychology*, *54*, 616–628.

Buss, D. M. (1989). Sex differences in human mate preferences: evolutionary hypotheses tested in 37 cultures. *Behavioral and Brain Sciences*, *12*, 1–49.

Buss, D. M., & Dedden, L. A. (1990). Derogation of competitors. *Journal of Social and Personal Relationships*, *7*, 395–422.

Buss, D. M., & Schmitt, D. P. (1993). Sexual strategies theory: an evolutionary perspective on human mating. *Psychological Review*, *100*, 204–232.

Buss, D. M., & Shackelford, T. K. (2008). Attractive women want it all: good genes, economic investment, parenting proclivities, and emotional commitment. *Evolutionary Psychology*, *6*, 134–146.

Buss, D. M., Larsen, R., Westen, D., & Semmelroth, J. (1992). Sex differences in jealousy: evolution, physiology, and psychology. *Psychological Science*, *3*, 251–255.

Buss, D. M., Abbott, M., Angleitner, A., Asherian, A., Biaggio, A., Blancoe-Villasenor, A. et al., (1990). International preferences in selecting mates: a study of 37 cultures. *Journal of Cross-Cultural Psychology*, *21*, 5–47.

Buss, D. M., Shackelford, T. K., Choe, J., Buunk, B. P., & Dijkstra, P. (2000). Distress about mate rivals. *Personal Relationships*, *7*, 235–243.

Buunk, A. P., Park, J. H., & Duncan, L. A. (2010). Cultural variation in parental influence on mate choice. *Cross-Cultural Research*, *44*, 23–40.

Buunk, B. P., Angleitner, A., Oubaid, V., & Buss, D. M. (1996). Sex differences in jealousy evolutionary and cultural perspective: tests from Netherlands, Germany, and the United States. *Psychological Science*, *7*, 359–363.

Buunk, B. P., Park, J. H., &, Dubbs, S. L. (2008). Parent-offspring conflict in mate preferences. *Review of General Psychology*, *21*, 47–62.

Byers, E. S. (2005). Relationship satisfaction and sexual satisfaction: a longitudinal study of individuals in long-term relationships. *Journal of Sex Research, 42*, 113–118.

Byers, E. S., & Heinlein, L. (1989). Predicting initiations and refusals of sexual activities in married and cohabiting heterosexual couples. *Journal of Sex Research, 26*, 210–231.

Bylsma, W. H., Cozzarelli, C., & Sumer, N. (1997). Relation between adult attachment styles and global self-esteem. *Basic and Applied Social Psychology, 19*, 1–16.

Call, V., Sprecher, S., & Schwartz, P. (1995). The incidence and frequency of marital sex in a national sample. *Journal of Marriage & the Family, 57*, 639–652.

Campbell, J. C., Glass, N., Sharps, P. W., Laughon, K., & Bloom, T. (2007). Intimate partner homicide: review and implications of research and policy. *Trauma, Violence and Abuse, 8*, 246–269.

Campbell, J. C., Webster, D., Koziol-McLain, J., Block, C. R., Campbell, D. W., Curry, M. et al. (2003a). Assessing risk factors for intimate partner homicide. *National Institute of Justice Journal, 250*, 14–19.

Campbell, J. C., Webster, D., Koziol-McLain, J., Block, C. R., Campbell, D. W., Curry, M. et al. (2003b). Risk factors for femicide in abusive relationships: results from a multisite case control study. *American Journal of Public Health, 93*, 1089–1097.

Campbell, L., & Wilbur, C. (2009). Are the traits we prefer in potential mates the traits they value in themselves? An analysis of sex differences in the self-concept. *Self and Identity, 8*, 418–446.

Campbell, L., Cronk, L., Simpson, J. A., Milroy, A., Wilson, C. L., & Dunham, B. (2009). The association between men's ratings of women as desirable long-term mates and individual differences in women's sexual attitudes and behaviors. *Personality and Individual Differences, 46*, 509–513.

Campbell, L., Martin, R. A., & Ward, J. R. (2008). An observational study of humor use while resolving conflict in dating couples. *Personal Relationships, 15*, 41–55.

Campbell, L., Simpson, J. A., Boldry, J., & Kashy, D. A. (2005). Perceptions of conflict and support in romantic relationships: the role of attachment anxiety. *Journal of Personality and Social Psychology, 88*, 510–531.

Campbell, L., Simpson, J. A., Boldry, J. G., & Rubin, H. (2010). Trust, variability in relationship evaluations, and relationship processes. *Journal of Personality and Social Psychology, 99*, 14–31.

Campbell, L., Simpson, J. A., Kashy, D. A., & Fletcher, G. J. O. (2001). Ideal standards, the self, and flexibility of ideals in close relationships. *Personality and Social Psychology Bulletin, 27*, 447–462.

Campos, L., Otta, E., & de Oliveira Siqueira, J. (2002). Sex differences in mate selection strategies: content analyses and response to personal advertisements in Brazil. *Evolution and Human Behavior, 23*, 395–406.

Cantos, A. L., Neidig, P. H., & O'Leary, K. D. (1994). Injuries of women and men in a treatment program for domestic violence. *Journal of Family Violence, 9*, 113–124.

Caplan, L., Jr. (1984). *After Hinckley: The insanity Defense Reexamined*. Boston, MA: David R. Godine, Publisher.

Carael, M., Cleland, J., Deheneffe, J., Ferry, B., & Ingham, R. (1995). Sexual behavior in developing countries: implications for HIV control. *AIDS, 9*, 1171–1175.

Carmichael, M. S., Humbert, R., Dixen, J., Palmisano, G., Greenleaf, W., & Davidson, J. M. (1987). Plasma oxytocin increases in the human sexual response. *The Journal of Clinical Endocrinology and Metabolism, 64*, 27–31.

Carnelley, K. B., Wortman, C. B., Bolger, N., & Burke, T. (2006). The time course of grief reactions to spousal loss: evidence from a national probability sample. *Journal of Personality and Social Psychology, 91*, 476–492.

Carr, D., House, J. S., Kessler, R. C., Nesse, R. M., Sonnega, J., & Wortman, C. (2000). Marital quality and psychological adjustment to widowhood among older adults: a longitudinal analysis: erratum. *Journals of Gerontology: Series BL Psychological Sciences and Social Sciences, 55,* S374.

Carrado, M., George, M. J., Loxam, E., Jones, L., & Templar, D. (1996). Aggression in British heterosexual relationships: a descriptive analysis. *Aggressive Behavior, 22,* 401–415.

Carroll, S. B. (2006). *The Making of the Fittest: DNA and the Ultimate Forensic Record of Evolution.* New York, NY: Norton.

Carter, C. S. (2003). Developmental consequences of oxytocin. *Physiology and Behavior, 79,* 383–397.

Cascardi, M., O'Leary, K. D., & Schlee, K. A. (1999). Co-occurrence and correlates of posttraumatic stress disorder and major depression in physically abused women. *Journal of Family Violence, 14,* 227–249.

Cascardi, M., & Vivian, D. (1995). Context for specific episodes of marital violence: gender and severity of violence differences. *Journal of Family Violence, 10,* 265–293.

Case, R. B., Moses, A. J., Case, N., McDermott, M., & Eberly, S. (1992). Living alone after myocardial infarction: impact on prognosis. *Journal of the American Medical Association, 267,* 515–519.

Cassidy, J., & Berlin, L. J. (1994). The insecure/ambivalent pattern of attachment: theory and research. *Child Development, 65,* 971–991.

Centers for Disease Control and Prevention (2002). *Sexually Transmitted Disease Surveillance, 2001.* Atlanta, GA: US Department of Health and Human Services.

Chagnon, N. A. (1992). *Yanamamö: The Last Days of Eden.* San Diego, CA: Harcourt Brace Jovanovich.

Cherlin, A. J. (2004). The deinstitutionalization of American marriage. *Journal of Marriage and the Family, 66,* 848–861.

Chivers, M. L., Rieger, G., Latty, E., & Bailey, J. M. (2004). A sex difference in the specificity of sexual arousal. *Psychological Science, 15,* 736–744.

Christensen, A., & Heavey, C. L. (1990). Gender and social structure in the demand/withdraw pattern of marital conflict. *Journal of Personality and Social Psychology, 59,* 73–81.

Christensen, A., Atkins, D. C., Yi, J., Baucom, D. H., & George, W. H. (2006). Couple and individual adjustment for 2 years following a randomized clinical trial comparing traditional versus integrative behavioral couple therapy. *Journal of Consulting and Clinical Psychology, 74,* 1189–1191.

Christensen, A., Eldridge, K., Catta-Preta, A. B., Lim, V. R., Santagata, R. (2006). Cross-cultural consistency of the demand/withdraw interaction pattern in couples. *Journal of Marriage and Family, 68,* 1029–1044.

Church, A. T., & Lonner, W. J. (1998). The cross-cultural perspective in the study of personality: Rationale and current research. *Journal of Cross-Cultural Psychology, 29,* 32–62.

Cicerello, A., & Sheehan, E. P. (1995). Personal advertisements: a content analysis. *Journal of Social Behavior and Personality, 10,* 751–756.

Clark, M. S., & Taraban, C. (1991). Reactions to and willingness to express emotion in communal and exchange relationships. *Journal of Experimental Psychology, 27,* 324–336.

Clark, M. S., Fitness, J., & Brissette, I. (2001). Understanding people's perceptions of relationships is crucial to understanding their emotional lives. In G. J. O. Fletcher & M. Clark (Eds), *Blackwell Handbook of Social Psychology: Interpersonal Processes* (pp. 252–278). Malden, MA: Blackwell.

Clark, M. S., Pataki, S. P., & Carver, V. H. (1996). Some thoughts and findings on self-presentation of emotions in relationships. In G. J. O. Fletcher & J. Fitness (Eds), *Knowledge Structures in Close Relationships* (pp. 247–274). Mahwah, NJ: Lawrence Erlbaum.

Clark, R., & Hatfield, E. (1989). Gender differences in receptivity to sexual offers. *Journal of Psychology & Human Sexuality, 2,* 39–55.

Coan, J. A. (2008). Towards a neuroscience of attachment. In J. Cassidy & P. R. Shaver (Eds), *Handbook of Attachment: Theory, Research, and Clinical Applications* (2nd ed., pp. 241–265). New York, NY: Guilford.

Coan, J. A., Schaefer, H. S., & Davidson, R. J. (2006). Lending a hand: social regulation of the neural response to threat. *Psychological Science, 17,* 1032–1039.

Cobb, M. (2006). *Generation: the Seventeenth-Century Scientists Who Unraveled the Secrets of Sex, Life, and Growth.* New York, NY: Bloomsbury Publishing.

Cobb, R., Davila, J., & Bradbury, T. N. (2001). Attachment security and marital satisfaction: the role of positive perceptions and social support. *Personality and Social Psychology Bulletin, 27,* 1131–1143.

Cockburn, A. (2006). Prevalence of different modes of parental care in birds. *Biological Sciences, 273,* 1375–1383.

Coe, C. L., & Lubach, G. R. (2001). Social context and other psychological influences on the development of immunity. In C. D. Ryff & B. H. Singer (Eds), *Emotion, Social Relationships, and Health* (pp. 243–261). Oxford: Oxford University Press.

Cohan, C. L., & Bradbury, T. N. (1997). Negative life events, marital interaction, and the longitudinal course of newlywed marriage. *Journal of Personality and Social Psychology, 73,* 114–128.

Cohen, S., & Wills, T. A. (1985). Stress, social support, and the buffering hypothesis. *Psychological Bulletin, 98,* 310–357.

Cohen, S., Frank, E., Doyle, W. J., Skoner, D. P., Rabin, B. S., & Gwaltney, J. M., Jr. (1998). Types of stressors that increase susceptibility to the common cold in healthy adults. *Health Psychology, 17,* 214–223.

Collins, N. L., & Feeney, B. C. (2000). A safe haven: an attachment theory perspective on support seeking and caregiving in intimate relationships. *Journal of Personality and Social Psychology, 78,* 1053–1073.

Collins, N. L., & Feeney, B. C. (2004). Working models of attachment shape perceptions of social support: evidence from experimental and observational studies. *Journal of Personality and Social Psychology, 87,* 363–383.

Collins, N. L., & Read, S. J. (1990). Adult attachment, working models, and relationship quality in dating couples. *Journal of Personality and Social Psychology, 58,* 644–663.

Collins, N. L., & Read, S. J. (1994). Cognitive representations of attachment: the structure and function of working models. In K. Bartholomew & D. Perlman (Eds.), *Attachment processes in adulthood* (pp. 53–90). London: J. Kingsley Publishers.

Colson, M. H. (2010). Female orgasm: myths, facts and controversies. *Sexologies, 19,* 8–14.

Conger, R. E., Rueter, M. A., & Elder, G. H. (1999). Couple resilience to economic pressure. *Journal of Personality and Social Psychology, 76,* 54–71.

Coyne, J. A. (2009). *Why Evolution is True.* Oxford: Oxford University Press.

Crocker, J., Luhtanen, R. K., Cooper, M. L., & Bouvrette, A. (2003). Contingencies of self-worth in college students: theory and measurement. *Journal of Personality and Social Psychology, 85,* 894–908.

Crocker, W. H., & Crocker, J. (1994). *The Canela: Bonding through Kinship, Ritual, and Sex.* Fort Worth, TX: Harcourt Brace.

Cronin, H. (1991). *The Ant and the Peacock: Altruism and Sexual Selection from Darwin to Today.* Cambridge: Cambridge University Press.

Crowell, J., & Feldman, S. (1988). Mothers' internal models of relationships and children's behavioral and developmental status: a study of mother-child interaction. *Child Development, 59,* 1273–1285.

Crowell, J. A., Treboux, D., & Brockmeyer, S. (2009). Parental divorce and adult children's attachment representations and marital status. *Attachment and Human Development, 11,* 87–101.

Cunningham, M. R. (1986). Measuring the physical in physical attractiveness: quasi-experiments on the sociobiology of female facial beauty. *Journal of Personality and Social Psychology*, *50*, 925–935.

Cunningham, M. R., Barbee, A. P., & Pike, C. L. (1990). What do women want? Facialmetric assessment of multiple motives in the perception of male facial physical attractiveness. *Journal of Personality and Social Psychology*, *59*, 61–72.

Cunningham, M. R., Druen, P. B., & Barbee, A. P. (1997). *Angels, Mentors, and Friends: Trade-offs Among Evolutionary, Social, and Individual Variables in Physical Appearance* (pp. 109–140). Hillsdale, NJ: Lawrence Erlbaum Associates, Inc.

Cunningham, M. R., Roberts, A. R., Barbee, A. P., Druen, P. B., & Wu, C.-H. (1995). "Their ideas of beauty are, on the whole, the same as ours": consistency and variability in the cross-cultural perception of female physical attractiveness. *Journal of Personality and Social Psychology*, *68*, 261–279.

Cutrona, C. E. (1996). Social support as a determinant of marital quality. In G. R. Pierce, B. R. Sarason, & I. G. Sarason (Eds), *Handbook of Social Support and the Family* (pp. 173–194). New York, NY: Plenum Press.

Cutrona, C. E. & Suhr, J. A. (1992). Controllability of stressful events and satisfaction with spouse support behaviors. *Communication Research*, *19*, 154–174.

Cutrona, C. E., Hessling, R. M., & Suhr, J. A. (1997). The influence of husband and wife personality on marital social support interactions. *Personal Relationships*, *4*, 379–393.

Cutrona, C. E., Shaffer, P. A., Wesner, K. A., & Gardner, K. A. (2007). Optimally matching support and perceived spousal sensitivity. *Journal of Family Psychology*, *21*, 754–758.

D'Onofrio, B. M., Turkenheimer, E., Emery, E., Harden, K. P., Slutske, W. S., Heath, A. C. et al. (2007). A genetically informed study of the intergenerational transmission of marital instability. *Journal of Marriage and Family*, *69*, 793–809.

Dabbs, J. M., & Dabbs, M. G. (2000). *Heroes, Rogues, and Lovers: Testosterone and Behavior*. New York, NY: McGraw-Hill.

Daly, J. A., Hogg, E., Sacks, D., Smith, M., & Zimring, L. (1983). Sex and relationship affect social self-grooming. *Journal of Nonverbal Behavior*, *7*, 183–189.

Daly, M., & Wilson, M. (1988). *Homicide*. New York, NY: Aldine de Gruyter.

Daly, M., Wilson, M., & Weghorst, S. J. (1981). Male sexual jealousy. *Ethology and Sociobiology*, *3*, 11–27.

Damasio, A. R. (1994). *Descartes' Error: Emotion, Reason and the Human Brain*. New York, NY: G. P. Putnam.

Darwin, C. (1859). *On the Origin of the Species by Means of Natural Selection, or, Preservation of Favoured Races in the Struggle for Life*. London: Murray.

Darwin, C. (1871). *The Descent of Man, and Selection in Relation to Sex*. London: Murray.

Darwin, C. (1872). *The Expression of the Emotions in Man and Animals*. London: Murray.

Davenport, W. H. (1977). Sex in cross-cultural perspective. In F. A. Beach (Ed.), *Human Sexuality in Four Perspectives* (pp. 115–163). Baltimore, MD: The Johns Hopkins University Press.

Davies, P. T., Sturge-Apple, M. L., Winter, M. A., Cummings, E. M., & Farrell, D. (2006). Child adaptational development in contexts of interparental conflict over time. *Child Development*, *77*, 218–233.

Davis, M. H., & Kraus, L. A. (1997). Personality and empathic accuracy. In W. Ickes (Ed.), *Empathic Accuracy* (pp. 144–168). New York, NY: Guilford.

Dawkins, R. (2009). *The Greatest Show on Earth: The Evidence for Evolution*. London: Bantam.

DeHart, T., Murray, S. L., Pelham, B. W., & Rose, P. (2003). The regulation of dependence in parent-child relationships. *Journal of Experimental Social Psychology*, *39*, 59–67.

de Munck, V. C. (1996). Love and marriage in a Sri Lankan Muslim community: toward a reevaluation of Dravidian marriage practices. *American Ethnologist, 23,* 698–716.

de Munck, V. C. (1998). Lust, love, and arranged marriages in Sri Lanka. In V. C. de Munck (Ed.), *Romantic Love and Sexual Behavior: Perspectives from the Social Sciences* (pp. 285–300). Westport, CT: Praeger Publishers/Greenwood Publishing Group.

de Rougemont, D. ([1940] 1983). *Love in the Western World* (M. Belgion, Trans.). Princeton, NJ: Random House.

de Wolff, M., & van Ijzendoorn, M. (1997). Sensitivity and attachment: a meta-analysis on parental antecedents of infant attachment. *Child Development, 68,* 571–591.

Deaux, K., & Hanna, R. (1984). Courtship in the personals column: the influence of gender and sexual orientation. *Sex Roles, 11,* 363–375.

deGraff, P. M., & Kalmijn, M. (2006). Divorce motives in a period of rising divorce: evidence from a Dutch life-history survey. *Journal of Family Issues, 27,* 483–505.

Dehle, C., & Landers, J. E. (2005). You can't always get what you want, but can you get what you need? Personality traits and social support in marriage. *Journal of Social and Clinical Psychology, 24,* 1051–1076.

Del Carmen, R., Perdersen, F. A., Huffman, L. C., & Bryan, Y. E. (1993). Dyadic distress management predicts subsequent security of attachment. *Infant Behavior and Development, 16,* 131–147.

Dennet, D. C. (1995). *Darwin's Dangerous Idea: Evolution and the Meanings of Life.* New York, NY: Simon & Schuster.

DePaulo, B. M. & Kashy, D. A. (1998). Everyday lies in close and casual relationships. *Journal of Personality and Social Psychology, 74,* 63–79.

Depue, R. A., & Collins, P. F. (1999). Neurobiology of the structure of personality: dopamine, facilitation of incentive motivation, and extraversion. *Behavioral and Brain Sciences, 22,* 491–517.

Desmond, A., & Moore, J. (1991). *Darwin: The Life of a Tormented Evolutionist.* New York, NY: W. W. Norton.

DeSteno, D. A., & Salovey, P. (1996). Evolutionary origins of sex differences in jealousy: questioning the "fitness" of the model. *Psychological Science, 7,* 367–372.

Diamond, L. M. (2000). Sexual identity, attractions, and behavior among young sexual-minority women over a two-year period. *Developmental Psychology, 36,* 241–250.

Diamond, L. M. (2003). What does sexual orientation orient? A biobehavioral model distinguishing romantic love and sexual desire. *Psychological Review, 110,* 173–192.

Diamond, L. M. (2008). Female bisexuality from adolescence to adulthood: results from a 10-year longitudinal study. *Developmental Psychology, 44,* 5–14.

Dittmar, H., Halliwell, E., & Ive, S. (2006). Does Barbie make girls want to be thin? The effect of experimental exposure to images of dolls on the body image of 5- to 8-year-old girls. *Developmental Psychology, 42,* 283–292.

Ditzen, B., Schaer, M., Gabriel, B., Bodenmann, G., Ehlert, U., & Heinrichs, M. (2009). Intranasal oxytocin increases positive communication and reduces cortisol levels during couple conflict. *Biological Psychiatry, 65,* 728–731.

Dixson, A. F. (2009). *Sexual Selection and the Origins of Mating Systems.* Oxford: Oxford University Press.

Dixson, A. F. (2012). *Primate Sexuality: Comparative Studies of the Prosimians, Monkeys, Apes, and Humans.* New York: Oxford University Press.

Dobash, R. E., & Dobash, R. P. (1984). The nature and antecedents of violent events. *British Journal of Criminology, 24,* 269–288.

Dobash, R. P., Dobash, R. E., Wilson, M., & Daly, M. (1992). The myth of sexual symmetry in marital violence. *Social Problems, 39,* 71–91.

Domes, G., Heinrichs, M., Michel, A., Berger, C., & Herpertz, S. C. (2007). Oxytocin improves "mind-reading" in humans. *Biological Psychiatry, 61,* 731–733.

Donaldson, Z. R., & Young, L. J. (2008). Oxytocin, vasopressin, and the neurogenetics of sociality. *Science, 322*, 900–904.

Doss, B. D., Simpson, L. E., & Christensen, A. (2004). Why do couples seek marital therapy? *Professional Psychology: Research and Practice, 35*, 608–614.

Dovidio, J. F., Ellyson, S. L., Keating, C. F., Heltman, K., & Brown, C. E. (1988). The relationship of social power to visual displays of dominance. *Journal of Personality and Social Psychology, 54*, 233–242.

Downey, G., Frietas, A. L., Michaelis, B., & Khouri, H. (1998). The self-fulfilling prophecy in close relationships: rejection sensitivity and rejection by romantic partners. *Journal of Personality and Social Psychology, 75*, 545–560.

Drigotas, S. M., Whitney, G. A., & Rusbult, C. E. (1995). On the peculiarities of loyalty: a diary study of responses to dissatisfaction in everyday life. *Personality and Social Psychology Bulletin, 21*, 596–609.

Dunbar, R. I. M., & Duncan, N. D. C. (1997). Human conversational behavior. *Human Nature, 8*, 231–246.

Durante, K., Li, N., & Haselton, M. (2008). Changes in women's choice of dress across the ovulatory cycle: naturalistic and laboratory task-based evidence. *Personality and Social Psychology Bulletin, 34*, 1451.

Durkheim, E. (1963). *Suicide*. New York, NY: Free Press (original work published in 1897).

Dutton, D. G., & Nicholls, T. L. (2005). The gender paradigm in domestic violence research and theory: part 1 – the conflict of theory and data. *Aggression and Violent Behavior, 10*, 680–714.

Dyrenforth, P. S., Kashy, D. A., Donnellan, B., & Lucas, R. E. (2010). Predicting relationship and life satisfaction from personality in nationally representative samples from three countries: the relative importance of actor, partner, and similarity effects. *Journal of Personality and Social Psychology, 99*, 690–702.

Eagly, A. H., & Wood, W. (1999). The origins of aggression sex differences: Evolved dispositions versus social roles. *Behavioral and Brain Sciences, 22*, 223–224.

Eastwick, P. W. (2009). Beyond the Pleistocene: using phylogeny and constraint to inform the evolutionary psychology of human mating. *Psychological Bulletin, 135*, 794–821.

Eastwick, P. W. (in press). Cultural influences on attraction. In J. A. Simpson & L. Campbell (Eds), *The Handbook of Close Relationships*. Oxford: Oxford University Press.

Eastwick, P. W., & Finkel, E. J. (2008). Sex differences in mate preferences revisited: Do people know what they initially desire in a romantic partner? *Journal of Personality and Social Psychology, 94*, 245–364.

Eastwick, P. W., Finkel, E. J., & Eagly, A. H. (2011). When and why do ideal partner preferences affect the process of initiating and maintaining romantic relationships? *Journal of Personality and Social Psychology, 101*, 1012–1032.

Eastwick, P. W., Finkel, E. K., Krishnamurti, T., & Loewenstein, G. (2008). Mispredicting distress following romantic breakup: revealing the time course of the affective forecasting error. *Journal of Experimental Social Psychology, 44*, 800–807.

Eberhard, W. G. (1985). *Sexual Selection and Animal Genitalia*. Cambridge, MA: Harvard University Press.

Edelstein, R. S., Stanton, S. J., Henderson, M. M., & Sanders, M. R. (2010). Endogenous estradiol levels are associated with attachment avoidance and implicit intimacy motivation. *Hormones and Behavior, 57*, 230–236.

Edlund, J. E., Heider, J. D., Scherer, C. R., Farc, M., & Sagarin, B. J. (2006). Sex differences in jealousy in response to actual infidelity. *Evolutionary Psychology, 4*, 462–470.

Eens, M., & Pinxten, R. (2000). Sex-role reversal in vertebrates: behavioural and endocrinological accounts. *Behavioural Processes, 51*, 124–128.

eHarmony Scientific Match making (2012). Retrieved April 8 2012, from http://www.eharmony.com/why/science.

Eibl-Eibesfeldt, I. (1989). *Human Ethology*. New York, NY: Aldine de Gruyter.

Eisenberger, N. I., Master, S. L., Inagaki, T. K., Taylor, S. E., Shirinyan, D., Lieberman, M. D., & Naliboff, B. D. (2011). Attachment figures activate a safety signal-related neural region and reduce pain experience. *Proceedings of the National Academy of Sciences of the USA, 108*, 11721–11726.

Ekman, P. (1994). Strong evidence for universals in facial expressions – a reply to Russell's mistaken critique. *Psychological Bulletin, 115*, 268–287.

Ellis, B. J. (2004). Timing of pubertal maturation in girls. *Psychological Bulletin, 130*, 920–958.

Ellis, B., J., Figueredo, A. J., Brumbach, B. H., & Schlomer, G. L. (2009). Fundamental dimensions of risk: the impact of harsh versus unpredictable environments on the evolution and development of life history strategies. *Human Nature, 20*, 204–268.

Ellis, B. J., & Garber, J. (2000). Psychosocial antecedents of variation in girls' pubertal timing. *Child Development, 71*, 485–501.

Ellis, B. J., & Kelley, H. H. (1999). The pairing game: a classroom demonstration of the matching phenomenon. *Teaching of Psychology, 26*, 118–121.

Ellis, B. J., McFadyen-Ketchum, S., Dodge, K. A., Pettit, G. S., & Bates, J. E. (1999). Quality of early family relationships and individual differences in the timing of pubertal maturation in girls. *Journal of Personality and Social Psychology, 77*, 387–401.

Ellis, L., Robb, B., & Burke, D. (2005). Sexual orientation in United States and Canadian students. *Archives of Sexual Behavior, 34*, 569–581.

Emery, N. J., Seed, A. M., von Bayern, A. M. P., & Clayton, N. S. (2007). Cognitive adaptations of social bonding in birds. *Philosophical Transactions of the Royal Society, 362*, 489–505.

Emery, R. (1988). *Marriage, Divorce, and Children's Adjustment*. Beverly Hills, CA: Sage.

Epstein, N., & Baucom, D. H. (2002). *Enhanced Cognitive-Behavioral Therapy for Couples: a Contextual Approach*. Washington, DC: American Psychological Association.

Erickson, M. F., Sroufe, L. A., & Egeland, B. (1985). The relationship between quality of attachment and behavior problems in preschool in a high risk sample. In I. Bretherton & E. Waters (Eds), *Growing Points of Attachment Theory and Research* (pp. 147–193). *Monographs of the Society for Research in Child Development, 50* (1–2, Serial No. 209).

Eysenck, H. J. (1976). *Sex and Personality*. London: Open Books.

Feeney, B. C. (2004). A secure base: responsive support of goal strivings and exploration adult intimate relationships. *Journal of Personality and Social Psychology, 87*, 631–648.

Feeney, B. C., & Thrush, R. L. (2010). Relationship influences on exploration in adulthood: the characteristics and function of a secure base. *Journal of Personality and Social Psychology, 98*, 57–76.

Feeney, J. A. (1995). Adult attachment and emotional control. *Personal Relationships, 2*, 143–159.

Feeney, J. A. (1999). Adult attachment, emotional control, and marital satisfaction. *Personal Relationships, 6*, 169–185.

Feeney, J. A. (2008). Adult romantic attachment: Developments in the study of couple relationships. In J. Cassidy & P. R. Shaver (Eds), *Handbook of Attachment: Theory, Research and Clinical Applications* (2nd ed; pp. 456–481). New York, NY: Guilford Press.

Feeney, J. A., & Noller, P. (1990). Attachment style as a predictor of adult romantic relationships. *Journal of Personality and Social Psychology, 58*, 281–291.

Fehr, B. (1988). Prototype analysis of the concepts of love and commitment. *Journal of Personality and Social Psychology, 55*, 557–579.

Fehr, B. (1999). Layperson's perception of commitment. *Journal of Personality and Social Psychology, 76*, 90–103.

Fehr, B., & Baldwin, M. (1996). Prototype and script analyses of laypeople's knowledge of anger. In G. J. O. Fletcher & J. Fitness (Eds), *Knowledge Structures in Close Relationships* (pp. 219–245). Mahwah, NJ: Lawrence Erlbaum.

Fehr, B., & Russell, J. A. (1991). The concept of love viewed from a prototype perspective. *Journal of Personality and Social Psychology*, *60*, 425–438.

Feingold, A. (1992). Good-looking people are not what we think. *Psychological Bulletin*, *111*, 304–341.

Fernald, A. (1985). Four-month-old infants prefer to listen to motherese. *Infant Behavior Development*, *8*, 181–195.

Fernandez, M. (1997). Domestic violence by extended family members in India. *Journal of Interpersonal Violence*, *12*, 433–455.

Filson, J., Ulloa, E., Runfola, C., & Hokoda, A. (2010). Does powerlessness explain the relationship between intimate partner violence and depression? *Journal of Interpersonal Violence*, *25*, 400–415.

Fincham, F. D. (2001). Attributions in close relationships: from balkanization to integration. In G. J. O. Fletcher & M. S. Clark (Eds), *Blackwell Handbook of Social Psychology: Interpersonal Processes* (pp. 3–31). Oxford: Blackwell.

Fincham, F. D., Stanley, S. M., & Beach, S. R. H. (2007). Transformative processes in marriage: an analysis of emerging trends. *Journal of Marriage and Family*, *69*, 275–292.

Finkel, E. J., & Baumeister, R. F. (2010). Attraction and rejection. In R. F. Baumeister & E. J. Finkel (Eds), *Advanced Social Psychology: The State of the Science*. New York, NY: Oxford University Press.

Finkel, E. J., & Campbell, W. K. (2001). Self-control and accommodation in close relationships: an interdependence analysis. *Journal of Personality and Social Psychology*, *81*, 263–277.

Finkel, E. J., DeWall, C. N., Slotter, E. B., Oaten, M., & Foshee, V. A. (2009). Self-regulatory failure and intimate partner violence perpetration. *Journal of Personality and Social Psychology*, *97*, 483–499.

Finkel, E. J., Eastwick, P. W., Karney, B. R., Reis, H. T., & Sprecher, S. (2012). Online dating: a critical analysis from the perspective of psychological science. *Psychological Science in the Public Interest*. Advance online publication, doi: 10.1177/1529100612436522.

Fisher, H. E. (1992). *Anatomy of Love: a Natural History of Mating, Marriage, and Why We Stray*. New York, NY: Fawcett Columbine.

Fisher, H. E. (1998). Lust, attraction, and attachment in mammalian reproduction. *Human Nature*, *9*, 23–52.

Fisher, H. E. (2000). Lust, attraction, attachment: biology and evolution of the three primary emotion systems for mating, reproduction, and parenting. *Journal of Sex Education and Therapy*, *25*, 96–104.

Fisher, H. E. (January 19, 2004). Your brain in love. *Time Magazine*, p. 77.

Fisher, J. D., Nadler, A., & Whitcher-Alagna, S. (1982). Recipient reactions to aid. *Psychological Bulletin*, *91*, 27–54.

Fitness, J. (1996). Emotion knowledge structures in close relationships. In G. J. O. Fletcher & J. Fitness (Eds.), *Knowledge Structures in Close Relationships* (pp. 195–217). Mahwah, NJ: Lawrence Erlbaum.

Fitness, J. (2001). Betrayal, rejection, revenge, and forgiveness: an interpersonal script analysis. In M. Leary (Ed.), *Interpersonal Rejection* (pp. 73–103). New York, NY: Oxford University Press.

Fitness, J., & Fletcher, G. J. O. (1993). Love, anger, hate, and jealousy in close relationships: a prototype and cognitive appraisal analysis. *Journal of Personality and Social Psychology*, *65*, 942–958.

Fitness, J., Fletcher, G. J. O., & Overall, N. (2003). Interpersonal attraction and intimate relationships. In M. Hogg & J. Cooper (Eds.), *Sage Handbook of Social Psychology* (pp. 258–276). London: Sage.

Fletcher, G. J. O. (1984). Psychology and commonsense. *American Psychologist*, *39*, 203–213.

Fletcher, G. J. O. (1995). *The Scientific Credibility of Folk Psychology*. Mahwah, NJ: Lawrence Erlbaum.

Fletcher, G. J. O. (2002). *New Science of Intimate Relationships*. Malden, MA: Blackwell Publishers Inc.

Fletcher, G. J. O., & Fincham, F. (1991). Attributional processes in close relationships. In G. J. O. Fletcher & F. Fincham (Eds), *Cognition in Close Relationships* (pp. 6–34). Hillsdale, NJ: Lawrence Erlbaum.

Fletcher, G. J. O., & Fitness, J. (1990). Occurrent social cognition in close relationships: the role of proximal and distal variables. *Journal of Personality and Social Psychology*, 59, 464–474.

Fletcher, G. J. O., & Kerr, P. S. G. (2010). Through the eyes of love: reality and illusion in intimate relationships. *Psychological Bulletin*, 136, 627–658.

Fletcher, G. J. O., & Kininmonth, L. (1992). Measuring relationship beliefs: an individual differences scale. *Journal of Research in Personality*, 26, 371–397.

Fletcher, G. J. O., & Thomas, G. (1996). Close relationship lay theories: their structure and function. In G. J. O. Fletcher & J. Fitness (Eds), *Knowledge Structures in Close Relationships* (pp. 3–24). Mahwah, NJ: Lawrence Erlbaum.

Fletcher, G. J. O., & Thomas, G. (2000). Behavior and on-line cognition in marital interaction. *Personal Relationships*, 7, 111–130.

Fletcher, G. J. O., Fincham, F. D., Cramer, L., & Heron, N. (1987). The role of attributions in the development of dating relationships. *Journal of Personality and Social Psychology*, 53, 481–489.

Fletcher, G. J. O., Fitness, J., & Blampied, N. M. (1990). The link between attributions and happiness in close relationships: the roles of depression and explanatory style. *Journal of Social and Clinical Psychology*, 9, 243–255.

Fletcher, G. J. O., Rosanowski, J., & Fitness, J. (1994). Automatic processing in intimate contexts: the role of close relationship beliefs. *Journal of Personality and Social Psychology*, 67, 888–897.

Fletcher, G. J. O., Simpson, J., & Thomas, G. (2000a). The measurement of relationship quality components: a confirmatory factor analytic study. *Personality and Social Psychology Bulletin*, 26, 340–354.

Fletcher, G. J. O., Simpson, J. A., & Thomas, G. (2000b). Ideals, perceptions, and evaluations in early relationship development. *Journal of Personality and Social Psychology*, 79, 933–940.

Fletcher, G. J. O., Simpson, J. A., Thomas, G., & Giles, L. (1999). Ideals in intimate relationships. *Journal of Personality and Social Psychology*, 76, 72–89.

Fletcher, G. J. O., Tither, J. M., O'Loughlin, C., Friesen, M., & Overall, N. (2004). Warm and homely or cold and beautiful? Sex differences in trading off traits in mate selection. *Personality and Social Psychology Bulletin*, 30, 659–672.

Fletcher, G. J. O., Thomas, G., & Durrant, R. (1999). Cognitive and behavioral accommodation in relationship interaction. *Journal of Social and Personal Relationships*, 16, 705–730.

Flinn, M. V. (2011). Evolutionary anthropology of the human family. In C. A. Salmon & T. K. Shackelford (Eds), *Oxford Handbook of Evolutionary Family Psychology* (pp. 12–32). New York, NY: Oxford University Press.

Fodor, J. A. (1983). *The Modularity of Mind*. Cambridge, MA: MIT Press.

Forbes, C. E., & Grafman, J. (2010). The role of the human prefrontal cortex in social cognition and moral judgment. *Annual Review of Neuroscience*, 33, 299–324.

Fowers, B. J., Lyons, E., Montel, K. H., & Shaked, N. (2001). Positive illusions about marriage among married and single individuals. *Journal of Family Psychology*, 15, 95–109.

Fraley, R. C., & Brumbaugh, C. C. (2004). A dynamical systems approach to conceptualizing and studying stability and change in attachment security. In W. S. Rholes & J. A. Simpson (Eds), *Adult Attachment: Theory, Research, and Clinical Implications* (pp. 86–132). New York, NY: Guilford Press.

Fraley, R. C., & Brumbaugh, C. C. (2007). Adult attachment and preemptive defenses: converging evidence on the role of defensive exclusion at the level of encoding. *Journal of Personality*, *75*, 1033–1050.

Fraley, R. C., Garner, J. P., & Shaver, P. R. (2000). Adult attachment and the defensive regulation of attention and memory: examining the role of preemptive and postemptive defense processes. *Journal of Personality and Social Psychology*, *79*, 816–826.

Frank, E., Anderson, C., & Rubinstein, D. (1978). Frequency of sexual dysfunction in "normal" couples. *New England Journal of Medicine*, *299*, 111–115.

Frazier, P. A., & Cook, S. W. (1993). Correlates of distress following heterosexual relationship dissolution. *Journal of Social and Personal Relationships*, *10*, 55–67.

Frazier, P. A., Tix, A. P., & Barnett, C. L. (2003). The relational context of social support: relationship satisfaction moderates the relations between enacted support and distress. *Personality and Social Psychology Bulletin*, *29*, 113–146.

Frieze, I. H., & Ramsey, S. J. (1976). Nonverbal maintenance of traditional sex roles. *Journal of Social Issues*, *32*, 133–141.

Funder, D. C. (1995). On the accuracy of personality judgment: A realistic approach. *Psychological Review*, *102*, 652–670.

Funder, D. C., & Dobroth, K. M. (1987). Differences between traits: properties associated with interjudge agreement. *Journal of Personality and Social Psychology*, *52*, 409–418.

Furlow, B., Gangestad, S. W., & Armijo-Prewitt, T. (1998). Developmental stability and human violence. *Proceedings of the Royal Society B*, *265*, 1–6.

Furman, W., & Simon, V. A. (1999). Cognitive representations of adolescent relationships. In W. Furman, B. B. Brown, & C. Feiring (Eds), *The Development of Romantic Relationships in Adolescence* (pp. 75–98). New York, NY: Cambridge University Press.

Gable, S. L., & Impett, E. A. (2012). Approach and avoidance motives and close relationships. *Social and Personality Psychology Compass*, *6*, 95–108.

Gable, S. L., Reis, H. T., Impett, E. A., & Asher, E. R. (2004). What do you do when things go right? The intrapersonal and interpersonal benefits of sharing positive events. *Journal of Personality and Social Psychology*, *87*, 228–245.

Gagné, F. M., & Lydon, J. E. (2001). Mind-set and close relationships: when bias leads to (in)accurate predictions. *Journal of Personality and Social Psychology*, *81*, 85–96.

Gagnon, J. H. (1977). *Human Sexualities*. Glenview, IL: Scott & Foresman.

Gagnon, J. H., & Simon, W. (1968). The social meaning of prison homosexuality. *Federal Probation*, *32*, 28–29.

Gallup, G. G., Burch, R. L., Zappieri, M. L., Parvez, R. A., Stockwell, M. L., & Davis, J. A. (2003). The human penis as a semen displacement device. *Evolution and Human Behavior*, *24*, 277–289.

Gangestad, S. W., Garver-Apgar, C. E., Simpson, J. A., & Cousins, A. J. (2007). Changes in women's mate preferences across the ovulatory cycle. *Journal of Personality and Social Psychology*, *92*, 151–163.

Gangestad, S. W., & Simpson, J. A. (2000). The evolution of human mating: trade-offs and strategic pluralism. *Behavioral and Brain Sciences*, *23*, 573–644.

Gangestad, S. W., & Simpson, J. A. (1990). Toward an evolutionary history of female sociosexual variation. *Journal of Personality*, *58*, 69–96.

Gangestad, S. W., Simpson, J. A., Cousins, A. J., Garver-Apgar, C. E., & Christensen, P. N. (2004). Women's preferences for male behavioral displays change across the menstrual cycle. *Psychological Science*, *15*, 203–207.

Gangestad, S. W., & Thornhill, R. (1997). The evolutionary psychology of extrapair sex: the role of fluctuating asymmetry. *Evolution and Human Behavior*, *18*, 69–88.

Gangestad, S. W., & Thornhill, R. (1998). Menstrual cycle variation in women's preference for the scent of symmetrical men. *Proceedings of the Royal Society B*, *265*, 927–933.

Gangestad, S. W., & Thornhill, R. (2008). Human oestrus. *Proceedings of the Royal Society B, 275*, 991–1000.

Ganong, L., Coleman, M., & Hans, J. (2006). Divorce as a prelude to stepfamily living and the consequences of redivorce. In: M. A. Fine & J. H. Harvey (Eds), *Handbook of Divorce and Relationship Dissolution* (pp. 409–434). New Jersey, NJ: Lawrence Erlbaum.

Gardner, K. A., & Cutrona, C. E. (2004). Social support communication in families. In A. L. Vangelisti (Ed.), *Handbook of Family Communication* (pp. 495–512). Mahwah, NY: Lawrence Erlbaum.

Geary, D. C. (2000). Evolution and proximate expression of human paternal investment. *Psychological Bulletin, 126*, 55–77.

Geary, D. C. (2010). *Male, Female: the Evolution of Human Sex Differences* (2nd ed). Washington, DC: American Psychological Association.

Geary, D. C., Bailey, D. H., & Oxford, J. K. (2011). Reflections on the human family. In C. A. Salmon & T. K. Shackelford (Eds), *Oxford Handbook of Evolutionary Family Psychology* (pp. 365–385). New York, NY: Oxford University Press.

Geiss, S. K., & O'Leary, K. D. (1981). Therapist ratings of frequency and severity of marital problems: implications for research. *Journal of Marital and Family Therapy, 7*, 515–520.

Gerin, W., Pieper, C., Levy, R., & Pickering, T. G. (1992). Social support in social interaction: a moderator of cardiovascular reactivity. *Psychosomatic Medicine, 54*, 324–336.

Gettler, L. T., McDade, T. W., Feranil, A. B., & Kuzawa, C. W. (2011). Longitudinal evidence that fatherhood decreases testosterone in human males. *Proceedings of the National Academy of Science, 108*, 16194–16199.

Gillath, O., Bunge, S. A., Shaver, P. R., Wendelken, C., & Mikulincer, M. (2005). Attachment-style differences in the ability to suppress negative thoughts: exploring the neural correlates. *NeuroImage, 28*, 835–847.

Gillath, O., Mikulincer, M., Fitzsimons, G. M., Shaver, P. R., Schachner, D. A., & Bargh, J. A. (2006). Automatic activation of attachment-related goals. *Personality and Social Psychology Bulletin, 32*, 1375–1388.

Glass, S. P., & Wright, T. L. (1992). Justifications for extramarital relationships: the associations between attitudes, behaviors, and gender. *Journal of Sex Research, 29*, 361–387.

Gleason, M. E. J., Iida, M., Bolger, N., & Shrout, P. E. (2003). Daily supportive equity in close relationships. *Personality and Social Psychology Bulletin, 29*, 1036–1045.

Gleason, M. E. J., Iida, M., Shrout, P. E., & Bolger, N. (2008). Receiving support as a mixed blessing: evidence for dual effects of support on psychological outcomes. *Journal of Personality and Social Psychology, 94*, 824–838.

Glynn, J. R., Caraël, M., Auvert, B., Kahindo, M., Chege, J., Musonda, R., . . . Study Group on the Heterogeneity of HIV Epidemics in African Cities. (2001). Why do young women have a much higher prevalence of HIV than young men? A study of Kisumu, Kenya and Ndola Zambia. *AIDS, 15*, S51–S60.

Godbout, N., Dutton, D. G., Lussier, Y., & Sabourin, S. (2009). Early exposure to violence, domestic violence, attachment representations, and marital adjustment. *Personal Relationships, 16*, 1350–4126.

Goetz, A. T., Shackelford, T. K., Platek, S. M., Starratt, V. G., & McKibbin, W. F. (2007). Sperm competition in humans: implications for male sexual psychology, physiology, anatomy, and behavior. *Annual Review of Sex Research, 18*, 1–22.

Goetz, A. T., Shackelford, T. K., Weekes-Shackelford, V. A., Euler, H. A., Hoier, S., Schmitt, D. P., & LaMunyon, C. W. (2005). Mate retention, semen displacement, and human sperm competition: a preliminary investigation of tactics to prevent and correct female infidelity. *Personality and Individual Differences, 38*, 749–763.

Goldey, K. L., & van Anders, S. M. (2010). Sexy thoughts: Effects of sexual cognitions on testosterone, cortisol, and arousal in women. *Hormones and Behavior, 59*, 754–764.

Gonzaga, G. C., Haselton, M. G., Smurda, J., Davies, M. S., & Poore, J. C. (2008). Love, desire, and the suppression of thoughts of romantic alternatives. *Evolution and Human Behavior, 29*, 119–126.

Gonzaga, G. C., Keltner, D., Londahl, E. A., & Smith, M. D. (2001). Love and the commitment problem in romantic relations and friendship. *Journal of Personality and Social Psychology, 81*, 247–262.

Gonzaga, G. C., Turner, R. A., Keltner, D., Campos, B. C., & Altemus, M. (2006). Romantic love and sexual desire in close relationships. *Emotion, 6*, 163–179.

Goodwin, J. S., Hunt, W. C., Key, C. R., & Samet, J. M. (1987). The effect of marital status on stage, treatment, and survival of cancer patients. *Journal of the American Medical Association, 34*, 20–26.

Gottman, J. M. (1979). *Marital Interaction: Experimental Investigations.* New York, NY: Academic Press.

Gottman, J. M. (1994). *What Predicts Divorce?* Hillsdale, NJ: Lawrence Erlbaum.

Gottman, J. M. (1998). Psychology and the study of marital processes. *Annual Review of Psychology, 49*, 169–197.

Gottman, J. M. & Krokoff, L. J. (1989). Marital interaction and satisfaction: a longitudinal view. *Journal of Consulting and Clinical Psychology, 57*, 47–52.

Gottman, J. M., Jacobson, N. S, Rushe, R. G., Shortt, J. W., Babcock, J., Lataillade, J. J., & Waltz, J. (1995). The relationship between heart-rate reactivity, emotionally aggressive behavior, and general violence in batterers. *Journal of Family Psychology, 9*, 227–248.

Gouin, J., Carter, C. S., Pournajafi-Nazarloo, H., Glaser, R., Malarkey, W. B., Loving, T. J. *et al.* (2010). Marital behavior, oxytocin, vasopressin, and wound healing. *Psychoneuroendocrinology, 35*, 1082–1090.

Gould, S. J. (1992). *Bully for Brontosaurus: Reflections on Natural History.* New York, NY: W.W. Norton.

Gove, W. R., Style, C. B., & Hughes, M. (1990). The effect of marriage on the well-being of adults: a theoretical analysis. *Journal of Family Issues, 11*, 4–35.

Graham, K., Bernards, S., Wilsnack, S. C., & Gmel, G. (2011). Alcohol may not cause partner violence but it seems to make it worse: a cross national comparison of the relationship between alcohol and severity of partner violence. *Journal of Interpersonal Violence, 26*, 1503–1523.

Graham, S. (1834). *A Lecture to Young Men.* Providence: Weeden and Cory. Facsimile repr. edn. (1974). New York, NY: Arno.

Grammer, K. (1993). 5-a-androst-16en-3-a-on: a male pheromone? A brief report. *Ethology and Sociobiology, 14*, 201–208.

Gray, P. B, & Campbell, B. C. (2009). Human male testosterone, pair bonding, and fatherhood. In P. B. Gray & P. T. Ellison (Eds), *Endocrinology of Social Relationships* (pp. 270–293). Cambridge, MA: Harvard University Press.

Gray, P. B., Chapman, J. F., Burnham, T. C., McIntyre, M. H., Lipson, S. F., & Ellison, P. T. (2004). Human male pair bonding and testosterone. *Human Nature, 15*, 119–131.

Gray, P. B., Kahlenberg, S. M., Barrett, E. S., Lipson, S. F., & Ellison, P. T. (2002). Marriage and fatherhood are associated with lower testosterone in males. *Evolution and Human Behavior, 23*, 193–201.

Green, R. E., Krause, J., Briggs, A. W., Maricic, T., Stenzel, U., Kircher, M. *et al.* (2010). A draft sequence of the neandertal genome. *Science, 328*, 710–722.

Greenblat, C. S. (1983). The salience of sexuality in the early years of marriage. *Journal of Marriage and the Family, 45*, 289–299.

Greiling, H., & Buss, D. M. (2000). Women's sexual strategies: the hidden dimension of extra-pair mating. *Personality and Individual Differences, 28*, 929–963.

Grewen, K. M., Girdler, S. S., Amico, J. A., & Light, K. C. (2005). Effects of partner support on resting oxytocin, cortisol, nore-pinephrine and blood pressure before and after warm partner contact. *Psychosomatic Medicine*, *67*, 531–538.

Grieser, D. L., & Kuhl, P. K. (1988). Maternal speech to infants in a tonal language: support for universal prosodic features in motherese. *Developmental Psychology*, *24*, 14–20.

Grote, N. K., & Frieze, I. H. (1994). The measurement of friendship-based love in intimate relationships. *Personal Relationships*, *1*, 275–300.

Gupta, G. R. (1976). Love, arranged marriage, and the Indian social structure. *Journal of Comparative Family Studies*, *7*, 75–85.

Gurven, M., Allen-Arave, W., Hill, K., & Hurtado, M. (2000). "It's a Wonderful Life": Signaling generosity among the Ache of Paraguay. *Evolution and Human Behavior*, *21*, 263–282.

Gutierres, S. E., Kenrick, D. T., & Partch, J. J. (1999). Beauty, dominance, and the mating game: contrast effects in self-assessment reflect gender differences in mate selection. *Personality and Social Psychology Bulletin*, *25*, 1126–1134.

Halberstam, D. (1994). *The Fifties*. New York, NY: Random House.

Halford, W. K., Gravestock, R. M., Lowe, R., & Scheldt, S. (1992). Toward a behavioral ecology of stressful marital interactions. *Behavioral Assessment*, *14*, 199–217.

Hall, D. R., & Zhao, J. Z. (1995). Cohabitation and divorce in Canada: testing the selectivity hypothesis. *Journal of Marriage and the Family*, *57*, 421–427.

Hamer, D. H., Hu, S., Magnuson, V. L., Hu, N., & Pattatucci, A. M. L. (1993). A linkage between DNA markers on the X chromosome and male sexual orientation, *Science*, *261*, 321–327.

Hamilton, W. (1964). The genetical evolution of social behavior: 1 and 2. *Journal of Theoretical Biology*, *1*, 1–52.

Hanly, M. J., & O'Neill, P. (1997). Violence and commitment: a study of dating couples. *Journal of Interpersonal Violence*, *12*, 685–703.

Hanson, T. L., McLanahan, S. S., & Thomson, E. (1998). Windows on divorce: before and after. *Social Sciences Research*, *27*, 329–349.

Harlow, H. F. (1959). Love in infant monkeys. *Scientific American*, *200*, 68–86.

Harris, C. R. (2003). A review of sex differences in sexual jealousy, including self-report data, psychophysiological responses, interpersonal violence, and morbid jealousy. *Personality and Social Psychology Review*, *7*, 102–128.

Haselton, M. G., & Buss, D. M. (2000). Error management theory: a new perspective on biases in cross-sex mind reading. *Journal of Personality and Social Psychology*, *78*, 81–91.

Haselton, M. G., & Gangestad, S. W. (2006). Conditional expression of women's desires and men's mate guarding across the ovulatory cycle. *Hormones and Behavior*, *49*, 509–518.

Haselton, M. G., Mortezaie, M., Pillsworth, E. G., Bleske-Recheck, A. E., & Frederick, D. A. (2007). Ovulation and human female ornamentation: near ovulation, women dress to impress. *Hormones and Behavior*, *51*, 41–45.

Hassebrauck, M. (1997). Cognitions of relationship quality: a prototype analysis of their structure and consequences. *Personal Relationships*, *4*, 163–185.

Hatch, L. R., & Bulcroft, K. (1992). Contact with friends in later-life: disentangling the effects of gender and marital status. *Journal of Marriage and Family*, *54*, 222–232.

Hatfield, E. (June, 2006). The Golden Fleece Award: Love's labors (almost) lost. *The Observer*, *19*, Washington, DC: Association for Psychological Science, 16–17.

Hatfield, E., & Rapson, R. L. (2006). Passionate love, sexual desire, and mate selection: cross-cultural and historical perspectives. In P. Noller & J. Feeney (Eds), *Close Relationships: Functions, Forms and Processes* (pp. 227–243). London: Psychology Press.

Hatfield, E., & Sprecher, S. (1986). Measuring passionate love in intimate relationships. *Journal of Adolescence*, *9*, 383–410.

Hatfield, E., Pillemer, J. T., O'Brien, M. U., &
Le, Y. C. L. (2008). The endurance of love:
passionate and companionate love in newlywed and long-term marriages. *Interper-
sona*, *2*, 35–64.

Haviland, J. B. (1977). *Gossip, Reputation and
Knowledge in Zinacantan*. Chicago, IL: University of Chicago Press.

Havlicek, J., Bartos, L., Dvorakova, R., & Flegr, J.
(2006) Non-advertised does not mean con-
cealed. Body odour changes across the human
menstrual cycle. *Ethology*, *112*, 81–90.

Havlicek, J., Roberts, S. C., & Flegr, J. (2005)
Women's preference for dominant male
odour: effects of menstrual cycle and relationship status. *Biology Letters*, *1*, 256–259.

Hawkes, K. (1991). Showing off: tests of an
hypothesis about men's foraging goals.
Ethology and Sociobiology, *12*, 29–54.

Hawkins, A. J., Blanchard, V. L., Baldwin, S. A.,
& Fawcett, E. B. (2008). Does marriage
and relationship education work? A meta-
analytic study. *Journal of Consulting and
Clinical Psychology*, *76*, 723–734.

Hawks, J. (2010). What is the human mutation
rate? Retrieved May 13, 2011, from http://
johnhawks.net/weblog/reviews/genomics/
variation/human-mutation-rate-review-
2010.html.

Hayes, A., Weston, R., Qu, L., & Gray, M.
(2010). Australian Institute of Family
Studies. *Families Then and Now: 1980–2010.*
Retrieved from http://www.aifs.gov.au/.

Hazan, C., & Shaver, P. R. (1987). Romantic
love conceptualized as an attachment
process. *Journal of Personality and Social
Psychology*, *52*, 511–524.

Hazan, C., & Shaver, P. R. (1992). Attachment
theory and relationship loss. In T. L. Orbuch
(Ed)., *Close Relationship Loss* (pp. 90–108).
New York, NY: Springer-Verlag.

Hazan, C., & Shaver, P. R. (1994). Attachment
as an organizational framework for research
on close relationships. *Psychological Inquiry*,
5, 1–22.

Hazan, C., & Zeifman, D. (1999). Pair bonds
as attachments: evaluating the evidence. In
J. Cassidy & P. R. Shaver (Eds), *Handbook of
Attachment: Theory, Research, and Clinical
Applications* (pp. 336–354). New York, NY:
Guilford Press.

Heaton, T. B. (2002). Factors contributing
to increasing marital stability in the
United States. *Journal of Family Issues*, *23*,
392–409.

Heavey, C. L., Christensen, A., & Malamuth,
N. M. (1995). The longitudinal impact of
demand and withdrawal during marital
conflict. *Journal of Consulting and Clinical
Psychology*, *63*, 797–801.

Heavey, C. L., Layne, C., & Christensen, A.
(1993). Gender and conflict structure in
marital interaction: a replication and extension. *Journal of Consulting and Clinical Psychology*, *61*, 16–27.

Hed, H. M. E. (1987). Trends in opportunity
for natural selection in the Swedish population during the period 1650–1980. *Human
Biology*, *59*, 785–797.

Heelas, P. (1989). Identifying peaceful societies. In S. Howell & R. Willis (Eds), *Societies
at Peace: Anthropological Perspectives* (pp.
225–243). New York, NY: Routledge.

Heider, F. (1958). *The Psychology of Interpersonal Relations*. New York, NY: Wiley.

Hellmuth, J. C., & McNulty, J. K. (2008). Neuroticism, marital violence, and the moderating role of stress and behavioral skills.
Journal of Personality and Social Psychology,
95, 166–180.

Hendrick, C., & Hendrick, S. S. (2003).
Romantic love: Measuring cupid's arrow.
In S. J. Lopez & C. R. Snyder (Eds), *Posi-
tive Psychological Assessment: A Handbook
of Models and Measures.* (pp. 235–249).
Washington, DC: American Psychological
Association.

Hendrick, C., Hendrick, S. S., & Dicke, A.
(1998). The love attitudes scale: short form.
Journal of Social and Personal Relationships,
15, 147–159.

Hendrick, S. S., & Hendrick, C. (1993). Lovers
as friends. *Journal of Social and Personal
Relationships*, *10*, 459–466.

Henrich, J., Boyd, R., & Richerson, P. J. (2012).
The puzzle of monogamous marriage. *Phil-*

osophical Transactions of the Royal Society, 367, 657–669.

Herbert, T. B., & Cohen, S. (1993). Stress and immunity in humans: a meta-analytic review. Psychosomatic Medicine, 55, 364–379.

Herdt, G. H. (1981). Guardians of the Flutes: Idioms of Masculinity. New York, NY: McGraw-Hill.

Herold, E. S., & Milhausen, R. R. (1999). Dating preferences of university women: an analysis of the nice guy stereotype. Journal of Sex and Marital Therapy, 25, 333–343.

Hewitt, B., & de Vaus, D. (2009). Change in the association between premarital cohabitation and separation, Australia 1945–2000. Journal of Marriage and the Family, 71, 353–361.

Hill, K., & Hurtado, A. M. (1996). Ache Life History: The Ecology and Demography of a Foraging People. Hawthorne, NY: Aldine de Gruyter.

Hill, K., Boesch, C., Goodall, J., Pusey, A., Williams, J., & Wrangham, R. (2001). Mortality rates among wild chimpanzees. Journal of Human Evolution, 40, 437–450.

Hinde, R. A. (1976). On describing relationships. Journal of Child Psychology, 17, 1–19.

Hirschfeld, L. A., & Gelman, S. A. (Eds), (1994) Mapping the Mind: Domain Specificity in Cognition and Culture. New York, NY: Cambridge University Press.

Hitsch, G. J., Hortaçsu, A., & Ariely, D. (2010). What makes you click? – Mate preferences in online dating. Quantitative Marketing and Economics, 8, 393–427.

Holmes, J. G. (1991). Trust and the appraisal process in close relationships. In W. H. Jones & D. Perlman (Eds), Advances in Personal Relationships: a Research Annual (Vol. 2., pp. 57–104). Oxford: Jessica Kingsley Publishers.

Holmes, J. G., & Murray, S. L. (1996). Conflict in close relationships. In E. T. Higgins & A. Kruglanski (Eds), Social Psychology: Handbook of Basic Principles (pp. 622–654). New York, NY: Guilford.

Holmes, J. G., & Rempel, J. K. (1989). Trust in close relationships. In C. Hendrick (Ed.), Close Relationships. (pp. 187–220). Thousand Oaks, CA: Sage Publications, Inc.

Holmes, T. H., & Rahe, R. H. (1967). The social readjustment rating scale. Journal of Psychosomatic Research, 11, 213–218.

Holtzworth-Munroe, A., & Jacobson, N. S. (1985). Causal attributions of married couples – when do they search for causes – what do they conclude when they do? Journal of Personality and Social Psychology, 48, 1398–1412.

Holtzworth-Munroe, A., & Stuart, G. L. (1994). Typologies of male batterers: three subtypes and the differences among them. Psychological Bulletin, 116, 476–497.

Howell, N. (1979). Demography of the Dobe !Kung. New York, NY: Walter de Gruyter.

Howland, M., & Simpson, J. A. (2010). Getting in under the radar: a dyadic view of invisible support. Psychological Science, 21, 1878–1885.

Hrdy, S. B. (2009). Mothers and Others: the Evolutionary Origins of Mutual Understanding. Cambridge, MA: Harvard University Press.

Hughes, J. F., Skaletsky, H., Pyntikova, T., Graves, T. A., van Daalen, S. K. M., Minx, P. J. et al. (2010). Chimpanzee and human Y chromosomes are remarkably divergent in structure and gene content. Nature, 463, 536–539.

Hunt, M. (1974). Sexual Behavior in the 1970s. Chicago, IL: Playboy Press.

Huston, T. & Houts, R. (1998). The psychological infrastructure of courtship and marriage: the role of personality and compatibility in romantic relationships. In T. Bradbury (Ed.), The Developmental Course of Marital Dysfunction (pp. 114–151). New York, NY: Cambridge University Press.

Huston, T. L., & Vangelisti, A. L. (1991). Socioemotional behavior and satisfaction in marital relationships: a longitudinal study. Journal of Personality and Social Psychology, 61, 721–733.

Ickes, W. (1993). Empathic accuracy. *Journal of Personality, 61*, 587–610.

Ickes, W., Stinson, L., Bissonnette, V., & Garcia, S. (1990). Naturalistic social cognition – empathic accuracy in mixed-sex dyads. *Journal of Personality and Social Psychology, 59*, 730–742.

Inglehart, R. (1990). *Culture Shift in Advanced Industrial Society*. Princeton, NJ: Princeton University Press.

Insel, T. R. (2010). The challenge of translation in social neuroscience: a review of oxytocin, vasopressin, and affiliative behavior. *Neuron, 65*, 768–779.

Isabella, R., & Belsky, J. (1990). Interactional synchrony and the origins of infant-mother attachment: a replication study. *Child Development, 62*, 373–384.

Isabella, R., Belsky, J., & von Eye, A. (1989). Origins of infant-mother attachment: an examination of interactional synchrony during the infant's first year. *Developmental Psychology, 25*, 12–21.

Isler, K., & van Schaik, C. P. (2009). The expensive brain: a framework for explaining evolutionary changes in brain size. *Journal of Human Evolution, 57*, 392–400.

Izard, C. E. (1994). Innate and universal facial expressions – evidence from developmental and cross-cultural research. *Psychological Bulletin, 115*, 228–299.

Jacobson, N. S., & Christensen, A. (1998). *Acceptance and Change in Couple Therapy: a Therapist's Guide to Transforming Relationships*. New York, NY: Norton.

Jacobson, N. S., & Margolin, G. (1979). *Marital Therapy: Strategies Based on Social Learning and Behavior Exchange Principles*. New York, NY: Brunner/Mazel.

Jain, S. (2007). Lifetime marriage and divorce trends. Australian Social Trends 2007. Canberra: Australian Bureau of Statistics. Retrieved August 12, 2011, from http://www.abs.gov.au/ausstats.

James, W. H. (1981). The honeymoon effect on marital coitus. *The Journal of Sex Research, 17*, 114–123.

James, W. H. (1993). The incidence of superfecundation and of double paternity in the general population. *Acta Geneicae Medicae et Gemellologiae, 42*, 257–262.

Jankowiak, W. R., & Fischer, E. F. (1992). A cross-cultural perspective on romantic love. *Ethnology, 21*, 149–155.

Jasieńska, G., Ziomkiewicz, A., Ellison, P. T., Lipson, S. F., Thune, I., 2004. Large breast and narrow waist indicate high reproductive potential in women. *Proceedings of the Royal Society of London B, 271*, 1213–1217.

Jobling, M. A. (2011). Father figures. *Investigative Genetics, 2*, 21.

Johnson, D. J., & Rusbult, C. E. (1989). Resisting temptation: devaluation of alternative partners as a means of maintaining commitment in close relationships. *Journal of Personality and Social Psychology, 57*, 967–980.

Johnson, M. P. (1995). Patriarchal terrorism and common couple violence: two forms of violence against women. *Journal of Marriage and the Family, 57*, 283–294.

Johnson, S. (2004). *The Practice of Emotionally Focused Marital Therapy* (2nd ed.). New York, NY: Brunner/Routledge.

Josephs, R. A., Markus, H. R., & Tafarodi, R. W. (1992). Gender and self-esteem. *Journal of Personality and Social Psychology, 63*, 391–402.

Julien, D., Chartrand, E., Simard, M., Bouthillier, D., & Begin, J. (2003). Conflict, social support, and relationship quality: an observational study of heterosexual, gay male, and lesbian couples' communication. *Journal of Family Psychology, 17*, 419–428.

Kahn, M. (1970). Non-verbal communication and marital satisfaction. *Family Processes, 9*, 449–456.

Kaighobadi, F., Shackelford, T. K., & Goetz, A. T. (2009). From mate retention to murder: evolutionary psychological perspectives on men's partner-directed violence. *Review of General Psychology, 13*, 327–334.

Kaplan, H., Lancaster, J. B., & Anderson, K. G. (1998). Human parental investment and fertility: the life histories of men in Albuquerque. In A. Booth & N. Crouter (Eds), *Men in Families: When Do They Get Involved? What Difference Does It Make?*

(pp. 55–111). New York, NY: Lawrence Erlbaum.

Karamagi, C. A. S., Tumwine, J. K., Tylleskar, T., & Heggenhougen, K. (2006). Intimate partner violence against women in eastern Uganda: implications for HIV prevention. *BMC Public Health*, 6. Online publication. doi 10.1186/1471-2458-6-284.

Karney, B. R., & Bradbury, T. N. (1995). The longitudinal course of marital quality and stability: a review of theory, methods, and research. *Psychological Bulletin*, *118*, 3–34.

Karney, B. R., & Bradbury, T. N. (1997). Neuroticism, marital interaction, and the trajectory of marital satisfaction. *Journal of Personality and Social Psychology*, *72*, 1075–1092.

Karney, B. R., & Bradbury, T. N. (2000). Attribution processes in marriage: state or trait? A growth curve analysis. *Journal of Personality and Social Psychology*, *78*, 295–309.

Karney, B. R., & Frye, N. E. (2002). "But we've been getting better lately": comparing prospective and retrospective views of relationship development. *Journal of Personality and Social Psychology*, *82*, 222–238.

Karremans, J. C., & Aarts, H. (2007). The role of automaticity in determining the inclination to forgive close others. *Journal of Experimental Social Psychology*, *43*, 902–917.

Kee, E., & Farid, H. (2011). A perceptual metric for photo retouching. *Proceedings of the National Academy of Sciences of the USA*, *108*, 19907–19912.

Kelley, H. H. (1979). *Personal Relationships: Their Structures and Processes*. New York, NY: Wiley.

Kelley, H. H., Berscheid, E., Christensen, A., Harvey, J. H., Huston, T. L., Levinger, G. et al. (1983). *Close Relationships*. San Francisco, CA: Freeman.

Kelley, H. H., & Thibaut, J. W. (1978). *Interpersonal Relations: a Theory of Interdependence*. New York: Wiley.

Kellogg, J. H. (1888). *Plain Facts for Old and Young: Embracing the Natural History and Hygiene of Organic Life*. Burlington, Iowa:

I. F. Segner. Facsimile repr. edn. (1974). New York, NY: Arno.

Kelly, R. L. (1995). *The Foraging Spectrum: Diversity in Hunter-Gatherer Lifeways*. Washington, DC: Smithsonian Institution.

Kenny, D. A. (1994). *Interpersonal Perception: a Social Relations Analysis*. New York, NY: Guilford.

Kenny, D. A., & Acitelli, L. K. (2001). Accuracy and bias in the perception of the partner in a close relationship. *Journal of Personality and Social Psychology*, *80*, 439–448.

Kenrick, D. T., & Keefe, R. C. (1992). Age preferences in mates reflect sex differences in human reproductive strategies. *Behavioral and Brain Sciences*, *15*, 75–133.

Kenrick, D. T., Groth, G. E., Trost, M. R., & Sadalla, E. K. (1993). Integrating evolutionary and social exchange perspectives on relationships: effects of gender, self-appraisal, and involvement level on mate selection criteria. *Journal of Personality and Social Psychology*, *64*, 951–969.

Kenrick, D. T., Gutierres, S. E., & Goldberg, L. L. (1989). Influence of popular erotica on judgments of strangers and mates. *Journal of Experimental Social Psychology*, *25*, 159–167.

Kenrick, D. T., Sundie, J. M., Nicastle, L. D., & Stone, G. O. (2001). Can one ever be too wealthy or too chaste? Searching for nonlinearities in mate judgment. *Journal of Personality and Social Psychology*, *80*, 462–471.

Kiecolt-Glaser, J. K., & Newton, T. L. (2001). Marriage and health: his and hers. *Psychological Bulletin*, *127*, 427–503.

Kiecolt-Glaser, J. K., Bane, C., Glaser, R., & Malarkey, W. B. (2003). Love, marriage and divorce: newlyweds' stress hormones foreshadow relationship changes. *Journal of Consulting and Clinical Psychology*, *71*, 176–188.

Kiecolt-Glaser, J. K., Malarkey, W. B., Cacioppo, J. T., & Glaser, R. (1994). Stressful personal relationships: immune and endocrine function. In R. Glaser & J. K. Kiecolt-Glaser (Eds), *Handbook of Human Stress and Immunity* (pp. 321–339). San Diego, CA: Academic Press.

Kilchevsky, A., Vardi, Y., Lowenstein, L., & Gruenwald, I. (2012). Is the female G-spot truly a distinct anatomic entity? *Journal of Sexual Medicine, 9,* 719–726.

Kinsey, A. C., Pomeroy, W. B., & Martin, C. E. (1948). *Sexual Behavior in the Human Male.* Oxford: Saunders.

Kinsey, A. C., Pomeroy, W. B., Martin, C. E., & Gebhard, P. H. (1953). *Sexual Behavior in the Human Female.* Oxford: Saunders.

Kirkpatrick, L. A., & Davis, K. E. (1994). Attachment style, gender and relationship stability. *Journal of Personality and Social Psychology, 66,* 502–512.

Kirkpatrick, L. A., & Hazan, C. (1994). Attachment styles and close relationships. *Personal Relationships, 1,* 123–142.

Kitson, G. C., Babri, K. B., & Roach, M. J. (1985). Who divorces and why: a review. *Journal of Family Issues, 6,* 255–293.

Klaus, M., & Kennell, J. (1976). Parent-to-infant attachment. In D. Hull (Ed.), *Recent Advances in Pediatrics* (pp. 129–152). New York, NY: Churchill Livingstone.

Klinetob, N. A., & Smith, D. A. (1996). Demand-withdraw communication in marital interaction: tests of interpersonal contingency and gender role hypotheses. *Journal of Marriage and the Family, 58,* 945–957.

Klusmann, D. (2002). Sexual motivation and the duration of partnership. *Archives of Sexual Behavior, 31,* 275–287.

Kluwer, E. S., & Johnson, M. D. (2007). Conflict frequency and relationship quality across the transition to parenthood. *Journal of Marriage and the Family, 69,* 1089–1106.

Kobak, R. R., & Hazan, C. (1991). Attachment in marriage. *Journal of Personality and Social Psychology, 60,* 861–869.

Konner, M. (2010). *The Evolution of Childhood: Relationships, Emotion, Mind.* Cambridge, MA: Harvard University Press.

Kosfeld, M., Heinrichs, M., Zak, P. J., Fischbacher, U., & Fehr, E. (2005). Oxytocin increases trust in humans. *Nature, 435,* 673–676.

Kross, E., Berman, M. G., Mischel, W., Smith, E. E., & Wager, T. D. (2011). Social rejection shares somatosensory representations with physical pain. *Proceedings of the National Academy of Sciences of the USA, 108,* 6270–6275.

Kulu, H., & Boyle, P. J. (2010). Premarital cohabitation and divorce: support for the "trial marriage" theory? *Demographic Research, 23,* 879–904.

Kurdek, L. A. (1993). Predicting marital dissolution – a 5-year prospective longitudinal-study of newlywed couples. *Journal of Personality and Social Psychology, 64,* 221–242.

Kurdek, L. A. (2002). Predicting the timing of separation and marital satisfaction: an eight-year prospective longitudinal study. *Journal of Marriage and the Family, 64,* 163–179.

Kurosu, S. (2011). Divorce in early modern rural Japan: household and individual life course in northeastern villages. *Journal of Family History, 36,* 118–141.

Kurz, D. (1997). Physical assaults by male partners: a major social problem. In M. R. Walsh (Ed.), *Women, Men, & Gender* (pp. 222–231). New Haven, CT: Yale University Press.

Kurzban, R., & Weeden, J. (2007). Do advertised preferences predict the behavior of speed daters? *Personal Relationships, 14,* 623–632.

Lackenbauer, S. D., Campbell, L., Rubin, H., Fletcher, G. J. O., & Troister, T. (2010). Seeing clearly through rose-colored glasses: the unique and combined benefits of being perceived accurately and in a positively biased manner by romantic partners. *Personal Relationships, 17,* 475–493.

LaFreniere, P. J., & Sroufe, L. A. (1985). Profiles of peer competence in the preschool: interrelations between measures, influence of social ecology, and relation to attachment history. *Developmental Psychology, 21,* 56–69.

Lalueza-Fox, C., Rosas, A., Estalrrich, A., Gigli, E., Campos, P. F., Garcia-Tabernero, A. *et al.*

(2010). Genetic evidence for patrilocal mating behavior among neandertal groups. *Proceedings of the National Academy of Sciences of the USA, 108*, 250–253.

Langhinrichsen-Rohling, J. (2010). Controversies involving gender and intimate partner violence in the United States. *Sex Roles, 62*, 179–193.

Langlois, J. H., Kalakanis, L., Rubenstein, A. J., Larson, A., Hallam, M., & Smoot, M. (2000). Maxims or myths of beauty? A meta-analytic and theoretical review. *Psychological Bulletin, 126*, 390–423.

Långström, N., Rahman, Q., Carlström, E., & Lichtenstein, P. (2010). Genetic and environmental effects on same-sex sexual behavior: a population study of twins in Sweden. *Archives of Sexual Behavior, 39*, 75–80.

Larson, J. H., Anderson, S. M., Holman, T. B., & Niemann, B. K. (1998). A longitudinal study of the effects of premarital communication, relationship stability, and self-esteem on sexual satisfaction in the first year of marriage. *Journal of Sex and Marital Therapy, 24*, 193–206.

Latane, B., & Glass, D. C. (1968). Social and nonsocial attraction in rats. *Journal of Personality and Social Psychology, 9*, 142–146.

Laurenceau, J., Feldman Barrett, L., & Pietromonaco, P. R. (1998). Intimacy as an interpersonal process: the importance of self-disclosure, partner disclosure, and perceived partner responsiveness in interpersonal exchanges. *Journal of Personality and Social Psychology, 74*, 1238–1251.

Laurenceau, J., Troy, A. B., & Carver, C. S. (2005). Two distinct emotional experiences in romantic relationships: effects of perceptions regarding approach of intimacy and avoidance of conflict. *Personality and Social Psychology Bulletin, 31*, 1123–1133.

Law-Smith, M. J., Deady, D. K., Moore, F. R., Jones, B. C., Cornwell, R. E., Stirrat, M. *et al.* (2012). Maternal tendencies in women are associated with estrogen levels and facial femininity. *Hormones and Behavior, 61*, 12–16.

Law Smith, M. J., Perrett, D. I., Jones, B. C., Cornwell, R. E., Moore, F. R., Feinberg, D. R. *et al.* (2006). Facial appearance is a cue to oestrogen levels in women. *Proceedings of the Royal Society B: Biological Sciences, 273*, 135–140.

Lawler, K. A., Younger, J. W., Piferi, R. L., Billington, E., Jobe, R., Edmonson, K., & Jones, W. H. (2003). A change of heart: cardiovascular correlates of forgiveness in response to interpersonal conflict. *Journal of Behavioral Medicine, 26*, 373–393.

Lawrence, E., & Bradbury, T. N. (2001). Physical aggression and marital dysfunction: a longitudinal analysis. *Journal of Family Psychology, 15*, 135–154.

Lawrence, E., Bunde, M., Barry, R., Brock, R., Sullivan, K., Pasch, L. *et al.* (2008). Partner support and marital satisfaction: support amount, adequacy, provision, and solicitation. *Personal Relationships, 15*, 445–463.

Lawrence, E., Rothman, A. D., Cobb, R. J., Rothman, M. T., & Bradbury, T. N. (2008). Marital satisfaction across the transition to parenthood. *Journal of Family Psychology, 22*, 41–50.

Le, B., & Agnew, C. R. (2003). Commitment and its theorized determinants: a meta-analysis of the investment model. *Personal Relationships, 10*, 37–57.

Le, B., Dove, N. L., Agnew, C. R., Korn, M. S., & Mutso, A. A. (2010). Predicting nonmarital romantic relationship dissolution: a meta-analytic synthesis. *Personal Relationships, 17*, 377–390.

Leary, M. R. (2001). The self we know, the self we show, self-esteem, self-presentation, and the maintenance of interpersonal relationships. In G. J. O. Fletcher & M. S. Clark (Eds), *Blackwell Handbook of Social Psychology: Interpersonal Processes* (pp. 457–477). Oxford: Blackwell.

Leary, M. R, & Baumeister, R. F. (2000). The nature and function of self-esteem: sociometer theory. In M. P. Zanna (Ed.), *Advances in Experimental Social Psychology* (Vol. 32., pp. 1–62). San Diego, CA: Academic Press.

Leary, M. R., Tambor, E. S., Terdal, S. K., & Downs, D. L. (1995). Self-esteem as an interpersonal monitor: the sociometer hypothesis. *Journal of Personality and Social Psychology*, *68*, 518–530.

Lee, G. R., & DeMaris, A. (2007). Widowhood, gender and depression: a longitudinal analysis. *Research on Aging*, *29*, 56–72.

Lee, J. A. (1977). A typology of styles of loving. *Personality and Social Psychology Bulletin*, *3*, 173–182.

Lee, R. B. (1978). Politics, sexual and nonsexual in an egalitarian society. *Social Science Information*, *17*, 871–895.

Lempers, J., Clark-Lempers, D., & Simons, R. (1989). Economic hardship, parenting, and distress in adolescence. *Child Development*, *60*, 25–49.

Leonard, K. E., & Roberts, L. J. (1998). The effects of alcohol on the marital interactions of aggressive and nonaggressive husbands and their wives. *Journal of Abnormal Psychology*, *107*, 602–615.

Leung, B., & Forbes, M. R. (1996). Fluctuating asymmetry in relation to stress and fitness: effects of trait type as revealed by meta-analysis. *Ecoscience*, *3*, 400–413.

LeVay, S. (1991). A difference in hypothalamic structure between heterosexual and homosexual men. *Science*, *253*, 1034–1037.

LeVay, S. (2009). *Human Sexuality* (3rd ed.) Sunderland, MA: Sinauer Associates.

Levin, R. J. (2012). The human female orgasm: a critical evaluation of its proposed reproductive functions. *Sexual and Relationship Therapy*, 1–14. Advance online publication. doi: 10.1080/14681994.2011.649692.

Levine, R., Sato, S., Hashimoto, T., & Verma, J. (1995). Love and marriage in eleven cultures. *Journal of Cross-Cultural Psychology*, *26*, 554–571.

Levinson, D. (1989). *Family Violence in Cross-Cultural Perspective*. Newbury Park, CA: Sage.

Lewandowski Jr., G. W., Aron, A., Bassis, S., & Kunak, J. (2006). Losing a self-expanding relationship: implications for the self-concept. *Personal Relationships*, *13*, 317–331.

Lewin, K. (1951). *Field Theory in Social Science*. New York, NY: Harper & Row.

Lewis, M., & Feiring, C. (1989). Infant, mother, and mother-infant interaction behavior and subsequent attachment. *Child Development*, *60*, 831–837.

Li, N. P., Bailey, J. M., Kenrick, D. T., & Linsenmeiser, J. A. W. (2002). The necessities and luxuries of mate preferences: testing the tradeoffs. *Journal of Personality and Social Psychology*, *82*, 947–955.

Lindau, S. T., Schumm, L. P., Laumann, E. O., Levinson, W., O'Muircheartaigh, C. A., & Waite, L. J. (2007). A study of sexuality and health among older adults in the United States. *The New England Journal of Medicine*, *357*, 762–775.

Lippa, R. A. (2000). Gender-related traits in gay men, lesbian women, and heterosexual men and women: the virtual identity of homosexual-heterosexual diagnosticity and gender diagnosticity. *Journal of Personality*, *68*, 899–926.

Lippa, R. A. (2007). The preferred traits of mates in a cross-national study of heterosexual and homosexual men and women: an examination of biological and cultural influences. *Archives of Sexual Behavior*, *36*, 193–-208.

Lippa, R. A., & Arad, S. (1997). The structure of sexual orientation and its relation to masculinity, femininity, and gender diagnosticity: different for men and women. *Sex Roles*, *37*, 187–208.

Litzinger, S., & Gordon, K. C. (2005). Exploring relationships among communication, sexual satisfaction, and marital satisfaction. *Journal of Sex and Marital Therapy*, *31*, 409–424.

Long, E. C. J., Cate, R. M., Fehsenfeld, D. A., & Williams, K. M. (1996). A longitudinal assessment of a measure of premarital sexual conflict. *Family Relations*, *45*, 302–308.

Loving, T. J., Crockett, E. E., & Paxson, A. A. (2009). Passionate love and relationship thinkers: Experimental evidence for acute cortisol elevations in women. *Psychoneuroendocrinology*, *34*, 939–946.

Lucas, R. E. (2005). Time does not heal all wounds: a longitudinal study of reaction and adaptation to divorce. *Psychological Science, 16*, 945–950.

Luchies, L. B., Finkel, E. J., & Fitzsimons, G. M. (2011). The effects of self-regulatory strength, content, and strategies on close relationships. *Journal of Personality, 79*, 1251–1279.

Luo, S., Chen, H., Yue, G., Zhang, G., Zhaoyang, R., & Xu, D. (2008). Predicting marital satisfaction from self, partner, and couple characteristics: is it me, you, or us? *Journal of Personality, 76*, 1231–1266.

Lydon, J. E., Meana, M., Sepinwall, D., Richards, N., & Mayman, S. (1999). The commitment calibration hypothesis: when do people devalue attractive alternatives? *Personality and Social Psychology Bulletin, 25*, 152–161.

Mackey, W. C., & Immerman, R. S. (2000). Sexually transmitted diseases, pair bonding, fathering, and alliance formation: disease avoidance behaviors as a proposed element in human evolution. *Psychology of Men and Masculinity, 1*, 49–61.

Magdol, L., Moffitt, T. E., Caspi, P. A., Newman, D. L., Fagan, J., & Silva, P. A. (1997). Gender differences in partner violence in a birth cohort of 21-year-olds: bridging the gap between clinical and epidemiological approaches. *Journal of Consulting and Clinical Psychology, 65*, 68–78.

Main, M. (1981). Avoidance in the service of attachment: a working paper. In K. Immelmann, G. Barlow, M. Main, & L. Petrinovich (Eds), *Behavioral Development: the Bielefeld Interdisciplinary Project* (pp. 651–693). New York, NY: Cambridge University Press.

Main, M., & Solomon, J. (1986). Discovery of an insecure-disorganized/disoriented attachment pattern: procedures, findings, and implications for the classification of behavior. In T. B. Brazelton & M. Yogman (Eds), *Affective Development in Infancy* (pp. 95–124). Norwood, NJ: Ablex.

Maisel, N. C., & Gable, S. L. (2009). The paradox of received social support: the importance of responsiveness. *Psychological Science, 20*, 928–932.

Maner, J. K., Gailliot, M. T., & Miller, S. L. (2009). The implicit cognition of relationship maintenance: inattention to attractive alternatives. *Journal of Experimental Social Psychology, 45*, 174–179.

Mantegazza, P. (1894). *The Physiology of Love.* New York, NY: The Cleveland Publishing Company.

Marazziti, D., & Canale, D. (2004). Hormonal changes when falling in love. *Psychoneuroendocrinology, 29*, 931–936.

Marcus, D. K., & Miller, R. S. (2003). Sex differences in judgments of physical attractiveness: a social relations analysis. *Personality and Social Psychology Bulletin, 29*, 325–35.

Markman, H., Stanley, S., & Blumberg, S. L. (1994). *Fighting for Your Marriage.* San Francisco, CA: Jossey-Bass.

Marsiglio, W., & Donnelly, D. (1991). Sexual relations in later life: a national study of married persons. *Journals of Gerontology, 46*, S338–S344.

Martin, S. L., Tsui, A. O., Maitra, K., & Marinshaw, R. (1999). Domestic violence in northern India. *American Journal of Epidemiology, 150*, 417–426.

Mastekaasa, A. (1994). Psychological well-being and marital dissolution: selection effects? *Journal of Family Issues, 15*, 208–228.

Masumura, W. T. (1979). Wife abuse and other forms of aggression. *Victimology: an International Journal, 4*, 46–59.

Matas, L., Arend, R., & Sroufe, L. A. (1978). Continuity in adaptation in the second year: the relationship between quality of attachment and later competence. *Child Development, 49*, 547–556.

Mazur, A., & Michalek, J. (1998). Marriage, divorce, and male testosterone. *Social Forces, 77*, 315–330.

McGue, M., & Lykken, D. T. (1992). Genetic influence on risk of divorce. *Psychological Science, 3*, 368–373.

McLean, C. Y., Reno, P. L., Pollen, A. A., Bassan, A. I., Capellini, T. D., Guenther, C. *et al.*

(2011). Human-specific loss of regulatory DNA and the evolution of human-specific traits. *Nature, 471,* 216–219.

McLoyd, V. (1990). The declining fortunes of black children: psychological distress, parenting, and socioemotional development in the context of economic hardship. *Child Development, 61,* 311–346.

McNulty, J. K. (2008). Tendencies to forgive in marriage: putting the benefits into context. *Journal of Family Psychology, 22,* 171–175.

McNulty, J. K. (2010). When positive processes hurt relationships. *Current Directions in Psychological Science, 19,* 167–171.

McNulty, J. K., & Fisher, T. D. (2008). Gender differences in response to sexual expectancies and changes in sexual frequency: a short-term longitudinal study of sexual satisfaction in newly married couples. *Archives of Sexual Behavior, 37,* 229–240.

McNulty, J. K. & Karney, B. R. (2004). Positive expectations in the early years of marriage: Should couples expect the best or brace for the worst? *Journal of Personality and Social Psychology, 86,* 729–743.

McNulty, J. K. & Russell, V. M. (2010). When "negative" behaviors are positive: a contextual analysis of the long-term effects of interpersonal communication. *Journal of Personality and Social Psychology, 98,* 587–604.

McNulty, J. K., O'Mara, E. M., & Karney, B. R. (2008). Benevolent cognitions as a strategy of relationship maintenance: "Don't sweat the small stuff". . . . But it is not all small stuff. *Journal of Personality and Social Psychology, 94,* 631–646.

Meyer-Bahlburg, H. F. L. (2001). Gender and sexuality in classic congenital adrenal hyperplasia. *Endocrinology and Metabolism clinics of North America, 30,* 155–171.

Meyers, S. A., & Berscheid, E. (1997). The language of love: the difference a preposition makes. *Personality and Social Psychology Bulletin, 23,* 347–362.

Michael, R. T., Gagnon, J. H., Laumann, E. O., & Kolata, G. (1994). *Sex in America: A definitive survey.* Boston, MA: Little & Brown.

Mikulincer, M. (1998). Attachment working models and the sense of trust: an exploration of interaction goals and affect regulation. *Journal of Personality and Social Psychology, 74,* 1209–1224.

Mikulincer, M., Birnbaum, G., Woddis, D., & Nachmias, G. (2000). Stress and accessibility of proximity-related thoughts: exploring the normative and intraindividual components of attachment theory. *Journal of Personality and Social Psychology, 78,* 509–523.

Mikulincer, M., Gillath, O., & Shaver, P. R. (2002). Activation of the attachment system in adulthood: Threat-related primes increase the accessibility of mental representations of attachment figures. *Journal of Personality and Social Psychology, 83,* 881–895.

Mikulincer, M., Gillath, O., Halevy, V., Avihou, N., Avidan, S., & Eshkoli, N. (2001). Attachment theory and reactions to others' needs: evidence that activation of the sense of attachment security promotes empathic responses. *Journal of Personality and Social Psychology, 81,* 1205–1224.

Mikulincer, M., & Nachshon, O. (1991). Attachment styles and patterns of self-disclosure. *Journal of Personality and Social Psychology, 61,* 321–331.

Mikulincer, M., & Shaver, P. R. (2003). The attachment behavioral system in adulthood: Activation, psychodynamics, and interpersonal processes. In M. P. Zanna (Ed.), *Advances in Experimental Social Psychology* (Vol. 35, pp. 53–152). San Diego, CA: Academic Press.

Mikulincer, M., & Shaver, P. R. (2007). *Attachment in adulthood: Structure, dynamics, and change.* New York, NY: Guilford Press.

Miller, G. E., & Chen, E. (2007). Unfavorable socioeconomic conditions in early life presage expression of proinflammatory phenotype in adolescence. *Psychosomatic Medicine, 69,* 402–409.

Miller, G. E., Chen, E., & Parker, J. K. (2011). Psychological stress in childhood and susceptibility to the chronic diseases of aging:

moving toward a model of behavioral and biological mechanisms. *Psychological Bulletin, 137*, 959–997.

Miller, G. F. (1998). How mate choice shaped human nature: a review of sexual selection and human evolution. In C. Crawford & D. L. Krebs (Eds), *Handbook of Evolutionary Psychology: Ideas, Issues and Applications* (pp. 87–129). Mahwah, NJ: Lawrence Erlbaum.

Miller, G. F. (2000). *The Mating Mind: How Sexual Choice Shaped the Evolution of Human Nature.* New York, NY: Doubleday.

Miller, G. F., Tybur, J. M., & Jordan, B. D. (2007). Ovulatory cycle shifts on earnings by lap dancers: economic evidence for human estrus? *Evolution and Human Behavior, 28*, 375–381.

Miller, L. C., & Fishkin, S. A. (1997). On the dynamics of human bonding and reproductive success: seeking windows on the adapted-for human-environment interface. In J. A. Simpson & D. T. Kenrick (Eds), *Evolutionary Social Psychology* (pp. 197–235). Mahwah, NJ: Lawrence Erlbaum.

Miller, R. S. (1997). Inattentive and contented: relationship commitment and attention to alternatives. *Journal of Personality and Social Psychology, 73*, 758–766.

Miller, S. L., & Maner, J. K. (2010). Evolution and relationship maintenance: fertility cues lead committed men to devalue relationship alternatives. *Journal of Experimental Social Psychology, 46*, 1081–1084.

Moffitt, T. E., Caspi, A., Belsky, J., & Silva, P. A. (1992). Childhood experience and the onset of menarche: a test of a sociobiological model. *Child Development, 63*, 47–58.

Moller, A. P. (1997). Developmental stability and fitness: a review. *American Naturalist, 149*, 916–942.

Moller, A. P., & Swaddle, J. P. (1997). *Asymmetry, Developmental Stability and Evolution.* Oxford: Oxford University Press.

Moller, A. P., & Thornhill, R. (1998). Bilateral symmetry and sexual selection: a meta-analysis. *The American Naturalist, 151*, 174–192.

Montoya, R. M., Horton, R. S., & Kirchner, J. (2008). Is actual similarity necessary for attraction? A meta-analysis of actual and perceived similarity. *Journal of Social and Personal Relationships, 25*, 889–922.

Moore, D. E., & Cates, W. (1990). Sexually transmitted diseases and infertility. In K. K. Holmes, P. A. March, P. F. Sparling, & P. J. Wiesner (Eds), *Sexually Transmitted Diseases* (2nd ed., pp. 19–29). New York, NY: McGraw-Hill.

Moriceau, S., & Sullivan, R. M. (2005). Neurobiology of infant attachment. *Developmental Psychobiology, 47*, 230–242.

Moss, C. (2000). *Elephant Memories: Thirteen Years in the Life of an Elephant Family.* Chicago, IL: University of Chicago Press.

Munsch, C. L. (2012). The science of two-timing: the state of infidelity research. *Sociology Compass, 6*, 46–59.

Murphy, M. R., Seckl, J. R., Burton, S., Checkley, S. A., & Lightman, S. L. (1987). Changes in oxytocin and vasopressin secretion during sexual activity in men. *The Journal of Clinical Endocrinology and Metabolism, 65*, 738–741.

Murphy, S. (1992). *A Delicate Dance: Sexuality, Celibacy, and Relationships among Catholic Clergy and Religious.* New York, NY: Crossroad.

Murray, S. L. (2001). Seeking a sense of conviction: motivated cognition in close relationships. In G. J. O. Fletcher & M. S. Clark (Eds), *Blackwell Handbook of Social Psychology: Interpersonal Processes* (pp. 107–126). Malden, MA: Blackwell.

Murray, S. L., & Holmes, J. G. (1993). Seeing virtues in faults: negativity and the transformation of interpersonal narratives in close relationships. *Journal of Personality and Social Psychology, 65*, 707–722.

Murray, S. L., & Holmes, J. G. (2009). The architecture of interdependent mind: a motivation-management theory of mutual responsiveness. *Psychological Review, 116*, 908–928.

Murray, S. L., Bellavia, G. M., Rose, P., & Griffin, D. W. (2003a). Once hurt, twice hurtful: how perceived regard regulates daily marital interactions. *Journal of Personality and Social Psychology*, *84*, 126–147.

Murray, S. L., Derrick, J. L., Leder, S., & Holmes, J. G. (2008). Balancing connectedness and self-protection goals in close relationships: a levels-of-processing perspective on risk regulation. *Journal of Personality and Social Psychology*, *94*, 429–459.

Murray, S. L., Griffin, D. W., Rose, P., & Bellavia, G. M. (2003b). Calibrating the sociometer: the relational contingencies of self-esteem. *Journal of Personality and Social Psychology*, *85*, 63–84.

Murray, S. L., Holmes, J. G., Bellavia, G., Griffin, D. W., & Dolderman, D. (2002). Kindred spirits? The benefits of egocentrism in close relationships. *Journal of Personality and Social Psychology*, *82*, 563–581.

Murray, S. L., Holmes, J. G., & Collins, N. L. (2006). Optimizing assurance: the risk regulation system in relationships. *Psychological Bulletin*, *132*, 641–666.

Murray, S. L., Holmes, J. G., & Griffin, D. W. (1996a). The benefits of positive illusions: idealization and the construction of satisfaction in close relationships. *Journal of Personality and Social Psychology*, *70*, 79–98.

Murray, S. L., Holmes, J. G., & Griffin, D. W. (1996b). The self-fulfilling nature of positive illusions in romantic relationships: love is not blind, but prescient. *Journal of Personality and Social Psychology*, *71*, 1155–1180.

Murray, S. L., Holmes, J. G., & Griffin, D. W. (2000). Self-esteem and the quest for felt security: how perceived regard regulates attachment processes. *Journal of Personality and Social Psychology*, *78*, 478–498.

Muscarella, F. (2000). The evolution of homoerotic behavior in humans. *Journal of Homosexuality*, *40*, 51–77.

Myers, D. G. (1999). Close relationships and quality of life. In D. Kahneman, E. Diener, & N. Schwarz (Eds), *Well-being: the Foundations of Hedonic Psychology* (pp. 374–391). New York, NY: Russell Sage Foundation.

Myers, D. G., & Diener, E. (1995). Who is happy? *Psychological Science*, *6*, 10–19.

National Centre for Family & Marriage Research (2010). *Trends in Cohabitation: Twenty Years of Change, 1987–2008*. Retrieved August 6, 2011, from http://ncfmr.bgsu.edu/page78050.html.

Neff, L. A., & Karney, B. R. (2004). How does context affect intimate relationships? Linking external stress and cognitive processes within marriage. *Personality and Social Psychology Bulletin*, *30*, 134–148.

Neff, L. A., & Karney, B. R. (2005). Gender differences in social support: a question of skill or responsiveness? *Journal of Personality and Social Psychology*, *88*, 79–90.

Neff, L. A., & Karney, B. R. (2009). Stress and reactivity to daily relationship experiences: how stress hinders adaptive processes in marriage. *Journal of Personality and Social Psychology*, *71*, 1155–1188.

Nelson, E. E., & Panksepp, J. (1998). Brain substrates of infant-mother attachment: contributions of opioids, oxytocin and norepinephrine. *Neuroscience and Biobehavioral Reviews*, *22*, 437–452.

Neumann, I. D. (2008). Brain oxytocin mediates beneficial consequences of close social interactions: from maternal love and sex. In D. W. Pfaff, C. Kordon, P. Chanson, & Y. Christen (Eds), *Hormones and Social Behavior* (pp. 81–102). London: Springer.

New Zealand Ministry of Justice Report (1996). *A Summary of Crime Victims and Women's Safety Surveys*. Retrieved 8 August, 2010, from http://www.justice.govt.nz/publications/publications.

Newsom, J. T. (1999). Another side to caregiving: negative reactions to being helped. *Current Directions in Psychological Science*, *8*, 183–187.

Norris, M., & Pawlowski, W. (2010) (Eds), *Business of Consumer Book Publishing 2010*. Stamford, CT: Simba Information.

Nowick, K., Gernat, T., Almaas, E., & Stubbs, L. (2009). Differences in human and gene expression patterns define an evolving network of transcription factors in brain. *Proceedings of National Academy of Sciences, 106,* 22358–22363.

Obama, B. (2004). *Dreams from my Father.* New York, NY: Random House.

OECD Social Policy Division Family Database (2010). Retrieved July 10, 2011, from www.oecd.org/els/social/family/database.

OECD (2011) Based on data from chart "SF3.1.E: The increase in crude divorce rates from 1970 to 2008" from OECD (2011), OECD Family Database, OECD, Paris. Retrieved December 6, 2011, from www.oecd.org/social/family/database.

O'Leary, K. D., Malone, J., & Tyree, A. (1994). Physical aggression in early marriage: pre-relationship and relationship effects. *Journal of Consulting and Clinical Psychology, 62,* 594–602.

Oliver, M. B., & Hyde, J. S. (1996). Gender differences in sexuality: a meta-analysis. *Psychological Bulletin, 114,* 29–51.

Orbuch, T. L., Veroff, J., Hassan, H., & Horrocks, J. (2002). Who will divorce: a 14-year longitudinal study of black couples and white couples. *Journal of Social and Personal Relationships, 19,* 179–202.

Overall, N. C., & Sibley, C. G. (2008). When accommodation matters: situational dependency within daily interactions with romantic partners. *Journal of Experimental Social Psychology, 44,* 238–249.

Overall, N. C., & Sibley, C. G. (2009a). When rejection-sensitivity matters: regulating dependence within daily interactions with family and friends. *Personality and Social Psychology Bulletin, 35,* 1057–1070.

Overall, N. C., & Sibley, C. G. (2009b). Attachment and dependence regulation within daily interactions with romantic partners. *Personal Relationships, 16,* 239–261.

Overall, N. C., Fletcher, G. J. O., & Friesen, M. D. (2003). Mapping the intimate relationship mind: comparisons between three models of attachment representations. *Personality and Social Psychology Bulletin, 29,* 1479–1493.

Overall, N. C., Fletcher, G. J. O., & Kenny, D. A. (2012). When bias and insecurity promote accuracy: mean-level bias and tracking accuracy in couples' conflict discussions. *Personality and Social Psychology Bulletin, 38,* 642–655.

Overall, N. C., Fletcher, G. J. O., & Simpson, J. A. (2006). Regulation processes in intimate relationships: the role of ideal standards. *Journal of Personality and Social Psychology, 91,* 662–685.

Overall, N. C., Fletcher, G. J. O., Simpson, J. A., & Sibley, C. G. (2009). Regulating partners in intimate relationships: the costs and benefits of different communication strategies. *Journal of Personality and Social Psychology, 96,* 620–639.

Overall, N. C., Sibley, C. G., & Travaglia, L. K. (2010). Loyal but ignored: the benefits and costs of constructive communication behavior. *Personal Relationships, 17,* 127–148.

Palombit, R. (1994). Dynamic pair bonds in hylobatids: implications regarding monogamous social systems. *Behavior, 128,* 65–101.

Pasch, L., & Bradbury, T. N. (1998). Social support, conflict and the development of marital dysfunction. *Journal of Consulting and Clinical Psychology, 66,* 219–230.

Pasch, L., Bradbury, T. N., & Davila, J. (1997). Gender, negative affectivity, and observed social support behavior in marital interaction. *Personal Relationships, 4,* 361–378.

Pasch, L., Bradbury, T. N., & Sullivan, K. T. (1997). Social support in marriage: an analysis of intraindividual and interpersonal components. In G. R. Pierce, B. Lakey, & I. G. Sarason (Eds), *Sourcebook of Social Support and Personality* (pp. 229–256). New York, NY: Plenum Press.

Pawlowski, B., & Koziel, S. (2002). The impact of traits offered in personal advertisements on response rates. *Evolution and Human Behavior, 23,* 139–149.

Penton-Voak, I. S., & Chen, J. Y. (2004). High salivary testosterone is linked to masculine male facial appearance in humans. *Evolution and Human Behavior, 25,* 229–241.

Penton-Voak, I. S. & Perrett, D. I. (2000). Female preference for male faces changes cyclically: further evidence. *Evolution and Human Behavior, 21,* 39–48.

Penton-Voak, I. S., Perrett, D. I., Castles, D. L., Burt, D. M., Kobayashi, T., Murray, L. K., & Minamisawa, R. (1999). Menstrual cycle alters face preference. *Nature, 399,* 741–742.

Peplau, L. A. (2001). Rethinking women's sexual orientation: an interdisciplinary relationship-focused approach. *Personal Relationships, 8,* 1–19.

Peplau, L. A., & Garnets, L. D. (2000). A new paradigm for understanding women's sexuality and sexual orientation. *Journal of Social Issues, 56,* 329–350.

Peplau, L. A., Spalding, L. R., Conley, T. D., & Veniegas, R. C. (1999). The development of sexual orientation in women. *Annual Review of Sex Research, 10,* 70–99.

Perilloux, H. K., Webster, G. D., & Gaulin, S. J. C. (2010). Signals of genetic quality and maternal investment capacity: the dynamic effects of fluctuating asymmetry and waist-to-hip ratio on men's ratings of women's attractiveness. *Social Psychological and Personality Science, 1,* 34–42.

Petrie, M. (1994). Improved growth and survival of offspring of peacocks with more elaborate trains. *Nature, 371,* 598–599.

Petrie, M., & Halliday, T. (1994). Experimental and natural changes in the peacock's (Pavo cristatus) train can affect mating success. *Behavioral Ecology and Sociobiology, 35,* 213–217.

Pinker, S. (2002). *The Blank Slate: the Modern Denial of Human Nature.* London: Viking Penguin.

Pipitone, R. N., & Gallup, G. G. Jr. (2008). Women's voice attractiveness varies across the menstrual cycle. *Evolution and Human Behavior, 29,* 268–274.

Place, S. S., Todd, P. M., Penke, L., & Asendorpf, J. B. (2009). The ability to judge the romantic interest of others. *Psychological Science, 20,* 22–26.

Plant, E. A., Kunstman, J. W., & Maner, J. K. (2010). You do not only hurt the one you love: self-protective responses to attractive relationship alternatives. *Journal of Experimental Social Psychology, 46,* 474–477.

Polk, K. (1994). *When Men Kill: Scenarios of Masculine Violence.* Cambridge: Cambridge University Press.

Powers, S. I., Pietromonaco, P. R., Gunlicks, M., & Sayer, A. (2006). Dating couples' attachment styles and patterns of cortisol reactivity and recovery in response to a relationship conflict. *Journal of Personality and Social Psychology, 90,* 613–668.

Puts, D. A. (2005). Mating context and menstrual phase affect women's preference for male voice pitch. *Evolution and Human Behavior, 26,* 388–397.

Quinlan, R. J. (2003). Father absence, parental care, and female reproductive development. *Evolution and Human Behavior, 24,* 376–390.

Rapoport, Y. (2005). *Marriage, Money and Divorce in Medieval Islamic Society.* Cambridge: Cambridge University Press.

Regan, P. C. (1998). Minimum mate selection standards as a function of perceived mate value, relationship context, and gender. *Journal of Psychology and Human Sexuality, 10,* 53–73.

Regan, P. C. (1999). Hormonal correlates and causes of sexual desire: a review. *Canadian Journal of Human Sexuality, 8,* 1–16.

Reich, J. W., & Zautra, A. (1981). Life events and personal causation: some relationships with satisfaction and distress. *Journal of Personality and Social Psychology, 41,* 1002–1012.

Reis, H. T. (2007). Steps toward the ripening of relationship science. *Personal Relationships, 14,* 1–23.

Reis, H. T., & Downey, G. (1999). Social cognition in relationships: building essential bridges between two literatures. *Social Cognition, 17,* 97–117.

Reis, H. T., & Patrick, B. C. (1996). Attachment and intimacy: component processes. In E. T. Higgens & A. Kruglanski (Eds), *Social Psychology: Handbook of Basic Principles* (pp. 367–389). New York, NY: Guilford Press.

Reis, H. T., & Shaver, P. (1988). Intimacy as an interpersonal process. In S. Duck, D. F. Hay, S. E. Hobfoll, W. Ickes, & B. M. Montgomery (Eds), *Handbook of Personal Relationships: Theory, Research and Interventions.* (pp. 367–389). Oxford: John Wiley & Sons.

Reis, H. T., Clark, M. S., & Holmes, J. G. (2004). Perceived partner responsiveness as an organizing construct in the study of intimacy and closeness. In D. J. Mashek & A. P. Aron (Eds), *Handbook of Closeness and Intimacy.* (pp. 201–225). Mahwah, NJ: Lawrence Erlbaum.

Rempel, J. K., Ross, M., & Holmes, J. G. (2001). Trust and communicated attributions in close relationships. *Journal of Personality and Social Psychology, 81*, 57–64.

Rendall, M. S., Weden, M. S., Favreault, M. M., & Waldron, H. (2011). The protective effect of marriage for survival: A review and update. *Demography, 48*, 481–506.

Rhodes, G., Proffitt, F., Grady, J. M., & Sumich, A. (1998). Facial symmetry and the perception of beauty. *Psychonomic Bulletin and Review, 5*, 659–669.

Rholes, W. S., Simpson, J. A., & Blakely, B. S. (1995). Adult attachment styles and mothers' relationships with their young children. *Personal Relationships, 2*, 35–54.

Rholes, W. S., Simpson, J. A., Blakely, B. S., Lanigan, L., & Allen, E. A. (1997). Adult attachment styles, the desire to have children, and working models of parenthood. *Journal of Personality, 65*, 357–385.

Rice, G., Anderson, C., Risch, N., & Ebers, G. (1999). Male homosexuality: absence of linkage to microsatellite markers at Xq28. *Science, 284*, 665–667.

Ridley, M. (1999). *Genome: the Autobiography of a Species in 23 Chapters.* London: Harper Collins.

Rietveld, S., & van Beest, I. (2007). Roller-coaster asthma: when positive emotional stress interferes with dyspnea perception. *Behaviour Research and Therapy, 45*, 977–987.

Riggs, S. A. (2010). Childhood emotional abuse and the attachment system across the life cycle: what theory and research tell us. *Journal of Aggression, Maltreatment, and Trauma, 19*, 5–51.

Rikowski, A., & Grammer, K. (1999). Human body odour, symmetry, and attractiveness. *Proceedings of the Royal Society B, 266*, 869–874.

Rogers, A. (1999). *Barbie Culture.* Thousand Oaks, CA: Sage.

Rogers, R. G. (1995). Marriage, sex, and mortality. *Journal of Marriage and Family, 57*, 515–526.

Ronay, R., & von Hippel, W. (2010). The presence of an attractive woman elevates testosterone and physical risk taking in young men. *Social Psychological and Personality Science, 1*, 57–64.

Roney, J. R. (2003). Effects of visual exposure to the opposite sex: cognitive aspects of mate attraction in human males. *Personality and Social Psychology Bulletin, 29*, 393–404.

Roney, J. R., & Maestripieri, D. (2004). Relative digit lengths predict men's behavior and attractiveness during social interactions with women. *Human Nature, 15*, 271–282.

Rosenfeld, M. J., & Thomas, R. J. (2010). *Meeting Online: The Rise of the Internet as a Social Intermediary.* Unpublished manuscript, Department of Sociology, Stanford University, Stanford, CA.

Rowe, D. C. (2000). Environmental and genetic influences on pubertal development. In J. L. Rodgers, D. C. Rowe, & W. B. Miller (Eds), *Genetic Influences on Human Fertility and Sexuality* (pp. 147–168). Boston, MA: Kluwer.

Rubin, H., & Campbell, L. (2012). Day-to-day changes in intimacy predict heightened relationship passion, sexual occurrence, and sexual satisfaction: a dyadic diary analysis. *Social Psychological and Personality Science*, *3*, 224–231.

Rubin, Z. (1970). Measurement of romantic love. *Journal of Personality and Social Psychology*, *16*, 265–273.

Rubin, Z. (1973). *Liking and Loving: an Invitation to Social Psychology*. New York, NY: Holt, Rinehart & Winston.

Rusbult, C. E. (1983). A longitudinal test of the investment model: the development (and deterioration) of satisfaction and commitment in heterosexual involvements. *Journal of Personality and Social Psychology*, *45*, 101–117.

Rusbult, C. E., & Martz, J. M. (1995). Remaining in an abusive relationship – an investment model analysis of nonvoluntary dependence. *Personality and Social Psychology Bulletin*, *21*, 558–571.

Rusbult, C. E., Arriaga, X. B., & Agnew, C. R. (2001). Interdependence in close relationships. In G. J. O. Fletcher and M. S. Clark (Eds). *Blackwell Handbook of Social Psychology: Interpersonal Processes* (pp 359–387). Malden, MA: Blackwell.

Rusbult, C. E., Bissonnette, V. L., Arriaga, X. B., & Cox, C. L. (1998). Accommodation processes during the early years of marriage. In T. N. Bradbury (Ed.), *The Developmental Course of Marital Dysfunction* (pp. 74–113). New York, NY: Cambridge.

Rusbult, C. E., Johnson, D. J., & Morrow, G. D. (1986a). Impact of couple patterns of problem solving on distress and nondistress in dating relationships. *Journal of Personality and Social Psychology*, *50*, 744–753.

Rusbult, C. E., Johnson, D. J., & Morrow, G. D. (1986b). Determinants and consequences of exit, voice, loyalty, and neglect: responses to dissatisfaction in adult romantic involvements. *Human Relations*, *39*, 45–63.

Rusbult, C. E., Martz, J. M., & Agnew, C. R. (1998). The investment model scale: measuring commitment level, satisfaction level, quality of alternatives, and investment size. *Personal Relationships*, *5*, 357–391.

Rusbult, C. E., & Van Lange, P. A. M. (2003). Interdependence, interaction, and relationships. *Annual Review of Psychology*, *54*, 351–375.

Rusbult, C. E., Van Lange, P. A. M., Wildschut, T., Yovetich, N. A., & Verette, J. (2000). Perceived superiority in close relationships: why it exists and persists. *Journal of Personality and Social Psychology*, *79*, 521–545.

Rusbult, C. E., Verette, J., Whitney, G. A., Slovik, L. F., & Lipkus, I. (1991). Accommodation processes in close relationships: theory and preliminary empirical evidence. *Journal of Personality and Social Psychology*, *60*, 53–78.

Rusbult, C. E., Zembrodt, I. M., & Gunn, L. K. (1982). Exit, voice, loyalty, and neglect: responses to dissatisfaction in romantic involvements. *Journal of Personality and Social Psychology*, *43*, 1230–1242.

Russell, J. A. (1994). Is there universal recognition of emotion from facial expression? A review of the cross-cultural studies. *Psychological Bulletin*, *115*, 102–141.

Russell, J. A. (1995). Facial expressions of emotion – what lies beyond minimal universality. *Psychological Bulletin*, *118*, 379–391.

Ryff, C. D., Singer, B. H., Wing, E., & Love, G. D. (2001). Elective affinities and uninvited agonies: mapping emotion with significant others onto health. In C. D. Ryff & H. B. Singer (Eds), *Emotion, Social Relationships, and Health* (pp. 133–175). Oxford: Oxford University Press.

Saitzyk, A., Floyd, F., & Kroll, A. (1997). Sequential analysis of autonomy-interdependence and affiliation-disaffiliation in couples' social support interactions. *Personal Relationships*, *4*, 341–360.

Salzman, C. D., & Fusi, S. (2010). Emotion, cognition, and mental state representation in amygdala and prefrontal cortex. *Annual Review of Neuroscience*, *33*, 173–202.

Sanchez, R., Parkin, J. C., Chen, J., & Gray, P. B. (2009). Oxytocin, vasopressin and human social behavior. In P. T. Ellison & P. B. Gray (Eds), *Endocrinology of Social Relationships* (pp. 319–339). Cambridge, MA: Harvard University Press.

Sanders, S. A., & Reinisch, J. M. (1999). Would you say you "had sex" if . . . ? *Journal of the American Medical Association*, *281*, 275–277.

Sassler, S. (2010). Partnering across the life course: sex, relationships, and mate selection. *Journal of Marriage and Family*, *72*, 557–575.

Savini, T., Boesch, C., & Reichard, U. H. (2009). Varying ecological quality influences the probability of polyandry in white-handed gibbons (Hylobates lar) in Thailand. *Biotropica*, *41*, 503–513.

Sayre, K. M. (1995). *Plato's Literary Garden: How to Read a Platonic Dialogue*. Notre Dame, IN: University of Notre Dame Press.

Sbarra, D. A. (2006). Predicting the onset of emotional recovery following nonmarital relationship dissolution: survival analysis of sadness and anger. *Personality and Social Psychology Bulletin*, *32*, 298–312.

Sbarra, D. A., & Emery, R. E. (2005). Co-parenting conflict, nonacceptance, and depression among divorced adults: results from a 12-year follow-up study of child custody mediation using multiple imputation. *American Journal of Orthopsychiatry*, *75*, 73–75.

Sbarra, D. A., & Ferrer, E. (2006). The structure and process of emotional experience following nonmarital relationship dissolution: Dynamic factor analyses of love, anger, and sadness. *Emotion*, *6*, 224–238.

Sbarra, D. A., & Nietert, P. J. (2009). Divorce and death: forty years of the Charleston Heart Study. *Psychological Science*, *20*, 107–113.

Sbarra, D. A., Law, R. W., & Portley, R. M. (2011). Divorce and death: a meta-analysis and research agenda for clinical, social, and health psychology. *Perspectives on Psychological Science*, *6*, 454–474.

Scarbrough, P. S., & Johnston, V. S. (2005). Individual differences in women's facial preferences as a function of digit ratio and mental rotation ability. *Evolution and Human Behavior*, *26*, 509–526.

Schmitt, D. P. (2005). Sociosexuality from Argentina to Zimbabwe: a 48-nation study of sex, culture, and strategies of human mating. *Behavioral and Brain Sciences*, *28*, 247–311.

Schmitt, D. P., Alcalay, L., Allensworth, M., Allik, J., Ault, L., Austers, I. *et al.* (2003). Are men universally more dismissing than women? Gender differences in romantic attachment across 62 cultural regions. *Personal Relationships*, *10*, 309–333.

Schmitt, D. P., and 118 members of the International Sexuality Description Project. (2003). Universal sex differences in desire for sexual variety: tests from 52 nations, 6 continents, and 13 islands. *Journal of Personality and Social Psychology*, *85*, 85–104.

Scholmerich, A., Fracasso, M., Lamb, M., & Broberg, A. (1995). Interactional harmony at 7 and 10 months of age predicts security of attachment as measured by Q-sort ratings. *Social Development*, *34*, 62–74.

Schul, Y., & Vinokur, A. D. (2000). Projection in person perception among spouses as a function of the similarity in their shared experiences. *Personality and Social Psychology Bulletin*, *26*, 987–1001.

Schulz, K. F., Murphy, F. K., Patamasucon, P., & Meheus, A. Z. (1990). Congenital syphilis. In K. K. Holmes, P. A. March, P. F. Sparling, & P. J. Wiesner (Eds), *Sexually Transmitted Diseases* (2nd ed., pp. 821–842). New York, NY: McGraw-Hill.

Scott, S. J., Trent, K., & Shen, Y. (2001). Changing partners: toward a macrostructural-opportunity theory of marital dissolution. *Journal of Marriage and the Family*, *63*, 743–754.

Scutt, J. (1983). *Even in the Best of Homes.* Melbourne: Penguin.

Seal, D. W., Agostinelli, G., & Hannett, C. A. (1994). Extradyadic romantic involvement: moderating effects of sociosexuality and gender. *Sex Roles, 31,* 1–22.

Sear, R., & Gibson, M. A. (2009). Introduction to special issue on "Trade-offs in female life histories: integrating evolutionary frameworks". *American Journal of Human Biology, 21,* 417–420.

Sear, R., & Mace, R. (2008). Who keeps children alive? A review of the effects of kin on child survival. *Evolution and Human Behavior, 29,* 1–18.

Sear, R., Mace, R., & McGregor, I. A. (2000). Maternal grandmothers improve nutritional status and survival of children in rural Gambia. *Proceedings of the Royal Society of Biological Sciences, 267,* 1641–1647.

Seeman, T. E. (1996). Social ties and health: the benefits of social integration. *Annuals of Epidemiology, 6,* 442–451.

Seeman, T. E. (2001). How do others get under our skin? Social relationships and health. In C. D. Ryff & B. H. Singer (Eds), *Emotion, Social Relationships, and Health* (pp. 189–210). Oxford: Oxford University Press.

Segraves, K., & Segraves, R. T. (1991). Hypoactive sexual desire disorder: prevalence and comorbidity in 906 subjects. *Journal of Sex and Marital Therapy, 17,* 55–58.

Seligman, M. E. P. (1995). The effectiveness of psychotherapy: the Consumer Reports study. *American Psychologist, 50,* 965–974.

Shadish, W. R., & Baldwin, S. A. (2003). Meta-analysis of MFT interventions. *Journal of Marital and Family Therapy, 29,* 547–570.

Shadish, W. R., & Baldwin, S. A. (2005). Effects of behavioral martial therapy: a meta-analysis of randomized controlled trials. *Journal of Consulting and Clinical Psychology, 73,* 6–14.

Shadish, W. R., Montgomery, L. M., Wilson, P., Bright, I, & Okwumabua, T. (1993). Effects of family and marital psychotherapies: a meta-analysis. *Journal of Consulting and Clinical Psychology, 61,* 992–1002.

Shaver, P. R., Hazan, C., & Bradshaw, D. (1988). Love as attachment. In R. J. Sternberg & M. L. Bares (Eds), *The Psychology of Love.* (pp. 68–99). New Haven, CT: Yale University Press.

Short, R. V. (1984). Testes size, ovulation rate and breast cancer. In O. A. Ryder & M. L. Byrd (Eds), *One Medicine* (pp. 32–44). Berlin: Springer-Verlag.

Shostak, M. (1981). *Nisa: The Life and Words of a !Kung Woman.* London: Allen Lane.

Shultz, S., & Dunbar, R. I. M. (2010). Social bonds in birds are associated with brain size and contingent on the correlated evolution of life-history and increased parental investment. *Biological Journal of the Linnean Society, 100,* 111–123.

Sillars, A. L., & Vangelisti, A. L. (2006). Communication: basic properties and their relevance to relationship research. In A. L. Vangelisti & D. Perlman, *The Cambridge Handbook of Personal Relationships* (pp. 331–352). New York: Cambridge University Press.

Simmons, L. W., Firman, R. E. C., Rhodes, G., & Peters, M. (2004). Human sperm competition: testes size, sperm production and rates of extrapair copulation. *Animal Behavior, 68,* 297–302.

Simpson, J. A. (1990). Influence of attachment styles on romantic relationships. *Journal of Personality and Social Psychology, 59,* 971–980.

Simpson, J. A. (2007). Psychological foundations of trust. *Current Directions in Psychological Science, 16,* 264–268.

Simpson, J. A., & Belsky, J. (2008). Attachment theory within a modern evolutionary framework. In J. Cassidy & P. R. Shaver (Eds), *Handbook of Attachment: Theory, Research, and Clinical Applications* (2nd ed, pp. 131–157). New York, NY: Guilford Press.

Simpson, J. A., & Gangestad, S. W. (1991). Individual differences in sociosexuality:

evidence for convergent and discriminant validity. *Journal of Personality and Social Psychology*, 60, 870–883.

Simpson, J. A., & Gangestad, S. W. (1992). Sociosexuality and romantic partner choice. *Journal of Personality*, 60, 31–51.

Simpson, J. A., & Rholes, W. S. (1994). Stress and secure base relationships in adulthood. In K. Bartholomew, & D. Perlman (Eds), *Advances in Personal Relationships: Attachment Processes in Adulthood* (Vol. 5, pp. 181–204). London: Jessica Kingsley.

Simpson, J. A., & Rholes, W. S. (2002). Fearful-avoidance, disorganization, and multiple working models: some directions for future theory and research. *Attachment and Human Development*, 4, 223–229.

Simpson, J. A., Gangestad, S. W., & Biek, M. (1993). Personality and nonverbal social behavior: an ethological perspective of relationship initiation. *Journal of Experimental Social Psychology*, 29, 434–461.

Simpson, J. A., Gangestad, S. W., Christensen, P. N., & Leck, K. (1999). Fluctuating asymmetry, sociosexuality, and intrasexual competitive tactics. *Journal of Personality and Social Psychology*, 76, 159–172.

Simpson, J. A., Gangestad, S. W., & Lerma, M. (1990). Perception of physical attractiveness: mechanisms involved in the maintenance of romantic relationships. *Journal of Personality and Social Psychology*, 59, 1192–1201.

Simpson, J. A., Griskevicius, V., Kuo, S. I., Sung, S., & Collins, W. A. (2012). Evolution, stress, and sensitive periods: the influence of unpredictability in early versus late childhood on sex and risky behavior. *Developmental Psychology*, 48, 674–686.

Simpson, J. A., Ickes, W., & Blackstone, T. (1995). When the head protects the heart: empathic accuracy in dating relationships. *Journal of Personality and Social Psychology*, 69, 629–641.

Simpson, J. A., Ickes, W., & Grich, J. (1999). When accuracy hurts: reactions of anxious-ambivalent dating partners to a relationship-threatening situation. *Journal of Personality and Social Psychology*, 76, 754–769.

Simpson, J. A., Rholes, W. S., Campbell, L., & Wilson, C. L. (2003). Changes in attachment orientations across the transition to parenthood. *Journal of Experimental Social Psychology*, 39, 317–331.

Simpson, J. A., Rholes, W. S., Oriña, M., & Grich, J. (2002). Working models of attachment, support giving, and support seeking in a stressful situation. *Personality and Social Psychology Bulletin*, 28, 598–608.

Simpson, J. A., Rholes, W. S., & Nelligan, J. S. (1992). Support-seeking and support-giving within couples in an anxiety-provoking situation: the role of attachment styles. *Journal of Personality and Social Psychology*, 62, 434–446.

Simpson, J. A., Rholes, W. S., & Phillips, D. (1996). Conflict in close relationships: an attachment perspective. *Journal of Personality and Social Psychology*, 71, 899–914.

Simpson, J. A., Winterheld, H. A., Rholes, W. S., & Oriña, M. (2007). Working models of attachment and reactions to different forms of caregiving from romantic partners. *Journal of Personality and Social Psychology*, 93, 466–477.

Singh, D. (1993). Adaptive significance of female physical attractiveness: role of waist-to-hip ratio. *Journal of Personality and Social Psychology*, 65, 293–307.

Singh, D. (1994). Is thin really beautiful and good? Relationship between waist-to-hip ratio (WHR) and female attractiveness. *Personality and Individual Differences*, 16, 123–132.

Singh, D., & Bronstad, P. M. (2001). Female body odour is a potential cue to ovulation. *Proceedings of the Royal Society B*, 268, 797–801.

Singh, D., & Luis, S. (1995). Ethnic and gender consensus for the effect of waist-to-hip ratio on judgment of women's attractiveness. *Human Nature, 6*, 51–65.

Slater, A., Von der Schulenburg, C., Brown, E., Badenoch, M., Butterworth, G., Parsons, S., & Samuels, C. (1998). Newborn infants prefer attractive faces. *Infant Behavior and Development, 21*, 345–354.

Slob, A. K., & van der Werff Ten Bosch, J. J. (1991). Orgasm in nonhuman species. In P. Kohari & R. Patel (Eds), *Proceedings of the First International Conference on Orgasm* (pp. 135–149). Bombay: VRP.

Slotter, E. B., Gardner, W. L., & Finkel, E. J. (2010). Who am I without you? The influence of romantic breakup on the self-concept. *Personality and Social Psychology Bulletin, 36*, 147–160.

Smith, E. A., & Bird, R. L. B. (2000). Turtle hunting and tombstone opening: public generosity as costly signaling. *Evolution and Human Behavior, 21*, 245–261.

Snyder, D. K., Castellani, A. M., & Whisman, M. A. (2006). Current status and future directions in couple therapy. *Annual Review of Psychology, 57*, 317–344.

Solomon, J. & George, C. (Eds) (2011). *Disorganized Attachment and Caregiving*. New York, NY: Guilford.

Soons, J. P., & Kalmijn, M. (2009). Is marriage more than cohabitation? Well-being differences in 30 European countries. *Journal of Marriage and the Family, 71*, 1141–1157.

Spanier, G. B. (1976). Measuring dyadic adjustment: new scales for assessing the quality of marriage and similar dyads. *Journal of Marriage and the Family, 38*, 15–28.

Spielmann, S. S., MacDonald, G., & Wilson, A. E. (2009). On the rebound: focusing on someone new helps anxiously attached individuals let go of ex-partners. *Personality and Social Psychology Bulletin, 35*, 1382–1394.

Sprecher, S. (2002). Sexual satisfaction in premarital relationships: associations with satisfaction, love, commitment, and stability. *Journal of Sex Research, 39*, 190–196.

Sprecher, S., & Cate, R. M. (2004). Sexual satisfaction and sexual expression as predictors of relationship satisfaction and stability. In J. H. Harvey, A. Wenzel, & S. Sprecher (Eds), *The Handbook of Sexuality in Close Relationships* (pp. 235–256). Mahwah, NJ: Lawrence Erlbaum.

Sprecher, S. & Regan, P. C. (1988). Passionate and companionate love in courting and young married couples. *Sociological Inquiry, 68*, 163–185.

Sprecher, S., Christopher, F. S., & Cate, R. (2006). Sexuality in close relationships. In A. L. Vangelisti, & D. Perlman (Eds), *The Cambridge Handbook of Personal Relationships*. (pp. 463–482). New York, NY: Cambridge University Press.

Sprecher, S., Felmlee, D., Schmeeckles, M., & Shu, X. (2006). No breakup occurs on an island: social networks and relationship dissolution. In M. A. Fine & J. H. Harvey (Eds), *Handbook of Divorce and Relationship Dissolution* (pp. 457–478). Mahwah, NJ: Lawrence Erlbaum.

Sprecher, S., Sullivan, Q., & Hatfield, E. (1994). Mate selection preferences: gender differences examined in a national sample. *Journal of Personality and Social Psychology, 66*, 1074–1080.

Sroufe, L. A., & Waters, E. (1977a). Attachment as an organizational construct. *Child Development, 48*, 1184–1199.

Sroufe, L. A., & Waters, E. (1977b). Heart rate as a convergent measure in clinical and developmental research. *Merrill-Palmer Quarterly, 23*, 3–27.

Sroufe, L. A., Egeland, B., Carlson, E. A., & Collins, W. A. (2005). *The Development of the Person: The Minnesota Study of Risk and Adaptation from Birth to Adulthood*. New York, NY: Guilford Press.

Stafford, L., & Canary, D. J. (1991). Maintenance strategies and romantic relationship type, gender and relational characteristics. *Journal of Social and Personal Relationships, 8*, 217–242.

Steinmetz, S. K., & Lucca, J. S. (1988). Husband battering. In V. B. Van Hasselt, R. L. Morrison, A. S. Bellack, & M. S. Hersen (Eds), *Handbook of Family Violence* (pp. 233–246). New York, NY: Plenum.

Sternberg, R. J. (1986). A triangular theory of love. *Psychological Review, 93*, 119–135.

Sternberg, R. J. (1987). Liking versus loving: a comparative evaluation of theories. *Psychological Bulletin, 102*, 331–345.

Stillman, T. F. & Maner, J. K. (2009). A sharp eye for her SOI: perception and misperception of female sociosexuality at zero acquaintance. *Evolution and Human Behavior, 30*, 124–130.

Stith, S. M., Green, N. M., Smith, D. B., & Ward, D. B. (2008). Marital satisfaction and marital discord as risk markers for intimate partner violence: a meta-analytic review. *Journal of Family Violence, 23*, 149–160.

Stocker, C. M., Richmond, M. K., Low, S. M., Alexander, E. K., & Elias, N. M. (2003). Marital conflict and children's adjustment: parental hostility and children's interpretations as mediators. *Social Development, 12*, 149–161.

Storaasli, R. D., & Markman, H. J. (1990). Relationship problems in the early stages of marriage: a longitudinal investigation. *Journal of Family Psychology, 4*, 80–98.

Straus, M. A. (1979). Measuring intrafamily conflict and violence: the Conflict Tactics (CT) Scales. *National Council on Family Relations, 41*, 75–88.

Straus, M. A. (1997). Physical assaults by women partners: a major social problem. In M. R. Walsh (Ed.), *Women, Men, & Gender* (pp. 210–221). New Haven, CT: Yale University Press.

Straus, M. A. (1999). The controversy over domestic violence by women. In X. B. Arriaga & S. Oskamp (Eds), *Violence in Intimate Relationships* (pp. 17–44). Thousand Oaks, CA: Sage Publications.

Straus, M. A., & Gelles, R. J. (1988). Violence in American families: how much is there and why does it occur? In E. W. Nunnally, C. S. Chilman, & F. M. Cox (Eds), *Troubled Relationships* (pp. 141–162). Newbury Park, CA: Sage.

Straus, M. A., & Gelles, R. J. (Eds) (1990). *Physical Violence in American Families: Risk Factors and Adaptations to Violence in 8,145 Families.* New Brunswick, NJ: Transaction Publishers.

Straus, M. A., Gelles, R. J., & Steinmetz, S. K. (2006). *Behind Closed Doors: Violence in the American Family.* New Brunswick, NJ: Transaction Publishers.

Straus, M. A., Hamby, S. L., Boney-McCoy, S., & Sugarman, D. B. (1996). The revised conflict tactics scales (CTS2). *Journal of Family Issues, 17*, 283–316.

Straus, M. A., Kantor, G. K., & Moore, D. W. (1997). Change in cultural norms approving marital violence from 1968 to 1994. In G. K. Kantor & J. L. Jasinski (Eds), *Out of Darkness: Contemporary Perspectives on Family Violence* (pp. 3–16). Thousand Oaks, CA: Sage.

Stringer, C. (2012). *Lone Survivors: How We Came to be the Only Humans on Earth.* New York, NY: Times Books.

Stringer, C., & McKie, R. (1996). *African Exodus: the Origins of Modern Humanity.* New York, NY: Henry Holt.

Stroebe, W., & Stroebe, M. S. (1987). *Bereavement and Health: the Psychological and Physical Consequences of Partner Loss.* Cambridge: Cambridge University Press.

Stroebe, M., Schut, H., & Stroebe, W. (2007). Health outcomes of bereavement. *Lancet, 370*, 1960–1973.

Sullivan, K. T., Pasch, L. A., Johnson, M. S., & Bradbury, T. N. (2010). Social support, problem solving, and the longitudinal course of newlywed marriage. *Journal of Personality and Social Psychology, 98*, 631–644.

Surbey, M. (1990). Family composition, stress, and human menarche. In F. Bercovitch & T. Zeigler (Eds), *The Socioendocrinology of Primate Reproduction* (pp. 71–97). New York, NY: Liss.

Swaddle, J. P., & Reierson, G. W. (2002). Testosterone increases perceived dominance but not attractiveness of human males. *Proceedings of the Royal Society of London B, 269*, 2285–2289.

Swann, W. B., Jr., & Gill, M. J. (1997). Confidence and accuracy in person perception: do we know what we think we know about our relationship partners? *Journal of Personality and Social Psychology*, *73*, 747–757.

Swann, W. B., Jr., Bosson, J. K., & Pelham, B. W. (2002). Different partners, different selves: strategic verification of circumscribed identities. *Personality and Social Psychology Bulletin*, *28*, 1215–1228.

Sweeney, M. M., & Horowitz, A. V. (2001). Infidelity, initiation, and the emotional climate of divorce: are there implications for mental health? *Journal of Health and Social Behavior*, *42*, 295–309.

Swindle, R., Jr., Heller, K., Pescosolido, B., & Kikuzawa, S. (2000). Responses to nervous breakdowns in America over a 40-year period: mental health policy implications. *American Psychologist*, *55*, 740–749.

Sykes, B., & Irven, C. (2000). Surnames and the Y chromosome. *American Journal of Human Genetics*, *66*, 1417–1419.

Symons, D. (1979). *The Evolution of Human Sexuality*. New York, NY: Oxford University Press.

Szinovacz, M. E., & Egley, L. C. (1995). Comparing one-partner and couple data on sensitive marital behaviors: the case of marital violence. *Journal of Marriage and the Family*, *57*, 995–1010.

Tabak, B. A., McCullough, M. E., Szeto, A., Mendez, A. J., & McCabe, P. M. (2011). Oxytocin indexes relational distress following interpersonal harms in women. *Psychoneuroendocrinology*, *36*, 115–122.

Tashiro, T., Frazier, P., & Berman, M. (2006). Stress-related growth following divorce and relationship dissolution. In M. A. Fine & J. H. Harvey (Eds), *Handbook of Divorce and Relationship Dissolution* (pp. 361–384). Mahwah, NJ: Lawrence Erlbaum.

Tattersall, I., & Schwartz, J. H. (2009). Evolution of the genus *Homo*. *Annual Review of Earth and Planetary Sciences*, *37*, 67–92.

Taylor, S. E., Saphire-Bernstein, S., & Seeman, T. E. (2010). Are plasma oxytocin in women and plasma vasopressin in men biomarkers of distressed pair-bond relationships? *Psychological Science*, *21*, 3–7.

Tesser, A., & Beach, S. R. H. (1998). Life events, relationship quality, and depression: an investigation of judgment discontinuity in vivo. *Journal of Personality and Social Psychology*, *74*, 36–52.

Thibaut, J. W., & Kelley, H. H. (1959). *The Social Psychology of Groups*. New York, NY: Wiley.

Thomas, G., & Fletcher, G. J. O. (2003). Mind-reading accuracy in intimate relationships: assessing the roles of the relationship, the target, and the judge. *Journal of Personality and Social Psychology*, *85*, 1079–1094.

Thomas, G., Fletcher, G. J. O., & Lange, C. (1997). On-line empathic accuracy in marital interaction. *Journal of Personality and Social Psychology*, *72*, 839–850.

Thompson, M. E., Jones, J. H., Pusey, A. E., Brewer-Marsden, S., Goodall, J., Marsden, D. *et al.* (2007). Aging and fertility patterns in wild chimpanzees provide insights into the evolution of menopause. *Current Biology*, *17*, 2150–2156.

Thornhill, R., & Gangestad, S. W. (1994). Fluctuating asymmetry correlates with lifetime sex partner numbers and age at first sex in Homo sapiens. *Psychological Science*, *5*, 297–302.

Thornhill, R., & Gangestad, S. W. (1999). The scent of symmetry: a human sex pheromone that signals fitness? *Evolution and Human Behavior*, *20*, 175–201.

Thornhill, R., & Gangestad, S. W. (2006). Facial sexual dimorphism, developmental stability and susceptibility to disease in men and women. *Evolution and Human Behavior*, *27*, 131–144.

Thornhill, R., & Gangestad, S. W. (2008). *The Evolutionary Biology of Human Female Sexuality*. New York, NY: Oxford University Press.

Thornhill, R., & Moller, A. P. (1997). Developmental stability, disease and medicine. *Biological Reviews*, *72*, 497–548.

Thornhill, R., Gangestad, S. W., Miller, R., Scheyd, G., Knight, J., & Franklin, M.

(2003). MHC, symmetry, and body scent attractiveness in men and women. *Behavioral Ecology, 14,* 668–678.

Tiwari, G. (2008). Interplay of love, sex, and marriage in a polyandrous society in the high Himalayas of India. In W. R. Jankowiak (Ed.). *Intimacies.* (pp. 122–147). New York, NY: Columbia University Press.

Tjaden, P., & Thoennes, N. (2000). *Full Report of the Prevalence, Incidence, and Consequences of Violence Against Women Survey.* US Department of Justice, Office of Justice Programs.

Todd, P. M., Penke, L., Fasolo, B., & Lenton, A. P. (2007). Different cognitive processes underlie human mate choices and mate preferences. *Proceedings of the National Academy of Sciences of the USA, 104,* 15011–15016.

Tooby, J., & Cosmides, L. (1992). The psychological foundations of culture. In J. H. Barkow, L. Cosmides, & J. Tooby (Eds), *The Adapted Mind* (pp. 19–136). New York, NY: Oxford University Press.

Tooby, J., & Cosmides, L. (1997). Evolutionary psychology: a primer retrieved March 11, 2011, from http://www.psych.ucsb.edu/research/cep/primer.html.

Trivers, R. L. (1972). Parental investment and sexual selection. In B. Campbell (Ed.), *Sexual Selection and the Descent of Man 1871–1971* (pp. 136–179). Chicago, IL: Aldine.

Troisi, J. D., & Gabriel, S. (2011). Chicken soup really is good for the soul: "comfort food" fulfills the need to belong. *Psychological Science, 22,* 747–753.

Tuiten, A., Van Honk, J., Koppeschaar, H., Bernards, C., Thisjen, J., & Verbaten, R. (2006). Time course effects of testosterone administration on sexual arousal in women. *Archives of General Psychiatry, 57,* 149–154.

UK Crown Prosecution Service. (2007). Domestic violence monitoring snapshot: Cases finalised in December 2006. Retrieved 5 August, 2011, from http://www.cps.gov.uk/publications/prosecution/domestic/snapshot_2006_12.html

US Bureau of Justice Statistics. (2007). Homicide trends in the U.S. Retrieved October 24, 2011, retrieved from http://bjs.ojp.usdoj.gov/content/homicide/intimates.cfm

US Census Bureau (2007). American Community Survey 2007 Release Table S1101. Households and families. Retrieved October 25, 2011, from http://fact-finder.census.gov

Uchino, B. N., Cacioppo, J. T., & Kiecolt-Glaser, J. K. (1996). The relationship between social support and physiological processes: a review with emphasis on underlying mechanisms and implications for health. *Psychological Bulletin, 119,* 488–531.

van Anders, S. M., & Watson, N. V. (2006). Relationship status and testosterone in North American heterosexual and non-heterosexual men and women: cross-sectional and longitudinal data. *Psychoneuroendocrinology, 31,* 715–723.

van Anders, S. M., Hamilton, L. D., & Watson, N. V. (2007). Multiple partners are associated with higher testosterone in North American men and women. *Hormones and Behavior, 51,* 454–459.

van Lange, P. A. M., Rusbult, C. E., Drigotas, S. M., Arriaga, X. B., Witcher, B., & Cox, C. (1997). Willingness to sacrifice in close relationships. *Journal of Personality and Social Psychology, 72,* 1373–1395.

Vanderwater, E. A., & Landsford, J. E. (1998). Influences of family structure and parental conflict on children's well-being. *Family Relations, 47,* 323–330.

Verhofstadt, L. L., Buysse, A., Ickes, W., Davis, M., & Devoldre, I. (2008). Support provision in marriage: the role of emotional similarity and empathic accuracy. *Emotion, 8,* 792–802.

Verhofstadt, L. L., Buysse, A., Ickes, W., De Clercq, A., & Peene, O. J. (2005). Conflict and support interactions in marriage: an analysis of couples' interactive behavior and on-line cognition. *Personal Relationships, 12,* 23–42.

Vivian, D., & Langhinrichsen-Rohling, J. (1994). Are bi-directionally violent couples mutually victimized? In L. K. Hamberger

& C. Renzetti (Eds), *Domestic Partner Abuse* (pp. 23–52). New York, NY: Springer.

Vohs, K. D., & Baumeister, R. F. (2004). Sexual passion, intimacy, and gender. In D. J. Mashek & A. P. Aron (Eds), *Handbook of Closeness and Intimacy* (pp. 189–199). Mahwah, NJ: Lawrence Erlbaum.

Vohs, K. D., Finkenauer, C., & Baumeister, R. F. (2011). The sum of friends' and lovers' self-control scores predicts relationship quality. *Social Psychological and Personality Science, 2*, 138–145.

Vondra, J., Shaw, D., & Kevinides, M. (1995). Predicting infant attachment classification from multiple, contemporaneous measures of maternal care. *Infant Behavior and Development, 18*, 415–425.

Waage, J. K. (1979). Dual function of the damselfly penis: sperm removal and transfer. *Science, 203*, 916–918.

Waldinger, R. J., & Schulz, M. S. (2006). Linking hearts and minds in couple interactions: intentions, attributions and overriding sentiments. *Journal of Family Psychology, 20*, 494–504.

Walker, L. E. (1984). *The Battered Woman Syndrome*. New York, NY: Springer.

Walster, E. & Walster, G. W. (1978). *A New Look at Love*. Reading, MA: Addison-Wesley.

Walum, H., Lichtenstein, P., Neiderhiser, J. M., Reiss, D., Ganiban, J. M., Spotts, E. L. *et al.* (2012). Variation in the oxytocin receptor gene is associated with pair-bonding and social behavior. *Biological Psychiatry, 71*, 419–426.

Walum, H., Westberg, L., Henningsson, S., Neiderhiser, J. M., Reiss, D., Igl, W. *et al.* (2008). Genetic variation in the vasopressin receptor 1a gene (AVPR1A) associates with pair-bonding behavior in humans. *Proceedings of the National Academy of Sciences of the USA, 105*, 14153–14156.

Wan, C. K., Jaccard, J., & Ramey, S. L. (1996). The relationship between social support

and life satisfaction as a function of family structure. *Journal of Marriage and the Family, 58*, 502–512.

Wang, H., & Amato, P. R. (2000). Predictors of divorce adjustment: stressors, resources, and definitions. *Journal of Marriage and the Family, 62*, 655–668.

Waters, E., Wippman, J., & Sroufe, L. A. (1979). Attachment, positive affect, and competence in the peer group: two studies in construct validation. *Child Development, 50*, 821–829.

Wegner, D. M., & Bargh, J. A. (1998). Control and automaticity in social life. In D. T. Gilbert, S. T. Fiske, & G. Lindzey (Eds), *The Handbook of Social Psychology* (4th ed., Vol. 1, pp. 446–496). New York, NY: McGraw-Hill.

Weiner, B. (1985). An attributional theory of achievement motivation and emotion. *Psychological Review, 92*, 548–573.

Weiss, R. L., & Heyman, R. E. (1997). A clinical-research overview of couple's interactions. In W. K. Halford & H. J. Markman (Eds), *Clinical Handbook of Marriage and Couples Interventions* (pp. 13–41). Chichester: Wiley.

Weiss, R. L., & Summers, K. J. (1983). Marital interaction coding system-III. In E. Filsinger (Ed.), *Marriage and Family Assessment* (pp. 35–115). Beverly Hills, CA: Sage.

Weisse, C. S. (1992). Depression and immunocompetence: a review of the literature. *Psychological Bulletin, 111*, 475–489.

Weissman, M. M. (1987). Advances in psychiatric epidemiology: rates and risks for major depression. *American Journal of Public Health, 77*, 445–471.

Whisman, M. A., Dixon, A. E., & Johnson, B. (1997). Therapists' perspectives of couple problems and treatment issues in couple therapy. *Journal of Family Psychology, 11*, 361–366.

Whitam, F. L., Daskalos, C., Sobolewski, C. G., & Padilla, P. (1998). The emergence of lesbian sexuality and identity cross-culturally: Brazil, Peru, the Philippines, and the United States. *Archives of Sexual Behavior*, *27*, 31–56.

White, J. W., Smith, P. H., Koss, M. P., & Figueredo, A. J. (2000). Intimate partner aggression – What have we learned? Comment on Archer (2000). *Psychological Bulletin*, *126*, 690–696.

White, L. K., & Booth, A. (1991). Divorce over the life course: the role of marital happiness. *Journal of Family Issues*, *12*, 5–21.

Wickrama, K. A. S., Lorenz, F. O., Conger, R. D., & Elder, G H., Jr. (1997). Marital quality and physical illness: a latent growth curve analysis. *Journal of Marriage and the Family*, *59*, 143–155.

Wiederman, M. W. (1993). Evolved gender differences in mate preferences: evidence from personal advertisements. *Ethology and Sociobiology*, *14*, 331–352.

Wieselquist, J., Rusbult, C. E., Foster, C. A., & Agnew, C. R. (1999). Commitment, pro-relationship behavior, and trust in close relationships. *Journal of Personality and Social Psychology*, *77*, 942–966.

Wilbur, C. J., & Campbell, L. (2010). What do women want? An interactionist account of women's mate preferences. *Personality and Individual Differences*, *49*, 749–754.

Wilcox, A. J., Weinberg, C. R., & Baird, D. D. (1995). Timing of sexual intercourse in relation to ovulation: effects on the probability of conception, survival of the pregnancy and sex of the baby. *New England Journal of Medicine*, *333*, 1517–1521.

Williams, L. E., & Bargh, J. A. (2008). Experiencing physical warmth promotes interpersonal warmth. *Science*, *322*, 606–607.

Wilson, E. O. (1998). *Consilience: the Unity of Knowledge*. London: Little Brown.

Wilson, C. L., Rholes, W. S., Simpson, J. A., & Tran, S. (2007). Labor, delivery, and early parenthood: an attachment theory perspective. *Personality and Social Psychology Bulletin*, *33*, 505–518.

Wilson, M., & Daly, M. (1992). Who kills whom in spouse killings? On the exceptional sex ratio of spousal homicides in the United States. *Criminology*, *30*, 189–215.

Wilson, M., & Daly, M. (1993). An evolutionary psychological perspective on male sexual proprietariness and violence against wives. *Violence and Victims*, *18*, 271–294.

Wilson, M., & Daly, M. (1996). Male sexual proprietariness and violence against wives. *Current Directions in Psychological Science*, *5*, 2–7.

Wood, W., & Eagly, A. H. (2002). A cross-cultural analysis of the behavior of women and men: implications for the origins of sex difference. *Psychological Bulletin*, *128*, 699–727.

Woodin, E. M., & O'Leary, K. D. (2010). A brief motivational intervention for physically aggressive dating couples. *Prevention Science*, *11*, 371–383.

Woollett, K., & Maguire, E. A. (2011). Acquiring "the knowledge" of London's layout drives structural brain changes. *Current Biology*, *21*, 2109–2114.

Xu, X., Aron, A., Brown, L., Cao, G., Feng, T. & Weng, X. (2011). Reward and motivation systems: a brain mapping study of early-stage romantic love in Chinese participants. *Human Brain Mapping*, *32*, 249–257.

Young, H., & Uenukukopako, T. (1995). *Hinemoa & Tutenekai: A Te Arawa Legend*. New Zealand: Huia.

Youngblade, L. M., & Belsky, J. (1989). Child maltreatment, infant-parent attachment security, and dysfunctional peer relationships in toddlerhood. *Topics in Early Childhood Special Education*, *9*, 1–15.

Zaadstra, B. M., Seidell, J. C., van Noord, P. A. H., te Velde, E. R., Habbema, J. D. F., Vrieswijk, B., & Karbaat, J. (1993). Fat and female fecundity: prospective study of effect of body fat distribution on conception rates. *British Medical Journal*, *306*, 484–487.

Zaki, J., Weber, J., Bolger, N., & Ochsner, K. (2009). The neural bases of empathic accuracy. *Proceedings of the National Academy of Sciences of the USA, 106,* 11382–11387.

Zebrowitz, L. A., & Rhodes, G. (2002). Nature let a hundred flowers bloom: the multiple ways and wherefores of attractiveness. In G. Rhodes & L. A. Zebrowitz (Eds), *Facial Attractiveness: Evolutionary, Cognitive, Cul-*

tural, and Motivational Perspectives (pp. 261–293). Westport, CT: Ablex.

Zeifman, D., & Hazan, C. (1997). Attachment: The bond in pair-bonds. In J. A. Simpson & D. T. Kenrick (Eds.), *Evolutionary social psychology* (pp. 237–263). Mahwah, NJ: Erlbaum.

Author Index

Subject Index